ORDER WITHOUT LAW

Order without Law

How Neighbors Settle Disputes

Robert C. Ellickson

HARVARD UNIVERSITY PRESS

Cambridge, Massachusetts
London, England

Library of Congress Cataloging-in-Publication data

Ellickson, Robert C.
    Order without law: how neighbors settle disputes / Robert C.
Ellickson.
        p.   cm.
    Includes index.
    ISBN 0-674-64168-X (cloth)
    ISBN 0-674-64169-8 (pbk.)
    I. Sociological jurisprudence. 2. Dispute resolution (Law)—California—Shasta
County. 3. Compromise (Law)—California—Shasta County. 4. Trespass—Califor-
nia—Shasta County. 5. Cattle—California—Shasta County. 6. Social control.
I. Title.   K370.E45   1991
    340'.115—dc20   90-25710
                        CIP

To my mother and to the memory of my father, who in his youth ran cattle in North Dakota

＊ ＊ ＊

Preface

This book seeks to demonstrate that people frequently resolve their disputes in cooperative fashion without paying any attention to the laws that apply to those disputes. This thesis has broad implications for how political debates should be conducted, how lawyers should practice their profession, and how law schools and social-science departments should educate their students.

I did not appreciate how unimportant law can be when I embarked on this project. Until then I had devoted my scholarly career to examining land-use issues from a law-and-economics perspective. In those endeavors I made use of the Coase Theorem, a central proposition of law and economics that portrays people as bargaining to mutual advantage from whatever starting points the legal system has bestowed on them. (The more provocative aspect of the Coase Theorem is that, under certain assumptions, people will bargain to the *same* outcomes regardless of their original legal entitlements.)

In 1981 I had just finished coauthoring a casebook on land-use law and had grown vaguely dissatisfied with library-based legal scholarship. I decided to venture out into the world to learn more about how neighbors actually interact with one another, particularly when their legal rights vary from one place to the next. My first inspiration was to investigate how the law of lateral support influences which landowner pays to shore up an existing urban building whose foundations are threatened by an excavation on adjoining land. This line of research had to be abandoned when it turned out that federal regulations designed to protect the safety of workers had essentially preempted the widely varying common-law rules of lateral support.

I then turned to the issue of a cattleman's liability for cattle-trespass damages, in part because Ronald Coase had featured this issue in the famous article in which he set out his theorem. Based at the Stanford Law School at the time, I sought to identify a county in California that had both "open" and "closed" range—legal regimes in which a cattleman's legal liabilities for cattle trespass are dramatically different. Because university law libraries have few county ordinances in their collections, this search necessitated travel to various rural county seats. In the California Gold Country around Sacramento I discovered that Amador County, El Dorado County, and Placer County had all recently "opened" some of their range, but only in largely uninhabited territories in the high Sierra. Increasingly frustrated, on a sweltering day in August 1981 I left the Gold Country and drove north for three hours to pursue a lead involving Shasta County, at the top of the Central Valley. In the offices of the University of California Extension Service in Redding, I came upon Shasta County's farm advisor, Walt Johnson. With my first question Walt's face lit up and he began to talk. It was immediately apparent that my search for a field site was over.

Although vaguely confident from the outset that fieldwork in Shasta County would turn out to be enlightening in one way or another, I began with no particular hypotheses in mind. Nevertheless, after only a few interviews I could see that rural residents in Shasta County were frequently applying informal norms of neighborliness to resolve disputes even when they knew that their norms were inconsistent with the law. In short, contrary to standard law-and-economics analysis, in many contexts legal entitlements do not function as starting points for bargaining. This book is largely my attempt to integrate this finding with social-scientific analysis of the functions of law.

Details of my research methodology are provided in the Appendix, but a few words about usage are in order here. I have employed pseudonyms for most of the residents of Shasta County involved in the vignettes included in the book. Some public officials, such as Judge Richard Eaton and Supervisors John Caton, Dan Gover, and Norman Wagoner, are identified by their real names, as are the two individuals who most helped ease my immersion into Shasta County life—Bob Bosworth, then the president of the Shasta County Cattlemen's Association, and Walt Johnson. I extend my deepest thanks to them and to all the others in Shasta County who helped the stranger in shirtsleeves and necktie.

Chapters 1–3 draw on my earlier article "Of Coase and Cattle: Dispute Resolution among Neighbors in Shasta County," 38 *Stan. L. Rev.* 623 (1986). Chapters 7–8 derive from "A Critique of Economic and Sociological Theories of Social Control," 16 *J. Legal Stud.* 67 (1987). A portion of Chapter 11 is based on "A Hypothesis of Wealth-Maximizing Norms: Evidence from the Whaling Industry," 5 *J.L. Econ. & Org.* 83 (1989). I thank Richard A. Epstein, coeditor of the *Journal of Legal Studies,* and

Roberta Romano, coeditor of the *Journal of Law, Economics & Organization,* for allowing me to reprint material from the latter two sources.

I have many other debts to acknowledge as well. Portions of the text benefited from comments made during presentations at workshops at Boalt Hall, Boston University Law School, Chicago Law School, Harvard Law School, Michigan Law School, Stanford Business School, Stanford Law School, University of Toronto Law School, and Yale Law School. I received helpful suggestions from, among many others, Bruce Ackerman, Yoram Barzel, Bob Clark, Bob Cooter, Richard Epstein, Ron Gilson, Vic Goldberg, Mark Granovetter, Mark Handler, Henry Hansmann, Tom Jackson, Jim Krier, John Langbein, Geoff Miller, Bob Mnookin, Mitch Polinsky, Dick Posner, and Roberta Romano. I extend special thanks to four law-and-society scholars who, at different times and in different ways, reached across the chasm to educate me about what they do: Donald Black, Lawrence Friedman, Rick Lempert, and Stan Wheeler. The complete manuscript was greatly improved by three generous friends who had the steadfastness to make line-by-line comments—Dick Craswell, Carol Rose, and Gary Schwartz.

The Stanford Law School made this project possible by devoting a portion of a bequest from the Dorothy Redwine Estate to defray my field-research expenses. Jerry Anderson, Cheryl Davey, Tom Hagler, Keith Kelly, and Debbie Sivas contributed research assistance along the way; Simon Frankel provided exceptional research and editorial help during the manuscript's final stages. Jean Castle and Trish DiMicco reliably provided crucial secretarial support. At the Harvard University Press, I thank Elizabeth Gretz for her meticulous and sensible changes in the manuscript, and Mike Aronson, my editor, who patiently and skillfully pushed the project through to completion.

Lastly, I am grateful to my wife, Ellen, and my children, Jenny and Owen, for putting up with my years of work on this book. In January 1983, a few months after I had finished most of the fieldwork, the Shasta County Cattlemen's Association invited me to speak at their annual luncheon, which I was delighted to do. On this trip, Ellen and the children came with me. In the years since, when encouraging me to finish this project, Ellen has sometimes reminded me how small Jenny and Owen were then, playing on the deck of the cattlemen's meeting place while their father spoke inside, the snowy foothills of the Cascade Range stepping upward toward the distantly looming cone of Mount Shasta.

New Haven, December 1990

∗ ∗ ∗

Contents

ORDER WITHOUT LAW

*　*　*

Introduction

I think the whole thing is good neighbors. If you don't have good neighbors, you can forget the whole thing.

—Chuck Searle, Shasta County cattleman

My family believes in "live and let live." Have you heard of that?

—Phil Ritchie, Shasta County farmer

Events in a remote corner of the world can illuminate central questions about the organization of social life. The first half of what follows is an account of how residents of rural Shasta County, California, resolve a variety of disputes that arise from wayward cattle. A principal finding is that Shasta County neighbors apply informal norms, rather than formal legal rules, to resolve most of the issues that arise among them. This finding is used as a springboard for the development, in the second half of this book, of elements of a theory of how people manage to interact to mutual advantage without the help of a state or other hierarchical coordinator. The theory seeks to predict the content of informal norms, to expose the processes through which norms are generated, and to demarcate the domain of human activity that falls within—and beyond—the shadow of the law.

Stated most rashly, the aim of this work is to integrate three valuable—but overly narrow—visions of the social world: those of law and economics, sociology, and game theory. Expressed more modestly, the goal is to add a bit more realism and clarity to discussions of relations among neighbors and among members of other close-knit groups.

Why Stray Cattle? Why Shasta County?: The Coasean Parable

Investigation of the law in action in a specific setting can enhance general understanding of human affairs. Shasta County offers a saga replete with cowboys, scoundrels, barbed wire, citizen petitions, and other details that

1

connect to venerable traditions of the United States. Especially because there has been lamentably little legal scholarship in an anthropological mode, this story is informative (and colorful) in and of itself.[1]

The events reported here are of more than ordinary interest for another reason. One subarea of Shasta County is a microcosm perhaps uniquely suited to providing a real-world perspective on a hypothetical conflict much discussed in the literature on human cooperation. In a seminal work, "The Problem of Social Cost"—the most cited article on law—the economist Ronald Coase invoked as his fundamental example a conflict between a rancher running cattle and a neighboring farmer raising crops.[2] Coase used the Parable of the Farmer and the Rancher to illustrate what has come to be known as the Coase Theorem.[3] This counterintuitive proposition states, in its strongest form, that when transaction costs are zero a change in the rule of liability will have no effect on the allocation of resources. For example, as long as its admittedly heroic assumptions are met, the theorem predicts that making a rancher liable for damage done by his trespassing cattle would not cause the rancher to reduce the size of his herds, erect more fencing, or keep a closer watch on his livestock. A rancher who is liable for trespass damage has a legal incentive to implement all cost-justified measures to control his cattle. But even if the law were to decline to make the rancher liable, Coase reasoned that potential trespass victims would pay the rancher to implement the identical trespass-control measures. In short, market forces internalize all costs regardless of the rule of liability. This theorem has undoubtedly been both the most fruitful, and the most controversial, proposition to arise out of the law-and-economics movement.[4]

1. On the merits and methods of microlevel anthropology, see Clifford Geertz, *The Interpretation of Cultures* 3–30 (1973).

2. 3 *J.L. & Econ.* 1 (1960). During the 1957–1985 period the most cited article published in a conventional law review was Gerald Gunther, "The Supreme Court, 1971 Term—Foreword," 86 *Harv. L. Rev.* 1 (1972). See Fred R. Shapiro, "The Most-Cited Law Review Articles," 73 *Cal. L. Rev.* 1540, 1549 (1985). The *Social Sciences Citation Index,* which counts citations to articles appearing in law, economics, and other social science journals, provides a basis for comparing citations to the Coase and Gunther articles. This index indicates that during 1981–1988 the Coase article was cited in the surveyed journals almost twice as often as the Gunther article was.

3. Coase didn't, and no doubt wouldn't, use the label *parable.* This noun is nevertheless a useful shorthand way to refer to his example.

4. Some landmarks in the Coase Theorem literature are Robert Cooter, "The Cost of Coase," 11 *J. Legal Stud.* 1 (1982); John J. Donohue III, "Diverting the Coasean River: Incentive Schemes to Reduce Unemployment Spells," 99 *Yale L.J.* 549 (1989); and Donald H. Regan, "The Problem of Social Cost Revisited," 15 *J.L. & Econ.* 427 (1972).

Coase himself was fully aware that obtaining information, negotiating agreements, and litigating disputes are all potentially costly, and thus that his Farmer-Rancher Parable might not accurately portray how rural landowners would respond to a change in trespass law.[5] Some law-and-economics scholars, however, seem to believe that transaction costs are indeed often trivial when only two parties are in conflict.[6] These scholars therefore might assume, as Coase likely would not, that the Parable faithfully depicts how rural landowners would resolve cattle-trespass disputes.

Shasta County, California, is an ideal setting within which to explore the realism of the assumptions that underlie both the Farmer-Rancher Parable in particular and law and economics in general. Most of rural Shasta County is "open range." In open range an owner of cattle is typically not legally liable for damages stemming from his cattle's accidental trespass upon unfenced land. Since 1945, however, a special California statute has authorized the Shasta County Board of Supervisors, the county's elected governing body, to "close the range" in subareas of the county. A closed-range ordinance makes a cattleman strictly liable (that is, liable even in the absence of negligence) for any damage his livestock might cause while trespassing within the territory described by the ordinance. The Shasta County Board of Supervisors has exercised its power to close the range on dozens of occasions since 1945, thus changing for selected territories the exact rule of liability that Coase used in his famous example. The first part of this book reports how, if at all, the legal distinction between open and closed range influences behavior in rural areas. Shasta County neighbors, it turns out, do not behave as Coase portrays

5. Coase developed the parable not to describe behavior but rather to illustrate a purely theoretical point about the fanciful world of zero transaction costs. He himself has always been a militant in the cause of empiricism. See Ronald H. Coase, *The Firm, the Market, and the Law* 174–179 (1988).

6. Several of Coase's colleagues at the University of Chicago wedded themselves to this assumption in the 1960s. See, e.g., Walter J. Blum and Harry Kalven, Jr., *Public Law Perspectives on a Private Law Problem* 58–59 (1965); Harold Demsetz, "When Does the Rule of Liability Matter," 1 *J. Legal Stud.* 13, 16 (1972) (transaction costs "would seem to be negligible" when a baseball player negotiates with his club). The current consensus, even among Chicagoans, is that negotiations in bilateral-monopoly situations can be costly because the parties may act strategically. See, e.g., William M. Landes and Richard A. Posner, "Salvors, Finders, Good Samaritans, and Other Rescuers: An Economic Study of Altruism," 7 *J. Legal Stud.* 83, 91 (1978) ("transaction costs under bilateral monopoly are high"); Robert Cooter, Stephen Marks, and Robert Mnookin, "Bargaining in the Shadow of the Law: A Testable Model of Strategic Behavior," 11 *J. Legal Stud.* 225, 242–244 (1982). Other reasons why transaction costs might be high in simple two-party situations are explored in Ellickson, "The Case for Coase and against 'Coaseanism,'" 99 *Yale L.J.* 611 (1989).

them as behaving in the Farmer-Rancher Parable.[7] Neighbors in fact are strongly inclined to cooperate, but they achieve cooperative outcomes not by bargaining from legally established entitlements, as the parable supposes, but rather by developing and enforcing adaptive norms of neighborliness that trump formal legal entitlements. Although the route chosen is not the one that the parable anticipates, the end reached is exactly the one that Coase predicted: coordination to mutual advantage without supervision by the state.

The Pervasiveness of Order without Law

The Shasta County findings add to a growing library of evidence that large segments of social life are located and shaped beyond the reach of law. Despite this mounting evidence, the limits of law remain too little appreciated. In everyday speech, for example, one commonly hears the phrase "law and order," which implies that governments monopolize the control of misconduct. This notion is false—so utterly false that it warrants the implicit attack it receives in the title of this book.

Order often arises spontaneously. Although many other writers have recognized this point,[8] it remains counterintuitive and cannot be repeated too often. It is hardly surprising that the statists who favor expanding the role of government do not sufficiently appreciate nonhierarchical systems of social control. What is surprising is that some of the most militant supporters of decentralization often commit a similar error. The work of Coase is illustrative. Although Coase's writing reveals an unmistakable antigovernment streak, in "The Problem of Social Cost" he adopted the "legal centralist" view that the state functions as the sole creator of operative rules of entitlement among individuals. In so doing Coase repeated a blunder that dates back at least to Thomas Hobbes. According to Hobbes, without a Leviathan (government) to issue and enforce commands, all would be endless civil strife. The Shasta County evidence shows that Hobbes was much too quick to equate anarchy with chaos.

7. Besides exaggerating the reach of law, Coase's parable misidentifies the main risks associated with straying cattle. In Shasta County, the principal risks are not those posed to neighboring vegetation but those posed to motorists and to the animals themselves. See Chapter 5.

8. Two classic sources are Charles Lindblom, *The Intelligence of Democracy* 3–6 (1965) (lucid explanation of the possibility of coordination without hierarchy), and Friedrich Hayek, *The Road to Serfdom* 35–37 (1944) (reasons why planned economies can be expected to perform less well than unplanned ones). Some important subsequent works in the same vein are cited infra notes 19–21.

Many entitlements, especially workaday entitlements, can arise spontaneously. People may supplement, and indeed preempt, the state's rules with rules of their own.[9]

An alert observer can find in everyday life abundant evidence of the workings of nonhierarchical processes of coordination. Consider the development of a language. Millions of people have incrementally helped shape the English language into an enormously ornate and valuable institution.[10] Those who have contributed to this achievement have acted without the help of the state or any other hierarchical coordinator. The innovators who coined the words in this sentence, for example, are anonymous. *Time* magazine, a publication whose lifeblood is the English language, cannot possibly recognize (even retrospectively) any of its language's architects as Person of the Year.

Consider the growth of cities. In the nineteenth century several million people in the Midwest coordinated their efforts and built the city of Chicago. No one supervised this achievement and no single actor had more than a small part in it. Indeed, that Chicago's growth was largely undirected likely helped it develop so quickly.

Consider the operation of markets. Every day hundreds of thousands of people assist in supplying the food needed to sustain the seven million residents of New York City. No single individual knows how this aggregate feat is accomplished, and no one goes to work with this aggregate objective in mind. Nevertheless, New Yorkers invariably find food on their market shelves. This happens because a host of people consciously carry out tiny tasks that require them only to be aware of how their particular task meshes with the tasks of their immediate neighbors in the food-supply system. A Kansas wheat-farmer, for example, must know something about how his harvested grain is trucked to the local grain elevator, but he need not know how bread baked from his wheat is trucked from New York bakeries to New York supermarkets. Would a New York City mayor be wise to appoint a "czar" to supervise the vital activity of food supply? Anyone who answers in the negative implicitly understands that undirected market processes can supply food more economically than would an intentional hierarchy.

---

9. For fuller discussion, see infra Chapter 8, text accompanying notes 1–44. In recent years Hobbes has been kicked around almost as much as Richard Nixon was in his prime. See, e.g., Robert Axelrod, *The Evolution of Cooperation* 4 (1984); Peter Singer, *The Expanding Circle: Ethics and Sociobiology* 23–24 (1981); Michael Taylor, *Anarchy and Cooperation* 3, 7, 98–118 (1976).

10. English is employed as the illustrative language here because this book is written in it. Needless to say, many other languages are less irregular (more coordinated) than English is.

Last, and most pertinent, consider the operation of informal controls on behavior, as illustrated by the controversy that erupted in 1989 over flag burning. In June of that year a Supreme Court decision held that the First Amendment protects from criminal prosecution a person who burns a flag as a symbolic statement.[11] This ruling triggered a political melee. Opponents of flag burning declaimed that "there ought to be a law" against it. The President and many lesser political figures began to push for enactments, including a constitutional amendment, that would recriminalize the activity. Proponents of recriminalization doubtless understood that theirs was largely a symbolic battle. They apparently also believed, however, that the passage of legislation would serve the instrumental function of curbing flag burning. In this regard they seemed largely oblivious to the power of informal social controls. For better or worse, informal social forces in fact powerfully constrain the desecration of national symbols in public places. A demonstrator considering burning the national flag in the middle of a busy park can anticipate that observers will respond vehemently regardless of what the law says. Indeed, on July 4, 1989, when a handful of extremists scattered around the country tried to exercise the First Amendment flag-burning right that the Supreme Court had conspicuously recognized two weeks before, onlookers (mostly veterans) forcefully reminded them that informal rules against flag burning remained firmly in place.[12]

Out of the Swamp?: Bringing Theory to Law-and-Society Scholarship

An investigator of informal norms can find much of value in the works of scholars in the law-and-society movement, one of the significant social-scientific schools of legal research. Within law schools, the law-and-society scholars, especially those steeped in the tradition of Willard Hurst, are typically those most fervently committed to field work.[13] Most law-

11. Texas v. Johnson, 109 S. Ct. 2533 (1989). See also United States v. Eichman, 110 S. Ct. 2404 (1990) (Flag Protection Act of 1989 held to violate first amendment).

12. See L. Gordon Crovitz, "On the Flag, the Justices Make Dukakis's Mistake," *Wall St. J.,* July 6, 1989, at A12, col. 3 (reporting how onlookers used force to prevent and punish flag burnings attempted on July 4 in Albany, Little Rock, Minneapolis, and New York City). In the hope of encouraging this sort of response, some state legislators in Louisiana pushed for reduction of criminal sanctions applicable to informal punishers of flag-defacers. See *Wall St. J.,* June 5, 1990, at B8, col. 5.

13. It should be noted that a number of practitioners of law and economics have undertaken field research. Pioneering economic investigations into how people coordinate their activities in the face of transaction costs include Steven N. S. Cheung, "The Fable of the Bees:

and-society scholars have their roots not in economics but in the more humanistic social sciences such as history, sociology, and anthropology. Perhaps as a result, some of these scholars see patterns of human behavior as highly variable and contingent on historical circumstance. A scholar with this outlook tends to resist designing field research to test articulated hypotheses. In fact, if influenced by the anthropologist Clifford Geertz, the scholar might aspire only to produce "thick" anecdotal accounts that would display "local knowledge" of the culture examined.[14] Practitioners of law and economics, by contrast, rarely shrink from applying in every context the model of rational, self-interested, human behavior that they borrow from economics proper.

One might think that members of both camps would see irresistible benefits in blending law-and-economics theory with law-and-society field data. In fact, a chasm separates these two groups of scholars.[15] They publish separate journals.[16] They gather at separate conferences. They seem rarely to read, much less to cite, work by loyalists of the other camp. Although this absence of cross-fertilization may stem in part from a lack of familiarity with the working language of a foreign discipline, it is also due in part to a mutual lack of respect, and even a contempt, for the kind of work that the other group does. To exaggerate only a little, the law-and-economics scholars believe that the law-and-society group is deficient in both sophistication and rigor, and the law-and-society scholars believe that the law-and-economics theorists are not only out of touch with reality but also short on humanity.

This book was written with one foot firmly placed in each of these two

---

An Economic Investigation," 16 *J.L. & Econ.* 11 (1973), and Ronald H. Coase, "The Lighthouse in Economics," 17 *J.L. & Econ.* 357 (1974). See also Elizabeth Hoffman and Matthew L. Spitzer, "Experimental Law and Economics: An Introduction," 85 *Colum. L. Rev.* 99 (1985) (includes bibliography on laboratory experiments).

14. See C. Geertz, supra note 1. Many law-and-society scholars regard Geertzism as insufficiently scientific, and are more willing than he to generalize.

15. The best-known assertion of a chasm between academic outlooks is C. P. Snow's 1959 lecture, "The Two Cultures." Snow saw literary intellectuals and physical scientists as polar opposites, and speculated about whether social scientists represented yet a third culture. C. P. Snow, *The Two Cultures: and a Second Look* 8–9 (2d ed. 1965). That the two camps of social scientists interested in empirical research on law have had difficulty communicating suggests that Snow was right to be in a quandary about how to classify members of the social-scientific disciplines.

16. The core journals are entitled, appropriately enough, the *Journal of Law & Economics* and the *Law & Society Review*. In addition, although they are both slightly more catholic, the *Journal of Legal Studies* has tilted heavily toward law-and-economics articles, and *Law & Social Inquiry*, toward law-and-society articles.

opposing camps. Law and economics, the tradition in which I have mostly labored, provided the parable that inspired the study. Moreover, the theoretical analysis of informal order is based on the rational-actor model of human behavior that underlies most work in economics and game theory. The field work in Shasta County, however, uses the research methods of law-and-society stalwarts such as Stewart Macaulay and H. Laurence Ross.[17] After reading rather widely in both literatures, I must confess my suspicion that law-and-society scholars, because they better understand the importance of informal social controls, would currently be better able than law-and-economics scholars to predict the essentials of what was found in Shasta County.[18] Before members of the law-and-society camp begin to gloat, however, they should be warned that the latter part of this work, which strives to develop a theory of norms, is a gauntlet thrown in their direction.

The Dynamics of Cooperation:
The Promise of Game Theory

Most residents of rural Shasta County self-consciously aspire to be good neighbors. For them cooperation is the norm, conflict the exception. Thanks to Robert Axelrod as much as anyone, the evolution of cooperation is a topic that currently excites scholars across a broad spectrum of

---

17. Their best-known works are Stewart Macaulay, "Non-Contractual Relations in Business: A Preliminary Study," 28 *Am. Soc. Rev.* 55 (1963), and H. Laurence Ross, *Settled Out of Court* (rev. ed. 1980). Law-and-society scholars themselves have bemoaned the paucity of field studies on dispute settlement in the contemporary United States. "Ironically, we have better data about dispute processing in Indian villages, Mexican towns, and East African tribes than we have about that process in American communities." William L. F. Felstiner, "Influences of Social Organization on Dispute Processing," 9 *L. & Soc'y Rev.* 63, 86 n.28 (1974). The field study most similar to the one undertaken in Shasta County is Julio L. Ruffini, "Disputing over Livestock in Sardinia," in *The Disputing Process: Law in Ten Societies* 209 (Laura Nader and Harry F. Todd, Jr., eds. 1978). Ruffini found that shepherds in Sardinia relied on self-help, not formal legal processes, to resolve rustling disputes. A related library-research project is Kenneth Vogel, "The Coase Theorem and California Animal Trespass Law," 16 *J. Legal Stud.* 149 (1987), an econometric assessment of the effect of closed-range ordinances in nineteenth-century California. For criticism of Vogel's methods, see Donohue, supra note 4, at 551 n.6.

18. Most economists might well not predict, for example, that settlements between neighbors in Shasta County usually involve in-kind, not monetary, payments, and that rural residents who engage in political battles over trespass law seem mostly concerned about symbolic, not material, outcomes. These observations are offered not to denigrate economic analysis but to point out how it might be enriched. See generally Ellickson, "Bringing Culture and Human Frailty to Rational Actors: A Critique of Classical Law-and-Economics," 65 *Chi.-Kent L. Rev.* 23 (1989).

disciplines.[19] In particular, biologists and economists, whose theories assume that in the crunch an organism will maximize its own welfare at the expense of others', are trying to reconcile the widespread phenomenon of cooperation with their axioms of individual selfishness.

Game theory is currently the main vehicle for the investigation of cooperation. Axelrod has shown that when two self-regarding individuals are situated in a highly stylized setting that ensures continuing encounters, they will often be able to bring their relations into a cooperative mode by adopting a simple strategy of Tit-for-Tat. In brief, a person adopting this strategy acts cooperatively until crossed, in which event he applies eye-for-an-eye remedies.[20] The theory developed here borrows some simple ideas from game theory. Chapter 12 even goes so far as to outline a specific strategy, Even-Up, that is asserted to be better designed than Tit-for-Tat to fit unstylized, real-world conditions, such as those observed in Shasta County. Although Even-Up is hardly rigorously developed, it may serve to prod game theorists toward somewhat greater realism.[21]

The Plan of the Book

Part I is largely descriptive. Chapter 1 provides a general introduction to Shasta County, the cattlemen who live there, and their methods of cattle husbandry. Chapter 2 describes several heated political battles that trespassing cattle have provoked in the county. With this background in place, Chapters 3–5 deal respectively with the three sorts of disputes among rural residents to which the legal distinction between open and closed range is potentially relevant. First, disputes may arise when livestock stray and cause damage to adjoining property. Second, rural neighbors may wrangle over how they should split the costs of building and maintaining boundary fences, the main device used to prevent cattle from wandering. Third, motorists sometimes collide with cattle that have ambled onto rural highways, often with tragic consequences. Chapters 3–5

19. See, e.g., *Trust: Making and Breaking Cooperative Relations* (Diego Gambetta ed. 1988); Eric Livingston, *Making Sense of Ethnomethodology* (1987); John Maynard Smith, *Evolution and the Theory of Games* (1982); Robert Sugden, *The Economics of Rights, Co-operation, and Welfare* (1986).

20. See Robert Axelrod, *The Evolution of Cooperation* (1984), and infra Chapter 9, text accompanying notes 19–22.

21. Game-theoretical work on cooperation has proceeded largely in the absence of empirical understanding of how people behave in workaday situations. See Russell Hardin, *Collective Action* 229–230 (1982).

examine both the legal rules that formally apply to these disputes in Shasta County and the ways in which rural neighbors actually resolve grievances over these matters. Chapter 6 addresses the paradox of why there is so much political excitement about legal rules that have almost no practical relevance in the settlement of the disputes to which they formally apply.

Shifting from the particular to the general, Part II sets out a theory of norms. Chapter 7 begins this endeavor by providing an overview of systems of social control. Chapter 8 applies this taxonomy to reveal some shortcomings in both the law-and-economics and law-and-society movements. Most law professors, including most law-and-economics scholars, implicitly propagate the Hobbesian notion that the legal system is the wellspring of social order (perhaps because this view lends significance to what they teach). Chapter 8 shows that Hobbes is off the mark, and not just in Shasta County. The chapter also discusses the antithetical tradition that correctly emphasizes that much social order can emerge without law, but criticizes the thinness of the theory underlying this view.

The balance of Part II moves beyond criticism. Building on a game-theoretic framework introduced in Chapter 9, Chapter 10 offers the hypothesis that, to govern their workaday interactions, members of a close-knit group develop informal norms that are utilitarian—that is, that maximize the objective welfare of group members. The analysis also identifies social imperfections whose existence would tend to undermine systems of informal social control. Formal theorists should be forewarned that these pivotal sections rely mainly on the induction of propositions from observations, rather than on the deduction of proofs from axioms.

A legal system includes various types of laws—for example, substantive, remedial, procedural, and jurisdictional laws. Each of these has an analogue in a system of informal norms. Just as the doctrine of laches prohibits the bringing of stale lawsuits, a procedural norm instructs people to "let bygones be bygones." Chapters 11–14 discuss the functions and contents of the main types of norms that a nonhierarchical group must generate to have a system of informal order. Informal norms serve, among other functions, to create property rights, to govern the use of remedial violence, and to punish persons who wrongly invoke the legal system. From Shasta County, whaling fisheries, university copycenters, and elsewhere, Chapters 11–14 adduce examples of each of the major varieties of norms, thereby sketching out some initial lines on the largely blank map of informal doctrine.

Chapters 15 and 16, which make up Part III, explore the shortcomings and implications of some of the propositions previously developed, particularly the general hypothesis that the diverse strands in the web of informal control tend to be utilitarian in content. The plunge into life in rural Shasta County that begins the book serves as the foundation for the theoretical discussions that come later.

PART I

Shasta County

1

—

Shasta County and Its Cattle Industry

Shasta County journalists sometimes refer to their region as "Superior California," a prideful designation that, unlike "Northern California," distinguishes the state's northernmost counties from the San Francisco Bay Area. As Figure 1.1 indicates, the county lies at the northern end of the four-hundred-mile-long Central Valley of California, not far from the Oregon border. The Sacramento River, which drains the northern half of the Central Valley, bisects the county. Redding, Shasta County's county seat and largest city, is situated at an elevation of five hundred feet at the spot where the Sacramento River emerges from the mountains north of the valley to begin a two-hundred-mile trip south toward San Francisco Bay.

Physical Environment

High mountain peaks lie within sight of Redding in all directions except south. The Trinity Mountains lie to the west; the towering cone of Mount Shasta, actually in Siskiyou County, stands fifty miles due north; and to the east lie other peaks of the volcanic Cascade Range—notably Mount Lassen, which sits in Shasta County's southeastern corner. To the east, north, and west of Redding, foothills rise irregularly toward these distant mountain peaks.

Weather dictates Shasta County's ranching practices. Like the rest of California, the county has a wet season and a dry season. Redding receives an average annual rainfall of 38.74 inches, most of it concentrated in the winter months. Little rain falls between mid-May and November. During the summer months intense sunlight bakes Redding, and the surrounding mountains block cooling winds. The city's average daily high temperature in July is 98 degrees. In the spring the grasslands near Redding are lush and green from the heavy winter rains; by summer, the extreme heat has turned the ground cover brown.

Most of Shasta County's terrain is too mountainous and its soils too

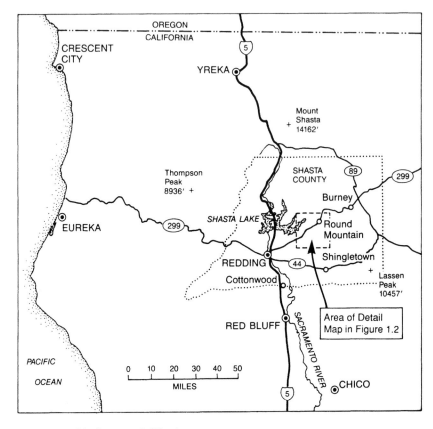

Figure 1.1   Northwestern California

poor to support significant agricultural activity. The majority of the land area in the county is commercial-quality forest, most of which the United States Forest Service and a handful of private timber companies own.[1] Census data describe 16 percent of the county as "land in farms."[2] The bulk of this agricultural land is unirrigated and used only as seasonal pasture for livestock—principally cattle, the county's major agricultural product. Only 1 percent of the county's land is used for raising harvested

1. Of the 2.4 million acres of land in Shasta County, 1.3 million have been identified as "commercial forest." The United States Forest Service owns 35 percent of this commercial forest, and forest industry companies own 46 percent. Cal. Dep't of Finance, *Cal. Statistical Abstract* 2, 129 (1983).

2. Id. at 111 (citing data from the 1978 U.S. Census of Agriculture).

SHASTA COUNTY AND ITS CATTLE INDUSTRY ✕✕✕ 17

crops,[3] and a majority of this field-crop acreage is devoted to alfalfa or other hay grown as feed for livestock.[4]

In 1973, the Shasta County Board of Supervisors voted to "close the range" in a fifty-six-square-mile rectangle of territory around Round Mountain, a rural hamlet thirty miles northeast of Redding. This ordinance, which county cattlemen later called "Caton's Folly" to embarrass a supervisor who helped pass it, provided the best opportunity in Shasta County to test the effects of an *actual* change in the rule of liability for cattle trespass. Nine years later, in 1982, the Board of Supervisors considered, but rejected, a petition to close the range in the Oak Run area immediately southwest of Caton's Folly. The Oak Run controversy promised to reveal the effects of a *threatened* change in liability rules. Residents of the Oak Run and Round Mountain areas were interviewed to shed more light on these effects. The general area northeast of Redding—referred to here as the Northeastern Sector—thus warrants closer description.

The Northeastern Sector consists of three ecological zones: grassy plains, foothills, and mountain forest. The elevation of the land largely determines the boundaries of these zones; the higher the terrain, the more rain it receives, and the cooler its summer weather.

The zone between 500 and 1500 feet in elevation, which is the zone closest to Redding, consists of grassy plains. This idyllic, oak-dotted country provides natural pasture during the spring and, if irrigated, can support a herd year-round. A water supply adequate for irrigation is available, however, only near the streams that flow through the area. Moreover, the soil in much of the grassy plains is infertile hardpan. Because of these natural constraints, a full-time rancher who operates in this zone typically needs at least several square miles of pasture for his herds.

The foothills lie roughly between 1500 and 3500 feet in elevation. As Figure 1.2 indicates, both Caton's Folly and the Oak Run area fall within this transition zone. Much of the foothill area has a mixed natural tree cover of pine and oak. In open areas the natural ground cover is less likely to be grass than an unpalatable chaparral of manzanita, buckbrush, and like shrubs. To foothill ranchers this brush is almost as repulsive a thought as the importation of Argentine beef; the more enterprising of

3. Id. at 2, 111.
4. Edward Peterson, *In the Shadow of the Mountain: A Short History of Shasta County, California* 110 (1965). Coase's Parable of the Farmer and the Rancher involved a pasture adjoining a field of annually harvested crops. Such land uses are rarely contiguous in Shasta County.

them spend much of their energies killing brush to enable forage grasses to grow.

Mountain forest, the third zone, starts at about 3500 feet. Ponderosa pine, Douglas fir, and other conifers that have supplanted the deciduous oaks cover the mountainsides at this elevation. The mountain forests remain green year-round, but most are too cold in winter and too hard to clear to be suitable sites for cattlemen's base ranches. The Roseburg Lum-

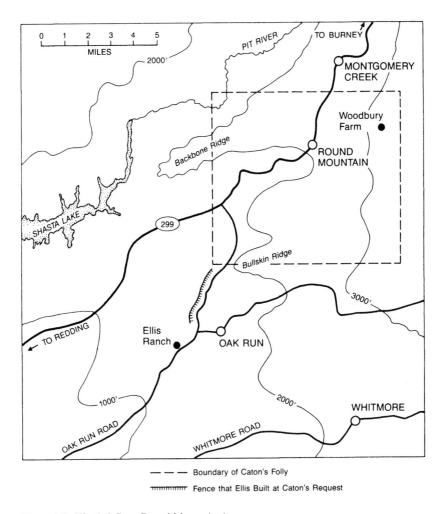

Figure 1.2 *The Oak Run–Round Mountain Area*

ber Company owns much of the mountain forest in the Northeastern Sector.[5] Like other private timber companies in the county, Roseburg has not shown any interest in subdividing its lands for development. For many decades, however, Roseburg and its predecessors in ownership have leased their forests to Shasta County cattlemen for summer range.

Social Environment

Shasta County has experienced rapid population growth. Redding's location at the northern end of the Central Valley makes it a natural transportation hub. It serves as the gateway to mountain recreation areas lying in three directions, and has emerged as the major regional center on Interstate 5 between Sacramento, California, and Eugene, Oregon. Between 1930 and 1980, the number of county residents increased ninefold,[6] and in the decade from 1970 to 1980, total county population rose from 78,000 to 116,000.[7] The county's population growth rate of 49.0 percent in the 1970s was substantially higher than the overall state rate (18.5 percent) and was somewhat higher than the aggregate rate for California's nonmetropolitan counties (36.4 percent). Indications of social instability have accompanied the influx of migrants. In 1981, Shasta had the highest divorce rate of any county in California,[8] and in 1980, the county's unemployment rate was twice that of the state as a whole.[9]

Precise figures on population trends within the Northeastern Sector are not available. It appears, however, that during the 1970s, the sector's

5. The Roseburg Lumber Company is a closely held corporation based in Roseburg, Oregon. It is controlled by Kenneth Ford, a self-made man whom Forbes Magazine has listed as one of the forty wealthiest individuals in the United States. *S.F. Chron.,* Aug. 28, 1982, at 14, col. 4. When Roseburg purchased its forests in the Northeastern Sector in 1979 from the Kimberly-Clark Corporation, it became the fourth timber company to own these lands since the early 1940s.

6. The 1930 United States Census recorded a county population of 13,927.

7. Bureau of the Census, *1980 Census of Population.* In 1980, 42,000 people lived in the city of Redding. By 1984, because Redding's estimated population had surpassed 50,000, it was awarded the status of a Metropolitan Statistical Area.

8. In 1981, Shasta County had 8.7 dissolutions and nullities of marriage per 1000 estimated persons, compared with a statewide figure of 5.8 per thousand. State of Cal., Dep't of Health Servs., *Vital Statistics of California—1981* 128 (1983).

9. Census data placed the county's unemployment rate at 13.8 percent, compared with the state's 6.5 percent. Bureau of the Census, *1980 Census of Population and Housing, Advance Estimates of Social, Economic, and Housing Characteristics.* The timber industry, an important factor in the Shasta County economy, was in a deep slump in 1980, a factor that no doubt contributed to this disparity.

population grew by an even larger percentage than did the county's.[10] Not surprisingly, the demographic histories of the three ecological zones within the sector are rather different.

Residential patterns in the grassy plains have not changed much in recent years. The first pioneers to settle east and northeast of Redding used the grasslands and lower foothills to raise livestock. The descendants of the nineteenth-century pioneer families, such as the Coombses, Donaldsons, and Wagoners, still hold a special place in rural Shasta County society. Oldtimers are quick to identify their roots in the county, and sometimes refer to families who arrived a generation ago as "people who haven't been here very long." Prior to the 1920s, the Southern Pacific Railroad owned alternate sections of the grassy plains—a reward from the United States for laying track to Redding.[11] During the 1920s, Southern Pacific sold off most of its grassland sections at the then market price of $2.50 to $5.00 per acre, thereby enabling the pioneer ranching families to consolidate their holdings. Abandoning their prior practice of running their herds at large, these families erected fences around their multi-thousand-acre spreads, cleared patches of brush, and began to irrigate their better pastures.

Beyond the suburbs of Redding most of the acreage in the grasslands and lower foothills remains divided into ranches at least several square miles in size. Approximately half of these ranches are owned by descendants of families that have been in the county for several generations. Although many of these ranches have a current market value of $1 million or more, the ranchers typically have modest annual incomes. For decades, ranchlands in Shasta County have generated an annual cash return of only 1 or 2 percent of their market value.[12] The cattlemen who

10. The population of what the Census Bureau calls the Central Shasta division increased from 3049 in 1970 to 6784 in 1980, or by 122 percent. Bureau of the Census, *1980 Census of Population*, vol. 1, pt. 6, ch. A, table 4, n.41 (1982). This division includes both the Northeastern Sector and larger rural territories to the north, south, and southeast.

11. The government gift consisted of alternate sections of land for a distance of twenty miles on either side of the railroad right-of-way. Stuart Daggett, *Chapters on the History of the Southern Pacific* 50, 122 (1922). A section of land is a square whose area is one square mile (640 acres).

12. Interview with Robert Shaw, Redding-based appraiser (July 19, 1982). Mr. Shaw attributed the low returns to the tax benefits and psychic income that ranching confers. Cattle ranching is noted for skimpy financial returns. See Arthur D. Little, Inc., *Final Environmental Statement, Proposed Livestock Grazing Program, BLM Cerbat/Black Mountain Planning Units* (II) 139–142 (1978) (returns to cattle ranching in Arizona range from negative to a positive 1 to 2 percent; ranchers do it for love); Marj Charlier, "Home on the Range Is a Part-Time Deal for Many Cowboys," *Wall St. J.*, Jan. 8, 1985, at 1, col. 4.

own and operate the large family ranches tend to follow self-imposed seven-day-a-week work schedules and live in houses less imposing than those one would find in an average American suburb. When estate taxes or property taxes have squeezed a ranching family financially, the family may sell its entire holding to another rancher or to investors seeking tax shelters or, more commonly, may deal off tree-covered pieces of its ranch to developers for subdivision into ranchettes.

The foothills have seen more subdivision activity and absolute population growth than have the grassy plains. Both supply and demand conditions explain this pattern. Because the foothills are somewhat less suited than the grasslands for agriculture, foothill landowners are more likely to subdivide their holdings. Most home buyers would also prefer the foothills to the grasslands as a residential location because the higher elevations are cooler in summer and offer more tree cover. As a result, the foothills within commuting distance of Redding have experienced a multifold increase in population over the past twenty years.[13]

Many of the recent settlers in the foothills are either retirees or younger migrants from California's major urban areas. These newcomers tend to live on minimally improved lots of from five to forty acres, either in owner-built houses or in mobile homes. Many of these ranchettes have sprung up near hamlets, such as Oak Run and Round Mountain, that contain a general store, a post office, an elementary school, and other basic community facilities. Despite these clusters of growth, development in the foothills has been rather diffuse. Especially since the mid-1960s, small-scale developers have subdivided forested areas in every sector of the foothills.[14] Thus virtually all foothill ranchers have some ranchette owners as neighbors. Ranchette owners may keep a farm animal or two as a hobby, but few of them make significant income from agriculture. The ranchette owners nevertheless admire both the cattlemen and the folkways traditionally associated with rural Shasta County.

13. Some of the new development has been for second homes. Celebrities such as Vida Blue, Clint Eastwood, Merle Haggard, and the former congressman Pete McCloskey are among those who have purchased properties in the rural areas east of Redding.

14. John Williams of the Redding office of the Title Insurance & Trust Company generously permitted access to the firm's tract indexes. These indexes showed that in twenty-four sections near the southern border of Caton's Folly, the number of land parcels increased from 61 in 1930, to 145 in 1972, to 295 in 1982. Countywide the number of land parcels quadrupled between 1967 and 1982. Interview with Tony Estacio, Chief, Administrative Services, Assessor's Office of Shasta County (July 8, 1982). These rates of parcelization appear to be atypically high for rural land markets. See Robert G. Healy and James L. Short, *The Market for Rural Land* 22 (1981) (in only one of five counties studied did the number of rural land parcels double between 1954 and 1976).

Work Environment: Modes of Cattle Ranching

Most Shasta County ranchers are men. Although women own, manage, and provide most of the physical labor on a number of ranches, rural culture generally supports the differentiation of sex roles. Thus a woman rancher who wishes to be active in the county Cattlemen's Association is likely to participate only in the CowBelles, the women's auxiliary. (In 1985 the National Cattlemen's Association elected its first woman president, JoAnn Smith, but she had come to prominence by serving as president of the Florida CowBelles.)[15]

Despite their long hours of work, few ranchers in Shasta County find raising beef cattle a road to prosperity. The typical rancher runs a cow and calf operation. When his calves are seven to twelve months old, he trucks them a dozen miles south of Redding to the Shasta County auction yard at Cottonwood, where each Friday some three thousand head change hands. Agents for feedlot operators and pasture owners buy the calves, take them to feedlots and pastures outside the county, and feed and fatten them for a few months to prepare them for slaughter. Beginning in the 1970s per capita consumption of beef in the United States began to fall.[16] In 1982, a six-hundred-pound yearling auctioned in Cottonwood brought about $375, compared with about $500 in 1979. Shasta County is at best marginal terrain for cattle ranching. In the early 1980s some cattlemen there were understandably fearful that they would be casualties in a shakeout of their beleaguered industry.

The Traditionalists

Shasta County cattlemen may be loosely grouped into two categories: the traditionalists and the modernists. Traditionalists tend to be more marginal economically, and to have a greater stake in fighting closed-range ordinances.

Traditional cattlemen continue to follow the husbandry practices that were nearly universal in the county as late as the 1920s. A traditionalist's trademark is that he lets his cattle roam, essentially untended, in unfenced mountain areas during the summer.[17] This customary practice

---

15. *N.Y. Times,* Apr. 24, 1985, at C1, col. 1.

16. Per capita beef consumption fell from 87.9 lbs. in 1975 to 77.2 lbs. in 1982, as consumers shifted toward poultry and pork. Bureau of the Census, *Statistical Abstract of the United States* 110 (1987).

17. The classic study of cattlemen operating on unfenced range is Ernest Staples Osgood, *The Day of the Cattleman* (1929) (emphasizing practices in Wyoming and Montana during the latter part of the nineteenth century). On the history of traditionalist practices in California,

evolved in response to the severity of Shasta County's dry season. In the area northeast of Redding, a rancher lacking irrigated pasture needs about ten to twenty acres per animal unit[18] for winter and spring pasture. Thus, to support two hundred cattle—a substantial herd by Shasta County standards—a rancher without irrigated pasture needs at least two thousand acres, or just over three square miles of land. During the dry season the brutal heat makes unirrigated grasslands almost worthless. To feed his animals during the summer, a lowland cattleman must therefore either have access to irrigated pasture or be able to move his animals to the high foothills and mountains, where cooler dry season temperatures enable natural forage to survive. The traditionalist solution is a summer grazing lease on a large tract of mountain forest.

The United States Forest Service, the Bureau of Land Management,[19] and the major private timber companies have all regularly entered into grazing leases with county cattlemen. Although the timber-company grazing leases typically have only a one-year term, the companies have allowed cattlemen to renew them as a matter of course.[20] Federal leases may run for any period up to ten years[21] and they also tend to be automatically renewable.[22] A cattleman who has been leasing a tract of forest for summer range thus tends to regard that leasehold as a part of his normal operations. Although the forest areas remain green in summer, they contain too few open meadows to support many cattle. Traditionalists may have to lease three hundred acres of forest per animal unit. Consequently, a traditionalist with a herd of only a hundred animals may have a summer lease on a forest equal in area to the city of San Francisco.

The fencing of remote forest leaseholds has never been cost-justified in the eyes of either the timber owners or their traditionalist lessees. To

---

see Robert Glass Cleland, *The Cattle on a Thousand Hills* (2d ed. 1951); David Dary, *Cowboy Culture* 44–66 (1981).

18. An "animal unit" is a mature cow plus calf, or the equivalent in terms of forage consumption. A horse converts to 1.25 animal units, a sheep to 0.2 animal units, and so on. An "animal unit month" (AUM) is the amount of forage an animal unit consumes in one month of grazing. Harold F. Heady, *Rangeland Management* 117 (1975).

19. The USFS and the BLM manage most of the vast federal holdings in the county. Altogether, federal agencies own 40 percent of the county's acreage. *California Almanac* 8-2 (1986–87 ed.).

20. A specialist in brokering private grazing leases stated that most of his landowner-lessee relationships had endured for decades. Interview with Jim Cochran, Wm. Beatty & Assoc., in Redding, Cal. (July 21, 1982).

21. See 43 U.S.C.A. §§315b, 1752 (1982).

22. Interviews with Terry Brumley of the USFS, in Redding, Cal. (Aug. 9, 1982), and Paul McClain of the BLM, in Redding, Cal. (July 9, 1982).

reduce the risk that livestock will trespass on contiguous lands, natural barriers such as ridges and gulches are commonly picked as boundaries for grazing leaseholds. But adroit boundary drawing is hardly a foolproof method for controlling strays. Mountain cattle tend to drift down drainage areas to lower elevations, especially after the weather has turned cold or a drought has dried upland creeks. Lessees occasionally erect drift fences across mountain valleys to block the most obvious of these migration routes. Because drift fences are easily destroyed by winter snows, however, many traditionalists let their animals roam in unfenced mountain range. As a result, even a forest lessee who has ridden his leasehold periodically during the summer may be unable to find part of the herd when he gathers his livestock in mid-October. After the October gathering, a traditionalist returns his animals to a base ranch at a lower elevation, and feeds them hay or other stored feed for a few months until the winter rains revive the natural grasses on the base-ranch pastures.[23]

The Modernists

Modernists among the Shasta County cattlemen keep their livestock behind fences at all times in order to increase their control over their herds. To satisfy the need for summer forage that originally caused traditionalist cattlemen to enter into forest leases, modernists install ditches and sprinklers to irrigate base-ranch pastures. One acre of irrigated pasture can support a cow and calf for an entire summer. A modernist who can irrigate about 10 percent of his lands is usually able to run a year-round, fenced operation.[24]

Modernists are more active than traditionalists in managing ranchland vegetation. If not controlled, the native brush that thrives in the foothill zone would consume much of the scarce ground water and soil nutrients that competing grasses need. Modernist foothill ranchers fight the brush by setting controlled burns, spreading herbicides, and dragging chains

23. Untimely grazing may damage rangeland. If grazing occurs too early, it may kill immature grass. If it occurs too late, the livestock may eat seeds needed for the following year's forage. Even though a long-term lessee might consider these risks on his own, grazing leases nevertheless typically specify entry and exit dates.

24. A cattleman needs at least ten acres of unirrigated land per AUM for winter range. If he were to irrigate 10 percent of this acreage, he would have enough irrigated pasture for summer range. Instead of irrigating, a modernist who prefers operating behind fences may move his herds to fenced summer grasslands located in the high mountain valleys of Superior California.

from tractors to uproot the larger plants.[25] Using these clearing techniques, leading modernist cattlemen have transformed unproductive foothill areas into valuable pasturelands.

Modernists tend to be younger than traditionalists, have more formal education, and be more active in the Cattlemen's Association. Some modernists view the traditionalists as old-fashioned and primitive. Traditionalists, however, see themselves as the "real" cattlemen—the ones who can recognize one of their cows at half a mile and sleep out under the stars in the tradition of the nineteenth-century cowboy.

Despite their stylistic differences, modernists and traditionalists have much in common. Members of both groups believe that the life of the cattleman is the best possible in western America. They enjoy riding horses and wearing blue jeans, cowboy hats, and cowboy boots. They are inclined to decorate their living rooms with an antique rifle above the door and a portrait of John Wayne on the wall. Although traditionalists have a much greater stake than modernists do in keeping the Board of Supervisors from closing the range, modernist cattlemen typically join the traditionalists in opposing proposed legal changes that would increase the liabilities of owners of stray cattle.

The Benefits and Costs of Boundary Fences

The study of cattle trespass incidents is inevitably a study of fencing. A fence demarcates boundaries, keeps out human and animal trespassers, and keeps in the fencebuilder's own animals. In the Farmer-Rancher Parable, Coase perceived the sole benefit of a fence to be the reduction of trespass damages to crops.[26] In fact, cattlemen enclose their lands largely to prevent damage to their own livestock. Predators, rustlers, winter snows, and poisonous plants such as larkspur all pose potentially lethal threats to cattle roaming unfenced countryside.[27] Cattlemen also worry

25. See generally H. Heady, supra note 18, at 253–255, 258, 280–329. On controlled burns, see also Cal. Pub. Res. Code §§4475–4494 (West 1984 & Supp. 1989) (delineating the role of the State Department of Forestry); Laurence A. Stoddart and Arthur D. Smith, *Range Management* 383–394 (1943) (describing the effects of burning on various types of rangeland).

26. See Ronald H. Coase, "The Problem of Social Cost," 3 *J.L. & Econ.* 1, 3, 5 (1960).

27. During the nineteenth century, when cattlemen let their stock loose on the Great Plains during the winter, even the best managers were likely to lose 5 percent of their mature animals each grazing season. Daniel J. Boorstin, *The Americans: The Democratic Experience* 10 (1973). In the Northwest during the same time period, losses ran about 10 percent. J. Orin Oliphant, *On the Cattle Ranges of the Oregon Country* 240–241 (1968). In Wyoming and Montana, during the disastrous winter of 1885–86, blizzards killed 85 percent or more of the livestock in some herds. E. Osgood, supra note 17, at 216–218.

that a bull of worthless pedigree will impregnate a wandering cow. By enclosing his lands, a cattleman can more easily provide salt and other useful dietary supplements and prevent the weight loss that occurs when cattle walk long distances.

The prices of grazing leases reflect the value that ranchers place on fences. In 1982, fenced land in the Northeastern Sector rented for about $10 per animal unit month, whereas unfenced land rented for about $3.[28] Because both arrangements yield the same quantity of forage, the rent differential provides a rough measure of how much ranchers value the protection and control that boundary fences provide.[29]

Since 1874, the year J. F. Glidden took out the first patent on barbed wire, the barbed-wire fence has been the standard American technology for enclosing livestock.[30] California's statutory standard for a "lawful fence" was set at the turn of the century. It calls for three tightly stretched strands of barbed wire stapled to posts situated 16½ feet (one rod) apart.[31] Today, Shasta County ranchers tend to use at least four strands of barbed wire in boundary fences.[32]

Instead of the cedar posts that were customary earlier in the century,[33]

28. These are rough averages of figures that ranchers and grazing-lease specialists offered in interviews.

29. The *quality* of forage of course varies from pasture to pasture.

30. D. Dary, supra note 17, at 308–331, recounts the influence of barbed wire on ranching practices nationally. Before barbed wire, the fencing-in of cattle was generally not economical in California. R. Cleland, supra note 17, at 62. A standard barbed-wire fence will not contain sheep or hogs. To fence in those animals, Shasta County landowners use woven wire (which they variously refer to as "netting," "hogwire," or "field fence") for the bottom 39 or 47 inches of fence, and top it off with one to three strands of barbed wire. Because many ranchers in Shasta County owned sheep and swine a half century ago, many boundary fences there still contain woven wire. Other types of boundary fences, such as electrified fencing, are uncommon. However, an owner of horses may use board fencing instead of barbed wire to eliminate the risk that barbs pose to the coats of show animals. A natural barrier such as a gulch or a dense growth of brush may obviate the need for any type of boundary fencing. On fence technology, see generally U.S. Dep't of Agric., Farmers' Bull. No. 2247, *Fences for the Farm and Rural Home* (1971).

31. Cal. Agric. Code §17121 (West 1968). See also infra Chapter 3, note 24.

32. Walt Johnson, the Shasta County farm advisor, recommends that barbed-wire boundary fences have five strands. A rancher often erects "cross" or "division" fences to subdivide his own pastureland into separate fields. These fences enable a rancher to rest a pasture that would be damaged by further grazing, to control breeding, and to keep livestock away from a controlled burn. Ranchers tend to invest less time and money in their cross fences than in their boundary fences, partly because a breach in a cross fence is less likely to result in the loss of an animal. Al Levitt admitted to using only four strands for his cross fences and to not maintaining them quite as well as his five-strand boundary fences.

33. A half century ago, most Shasta County ranchers made their own fence posts by splitting logs. Should his own ranchland lack an adequate supply of logs, a rancher would contract

fencebuilders now typically use steel posts, which are less expensive, easier to drive into rocky soil, and more likely to survive a controlled burn. (Wooden posts are still essential at corners, gates, stretch panels, and other places where extra strength is needed.)

In 1982, the materials for a new four-strand, barbed-wire fence in Shasta County cost about $2000 per mile. Fence contractors charge at least as much for labor and overhead.[34] Both ranchers and ranchette owners customarily build their own fences and thereby drastically reduce out-of-pocket labor expenditures. I found only one rancher, and no ranchette owner, who admitted having contracted out fencing work.[35]

Barbed-wire fences require periodic maintenance, especially in Shasta County, where many natural forces conspire against fence wire. The extreme summer heat loosens the wire; the winter cold pulls it taut. The deer that migrate through the foothills during the wet season are generally able to jump cattle fences; but when a jumping deer fails to clear a fence cleanly, its hoof may break a tightly stretched top wire.[36] Heavy winter rains, rotting posts, downed trees, unruly bulls, or wayward auto-

---

with a private timber company to obtain the right to split downed cedar trees in the mountain forests. Today farm supply stores offer ready-made wooden posts.

34. Interview with Carl Yokum of Northwest Fence, in Palo Cedro, Cal. (Aug. 11, 1982). Technological advances—particularly the invention of barbed wire—have made fencing much less expensive relative to land and labor than it was in Abraham Lincoln's log-splitting days. Today, a newcomer to rural Shasta County would spend in the neighborhood of $40,000 to purchase a forty-acre ranchette, but for one-tenth of that sum could hire a contractor to enclose it with barbed wire. In the 1850s, "[i]t was certainly a rare farm-maker who had not to invest more capital—or its equivalent in labor in the case of forested areas—in his fence than in land." Clarence H. Danhof, "Farm-Making Costs and the 'Safety Valve': 1850–60," 49 *J. Pol. Econ.* 317, 345 (1941). Fencing costs in California during the 1850s are estimated to have been $300 to $600 per mile in the currency of the time. Id. at 345 n.78. See also Meade v. Watson, 67 Cal. 591, 595, 8 P. 311, 313 (1885) (complaint asserted "value" of a stone boundary fence to be $1.75 per rod or $560 per mile). In the latter part of the nineteenth century, mean family income in the United States was on the order of $600–$800 per year. See 1 Bureau of the Census, *Historical Statistics of the United States: Colonial Times to 1970* 322 (1975). Before the arrival of barbed wire, a mile of fence thus cost on the order of an average family's annual income. In 1981, the mean family income in the United States was $24,000. See Bureau of the Census, *Statistical Abstract of the United States 1982–1983* 435 (1982). That income would then have been sufficient to purchase the installation of at least five miles of barbed-wire fence in Shasta County.

35. The fence contractors who were interviewed agreed that the vast majority of rural fencing is done on a do-it-yourself basis. When asked, Walt Johnson could not recall the name of any fence contractor.

36. To qualify as "lawful," a barbed-wire fence in California must have a top strand that is at least 48 inches above the ground. Cal. Agric. Code §17121 (West 1968). Farm experts recommend that the top wire of a five-strand fence be elevated 52 inches. See *Fences for the*

mobiles may also create a breach. A rancher or his hand therefore must spend a few days each spring, either on horseback or in a pickup truck, riding fence. A conscientious rancher also inspects his fences in the fall after the deer season, in part to see what damage trespassing hunters may have inflicted.[37] With emergency repairs needed frequently, fence maintenance chores weigh constantly on a rancher's mind.[38]

Ranchers believe that the many benefits of perimeter barriers outweigh fence construction and maintenance costs. Cattlemen with permanent ranches in either the grasslands or foothills almost invariably have perimeter fences, as well as cross fences to divide their spreads into separate pastures. A ranchette owner, however, is unlikely to fence the boundary of his land unless he has livestock. In forest pastures one observes either no fencing or only an occasional drift fence.[39]

Traditionalists running herds in unfenced mountain forests have provoked most of the closed-range political movements in Shasta County.[40] During the summer months mountain cattle may wander onto rural highways or ravage hay fields and gardens in the settled parts of the foothills. Since 1960, the proliferation of ranchettes in the foothills has aggravated these two risks and heightened opposition to the practice of running cattle at large. At times the rural political pot comes to a boil over these issues.

Farm and Rural Home, supra note 30, at 17. The risk of damage from jumping deer has induced some fence contractors to warn against placing the top strand too high.

37. The veteran rancher and former member of the county Board of Supervisors Norman Wagoner estimated that a cattleman working alone can inspect and repair a fence at a rate of about two miles per day.

38. The rancher Owen Shellworth calculated that he spent 25 percent of his work hours on fences, including corral fences.

39. In no instance had a forest owner (or a traditionalist cattleman who leased a forest for summer range) fenced a forest boundary.

40. But they have not provoked all of them. Walt Johnson could recall several instances in which the precipitator had been a rancher, ostensibly operating within a fenced perimeter, who had deliberately turned out his animals onto neighboring lands.

2

* *

The Politics of Cattle Trespass

Loose cattle often cause political flaps in Shasta County. Many rural residents know that the Board of Supervisors has the power to adopt closed-range ordinances. They believe that these ordinances increase the civil liabilities of owners of stray livestock not only for trespass damages but also, and more significantly, for damages stemming from highway collisions between vehicles and domestic animals. When residents and motorists in a particular area of the county suffer a rash of cattle-related incidents, they are likely to report their grievances to their local supervisor, whom they ask to mediate the conflict or to support a closed-range ordinance designed to cure the problem. If adopted, a closure indeed serves to reduce the number of loose cattle because fear of liability to motorists makes traditionalists reluctant to run cattle at large in closed range.[1]

At least since 1970, the Board of Supervisors has required constituents who propose adoption of a closed-range ordinance to follow a special procedure. The complainants must draw up a petition that identifies a specific territory for closure, gather signatures on copies of the petition, and forward the signed petition to the board. Although the board does not insist upon the submission of a particular minimum number of signatures, closure proponents gather as many as possible. Upon receiving a petition, the board's staff drafts an ordinance that will implement the closure and publicizes a hearing on the proposed measure.[2] In practice, opponents usually receive sufficient notice of an upcoming hearing to gather signatures on a counterpetition.[3] At the public hearing, the board hears statements from proponents and opponents and then votes on the

1. Rural residents actually exaggerate the effect of a closed-range ordinance on the legal allocation of losses arising out of vehicle-livestock collisions. See Chapters 5 and 6.
2. In the early 1980s the board held hearings on closed-range petitions no more than twice a year, in February and July.
3. In 1982 it was the board's standard practice, upon receiving a closed-range petition, to notify the Shasta County Cattlemen's Association by mail.

measure. Over the years, cattlemen have been quite successful in defeating proposed closures. Between 1946 and 1972, the board approved sixteen closures in various parts of Shasta County, but most of those ordinances only involved lands on Redding's urban fringe.[4]

Prior to the 1973 Caton's Folly ordinance that closed an area near Round Mountain, the Board of Supervisors approved only one closure that affected a significant amount of rural territory east of the Sacramento River. In the early 1960s, mountain cattle began to appear in number along a stretch of State Highway 44 in the Shingletown-Viola area, thirty miles east of Redding. Highway 44 is the major route between Redding and Mount Lassen National Park. In 1965 the board voted to close the range in a three-mile-wide strip of land straddling Highway 44 for a distance of twelve and a half miles.[5] This closure affected an area topographically similar to, but south of, the foothills of the Northeastern Sector. The entire sector remained open until the Caton's Folly closure. The history of that ordinance and of the board's rejection of the Oak Run closure petition in 1982 helps reveal the role of elected local officials in cattle trespass disputes.

Caton's Folly: The Closing of the Range at Round Mountain

The hamlet of Round Mountain lies thirty miles northeast of Redding. Scattered along State Highway 299, the main thoroughfare through the settlement, are a general store, an elementary school, and a substation in Pacific Gas & Electric's hydroelectric power grid. The hamlet is 2000 feet in elevation and is surrounded by higher foothills, the most prominent of which has given the place its name. During the 1960s, the area around Round Mountain, like the rest of the Shasta County foothills, became increasingly dotted with ranchettes. The frustration of these ranchette owners over the perceived misdeeds of three traditionalists, Paul Totten, Bob Moquet, and Ward Kearney, helped spawn the Caton's Folly ordinance of 1973. The particular activities of these three deserve brief description.

In the early 1970s, Totten, a small-scale traditionalist with a base ranch west of Redding, leased some thirty square miles of Roseburg Lumber

4. The county's Department of Public Works periodically prepares and sells to the public a map listing all closed-range ordinances and showing the territories they affect. The statement in the text is based on this map.

5. Shasta County, Cal., Ordinance 459 (Aug. 8, 1966).

Company forest lands for summer range.[6] The western boundary of Totten's leasehold was three miles east of the hamlet of Round Mountain and at a higher elevation. Just west of the boundary was an aging foothill farm with a sixty-acre irrigated field. John Woodbury had acquired this farm in 1966 and over a period of years had converted the irrigated field from natural grass to alfalfa. During the early 1970s Totten's mountain cattle found and repeatedly used a path that led from the meager offerings of the Roseburg forest to the banquet of Woodbury's unfenced alfalfa field. Whenever Woodbury telephoned him to complain about a trespass, Totten would eventually drive the cattle back up into the forest, but neither as promptly nor as irreversibly as Woodbury would have liked.

Bob Moquet's cattle were a more pervasive and longstanding nuisance. A tough and independent leader of a pioneer clan long settled in the Round Mountain area, Moquet aroused particular hostility because he was repeatedly unresponsive to his neighbors' complaints.[7] He seemed to believe that a cattleman had a divine right to let his cattle loose in the mountains during the summer. Steve Mattingly, a modernist cattleman who raised registered Galloway cattle on a fenced ranch on Buzzard Roost Road, became particularly concerned that Moquet's hybrid bulls might impregnate his cows.

In the early 1970s, Dr. Arthur Cooley, a Redding physician, obtained a summer grazing lease on a large tract of United States Forest Service land situated a few miles west of Round Mountain, on Backbone Ridge. To manage his mountain herd of several hundred animals, Cooley hired Ward Kearney, a traditionalist cowboy of exceptional ability. Kearney shared Moquet's view that people who object to stray cattle should fence them out. Consequently, after driving Cooley's cattle to Backbone Ridge, Kearney would allow them to drift down into the ranchette areas and heavily traveled stretches of Highway 299 near Round Mountain.

The mountain cattle owned by Cooley, Moquet, and Totten tipped the political balance in Round Mountain in favor of closure. In early 1973, Mattingly, Woodbury, and a few longtime area residents began meeting to discuss the problem of stray mountain cattle. These antitraditionalists eventually drafted and gathered signatures on a petition that asked the Board of Supervisors to convert from open to closed range a seven by

---

6. The lessor in the early 1970s was actually the Kimberly-Clark Corporation. Kimberly-Clark sold its forest lands in the Northeastern Sector to the Roseburg Lumber Company in 1979. For simplicity, the text treats Roseburg as the continuous owner of these lands.

7. Especially because he lived in the area, Moquet can be described as a deviant from prevailing rural norms. Totten lived elsewhere, and might be better characterized as an outsider.

eight mile rectangle of territory centered on Round Mountain. It is not clear who drew the exact boundaries of this rectangle. Not surprisingly, all of the activists' lands fell within its perimeter. In the end, seventy-two people, mostly Round Mountain residents, signed the closed-range petition.

On March 10, 1973, Mattingly mailed the signed petition to John Caton, the newly elected board member for the supervisorial district that included the foothills in the Northeastern Sector. Caton lived on a ranchette in Montgomery Creek, a hamlet situated three miles northeast of Round Mountain on Highway 299. Caton shared many of the cattlemen's values, yet he was aware that mountain cattle had been endangering both residents and motorists. The deepening conflict between traditionalist cattlemen and the residents of the Round Mountain area placed him in a delicate political position. He offered to help mediate and asked Mattingly and the other petitioners to wait a few months to see whether the problem would abate. It did not. During the summer of 1973, mountain cattle entered Woodbury's alfalfa field on over a dozen occasions. Woodbury said he telephoned Caton to complain each time.

On December 3, 1973, the Board of Supervisors finally held its hearing on the antitraditionalists' petition to close the fifty-six-square-mile rectangle. The hearing was lightly attended. John Woodbury, pasture owner Phil Ritchie, and ranchette owner Ted Plomeson spoke in favor of the closure. The only significant speaker in opposition was Dr. Cooley, whose protestations of economic hardship elicited little sympathy. The official minutes of the board's meeting contain no indication that a representative of the Shasta County Cattlemen's Association was present. At the end of the session, the board voted by a margin of 4 to 1, with Caton in the majority, to declare that the rectangle outlined in the March petition had "ceased to be devoted chiefly to grazing"—the legal language necessary to convert the area from open range to closed range.[8]

With the exception of a few modernists such as Mattingly, Shasta County cattlemen soon came to rue their failure to fight the Round Mountain closure. To chide Caton for supporting what they regarded as a lamentable precedent, they referred to the affected area as "Caton's Folly" or "Caton's Acres." Caton got the point. During the next decade, he successfully persuaded the Board of Supervisors to reject all petitions that would have closed additional territories in foothill areas of his district.

8. Shasta County, Cal., Ordinance 498 (Dec. 3, 1973).

Caton's Repentance: The Defeat of the Oak Run Closure Petition

Caton's change of heart is best illustrated by his handling of a 1981 petition that asked the board to close ninety-six square miles of range in the Oak Run area just southwest of Caton's Folly. The hamlet of Oak Run sits only three miles south of the southwestern corner of Caton's Folly. The hamlet's elevation is 1600 feet, a level where the grassy plains blend with the tangle of brush and trees that typify the foothills. During 1981–82, only a few months before I conducted most of my interviews, the Oak Run area had been the site of perhaps the most heated closed-range battle in the history of Shasta County. Frank Ellis, a recent entrant into the big-time cattle business, had single-handedly provoked the circulation of a petition that sought to triple the area of closed range in the foothills of the Northeastern Sector.

Frank Ellis

Ellis, accompanied by his wife and school-age children, moved to Shasta County in about 1973. A rancher and real estate broker by profession, Ellis was then in his late fifties. He immediately acquired a functioning 2500-acre ranch astride the Oak Run Road two miles west of Oak Run and just south of an area sprouting ranchettes. The size and prominent location of Ellis' base ranch helped to make him a conspicuous personality in the Northeastern Sector. Ellis, who declined my request for an interview, was by all reports a man capable of great charm. According to his neighbors, however, beneath this appealing surface lay a ruthless ambition for wealth and power. Many who dealt with Ellis came to regard him as capricious, spiteful, and not always good for his word. He became the target of numerous lawsuits, and for a time even had an attorney on retainer. Although Ellis' aggressive and colorful personality won him some admirers, his more upstanding neighbors came to view him as an untrustworthy bully.

During the late 1970s, Ellis built up the largest ranching empire in the Northeastern Sector. He started by obtaining a grazing lease on a section of Bureau of Land Management land to the west of his base ranch. Then in 1978 he persuaded the absentee owners of the largest ranching estate in the area to hire him to manage their scattered grasslands and foothills. By this one stroke, Ellis won control over another twenty square miles of pasture. Ellis eventually purchased hundreds of cattle on credit and hired a band of Mexican farmworkers, *braceros,* to tend them.

The various components of Ellis' ranching empire were not physically connected. Ellis knew that all his holdings were within open range, but he erroneously interpreted this to mean that he could legally herd his livestock onto any intervening land that was not fenced. When moving his livestock about, Ellis' cowboys not only deliberately crossed the unfenced private lands of others but also used those lands as free pasture.[9] By 1981, Ellis' drovers were aggressively running a herd of two to three thousand cattle at large in the grasslands and lower foothills northeast of Redding, an area where virtually all other cattlemen were modernists who kept their animals behind fences.

Ellis' Antagonists

Most of the lands that Ellis' livestock invaded were uncultivated and uninhabited tracts held by speculators, who, if anything, appreciated a herd coming through to beat back the brush. Yet in some areas, particularly those near Oak Run itself, the victims of Ellis' trespasses were ranchette owners who had recently moved to the foothills in search of a pastoral life. Ellis' marauding herds quickly became the bane of these ranchette owners. At least eight built fences at their own expense specifically to keep Ellis' animals off their lands. Although at least two of these ranchette owners saw Ellis as acting within his rights, most of them—particularly Doug Heinz—did not.

Heinz, a skilled craftsman from southern California, moved to Shasta County in 1978 with his wife and small children. The Heinzes acquired a house on a twenty-acre ranchette situated in open range west of Oak Run and about one mile from Ellis' base ranch. As a hobby, Heinz started to raise a few horses and cows on a twelve-acre portion of his ranchette that was enclosed by a five-strand barbed wire fence. The frequent passage of Ellis' herds punctured Heinz's dreams of small-scale squiredom.

According to Heinz, he and Ellis started off on polite terms. On three or four occasions in 1979, several of Ellis' cattle jumped over or broke through Heinz's fence. Heinz reacted to these early trespasses by telephoning Ellis. Ellis' response was to send his drovers to chase the cows within Heinz's field to tire them so they could then be coaxed through

---

9. Although they occurred in open range, these entries were intentional and therefore tortious. See infra Chapter 3, note 25.

the fence. This method of retrieval battered Heinz's fences, and Ellis' drovers never repaired the damage. Heinz's patience ran out one snowy day when he discovered that Ellis' hands had dropped hay for two hundred cattle in the narrow snowplowed driveway leading to his ranchette. The milling herd that flocked to the hay included cows that had just calved, and these skittish new mothers frightened Heinz's small children.

Although most of Heinz's ranchette-owning neighbors had passively endured indignities from Ellis' livestock, Heinz was relatively short-tempered. He purchased a shotgun and called the county sheriff to protest Ellis' activities. According to what Ellis later told acquaintances, Heinz also began to threaten that Ellis might find "dead cattle." On the next occasion that Ellis' cattle broke through the fence, Heinz seized three animals and held them for three months without notifying Ellis. This incident eventually led to a lawsuit by Heinz to recover boarding costs and to a countersuit by Ellis for mistreatment of Ellis' animals.[10]

In early 1981, while his lawsuit against Ellis was still pending, Heinz began a political crusade to stop Ellis' at-large grazing practices. Heinz anticipated recruiting a host of allies, and not just among his fellow ranchette owners. During 1978–1981, virtually every foothill motorist had reason to be annoyed at Ellis' failure to keep his livestock off the foothill roads. When Ellis' stock were being moved along the highways, motorists were often delayed for up to an hour. On at least six occasions vehicles collided with Ellis' animals on the Oak Run Road. Heinz succeeded in rallying to the anti-Ellis cause dozens of ranchette-owning newcomers, as well as members of at least one respected and long-established ranching family in the Oak Run area.

Caton's Mediation and the Battle of Petitions

During 1981 Heinz and his allies peppered their local supervisor, John Caton, with complaints about Ellis' herds. Since his christening in the Round Mountain incidents eight years earlier, Caton had become a veteran of political disputes over trespassing cattle. He knew that if he supported a closed-range ordinance for the Oak Run area, he would further alienate the powerful cattlemen's lobby, a group that had never forgiven him for supporting the Caton's Folly ordinance. If he opposed the closure, however, he would offend a potentially more numerous, if less organized, group, the ranchette owners and motorists that Ellis' herds endangered.

10. See infra Chapter 3, text accompanying notes 65–66.

Caton sought to defuse the controversy before a formal closure petition surfaced. Working in the spring of 1981 with the county animal control officer Brad Bogue, Caton threatened to support a closed-range ordinance for the Oak Run area if Ellis failed to build a fence along a three-mile stretch of the Oak Run Road that his herds made particularly dangerous. In response, Ellis promised Caton that he would build the fence. As the summer of 1981 dragged on without any sign of the fence, Caton began to regard circulation of a closed-range petition as inevitable.

Caton's political instincts proved to be accurate. Some members of the anti-Ellis group preferred to postpone circulating a petition until they had exhausted other types of mediation; this faction, for example, wanted to ask the Shasta County Cattlemen's Association to request Ellis to manage his herds more responsibly. But Heinz decided to force the issue. In the fall of 1981, without consulting some of his leading allies, he drafted and began to circulate a petition designed to close the range in a ninety-six-square-mile area southwest of, and abutting, Caton's Folly. Heinz drew the boundaries broadly in an effort to cast the entire Ellis empire into closed range. The petition did not mention Ellis by name, but it did state that "Our reasons for this stem mostly from the inconsideration and abuse of the open range law of one rancher."[11] Heinz and his allies gathered 42 signatures—an unimpressive total—and delivered their petition to John Caton in late November 1981.

The Board of Supervisors was scheduled to hold its next hearing on closure petitions three months later, in February 1982. The interval enabled Caton to minimize the political risks posed by the Heinz petition. He immediately publicized receipt of the petition, thereby helping the opposition to organize a countercampaign. Caton showed the Heinz petition to Wayne Thompson, a small-scale sheep rancher who lived on the Oak Run Road. Thompson enlisted his neighbor Larry Brennan, a college graduate who as a hobby raised horses on a large ranchette nearby, to draft a counterpetition urging the board to keep the area open. Brennan began the counterpetition with the following language: "We feel that

---

11. The petition continued:
    Our reasons to list a few are:
       1. Unsafe roadways due to poorly maintained fences, cows are continually on the roads and jepardizing [sic] the safety of school children.
       2. Property destruction of the trespassing cows on private property.
       3. Cutting of fences on private property to herd the cows with more ease to other areas of private property.
       4. Interference of range cows with private herds.

the 'open range' system serves many purposes for the large and small rancher: 1. Limits of liability. . . ."[12] Thompson tirelessly circulated the counterpetition in the vicinity of Oak Run. Prior to the February hearing, Thompson and his associates submitted to the board the names of 146 individuals, mostly residents of the Oak Run area, who had signed their counterpetition. Heinz's temperamental personality and lack of roots in the area limited his own success and aided Thompson, who outsolicited him by a margin of more than three to one.

The board also received a second counterpetition. Following standard procedures adopted after the Round Mountain controversy, the board's staff had automatically informed the Shasta County Cattlemen's Association that the board had received Heinz's closed-range petition. The association's leaders then circulated a petition on their own. Their petition to keep the range open attracted only 24 signers, but many were members of well-known ranching families operating northeast of Redding.

Caton's last major step after the Heinz petition surfaced was to remind Ellis that Caton's decision on the closure petition would rest largely on whether Ellis kept his promise to build the three miles of fence along Oak Run Road. Ellis finally responded, but grudgingly. By the time of the board's hearing on February 2, 1982, Ellis' employees had erected three miles of five-strand barbed-wire fence (shown in Figure 1.2), a project that probably cost Ellis $5,000 to $10,000. The fence was positioned on private lands (mostly owned by speculators) on which Ellis had grazed his herds without fee. Because the new fence helped to reassure motorists, it became a conspicuous monument to Caton's effectiveness. The fence offered no relief, however, to ranchette owners such as Heinz whose lands lay between Ellis' ranch and the new fence.

The Hearing and Its Aftermath

At the board's February 2 hearing, Caton kept his part of his bargain with Ellis. Caton's decision to oppose the closure had become an easy one. Not only had Thompson's counterpetition attracted far more signatories than the Heinz petition had, but Thompson and the cattlemen were also

12. The counterpetition continued:
    2. Fire protection—through grazing, keeping the grass down.
    3. Biological control—through natural fertilization of soil of rangeland, timber production, fuel-wood production.
    4. Natural predator control.
    5. Prevention of soil erosion due to stronger root system with annual grasses.

more successful than the Heinz group in turning out supporters at the board meeting. As Jeff Marotta, a ranchette owner and Heinz ally, stated, "When I saw all those cowboy hats [in the hearing room] I knew we were going to lose." At the hearing six speakers, including Doug Heinz, spoke in favor of the closure, but thirteen, including Bob Bosworth, president of the Shasta County Cattlemen's Association, spoke against it. Although the hall was packed, Ellis himself was not present. As someone said that night, "He wouldn't dare to be." [13]

Caton was also the beneficiary of an unexpected development: by early 1982 the Ellis ranching empire had begun to crumble. Ellis had bought hundreds of cattle on credit in anticipation that beef prices would rise. Instead, prices had fallen. This setback, arriving on top of a variety of other financial reverses, left Ellis without funds to pay creditors. A week or two before the board's hearing, Ellis' banks had begun repossessing his cattle. This juicy bit of news had spread quickly through the gossip mills of the Northeastern Sector foothills.

When the testimony at the hearing came to a close, the other supervisors stated that they would defer to John Caton, the supervisor in whose district the proposed closure lay. Caton recommended that the area remain as open range but added that, if the problem continued, the board should consider closing four sections of land where Heinz and most of the other complaining ranchette owners lived. The board promptly voted unanimously to deny the Heinz petition. To smooth the waters, Dan Gover, the board's chairman and a rancher himself, asked Bob Bosworth to meet with Ellis, Heinz, and county animal control officials to see what could be done to control Ellis' herds. [14] Caton had repented for Caton's Folly.

Within a few months of the hearing, both Heinz and Ellis were gone from the Oak Run area. At least as early as 1980 Heinz had planned to build a house in Redding for his family. Only a few days after the board rejected his petition, he moved out of the Oak Run ranchette and into his newly completed Redding house. Ellis' stay in Oak Run lasted only three months longer than Heinz's. The banks seized Ellis' cattle, and creditors lined up with claims on his ranch. In May 1982 Ellis moved his family

13. Just one speaker at the meeting, the cattleman Marty Fancher, referred to Ellis by name. Even the members of the anti-Ellis group discreetly spoke only of "one rancher" whose misdeeds had provoked the petition.

14. The proposed meeting was never held, in part because the cattlemen were only willing to administer informal sanctions, and, as Bosworth said at the hearing in response to a supervisor's question, this sort of pressure wouldn't work with Ellis because, "He hasn't been in [the county] all that long."

one hundred miles south to a farm in another California county in the Central Valley. As his parting shot to Shasta County, Ellis ordered his hands to destroy the three miles of fence along the Oak Run Road that he had had built just six months before. On the day the Board of Supervisors held its hearing, the two leading players in the Oak Run closure fight both knew that they were about to depart from the stage.[15]

15. This fact is consistent with the theoretical proposition, explored in subsequent chapters, that the lack of a prospective long-term future relationship makes disputants less likely to resolve their differences without the help of third parties, and hence more likely to resort to legal and political action.

3

* *

The Resolution of Cattle-Trespass Disputes

Trespass by cattle, the subject of Coase's Parable of the Farmer and the Rancher, is a common event in ranching country. A complex body of law, much of it of unusually ancient lineage, formally applies to these occurrences. In Shasta County, the rules of trespass law vary between open- and closed-range districts, and the location of district boundaries has been the focus of intense political controversy. Nevertheless, it turns out, perhaps counterintuitively, that legal rules hardly ever influence the settlement of cattle-trespass disputes in Shasta County.[1]

Animal Trespass Incidents

Each of the twenty-eight landowners interviewed, including each of the thirteen ranchette owners, reported at least one instance in which his lands had been invaded by someone else's livestock. Hay farmers grow what cattle especially like to eat and can thus expect frequent trespasses. For example, John Woodbury, an alfalfa grower, suffered almost weekly incursions in 1973. Woodbury's situation later improved when many traditionalist cattlemen declined to renew their grazing leases on mountain forest,[2] but he was still experiencing a couple of cattle trespasses a year in the early 1980s. Another hay farmer, Phil Ritchie, could identify six neighbors whose cattle had trespassed on his lands in recent years. Owners of large ranches are also frequent trespass victims because they cannot keep their many miles of aging perimeter fence cattle-tight. Thus, when

---

1. My field research relied heavily on face-to-face interviews. In all, seventy-three interviews were conducted, most of them in the summer of 1982. They were arranged with two sorts of people: landowners in the Oak Run–Round Mountain area, and a somewhat larger number of specialists—such as attorneys, claims adjusters, and government employees—thought likely to be knowledgeable about how rural residents resolve stray-cattle disputes. Various government records were also consulted, partly to have a cross-check on the landowners' version of history. The techniques used are more fully described in the Appendix.

2. See infra Chapter 6, text following note 9.

40

a rancher gathers his animals on his fenced pastures each spring, he is hardly startled to find a few head carrying a neighbor's brand.

Because beef cattle eat feed equal to about 2½ percent of their body weight each day,[3] a trespass victim's vegetation is always at risk. Nevertheless, a victim usually regards the loss of grass as trivial, provided that the animals are easy to corral and the owner removes them within a day or two. Trespassing livestock occasionally do cause more than nominal damage. Several ranchette owners reported incidents in which wayward cattle had damaged their fences and vegetable gardens; one farmer told of the ravaging of some of his ornamental trees.

The most serious trespasses reported were ones involving at-large cattle or bulls. A ranchette owner described how mountain cattle had once invaded his house construction site, broken the windows, and contaminated the creek. The part-time horsebreeder Larry Brennan told of buying seven tons of hay and stacking it on an unfenced portion of his fifty-acre ranchette, where it was then eaten by cattle that Frank Ellis had let roam free.

Rural residents especially fear trespasses by bulls. In a modern beef cattle herd, roughly one animal in twenty-five is a bull, whose principal function is to impregnate cows during their brief periods in heat.[4] Bulls are not only much more ornery but also much larger than other herd animals. A Hereford bull has a mature weight of 2000 pounds. By contrast, a mature Hereford cow weighs only 1100–1200 pounds, and Hereford steers (castrated males) are typically slaughtered when they weigh between 1000 and 1150 pounds.[5] Several ranchers who were interviewed had vivid memories of bull trespasses. A farmer who owned irrigated pasture was amazed at the depth of the hoof marks that an entering bull had made. A ranchette owner and a rancher told of barely escaping goring while attempting to corral invading bulls.[6] Because an alien bull often enters in pursuit of cows in heat, owners of female animals fear illicit couplings that might produce offspring of an undesired pedigree. Al-

3. Division of Agric. Sci., Univ. of Cal., Leaflet No. 21184, *Beef Production in California* 12–13 (Nov. 1980).

4. Cf. Cal. Agric. Code §16803 (West 1968) (cattlemen grazing herds on open range must include at least one bull for every thirty cows). The refinement of artificial insemination techniques has enabled some ranchers to increase the ratio of cows to bulls in herds kept behind fences.

5. *Beef Production in California*, supra note 3, at 3, 5.

6. None of the landowners interviewed mentioned an instance in which trespassing cattle had caused personal injury. Two insurance adjusters, who frequently had been called upon to settle dog-bite claims, could remember, between them, only one personal-injury claim arising from cattle—an instance in which a cow had stepped on someone's foot.

though no cow owner reported actual damages from misbreeding, several mentioned that this risk especially worried them.

Animal Trespass Law

One of the most venerable English common law rules of strict liability in tort is the rule that an owner of domestic livestock is liable, even in the absence of negligence, for property damage that his animals cause while trespassing. In the memorable words of Judge Blackburn:

> The case that has most commonly occurred, and which is most fre- quently to be found in the books, is as to the obligation of the owner of cattle which he has brought on his land, to prevent their escaping and doing mischief. The law as to them seems to be perfectly settled from early times; the owner must keep them in at his peril, or he will be answerable for the natural consequences of their escape; that is with regard to tame beasts, for the grass they eat and trample upon, though not for any injury to the person of others, for our ancestors have settled that it is not the general nature of horses to kick, or bulls to gore; but if the owner knows that the beast has a vicious propensity to attack man, he will be answerable for that too.[7]

This traditional English rule formally prevails in the closed-range areas of Shasta County.[8] In the open-range areas of the county—that is, in the great bulk of its rural territory—the English rule has been rejected in favor of the pro-cattleman "fencing-out" rule that many grazing states adopted during the nineteenth century.[9]

7. Fletcher v. Rylands, 1 L.R.-Ex. 265, 280 (1866) (dictum) (Blackburn, J.). See also 3 William Blackstone, *Commentaries* *211 ("A man is answerable for not only his own trespass, but that of his cattle also"). This rule was established in England by 1353 at the latest. 1 *Select Cases of Trespass from the King's Courts, 1307–1399* lxxviii (Morris S. Arnold ed. 1985). The details of animal-trespass law are explored more fully in Ellickson, "Of Coase and Cattle: Dispute Resolution among Neighbors in Shasta County," 38 *Stan. L. Rev.* 623, 659–667 (1986).

8. See, e.g., Montezuma Improvement Co. v. Simmerly, 181 Cal. 722, 724, 189 P. 100, 101 (1919). A trespass victim's own misconduct, such as failing to close a cattle gate or breaching a contractual duty to build a fence, may diminish or bar his recovery. See Glanville L. Williams, *Liability for Animals* 178–181 (1939). In California, misconduct by a plaintiff does not typically operate as a complete defense in a strict liability action. Daly v. General Motors Corp., 20 Cal. 3d 725, 575 P.2d 1162, 144 Cal. Rptr. 380 (1978) (products liability case).

9. Many authorities assert that the western states have been the chief followers of "fencing-out" rules. See, e.g., 2 Fowler V. Harper and Fleming James, *The Law of Torts* §14.10 (1956). Nineteenth-century treatises on fence law reveal, however, that in that era, fencing-out was the dominant rule throughout the United States, particularly in the *northern* states. See W. W. Thornton, *The Law of Railroad Fences and Private Crossings* §§8–10 (1892) (identifying thirteen states following the English rule and twenty-one states having fencing-out regimes);

In 1850, just after California attained statehood, an open-range rule was adopted for the entire state. In that year the legislature enacted a statute that entitled a victim of animal trespass to recover damages only when the victim had protected his lands with a "lawful fence."[10] This pro-cattleman policy grew increasingly controversial as California became more settled and field crops became more common. During the latter part of the nineteenth century, the California legislature enacted a series of statutes effectively closing the range in designated counties, thereby granting more protection to farmers who had not built fences.[11]

The closed-range exceptions eventually began to swamp California's traditional open-range rule and triggered a comprehensive legislative response. In the Estray Act of 1915,[12] the legislature adopted for most of California the traditional English rule that the owner of livestock is strictly liable for trespass damage.[13] This statute, however, retained the open-range rule in six counties in the lightly populated northern part of the state, where the tradition of running cattle at large remained strong. The six counties were Shasta, Del Norte, Lassen, Modoc, Siskiyou, and Trinity.[14]

Ransom H. Tyler, *The Law of Boundaries, Fences, and Window Lights* 361–512 (1874) (state-by-state review of fence law, indicating, at 451, that Michigan, for example, enacted a fencing-out statute in 1847).

10. 1850 Cal. Stat., ch. 49, 131. See Comerford v. Dupuy, 17 Cal. 308 (1861); Waters v. Moss, 12 Cal. 535 (1859) (dictum). Because lawful-fence rules draw brighter lines than do negligence rules, they tend to be easier to apply. Lawful-fence statutes are consequently suited to enforcement by lay "fence viewers," described infra note 27. For a more extended analysis of the merits of alternative rules of cattle-trespass liability, see infra Chapter 11, text accompanying notes 3–11.

11. See Note, "Torts: Trespass by Animals upon Unenclosed Lands in California," 7 *Cal. L. Rev.* 365 (1919).

12. 1915 Cal. Stat. 636 (current version at Cal. Agric. Code §§17001–17128 (West 1968 & Supp. 1986)).

13. Although the 1915 statute nominally dealt only with a trespass victim's rights to take up estrays (strays), California case law has consistently held that a statutory right to seize estrays on unfenced land carries with it the right to recover trespass damages under the traditional common law rule of strict liability. See, e.g., Montezuma Improvement Co. v. Simmerly, 181 Cal. 722, 189 P. 100 (1919); Williams v. Goodwin, 41 Cal. App. 3d 496, 116 Cal. Rptr. 200 (1974) (dictum).

14. 1915 Cal. Stat. 636 (current version at Cal. Agric. Code §§17123–17126 (West 1968)). Subsequent amendments repealed the exemptions applicable in all of Del Norte County, and in parts of Shasta and Trinity counties. See Cal. Agric. Code §§17123–17126 (West 1968). Cal. Agric. Code §17124 (West 1968) authorizes the board of supervisors of *any* county to convert closed-range areas to open range. Responding in part to lobbying efforts by local cattlemen's associations, an increasing number of California's foothill counties have "opened" parts of their mountain forest. See, e.g., Amador County, Cal., Ordinance 590 (Apr. 26, 1977); Placer County, Cal., Ordinance 2017-B (June 29, 1976).

In 1945 the legislature enacted two amendments that dealt exclusively with Shasta County, the least rural of the six exempt counties. The first stated that a prime agricultural area just south of Redding was "not . . . devoted chiefly to grazing"—a declaration that the legislature had decided to close the range in that small area of the county.[15] The second amendment empowered the Board of Supervisors of Shasta County to adopt ordinances designating additional areas of the county as places no longer devoted chiefly to grazing. A board action of this sort would make cattlemen strictly liable for trespass damage occurring in those locations.[16] Between 1945 and 1974 Shasta was the only California county to possess this special authority.[17] As a result Shasta County today has a crazy quilt of open- and closed-range areas that no other California county can match.[18]

The distinction between open range and closed range has formal legal significance in Shasta County trespass disputes. In closed range, the English rule governs and an animal owner is strictly liable for trespass damage to property.[19] In open-range areas, by contrast, even a livestock owner[20] who has negligently managed his animals is generally not liable for trespass damage to the lands[21] of a neighbor.

15. 1945 Cal. Stat. 1538–39 (current version at Cal. Agric. Code §17126 (West 1968)).

16. 1945 Cal. Stat. 1539 (current version at Cal. Agric. Code §17127 (West 1968 & Supp. 1986)).

17. In 1974 the state legislature granted similar authority to the Board of Supervisors of Trinity County, Shasta's neighbor to the west. 1974 Cal. Stat. 409 (current version at Cal. Agric. Code §17127 (West Supp. 1986)). A number of other western states that generally adhere to an open-range regime also authorize substate entities to "close" parts of their range. See, e.g., Maguire v. Yanke, 99 Idaho 829, 590 P.2d 85 (1978) (describing Idaho procedure through which landowners can petition to close range on a district-by-district basis); Wash. Rev. Code Ann. §16.24.010 (1962) (counties without townships granted power to close range).

18. A map issued by the Shasta County Department of Public Works in 1981 showed twenty-eight separate areas the Board of Supervisors had closed by ordinance since 1945. Although most of the closed areas were located near Redding, there were areas of closed range in the hinterland in every direction from the city.

19. Defenses based on the trespass victim's misconduct are discussed supra note 8.

20. Persons other than the animal's owner could conceivably be held liable for an animal's damage. The California courts (at least until the late 1980s) were as expansive as any state's in imposing tort liability. They would have been likely to hold a landlord who had leased land for grazing liable were he negligently to have abetted trespasses by a lessee's livestock. Cf. Uccello v. Laudenslayer, 44 Cal. App. 3d 504, 118 Cal. Rptr. 741 (1975) (residential landlord who knew of tenant's vicious dog and had the power to have it removed owed a duty of care to tenants' invitees and could be liable for negligence to dog-bite victim). But cf. Blake v. Dunn Farms, Inc., 274 Ind. 560, 413 N.E.2d 560 (1980) (landlord not liable for damages stemming from escape of tenant's horse that he knew little about).

21. Other rules may apply when livestock have caused personal injury or damage to chattels. In closed range, a cattle owner is strictly liable for foreseeable personal injuries that his

Even in open range in Shasta County, however, an animal owner is legally liable for animal-trespass damages of three significant sorts. First, owners of goats, swine, and vicious dogs are strictly liable for trespass throughout Shasta County.[22] Second, when a cattleman's livestock have trespassed in the face of a "lawful fence" that entirely enclosed the victim's open-range premises, the cattleman is also strictly liable.[23] (A California statute, unamended since 1915, defines the technological standard that a fence must meet to be "lawful.")[24] Third, common law decisions make a livestock owner liable for *intentional* open-range trespasses. Thus when Frank Ellis actively herded his cattle across the unfenced lands of his neighbors, he was legally liable for trespass. According to some precedents, he would also have been liable had he merely placed his cattle on his own lands in a way that would make it substantially certain that they would venture onto his neighbors' pastures.[25]

---

livestock have caused. See Williams v. Goodwin, 41 Cal. App. 3d 496, 116 Cal. Rptr. 200 (1974). But cf. *Restatement (Second) of Torts* §504 (1977) (denying possessor of unfenced land in open-range recovery for personal injuries on a strict liability theory). In both open and closed range, the owner of a trespassing animal would be strictly liable if that animal were to kill animals belonging to the owner of the premises invaded. See Cal. Civ. Code §3341 (West 1970).

22. See Cal. Agric. Code. §17128 (West 1968) (excepting owners of "goats, swine, or hogs" from benefits of open-range rule); Shasta County Ordinance Code §3306 (declaring it "unlawful" to permit "any vicious dog or other dangerous animal" to run at large).

23. Section 17122 of the Agricultural Code reads: "In any county or part of a county devoted chiefly to grazing and so declared pursuant to this article, a person shall not have the right to take up any estray animal found upon his premises, or upon premises to which he has the right of possession, nor shall he have a lien thereon, *unless the premises are entirely enclosed with a good and substantial fence.*" Cal. Agric. Code §17122 (West 1968) (emphasis added). Judicial decisions construe this sort of provision as also denying a person without such a fence the right to recover damages for cattle trespass. See supra note 13.

24. "A lawful fence is any fence which is good, strong, substantial, and sufficient to prevent the ingress and egress of livestock. No wire fence is a good and substantial fence within the meaning of this article unless it has three tightly stretched barbed wires securely fastened to posts of reasonable strength, firmly set in the ground not more than one rod [16½ feet] apart, one of which wires shall be at least four feet above the surface of the ground. Any kind of wire or other fence of height, strength and capacity equal to or greater than the wire fence herein described is a good and substantial fence within the meaning of this article. . . ." Cal. Agric. Code §17121 (West 1968). This statutory definition of a lawful fence has remained essentially unchanged since 1919. Compare 1919 Cal. Stat. 1150. The definition is technologically obsolete because, at least in Shasta County, cattlemen customarily use at least four strands of barbed wire in their boundary fences. California's statutory definitions of lawful fences before the invention of barbed wire are described in R. Tyler, supra note 9, at 482–484 (some samples: stone walls 4½ feet high; rail fences 5½ feet high; a 5-foot-high hedge).

25. In some states an open-range cattleman has been held liable for the trespass damages only when he has deliberately driven his livestock onto the lands of another. See, e.g., Garcia

When the law of either open or closed range entitles a trespass victim to relief, the standard legal remedy is an award of compensatory damages.[26] (In part because evidence of damage to forage is fleeting, some states, although currently not California, authorize the appointment of disinterested residents of the area to serve as "fence viewers" to assess the amount of the damages.)[27] A plaintiff who has suffered from continuing wrongful trespasses may also be entitled to an injunction against future incursions.[28] California's Estray Act additionally entitles a landowner whose premises have been wrongly invaded by cattle to seize the animals as security for a claim to recover boarding costs and other damages. A trespass victim who invokes this procedure must provide proper notice to the state director of agriculture; if certain statutory requirements are met, the animals can be sold to satisfy the claim.[29]

---

v. Sumrall, 58 Ariz. 526, 121 P.2d 640 (1942); Richards v. Sanderson, 39 Colo. 270, 89 P. 769 (1907). In other states, the entry of a cattleman's livestock has also been regarded as intentionally tortious when he has left them on a range from which it was substantially certain that they would enter the plaintiff's lands. See, e.g., Lazarus v. Phelps, 152 U.S. 81 (1894); Mower v. Olsen, 49 Utah 373, 164 P. 482 (1917). Two reported California decisions deal with the issue of intentional trespass by livestock owners; in both, applicable statutes prohibited the "herding" of livestock on the lands of others. The more recent decision, Cramer v. Jenkins, 82 Cal. App. 269, 255 P. 877 (1927), supports the proposition that leaving animals in a range from which they are substantially certain to trespass constitutes tortious misconduct. But cf. Logan v. Gedney, 38 Cal. 579 (1869) (implying that active herding may be required). The California Supreme Court's pro-plaintiff predilections during the early 1980s would have inclined it to follow the *Cramer* approach.

26. Some early California statutes authorized cattle-trespass victims to recover double damages in certain situations. See, e.g., 1850 Cal. Stat. 131 (victim enclosed by lawful fence can recover double damages for defendant's second offense). See also Nev. Rev. Stat. Ann. §569.440(1) (1986) (entitling trespass victim situated behind a lawful fence to recover double damages for second offense if the animal owner had been negligent).

27. See, e.g., Wash. Rev. Code Ann. §16.60.015 (Supp. 1989) ("damages [shall be] assessed by three reliable, disinterested parties and practical farmers, within five days next after the trespass has been committed . . . ."). See generally 35 *Am. Jur. 2d* Fences §§24–32 (1967). The practice of delegating valuation issues to fence viewers was widespread in the nineteenth century and before. See R. Tyler, supra note 9, at 395, 399, 459, 476 (describing statutes in New York, Maine, Wisconsin, and Kansas); William Cronon, *Changes in the Land: Indians, Colonists, and the Ecology of New England* 135 (1983) (colonial Massachusetts). At least one of the early California fence statutes provided for the appointment of fence viewers. See 1860 Cal. Stat. 142 (viewers' role is to assess the contributions that each adjoining landowner should make to build a sufficient partition fence).

28. See Montezuma Improvement Co. v. Simmerly, 181 Cal. 722, 189 P. 100 (1919); Blevins v. Mullally, 22 Cal. App. 519, 135 P. 307 (1913).

29. See Cal. Agric. Code §§17041, 17042, 17091–17095, 17122 (West 1968 & Supp. 1986). The animal owner may contest the propriety of the victim's invocation of this self-help remedy. See Yraceburn v. Cape, 60 Cal. App. 374, 212 P. 938 (1923) (victim wrongly invoked

The formal law provides trespass victims with only limited self-help remedies. A victim can use reasonable force to drive the animals off his land,[30] and is arguably privileged to herd them to a remote location he knows is inconvenient for their owner.[31] In addition, as just noted, a trespass victim willing to give the animals proper care can seize strays and bill the costs of their care to their owner. But a victim is generally not entitled to kill or wound the offending animals. For example, a fruit grower in Mendocino County (a closed-range county) was convicted in 1973 for malicious maiming of animals when, without prior warning to the livestock owner, he shot and killed livestock trespassing in his unfenced orchard.[32] In this respect, as we shall see, Shasta County mores diverge from the formal law.

The distinction between open range and closed range has formal relevance in public as well as private trespass law. Shasta County's law enforcement officials are entitled to impound cattle found running at large in closed range, but not those found in open range.[33] Brad Bogue, the county animal control officer, relies primarily on warnings when responding to reports of loose animals. Regardless of whether a trespass has occurred in open or closed range, Bogue's prime goal is to locate the owner of the livestock and urge the prompt removal of the offending animals. When talking to animal owners, he stresses that it is in the owner's self-interest to take better care of the livestock. When talking to ranchette owners living in open range who have called to complain about trespassing mountain cattle, Bogue informs them of the cattleman's open-

power to seize animals). The distraint procedure also poses potentially thorny state action and due process issues. Cf. Flagg Brothers, Inc. v. Brooks, 436 U.S. 149 (1978) (warehouseman's sale of entrusted goods). The "right to distrain animals damage feasant" has deep roots in the English common law. See 3 William Blackstone, *Commentaries* *211; G. Williams, supra note 8, at 7–123.

30. People v. Dunn, 39 Cal. App. 3d 418, 114 Cal. Rptr. 164 (1974) (dictum).

31. On the issue of whether this represents a reasonable exercise of self-help, compare Gilson v. Fisk, 8 N.H. 404 (1836) (trespass victim who drove herd three miles away held liable in damages for death of eight sheep), with Wells v. State, 13 S.W. 889 (Tex. Ct. App. 1890) (victim of intentional trespass did not violate criminal statute when he drove cattle three to four miles afield). Shasta County trespass victims sometimes adopt this time-honored self-help strategy. See infra note 56.

32. People v. Dunn, 39 Cal. App. 3d 418, 114 Cal. Rptr. 164 (1974). See also Annot., 12 A.L.R.3d 1103 (1967) (liability for accidentally or intentionally poisoning trespassing stock). But see Hummel v. State, 69 Okla. Crim. 38, 99 P.2d 913 (1940) (rancher was privileged to castrate a bull that threatened to impregnate pure-bred cows grazing on open range).

33. See Shasta County Ordinance Code §3306 (habitual animal trespasses declared to be a public nuisance, "provided that this section shall not apply to livestock upon the open range").

range rights. He asserts that this sort of mediation is all that is required in the usual case. In most years, Bogue's office does not impound a single head of cattle[34] or issue a single criminal citation for failure to prevent cattle trespass.[35]

Knowledge of Animal Trespass Law

The Shasta County landowners interviewed were quizzed about their knowledge of the complex legal rules of animal trespass law reviewed above. The extent of their knowledge is relevant for at least two reasons. First, Coase's parable is set in a world of zero transaction costs, where everyone has perfect knowledge of legal rules. In reality, legal knowledge is imperfect because legal research is costly and human cognitive capacities are limited. The following overview of the working legal knowledge of Shasta County residents provides a glimpse of people's behavior in the face of these constraints. Data of this sort have implications for the design of legal rules to achieve specific instrumental goals, because rules cannot have instrumental effects unless they are communicated to the relevant actors. Second, my research revealed that most residents resolve trespass disputes not according to formal law but rather according to workaday norms that are consistent with an overarching norm of cooperation among neighbors. How notable this finding is depends in part on how many residents know that their trespass norms might be inconsistent with formal legal rules.

Lay Knowledge of Trespass Law

To apply formal legal rules to a specific trespass incident, a Shasta County resident would first have to know whether it had occurred in an open-range or closed-range area of the county. Ideally, the resident would

34. The Shasta County Animal Control Office's Monthly Reports for 1980–1982 indicate that the office impounded one "bovine" during that period—a stray animal that Bogue said had been found within one block of the office's animal shelter. This figure understates the number of public impoundments because the brand inspector occasionally hauls stray cattle to the Cottonwood Auction Yard, which is better equipped than the animal shelter to board livestock.

35. Robert Baker, the county district attorney from 1965 to 1979, could not recall a single criminal prosecution for cattle trespass on private lands. Gary Glendenning, the livestock specialist in the detective's division of the county sheriff's office, affirmed that criminal trespass actions were "never" brought. Criminal proceedings have been initiated against owners of stray livestock, however, when the stray animals have repeatedly posed serious risks to *motorists*. See infra Chapter 5, note 41.

either have or know how to locate the map of closed-range areas published by the county's Department of Public Works. Second, a legally sophisticated person would have a working command of the rules of trespass law, including how they vary from open to closed range.

I found no one in Shasta County—whether an ordinary person or a legal specialist such as an attorney, judge, or insurance adjuster—with a complete working knowledge of the formal trespass rules just described. The persons best informed are, interestingly enough, two public officials without legal training: Brad Bogue, the animal control officer, and Bruce Jordan, the brand inspector. Their jobs require them to deal with stray livestock on almost a daily basis. Both have striven to learn applicable legal rules, and both sometimes invoke formal law when mediating disputes between county residents. Both Bogue and Jordan possess copies of the closed-range map and relevant provisions of the California Code. What they do *not* know is the decisional law; for example, neither is aware of the rule that an intentional trespass is always tortious, even in open range. Nevertheless, Bogue and Jordan, both familiar figures to the cattlemen and (to a lesser extent) to the ranchette owners of rural Shasta County, have done more than anyone else to educate the populace about formal trespass law.

What do ordinary rural residents know of that law? To a remarkable degree the landowners interviewed *did* know whether their own lands were within open or closed range. Of the twenty-five landowners asked to identify whether they lived in open or closed range, twenty-one provided the correct answer, including two who were fully aware that they owned land in both.[36] This level of knowledge is probably atypically high.[37] Most of the landowner interviews were conducted in the Round Mountain and Oak Run areas. The former was the site in 1973 of the Caton's Folly closed-range battle. More important, Frank Ellis' aggressive herding had provoked a furious closed-range battle in the Oak Run area just six months before the landowner interviews were conducted. Two well-placed sources—the Oak Run postmaster and the proprietor of the Oak Run general store—estimated that this political storm had caught the attention of perhaps 80 percent of the area's adult residents. In the summer of 1982, probably no populace in the United States was more

36. Eleven correctly stated they lived in open range; eight correctly stated they lived in closed range; one gave a flatly wrong answer; one, a partially wrong answer; and two "didn't know."

37. Two interviewees involved in open-range politics had obtained copies of the Department of Public Works' closed-range map.

alert to the legal distinction between open and closed range than were the inhabitants of the Oak Run area.[38]

What do laymen know of the substantive rules of trespass law? In particular, what do they know of how the rules vary from open to closed range? Individuals who are not legal specialists tend to conceive of these legal rules in black-and-white terms: either the livestock owners or the trespass victims "have the rights." We have seen, however, that the law of animal trespass is quite esoteric. An animal owner in open range, for example, is liable for intentional trespass, trespass through a lawful fence, or trespass by a goat. Only a few rural residents of Shasta County know anything of these subtleties. "Estray" and "lawful fence," central terms in the law of animal trespass, are not words in the cattlemen's everyday vocabulary. Neither of the two most sophisticated open-range ranchers interviewed was aware that enclosure by a lawful fence elevates a farmer's rights to recover for trespass. A traditionalist, whose cattle had often caused mischief in the Northeastern Sector foothills, thought estrays could never be seized in open range, although a lawful fence gives a trespass victim exactly that entitlement. No interviewee was aware that Ellis' intentional herding on his neighbors' lands in open range had been in excess of his legal rights.

As most laymen in rural Shasta County see it, trespass law is clear and simple. In closed range, an animal owner is strictly liable for trespass damages. (They of course never used, and would not recognize, the phrase "strict liability," which in the law of torts denotes liability even in the absence of negligence.) In open range, their basic premise is that an animal owner is never liable. When I posed hypothetical fact situations designed to put their rules under stress, the lay respondents sometimes backpedaled a bit, but they ultimately stuck to the notion that cattlemen have the rights in open range and trespass victims the rights in closed range.

Legal Specialists' Knowledge of Trespass Law

The laymen's penchant for simplicity enabled them to identify correctly the substance of the English strict-liability rule on cattle trespass that formally applies in closed range. In that regard, the laymen outperformed the judges, attorneys, and insurance adjusters who were interviewed. In two important respects the legal specialists had a poorer working knowledge of trespass and estray rules in Shasta County than did the lay land-

38. However, of eleven respondents asked, only three stated that they had known when buying their land what kind of "legal range" it lay in.

owners.[39] First, in contrast to the landowners, the legal specialists immediately invoked *negligence* principles when asked to analyze rights in trespass cases. In general, they thought that a cattleman would not be liable for trespass in open range (although about half seemed aware that this result would be affected by the presence of a lawful fence), and that he would be liable in closed range *only when negligent.* The negligence approach has so dominated American tort law during this century that legal specialists—insurance adjusters in particular—may fail to identify narrow pockets where strict liability rules, such as the English rule on cattle trespass, formally apply.[40]

Second, unlike the lay rural residents, the legal specialists knew almost nothing about the location of the closed-range districts in the county.[41] For example, two lawyers who lived in rural Shasta County and raised livestock as a sideline were ignorant of these boundaries; one incorrectly identified the kind of range in which he lived, and the other admitted he did not know what areas were open or closed. The latter added that this did not concern him because he would fence his lands under either legal regime.

Four insurance adjusters who settle trespass-damage claims in Shasta County were interviewed. These adjusters had little working knowledge of the location of closed-range and open-range areas or of the legal significance of those designations. One incorrectly identified Shasta County as an entirely closed-range jurisdiction. Another confused the legal designation "closed range" with the husbandry technique of keeping livestock behind fences; he stated that he did not keep up with the closed-range situation because the fence situation changes too rapidly to be worth following. The other two adjusters knew a bit more about the legal situation. Although neither possessed a closed-range map, each was able to guess how to locate one. However, both implied that they would not bother to find out whether a trespass incident had occurred in open or closed range before settling a claim. The liability rules that these adjusters apply to routine trespass claims seemed largely independent of formal law.[42]

39. This finding can be attributed to the fact, documented below, that trespass and estray claims are virtually never processed through the formal legal institutions of Shasta County.

40. Some legal specialists may also believe that the negligence principle is in every application normatively superior to the principle of strict liability.

41. In addition, neither of the two fence contractors interviewed had any notion of these boundaries. The county tax assessor assigned to the Oak Run–Round Mountain area was also unfamiliar with the closed-range map.

42. In his study of the settlement of automobile-liability claims, Ross found the law in action to be simpler and more mechanical than the formal law, but he did not find it to be

The Settlement of Trespass Disputes

If Shasta County residents were to act like the farmer and the rancher in Coase's parable, they would settle their trespass problems in the following way.[43] First, they would look to the formal law to determine who had what entitlements. They would regard those substantive rules as beyond their influence (as "exogenous," to use the economists' adjective). When they faced a potentially costly interaction, such as a trespass risk to crops, they would resolve it "in the shadow of"[44] the formal legal rules. Because transactions would be costless, enforcement would be complete: no violation of an entitlement would be ignored. For the same reason, two neighbors who interacted on a number of fronts would resolve their disputes front by front, rather than globally.

The field evidence casts doubt on the realism of each of these literal features of the parable. Because Coase himself was fully aware that transactions are costly and thus that the parable was no more than an abstraction, the contrary evidence in no way diminishes his monumental contribution in "The Problem of Social Cost." Indeed the evidence is fully consistent with Coase's central idea that, regardless of the content of law, people tend to structure their affairs to their mutual advantage. Nevertheless, the findings reported here may serve as a caution to law-and-economics scholars who have underestimated the impact of transaction costs on how the world works.[45]

Norms, Not Legal Rules, Are the Basic Sources of Entitlements

In rural Shasta County, where transaction costs are assuredly not zero, trespass conflicts are generally resolved not *in* "the shadow of the law" but, rather, *beyond* that shadow. Most rural residents are consciously com-

---

quite as disconnected as animal-trespass law is in Shasta County. See H. Laurence Ross, *Settled Out of Court* 134–135, 237–240 (rev. ed. 1980).

43. The scholars involved in the Civil Liability Research Project have attempted to standardize the vocabulary of dispute resolution. They use "grievance" to describe a perceived entitlement to pursue a claim against another, "claim" to describe a demand for redress, and "dispute" to describe a rejected claim. See, e.g., Richard E. Miller and Austin Sarat, "Grievances, Claims, and Disputes: Assessing the Adversary Culture," 15 *Law & Soc'y Rev.* 525, 527 (1980–81). The usage in this book is not as precise.

44. This now-familiar phrase originated in Robert H. Mnookin and Lewis Kornhauser, "Bargaining in the Shadow of the Law: The Case of Divorce," 88 *Yale L.J.* 950 (1979).

45. Law-and-economics scholars often employ models that explicitly assume that actors have perfect knowledge of legal rules. See infra Chapter 8, text accompanying notes 10–13.

mitted to an overarching norm of cooperation among neighbors.[46] In trespass situations, their applicable particularized norm, adhered to by all but a few deviants, is that an owner of livestock is responsible for the acts of his animals. Allegiance to this norm seems wholly independent of formal legal entitlements. Most cattlemen believe that a rancher should keep his animals from eating a neighbor's grass, regardless of whether the range is open or closed. Cattlemen typically couch their justifications for the norm in moral terms. Marty Fancher: "Suppose I sat down [uninvited] to a dinner your wife had cooked?" Dick Coombs: It "isn't right" to get free pasturage at the expense of one's neighbors. Owen Shellworth: "[My cattle] don't belong [in my neighbor's field]." Attorney-rancher Pete Schultz: A cattleman is "morally obligated to fence" to protect his neighbor's crops, even in open range.

The remainder of this chapter describes in greater detail how the norms of neighborliness operate and how deviants who violate these norms are informally controlled. The discussion also identifies another set of deviants: trespass victims who actually invoke their formal legal rights.

Incomplete Enforcement: The Live-and-Let-Live Philosophy

The norm that an animal owner should control his stock is modified by another norm that holds that a rural resident should put up with ("lump") minor damage stemming from isolated trespass incidents. The neighborly response to an isolated infraction is an exchange of civilities. A trespass victim should notify the animal owner that the trespass has occurred and assist the owner in retrieving the stray stock. Virtually all residents have telephones, the standard means of communication. A telephone report is usually couched not as a complaint but rather as a service to the animal owner, who, after all, has a valuable asset on the loose. Upon receiving a telephone report, a cattleman who is a good neighbor will quickly retrieve the animals (by truck if necessary), apologize for the occurrence, and thank the caller. The Mortons and the Shellworths, two ranching families in the Oak Run area particularly esteemed for their neighborliness, have a policy of promptly and apologetically responding to their neighbors' notifications of trespass.[47]

46. Although the rural landowners were emphatic about the importance of neighborliness and could offer many specific examples of neighborly behavior, they never articulated a general formula for how a rural resident should behave. Chapter 10 puts forward the hypothesis that the norms they honored served to maximize their objective welfare.

47. A trespass victim who cannot recognize the brand of the intruding animal—a quandary more common for ranchette owners than for ranchers—may telephone county authori-

Several realities of country life in Shasta County help explain why residents are expected to put up with trespass losses. First, it is common for a rural landowner to lose a bit of forage or to suffer minor fence damage. The area northeast of Redding lies on a deer migration route. During the late winter and early spring thousands of deer and elk move through the area, easily jumping the barbed-wire fences.[48] Because wild animals trespass so often, most rural residents come to regard minor damage from alien animals not as an injurious event but as an inevitable part of life.

Second, most residents expect to be on both the giving and the receiving ends of trespass incidents. Even the ranchette owners have, if not a few hobby livestock, at least several dogs, which they keep for companionship, security, and pest control. Unlike cattle, dogs that trespass may harass, or even kill, other farm animals. If trespass risks are symmetrical, and if victims bear all trespass losses, accounts balance in the long run. Under these conditions, the advantage of reciprocal lumping is that no one has to expend time or money to settle disputes.

The norm of reciprocal restraint that underlies the "live-and-let-live" philosophy also calls for ranchers to swallow the costs of boarding another person's animal, even for months at a time. A cattleman often finds in his herd an animal wearing someone else's brand. If he recognizes the brand he will customarily inform its owner, but the two will often agree that the simplest solution is for the animal to stay put until the trespass victim next gathers his animals, an event that may be weeks or months away. The cost of "cutting" a single animal from a larger herd seems to underlie this custom. Thus, ranchers often consciously provide other people's cattle with feed worth perhaps as much as $10 to $100 per animal. Although Shasta County ranchers tend to regard themselves as financially pinched, even ranchers who know that they are legally entitled to recover feeding costs virtually never seek monetary compensation for boarding estrays. The largest ranchers northeast of Redding who were interviewed reported that they had never charged anyone or been charged by anyone for costs of that sort. Even when they do not know to whom a stray animal belongs, they put the animal in their truck the next

---

ties. Calls of this sort are eventually referred to the brand inspector or animal control officer, who then regards the main priority to be the return of the animal to its owner.

48. One rancher reported that during the winter he expects to find thirty to forty deer grazing in his hayfield each night. The owner of a particularly large ranch estimated that about five hundred deer winter there, a condition he welcomes because he regards deer as "part of nature." John Woodbury, a key lobbyist for the passage of the Caton's Folly ordinance, stated that elk and deer had eaten more of the grass in his alfalfa field than mountain cattle ever had.

time they take a load of animals to the auction yard at Cottonwood and drop it off without charge so that the brand inspector can locate the owner.[49]

Mental Accounting of Interneighbor Debts

Residents who own only a few animals may of course be unable to see any average reciprocity of advantage in a live-and-let-live approach to animal trespass incidents. This would be true, for example, of a farmer whose fields frequently suffered minor damage from incursions by a particular rancher's livestock. Shasta County norms entitle a farmer in that situation to keep track of those minor losses in a mental account, and eventually to act to remedy the imbalance.

A fundamental feature of rural society makes this enforcement system feasible: Rural residents deal with one another on a large number of fronts, and most residents expect those interactions to continue far into the future. In sociological terms, their relationships are "multiplex," not "simplex."[50] In game-theoretic terms, they are engaged in iterated, not single-shot, play.[51] They interact on water supply, controlled burns, fence repairs, social events, staffing the volunteer fire department, and so on. Where population densities are low, each neighbor looms larger. Thus any trespass dispute with a neighbor is almost certain to be but one thread in the rich fabric of a continuing relationship.

A person in a multiplex relationship can keep a rough mental account of the outstanding credits and debits in each aspect of that relationship.[52]

49. Brand Inspector Bruce Jordan estimated that ranchers drop off approximately three hundred head of stray livestock at the auction yard each year, and that these ranchers typically decline to seek compensation from the owners of the strays.

50. See Robert L. Kidder, *Connecting Law and Society* 70–72 (1983). The phrase *multiplex relationship* was first coined in Max Gluckman, *The Judicial Process among the Barotse of Northern Rhodesia* 19 (1955).

51. The law-and-society literature has long emphasized that law is not likely to be important to parties enmeshed in a continuing relationship. For example, Marc Galanter has observed: "In the American setting, litigation tends to be between parties who are strangers. Either they never had a mutually beneficial continuing relationship, as in the typical automobile case, or their relationship—marital, commercial, or organizational—is ruptured. In either case, there is no anticipated future relationship. In the American setting, unlike some others, resort to litigation is viewed as an irreparable breach of the relationship." Marc Galanter, "Reading the Landscape of Disputes: What We Know and Don't Know (and Think We Know) about Our Allegedly Contentious and Litigious Society," 31 *UCLA L. Rev.* 4, 24–25 (1983). See also infra Chapter 10, text at notes 35–49 (discussion of close-knit groups).

52. Cf. Arthur J. Vidich and Joseph Bensman, *Small Town in Mass Society* 34 (rev. ed. 1968): "To a great extent these arrangements between friends and neighbors have a reciprocal character: a man who helps others may himself expect to be helped later on. In a way the

Should the aggregate account fall out of balance, tension may mount because the net creditor may begin to perceive the net debtor as an over-reacher. But as long as the aggregate account is in balance, neither party need be concerned that particular subaccounts are not. For example, if a rancher were to owe a farmer in the trespass subaccount, the farmer could be expected to remain content if that imbalance were to be offset by a debt he owed the rancher in, say, the water-supply subaccount.[53]

The live-and-let-live norm also suggests that neighbors should put up with minor imbalances in their aggregate accounts, especially when they perceive that their future interactions will provide adequate opportunities for settling old scores. Creditors may actually prefer having others in their debt. For example, when Larry Brennan lost seven tons of baled hay to Frank Ellis' cattle in open range, Brennan (although he did not know it) had a strong legal claim against Ellis for intentional trespass. Brennan estimated his loss at between $300 and $500, hardly a trivial amount. When Ellis learned of Brennan's loss he told Brennan to "come down and take some hay" from Ellis' barn. Brennan reported that he declined this offer of compensation, partly because he thought he should not have piled the bales in an unfenced area, but also because he would rather have Ellis in debt to him than be in debt to Ellis. Brennan was willing to let Ellis run up a deficit in their aggregate interpersonal accounts because he thought that as a creditor he would have more leverage over Ellis' future behavior.

The Control of Deviants: The Key Role of Self-Help

The rural Shasta County population includes deviants who do not ade-quately control their livestock and run up excessive debts in their infor-mal accounts with their neighbors. Frank Ellis, for example, was noto-riously indifferent about his reputation among his neighbors. In general, the traditionalists who let their animals loose in the mountains during the summer are less scrupulous than the modernists are in honoring the norms of neighborliness. This is likely due to the fact that traditionalists

---

whole system takes on the character of insurance. Of course some people are more conscious of their premium payments than others and keep a kind of mental bookkeeping on 'what they owe and who owes them what,' which is a perfectly permissible practice so long as one does not openly confront others with unbalanced accounts."

53. See Oliver E. Williamson, *Markets and Hierarchies* 256–257 (1975) (a participant in a continuing relationship seeks to achieve a favorable balance in the overall set of interactions, not in each separate interaction).

have less complex, and shorter-lived, interrelationships with the individuals who encounter their range cattle.

To discipline deviants, the residents of rural Shasta County use the following four types of countermeasures, listed in escalating order of seriousness: (1) self-help retaliation; (2) reports to county authorities; (3) claims for compensation informally submitted without the help of attorneys; and (4) attorney-assisted claims for compensation. The law starts to gain bite as one moves down this list.

Self-help. Not only are most trespass disputes in Shasta County resolved according to extralegal rules, but most enforcement actions are also extralegal. A measured amount of self-help—an amount that would serve to even up accounts[54]—is the predominant and ethically preferred response to someone who has not taken adequate steps to prevent his animals from trespassing.

The mildest form of self-help is truthful negative gossip. This usually works because only the extreme deviants are immune from the general obsession with neighborliness. Although the Oak Run–Round Mountain area is undergoing a rapid increase in population, it remains distinctly rural in atmosphere. People tend to know one another, and they value their reputations in the community. Some ranching families have lived in the area for several generations and include members who plan to stay indefinitely. Members of these families seem particularly intent on maintaining their reputations as good neighbors. Should one of them not promptly and courteously retrieve a stray, he might fear that any resulting gossip would permanently besmirch the family name.

Residents of the Northeastern Sector foothills seem quite conscious of the role of gossip in their system of social control. One longtime resident, who had also lived for many years in a suburb of a major California urban area, observed that people in the Oak Run area "gossip all the time," much more than in the urban area. Another reported intentionally using gossip to sanction a traditionalist who had been "impolite" when coming to pick up some stray mountain cattle; he reported that application of this self-help device produced an apology, an outcome itself presumably circulated through the gossip system.

The furor over Frank Ellis' loose cattle in the Oak Run area induced area residents to try a sophisticated variation of the gossip sanction. The ranchette residents who were particularly bothered by Ellis' cattle could see that he was utterly indifferent to his reputation among them. They thought, however, that as a major rancher, Ellis would worry about his

54. Even-Up strategies are discussed infra Chapter 12, text accompanying notes 39–48.

reputation among the large cattle operators in the county. They therefore reported Ellis' activities to the Board of Directors of the Shasta County Cattlemen's Association. This move proved unrewarding, for Ellis was also surprisingly indifferent to his reputation among the cattlemen.[55]

When milder measures such as gossip fail, a person is regarded as being justified in threatening to use, and perhaps even actually using, tougher self-help sanctions. Particularly in unfenced country, a victim may respond to repeated cattle trespasses by herding the offending animals to a location extremely inconvenient for their owner.[56] Another common response to repeated trespasses is to threaten to kill a responsible animal should it ever enter again. Although the killing of trespassing livestock is a crime in California,[57] six landowners—not noticeably less civilized than the others—unhesitatingly volunteered that they had issued death threats of this sort. These threats are credible in Shasta County because victims of recurring trespasses, particularly if they have first issued a warning, feel justified in killing or injuring the mischievous animals.[58] Despite the criminality of the conduct (a fact not necessarily known to the respondents), I learned the identity of two persons who had shot trespassing cattle. Another landowner told of running the steer of an uncooperative neighbor into a fence. The most intriguing report came from a rancher who had had recurrent problems with a trespassing bull many years before. This rancher told a key law enforcement official that he wanted to castrate the bull—"to turn it into a steer." The official replied that he would turn a deaf ear if that were to occur. The rancher asserted that he then carried out his threat.

It is difficult to estimate how frequently rural residents actually resort to violent self-help. Nevertheless, fear of physical retaliation is undoubtedly one of the major incentives for order in rural Shasta County. Ranchers who run herds at large freely admit that they worry that their tres-

---

55. See supra Chapter 2, note 14.

56. Two residents stated in interviews that they had done this. For some scattered precedents on the legality of this practice, see supra note 31.

57. Cal. Penal Code §597(a) (West Supp. 1989); People v. Dunn, 39 Cal. App. 3d 418, 114 Cal. Rptr. 164 (1974).

58. Violent self-help—occasionally organized on a group basis as vigilante justice—was a tradition in the nineteenth-century American West. "The laws [in Wyoming] appeared to require that a farmer fence his land to keep cattle out, but many a farmer preferred to save the cost of a fence, then wait until cattle came in his land, and with a shot or two secure a winter's supply of beef." Daniel J. Boorstin, *The Americans: The Democratic Experience* 30 (1973). See also Ernest Staples Osgood, *The Day of the Cattleman* (1929), at 157–160 (lynching of horse thieves); at 242 (killing of trespassing cattle); and at 252–253 (describing how large cattle companies mobilized an army to invade Johnson County, Wyoming, to prevent small ranchers from using violent self-help against the companies' cattle).

passing cattle might meet with violence. One traditionalist reported that he is responsive to complaints from ranchette owners because he fears they will poison or shoot his stock. A judge for a rural district of the county asserted that a vicious animal is likely to "disappear" if its owner does not control it. A resident of the Oak Run area stated that some area residents responded to Frank Ellis' practice of running herds at large by rustling Ellis' cattle. He suggested that Ellis print tee shirts with the inscription: "Eat Ellis Beef. Everyone in Oak Run Does!"

Complaints to public officials. The longtime ranchers of Shasta County pride themselves on being able to resolve their problems on their own. Except when they lose animals to rustlers, they do not seek help from public officials. Although ranchette owners also use the self-help remedies of gossip and violence, they, unlike the cattlemen, sometimes respond to a trespass incident by contacting a county official who they think will remedy the problem.[59] These calls are usually funneled to the animal control officer or brand inspector, who both report that most callers are ranchette owners with limited rural experience. As already discussed, these calls do produce results. The county officials typically contact the owner of the animal, who then arranges for its removal. Brad Bogue, the animal control officer, reported that in half the cases the caller knows whose animal it is. This suggests that callers often think that requests for removal have more effect when issued by someone in authority.

Mere removal of an animal may provide only temporary relief when its owner is a mountain lessee whose cattle have repeatedly descended upon the ranchettes. County officials therefore use mild threats to caution repeat offenders. In closed range, they may mention both their power to impound the estrays and the risk of criminal prosecution. These threats appear to be bluffs; as noted, the county never impounds stray cattle when it can locate an owner, and it rarely prosecutes cattlemen (and then only when their animals have posed risks to motorists). In open range, county officials may deliver a more subtle threat: not that they will initiate a prosecution, but that, if the owner does not mend his ways, the Board of Supervisors may face insuperable pressure to close the range in the relevant area. Because cattlemen perceive that a closure significantly diminishes their legal entitlements in situations where motorists have collided with their livestock, this threat can catch their attention.[60]

59. The role of complaints to public officials is explored in M. P. Baumgartner, *The Moral Order of a Suburb* 80–82 (1988) (New York suburb), and David M. Engel, "Cases, Conflict, and Accommodation: Patterns of Legal Interaction in an American Community," 1983 *Am. B. Found. Research J.* 803, 821 (rural Illinois county).

60. See infra Chapters 5 and 6.

A trespass victim's most effective official protest is one delivered directly to his elected county supervisor—the person best situated to change stray-cattle liability rules. Many Shasta County residents are aware that traditionalist cattlemen fear the supervisors more than they fear law enforcement authorities. Thus in 1973 the alfalfa farmer John Woodbury made his repeated phone calls about mountain cattle not to Brad Bogue but to Supervisor John Caton. When a supervisor receives many calls from trespass victims, his first instinct is to mediate the crisis. Supervisor Norman Wagoner's standard procedure was to assemble the ranchers in the area and advise them to put pressure on the offender or else risk the closure of the range. Wagoner's successor, Supervisor John Caton, similarly told Frank Ellis that he would support a closure at Oak Run unless Ellis built three miles of fence along the Oak Run Road. If a supervisor is not responsive to a constituent's complaint, the constituent may respond by circulating a closure petition, as Doug Heinz eventually did in Oak Run.

The rarity of claims for monetary relief. Because Shasta County residents tend to settle their trespass disputes beyond the shadow of the law, one might suspect that the norms of neighborliness include a norm against the invocation of formal legal rights. And this norm is indeed entrenched.[61] Owen Shellworth: "I don't believe in lawyers [because there are] always hard feelings [when you litigate]." Tony Morton: "[I never press a monetary claim because] I try to be a good neighbor." Norman Wagoner: "Being good neighbors means no lawsuits." Although trespasses are frequent, Shasta County's rural residents virtually never file formal trespass actions against one another. John Woodbury, for example, made dozens of phone calls to Supervisor John Caton, but never sought monetary compensation from the traditionalists whose cattle had repeatedly marauded his alfalfa field. Court records and conversations with court clerks indicate that in most years not a single private lawsuit seeking damages for either trespass by livestock or the expense of boarding estrays is filed in the county's courts.[62] Not only do the residents of the Northeastern Sector foothills refrain from filing formal lawsuits, but they

61. Norms against litigation are discussed more generally infra Chapter 14, text accompanying notes 36–43.

62. In the Central Valley Justice Court, no small claims for the August 1981 to June 1982 period were provoked by animal trespass, and the civil clerk who had worked there for eleven years could not remember any. The court's index of defendants for the 1975–1982 period indicated that Frank Ellis had been the only large rancher to become the target of any kind of legal action. In the Burney Justice Court, the small-claims files for 1980 showed no animal-trespass cases, and the clerks could recall no such cases in their four years on the job.

are also strongly disinclined to submit informal monetary claims to the owners of trespassing animals.[63]

The landowners who were interviewed clearly regard their restraint in seeking monetary relief as a mark of virtue. When asked why they did not pursue meritorious legal claims arising from trespass or fence-finance disputes, various landowners replied: "I'm not that kind of guy"; "I don't believe in it"; "I don't like to create a stink"; "I try to get along." The landowners who attempted to provide a rationale for this forbearance all implied the same one, a long-term reciprocity of advantage. Ann Kershaw: "The only one that makes money [when you litigate] is the lawyer." Al Levitt: "I figure it will balance out in the long run." Pete Schultz: "I hope they'll do the same for me." Phil Ritchie: "My family believes in 'live and let live.'"

Mutual restraint saves parties in a long-term relationship the costs of going through the formal claims process. Adjoining landowners who practice the live-and-let-live approach are both better off whenever the negative externalities from their activities are roughly in equipoise. Equipoise is as likely in closed range as in open. Landowners with property in closed range—the ones with the greatest formal legal rights—were the source of half of the quotations in the prior two paragraphs.

When a transfer *is* necessary to square unbalanced accounts, rural neighbors prefer to use in-kind payments, not cash. Shasta County landowners regard a monetary settlement as an arms' length transaction that symbolizes an unneighborly relationship. Should your goat happen to eat your neighbor's tomatoes, the neighborly thing for you to do would be to help replant the tomatoes; a transfer of money would be too cold and too impersonal.[64] When Kevin O'Hara's cattle went through a break in a fence and destroyed his neighbor's corn crop (a loss of less than $100), O'Hara had to work hard to persuade the neighbor to accept his offer of money to compensate for the damages. O'Hara insisted on making this payment because he "felt responsible" for his neighbor's loss, a feeling that would not have been in the least affected had the event occurred in open instead of closed range. There can also be social pressure against offering monetary settlements. Bob Bosworth's father agreed many decades ago to pay damages to a trespass victim in a closed-range area just

---

63. There were several reports that others had informally settled claims for the costs of boarding estrays. Only one rancher told of paying such a claim; he regarded the claimant's pursuit of the money as a "cheap move."

64. This pattern poses a puzzle for transaction-cost economists, because in-kind transfers tend to be more costly to effect than cash transfers. But see infra Chapter 13, text accompanying notes 14–17 (in-kind exchange among members contributes to a group's cohesion).

south of Shasta County; other cattlemen then rebuked him for setting an unfortunate precedent. The junior Bosworth, in 1982 the president of the Shasta County Cattlemen's Association, could recall no other out-of-pocket settlement in a trespass case.

Trespass victims who sustain an unusually large loss are more likely to take the potentially deviant step of making a claim for monetary relief. Among those interviewed were adjusters for the two insurance companies whose liability policies would be most likely to cover losses from animal trespass. The adjusters' responses suggest that in a typical year these companies receive fewer than ten trespass damage claims originating in Shasta County. In the paradigmatic case, the insured is not a rancher but rather a ranchette owner, whose family's horse has escaped and trampled a neighboring homeowner's shrubbery. The claimant is typically not represented by an attorney, a type of professional these adjusters rarely encounter. The adjusters also settle each year two or three trespass claims that homeowners or ranchette owners have brought against ranchers. Ranchers who suffer trespasses virtually never file claims against others' insurance companies. An adjuster for the company that insures most Shasta County ranchers stated that he could not recall, in his twenty years of adjusting, a single claim by a rancher for compensation for trespass damage.

Attorney-assisted claims. The landowners, particularly the ranchers, express a strong aversion to hiring an attorney to fight one's battles. To hire an attorney is to escalate a conflict. A good neighbor does not do such a thing because the "natural working order" calls for two neighbors to work out their problems between themselves. The files in the Shasta County courthouses reveal that the ranchers who honor norms of neighborliness—the vast majority—are not involved in cattle-related litigation of any kind.

I did uncover two instances in which animal-trespass victims in the Oak Run–Round Mountain area had turned to attorneys. In one of these cases the victim actually filed a formal complaint. Because lawyer-backed claims are so unusual, these two disputes, both of them bitter, deserve elaboration.

The first involved Tom Hailey and Curtis McCall. For three generations, Hailey's family has owned a large tract of foothill forest in an open-range area near Oak Run. In 1978 Hailey discovered McCall's cattle grazing on some of Hailey's partially fenced land. Hailey suspected that McCall had brought the animals in through a gate in Hailey's fence. When Hailey confronted him, McCall, who lived about a mile away, acted as if the incursion had been accidental. Hailey subsequently found a salt block on the tract—an object he could fairly assume that McCall had put there to service his trespassing herd. Hailey thus concluded that McCall had not only deliberately trespassed but had also aggravated the offense by untruthfully denying the charge. Hailey seized the salt block and consulted an attorney, who advised him to seek compensation from McCall. The two principals eventually agreed to a small monetary settlement.

Hailey is a semi-retired government employee who spends much of his time outside of Shasta County; he is regarded as reclusive and eccentric—certainly someone outside the mainstream of Oak Run society. McCall, a retired engineer with a hard-driving style, moved to Shasta County in the late 1970s to run a small livestock ranch. The Haileys refer to him as a "Texan"—a term that in Shasta County connotes someone who is both an outsider and lacks neighborly instincts.

The second dispute involved Doug Heinz and Frank Ellis. As described in Chapter 2, Heinz had the misfortune of owning a ranchette near Ellis' ranch. After experiencing repeated problems with Ellis' giant cattle herds, Heinz unilaterally seized three animals that had broken through his fence. Heinz boarded these animals for three months without notifying Ellis. Heinz later asserted he intended to return them when Ellis next held a roundup. According to Heinz, Ellis eventually found out that Heinz had the animals and asked for their return. Heinz agreed to return them if Ellis would pay pasturage costs. When Ellis replied, "You know I'm good for it," Heinz released the animals and sent Ellis a bill. Ellis refused to pay the bill, and further infuriated Heinz by calling him "boy" whenever Heinz brought up the debt.

On January 8, 1981, Heinz filed a small-claims action against Ellis to recover $750 "for property damage, hay and grain ate [sic] by defendant's cattle, boarding of animals."[65] Acting through the attorney he kept on retainer, Ellis responded eight days later with a separate civil suit against Heinz.[66] Ellis' complaint sought $1,500 compensatory and $10,000 punitive damages from Heinz for the shooting deaths of two Black Brangus cows that Ellis had pastured on Bureau of Land Management lands; it also sought compensation for the weight loss Ellis' three live animals had sustained during the months Heinz had been feeding them. The two legal actions were later consolidated. Heinz, who called Ellis' allegation that he had killed two cows "100 percent lies" and "scare tactics," hired an attorney based in Redding to represent him. This attorney threatened

65. Heinz v. Ellis, No. 81 SC 7 (Cent. Valley Just. Ct., filed Jan. 8, 1981).
66. Ellis v. Heinz, No. 81 CV 6 (Cent. Valley Just. Ct., filed Jan. 16, 1981).

to pursue a malicious prosecution action against Ellis if Ellis persisted in asserting that Heinz had slain the Black Brangus cows. In December 1981, the parties agreed to a settlement under the terms of which Ellis paid Heinz $300 in damages and $100 for attorney fees. Ellis' insurance company picked up the tab. By that time Heinz was spearheading a political campaign to close the range Ellis had been using.

The Heinz-Ellis and Hailey-McCall disputes share several characteristics. Although both arose in open range, in each instance legal authority favored the trespass victim: Hailey, because McCall's trespass had been intentional; and Heinz, because Ellis' animals had broken through an apparently lawful fence.[67] In both instances the victim, before consulting an attorney, had attempted to obtain informal satisfaction but had been rebuffed. Each victim came to believe that the animal owner had not been honest with him. Each dispute was ultimately settled in the victim's favor. In both instances, neither the trespass victim nor the cattle owner was a practiced follower of rural Shasta County norms. Thus other respondents tended to refer to the four individuals involved in these two claims as "bad apples," "odd ducks," or otherwise as people not aware of the natural working order. Ordinary people, it seems, do not often turn to attorneys to help resolve disputes.[68]

67. Heinz had technically imperiled his statutory claim for damages under the Estray Act when he failed to notify the proper public authorities that he had taken up Ellis' animals. See Cal. Agric. Code §§17042, 17095 (West 1967 & Supp. 1986).

68. See also William E. Nelson, *Dispute and Conflict Resolution in Plymouth Colony, Massachusetts, 1725–1825* (1981) (Plymouth's particularly litigious individuals during the 1725–1774 period tended to be people who were poorly socialized); Harry F. Todd, Jr., "Litigious Marginals: Character and Disputing in a Bavarian Village," in *The Disputing Process: Law in Ten Societies,* 86, 118 (Laura Nader and Harry F. Todd, Jr., eds. 1978) (socially marginal people were disproportionately represented in civil and criminal litigation).

4

×—×

Who Pays for Boundary Fences?

As Robert Frost recognized in his poem "Mending Wall," boundary fences can be a source of low-level drama in life among neighbors. In the language of economics, a boundary fence is a public good. When a landowner on one side of a boundary bears the entire cost of building or maintaining a boundary fence, that effort benefits the neighbor on the other side. Therefore each adjoining landowner may selfishly delay fence work in the hope of free-riding on efforts of the other.[1] As Frost saw, this strategically tricky situation can reveal much about both the character of individual neighbors and the organization of social life.

Fencing costs are a significant budget item for most Shasta County ranchers. Although many of the ranches in the grassy plains and foothills of the Northeastern Sector were first fenced over a half century ago, new fences nevertheless continue to appear as ranchette owners with orchards or hobby livestock enclose their lands. In 1982, new barbed-wire fences cost a total of about $1 per linear foot.[2] For landowners whose perimeters are already enclosed, fencing costs consist of the considerable time and money spent on the annual repair and the periodic replacement of existing structures.[3]

California law provides some formal rules on how neighbors should split the cost of building and maintaining boundary fences. Shasta County landowners tend to ignore these legal rules when settling fence disputes, just as they typically disregard trespass law when settling trespass disputes. The parties to disputes over fence costs are immediate neighbors and thus, more invariably than parties to cattle-trespass dis-

1. See Philip B. Heymann, "The Problem of Coordination: Bargaining and Rules," 86 *Harv. L. Rev.* 797, 819–820 (1973) (fence-finance example used to illustrate the general problem of coordination); Irwin Lipnowski and Shlomo Maital, "Voluntary Provision of a Pure Public Good as the Game of 'Chicken,'" 20 *J. Pub. Econ.* 381 (1983).

2. See supra Chapter 1, notes 34–35 and accompanying text.

3. There is something "that doesn't love a wall, that wants it down." Robert Frost, "Mending Wall," in *Complete Poems of Robert Frost* 47–48 (1949).

putes, caught in the civilizing grip of an ongoing multifaceted relationship. This close-knittedness enables them to apply informal norms to resolve most questions about who should pay for fences.

Formal Legal Rules on the Sharing of Boundary-Fence Costs

According to the strongest version of the Coase Theorem, whether a boundary fence would be built or maintained would be independent of the content of law. The cost-effectiveness of a fence project would entirely determine whether it would be undertaken. A boundary fence that was cost-justified from a social perspective would be built, and legal rules would only affect how much each neighbor would contribute to the mutually beneficial project.

In a zero-transaction-costs world two pockets of legal doctrine would primarily determine how adjoining landowners would split the costs of boundary fencing. First, the tort rules applicable to animal-trespass incidents (reviewed in Chapter 3) would be relevant. For example, as Coase's parable explains, a cattleman such as Frank Ellis would be willing to contribute more to a boundary fence in closed range than in open range, because his reduction in trespass liabilities would be greater. Conversely, an open-range farmer would be more willing to contribute to fencing than would a closed-range farmer. Second, the rules of restitution law that govern a fencebuilder's entitlements to compensation from a benefited neighbor would also directly govern how adjoining landowners would share fencing costs. This body of rules is taken up below.

In fact, rural neighbors in Shasta County often make deals about the financing of boundary fences. To one interested in the realism of Coase's parable, a central question is how much, if at all, the formal law influences the substance of their deals. Procedural questions also spring to mind. How often, if ever, do neighbors bother to put a deal in writing or to comply with other procedural steps that would increase the likelihood that a court would enforce a contract between them?

Substantive Law

In the absence of a contract or statute to the contrary,[4] a landowner who erects or maintains a boundary fence has no legal entitlement to recover

---

4. Some old cases, of doubtful authority today, also hold that unilateral maintenance of a fence for a lengthy period can give rise to a prescriptive duty to fence. See 35 *Am. Jur. 2d* Fences §7 (1967).

restitution from the adjoining landowner for benefits conferred.[5] Section 841 of the California Civil Code, however, creates circumscribed statutory rights to restitution. Unamended since 1872, when it was enacted as part of California's Field Code, section 841 sets forth cost-sharing rules for fencing similar to ones included in prior California statutes[6] and currently found in the codes of many other states.[7]

Section 841 establishes rights to restitution for both the construction and the maintenance of fences. The statutory provision dealing with construction costs prevents a subsequent encloser from freeloading on a neighbor's preexisting fence. It provides that, when a landowner has let his land lie without fencing, but "afterwards incloses it, he must refund to the other [coterminous landowner] a just proportion of the value, at that time, of any division fence made by the latter."[8] Restitution is thus due only when the later encloser has actually included a previously built fence as a part of his own enclosure. Over a half century ago the California Supreme Court applied this statute and its predecessors in a handful of cases to compel rural landowners to make restitution to neighbors who had previously constructed boundary fences.[9]

5. See *Cal. Jur. 3d* Adjoining Landowners §118 (1973); Glanville L. Williams, *Liability for Animals* 211, 227 (1939). But see Bliss v. Sneath, 103 Cal. 43, 36 P. 1029 (1894) (even in the absence of a statute, the common law of implied contracts may obligate the beneficiary of a neighbor's fence to contribute to its costs). See also, e.g., Day v. Caton, 119 Mass. 513 (1876), and Campbell v. Mesier, 4 Johns. Ch. 333 (N.Y. Chan. 1820), two instances in which the beneficiary of a party wall was held implicitly obligated to help pay for the wall's construction. See generally Robert C. Ellickson and A. Dan Tarlock, *Land-Use Controls* 598–604 (1981); Note, "Efficient Land Use and the Internalization of Beneficial Spillovers," 31 *Stan. L. Rev.* 459 (1979).

6. See, e.g., 1859 Cal. Stat., ch. 266, at 280 (applicable to five named counties, including Shasta); 1860 Cal. Stat., ch. 173, at 141–142.

7. See, e.g., Mass. Gen. Laws Ann., ch. 49, §§3, 10, 13 (West 1968); Wash. Rev. Code §§16.60.020–16.60.040 (1962). A nineteenth-century treatise on fence law indicates that statutory provisions like these were then common in the United States. See Ransom H. Tyler, *The Law of Boundaries, Fences, and Window Lights* (1874) (passim).

8. Cal. Civ. Code §841 (West 1982).

9. See Reusche v. Milhorn, 218 Cal. 696, 24 P.2d 792 (1933) (applying 1859 Cal. Stat. ch. 266, at 280, to affirm judgment of $91.33 in favor of a Shasta County fencebuilder); Bliss v. Sneath, 103 Cal. 43, 36 P. 1029 (1894) (§841 entitles defendant to setoff against rent due); Meade v. Watson, 67 Cal. 591, 8 P. 311 (1885) (1855 Cal. Stat. ch. 129, at 154, enables fencebuilder to state a cause of action to recover $280); Gonzales v. Wasson, 51 Cal. 295 (1876) (applying the same 1855 statute to affirm judgment for fencebuilder). (The 1855 and 1859 statutes were repealed by 1933 Cal. Stat., ch. 25, at 295.) A statute on fence-cost sharing may pose constitutional issues. See Sweeney v. Murphy, 39 A.D.2d 306, 334 N.Y.S.2d 239 (1972), aff'd per curiam, 31 N.Y.2d 1042, 294 N.E.2d 855, 342 N.Y.S.2d 70 (1973) (statute requiring defendant, who had no livestock, to bear one-half costs of maintaining boundary fence shared with plaintiff, who had livestock, is "arbitrary and confiscatory"); Choquette v. Perrault, 569

Section 841's rule on the sharing of fence maintenance costs is similarly qualified: when the lands on *both* sides of a boundary are enclosed, "co-terminous owners are mutually bound equally to maintain . . . the fences between them." This provision could presumably be construed to require enclosed neighbors to share equally the costs of replacing utterly dilapidated boundary fencing.

Common-law decisions regarding entitlements to dismantle structures might also influence the placement of boundary fences. A landowner who unilaterally builds a fence on a boundary line may be unable to raze it later without risk of liability to the adjoining landowner.[10] But because as a general rule an improvement placed inside a boundary line is the exclusive property of the landowner,[11] a rancher who deliberately built a fence a foot or two inside a boundary line might well be later able to remove it without legal consequence.[12]

Procedural Law

Because the Statute of Frauds might require an agreement in writing, a judge could decline to enforce an oral agreement to share fence costs.[13] Perhaps as a result, source books for attorneys contain suggested forms for fence construction and maintenance agreements.[14] For instance, a form in *American Jurisprudence Legal Forms* proposes that the two adjoining neighbors erect a mutually agreed-upon center post, and that each have exclusive maintenance responsibilities for the section of fence lying to the right of the post reckoned as each faces the fence from his own

---

A.2d 455 (Vt. 1989) (statute primarily benefits owners of livestock and therefore violates state constitution's provision against special-interest legislation). See generally Annot., 6 A.L.R. 212, 213–214 (1920).

10. See Allen v. McMillion, 82 Cal. App. 3d 211, 147 Cal. Rptr. 77 (1978) (destruction of boundary fence creates cause of action for trespass to real estate); Laughlin v. Franc, 247 Iowa 345, 73 N.W.2d 750 (1955) (adjoining landowners own fences built on boundary as tenants in common); Thompson v. Mattuschek, 134 Mont. 500, 333 P.2d 1022 (1959) (adjoiner who removed longstanding boundary fence is liable for other adjoiner's resulting livestock-trespass damages and for punitive damages as well).

11. Disman v. Union Oil Co. of California, 145 Cal. App. 2d 261, 266, 302 P.2d 326, 330 (1956).

12. Cf. Kimball v. Adams, 52 Wis. 554, 9 N.W. 170 (1881) (encroachee can remove fence that someone else placed on his land).

13. There is mixed authority on the issue of whether the Statute of Frauds prevents a court from enforcing an oral promise to maintain a fence. See 35 *Am. Jur. 2d* Fences §9 (1967).

14. See 8 *Am. Jur. Legal Forms 2d* Fences §§114:1–114:16, at 383–394 (1972).

side.[15] To help ensure that the covenants in such a written agreement would both bind and benefit successors in ownership, the formbook also suggests that the fencing agreement be recorded in official land records.[16] We shall see that Shasta County landowners proceed on a much more informal basis.

The Virtual Irrelevance of Fence Law

In contrast to the preceding period, for the past half century the California law reports have contained no cases involving disputes over the financing of rural fences. Reported cases are but the tip of the legal iceberg, of course. Still, the Shasta County evidence indicates that there is no tip because there is no iceberg. Rural landowners in Shasta County neither bring formal legal actions for fence-cost contribution nor negotiate fence-cost contracts in the shadow of the law. Instead, when confronted with a question of how to split the costs of boundary fences, they routinely apply informal norms that are largely consistent with, but apparently uninfluenced by, the provisions of section 841.

The Dearth of Claims and Lawsuits over Fence Costs

No litigation is initiated in Shasta County solely to resolve a dispute over responsibility for rural boundary fencing. The filing clerks in the relevant civil courts knew of none, and casual inspections of their files turned up nothing to cause one to question the reliability of their memories. Four trial-court judges with an aggregate of thirty years on the Shasta County bench were quizzed about disputes over fencing costs. Not one could recall a suit brought for restitution of expenditures on a rural fence.[17] Of the six attorneys interviewed, all with connections to rural Shasta County society, one stated that he had "perhaps" been involved twenty years ago in a case that raised fence-cost issues, but the other five said flatly that they had never been asked to help resolve such a dispute. Although fence repairs involve somewhat higher stakes than do routine cattle trespass incidents, the continuing relationships of adjoining landowners appar-

15. Id. at §114.11, p. 388. A legal book written for a popular audience asserts that rural landowners "ordinarily" divide fence maintenance responsibilities in this way. H. W. Hannah and Donald F. Storm, *Law for the Veterinarian and Livestock Owner* 124 (1959).

16. 8 *Am. Jur. Legal Forms 2d* Fences §114:3, at 386 (1972).

17. One judge recalled a plaintiff who had sought contribution toward the cost of fencing-in a swimming pool in an urban area. He denied the claim as unmeritorious.

ently enable them to resolve potential disputes without engaging in mutually disadvantageous formal battles.

Knowledge of Fence Law

Many rural landowners in Shasta County know something of the legal rules that might influence their sharing of the cost of boundary fences. As reported in Chapter 3, many know some rudiments of cattle-trespass law. Some landowners are also aware that situating a fence inside a boundary line increases a landowner's legal rights later to tear it down; there were two reports that this rule in fact had sometimes prompted fencebuilders to place perimeter fences several feet inside boundary lines.

The vast majority of rural landowners, however, are unaware of the existence of section 841, the California statute that deals directly with the allocation of boundary-fence costs. When questioned, not a single full-time rancher—not even the most savvy members of the Shasta County Cattlemen's Association—betrayed any knowledge of this statute. Some cattlemen guessed that the law might in fact entitle someone who fenced to force contributions from an adjoining landowner. Yet these same cattlemen added that no self-respecting rancher would ever pursue such a claim, much less hire a lawyer to enforce it.

Larry Brennan, who as a sideline raised horses on a large ranchette, was the only nonlawyer interviewed who knew anything of section 841. Brennan recalled that while taking a business course he had read a book that stated that in California a fencebuilder might under certain circumstances be entitled to force contributions from a passive neighbor. When Brennan himself later spent $1000 on a perimeter fence that he built unilaterally, however, he never considered enforcing his possible legal rights against the adjoining landowners.

Off the top of their heads, legal professionals in Shasta County know scarcely more fence law than nonlawyers do. Because there is virtually no litigation over fencing costs, most lawyers and judges have no occasion to become aware of section 841. When given a hypothetical problem on the sharing of fence costs, not one of the four judges responded by volunteering that there is, or might be, a statute right on point.

Of the six attorneys interviewed, four were unaware of section 841. The remaining two attorneys knew that a Civil Code section dealt specifically with the issue of who pays for boundary fences. One was the attorney who vaguely recalled being involved in litigation over fencing issues some twenty years before. The other attorney, Dennis Osborne, had come across section 841 when resolving a boundary dispute for a client some years earlier. Osborne, himself a small-scale rancher, nevertheless asserted that "no one enforces" section 841, and went on to tell of a personal incident that supported his contention. Osborne's ranch adjoins that of a particular neighbor for about a half mile. This neighbor had once owned cows that had occasionally flirted with Osborne's bull, which would then break through the aged fence separating the two premises. Osborne decided to upgrade the fence and had to shoulder the entire cost when his neighbor declined to contribute. Although Osborne knew that section 841 entitled him to force the neighbor to share this cost, he declined to pursue a formal claim. Osborne explained that he did not want to aggravate his neighbor, to whom he was otherwise indebted for keeping an eye on his place during the summer months, when Osborne tended to be away. Thus Brennan and Osborne, the two rural landowners with specific knowledge of section 841, had never considered actually invoking their entitlements under it.

Section 841 does occasionally matter, however, especially when neighbors have taken into the legal system a larger dispute that involves fencing as an ancillary matter. For example, the resolution of a boundary dispute may require the moving of an improperly located fence. Osborne had discovered section 841 when involved in a case of this sort.[18]

The Informal Norms That Govern Fence Finance

Because almost no Shasta County residents were following the music of section 841, I sought to identify the norms to which they were dancing. Although rural residents could quickly resolve simple hypothetical fence-cost disputes posed to them, they never articulated general principles of fence-cost allocation. Their statements and practices revealed, however, that they tend to follow a norm of proportionality. This norm calls for adjoining landowners to share fencing costs in rough proportion to the average density of livestock present on the respective sides of the boundary line.[19] In practice, this results in a choice among several focal-point solutions. The interviews also revealed the content of certain procedural and remedial norms that Shasta County residents apply to issues arising out of boundary-fence costs.

18. This suggests that efficiencies of scale may accrue when legal rules are applied to more and more disputes between a particular pair of antagonists.

19. Cf. Steven N. S. Cheung, "The Fable of the Bees: An Economic Investigation," 16 *J.L. & Econ.* 11, 30 (1973) (in Washington state, a "custom of the orchard" requires an orchardman to supply bees in proportion to his trees).

The Norm of Proportionality

The norm that allocates fence costs in proportion to the presence of live-stock is consistent with the norm, identified in Chapter 3, that currently makes a Shasta County owner of livestock responsible for the conduct of his animals. (By contrast, if Shasta County norms called for cropgrowers to "fence out" livestock, a norm that seems to have prevailed in the West during the mid-nineteenth century, fence-financing obligations might well be apportioned to the ownership of crops, not animals.)

Focal-point solutions. To be applied with mathematical nicety, the pro-portionality norm would require neighbors to keep a close count of the (ever-changing) number of animals present on each side of the common boundary. Everything else being equal, an abutter's fencing obligations would increase as the average density of livestock on his side of the boundary increased.

In fact, adjoining ranchers rarely closely compare the average densities of livestock populations, but instead resort to rough-and-ready "focal point" allocations of fence costs, such as fifty-fifty, all-or-nothing, you-materials/me-labor.[20] Just as diners often split a check in equal shares, or allow one of their number to pick up the entire check, cattlemen sacrifice precise equity for the convenience of simple rules of thumb.

When the base ranches of two full-time cattlemen adjoin, a well-engrained norm requires that they divide evenly the costs of building and maintaining their common stretch of fence. Eight ranchers who articu-lated this fifty-fifty rule went on to report at least one incident in which they and their rancher neighbors had honored it. Bob Bosworth said "everybody understands" the "custom" that ranchers split the costs of boundary fences equally.[21]

A different focal-point solution—namely, all-or-nothing—applies when an active rancher's pasture abuts a ranchette whose owner has few or no livestock; in these situations the proportionality norm requires the rancher to bear all the fencing expenses. Thus eight ranchers reported

---

20. The notion of focal points derives from Thomas C. Schelling, *The Strategy of Conflict* 111–113 (1960).

21. If one rancher were to further improve an already adequate fence, however, the adjoin-ing rancher would not be obligated to contribute. Thus a sheepman must bear the entire cost of adding the woven wire required to upgrade a barbed-wire fence from cattle-tight to sheep-tight. In two reported instances a land survey had revealed that an intended boundary fence had been wrongly situated; in both, the party who stood to gain land from the relocation of the fence paid the entire cost of shifting it to the proper location. In one of these instances five miles of fence had to be moved.

that they had unilaterally built and maintained fences on boundary lines adjoining lands of ranchette owners, and no interviewee cited an instance in which a full-time rancher had sought fence contributions from a small-fry neighbor before or after undertaking a fence project.[22]

The all-or-nothing solution is applied in other, slightly more ambiguous, cases. For example, the veteran rancher Owen Shellworth predicted that, when the time came, he would pick up the entire cost of rebuilding a fence he shared with a small-time rancher. Shellworth explained that this neighbor didn't know much about fences, and that the neighbor had fewer animals than he did. As another example, active ranchers shoulder the entire burden of fencing boundaries adjoining forests owned by federal agencies and timber companies, even when those forests are regularly leased for summer range.[23]

The allocation of fence costs is less predictable when the relative densities of animals make neither a fifty-fifty nor an all-or-nothing split the obvious choice. Rural residents are then likely to search for some intermediate fractional split, again one that makes use of a focal point. Two ranchette owners who had moved to the foothills of the Northeastern Sector from Southern California worked out the following solution. Joel Vance, who owned no livestock, was requested by his neighbor to the south, who owned some cattle and horses, to help share the costs of building a fence in a meadow area of their common boundary. In part because Vance aspired to lease his own land as pasture eventually, he agreed to hew the necessary fence posts from cedar trees on his ranchette. The southern neighbor in turn agreed both to provide the wire and other materials, and to perform all the labor. This solution placed over half the burden on Vance's neighbor, who expected to receive over half the benefits.

Ted Plomeson, a retired high-school teacher who had long lived on a large ranchette, told of a similar settlement decades before. In about 1940, cattle belonging to a neighbor who was a part-time rancher began to

22. Ranchers can exploit efficiencies of scale in fencebuilding that ranchette owners cannot. This helps explain why ranchers build boundary fences, but not why they decline to ask their smaller neighbors to bear part of the cost.

23. All four landowners who described the financing of fences between their lands and that of institutional neighbors stated that they had borne the entire expense. Two of these had land in open range and two in closed range. An official of the Roseburg Lumber Co., the largest private landowner in the Northeastern Sector, acknowledged that the company would not help defray the costs that neighbors incurred to fence the boundaries of its forests. Officials of the Bureau of Land Management and the United States Forest Service likewise said that their agencies would be highly unlikely to contribute.

trespass on Plomeson's ranchette. The trespass risk was partially reciprocated, however, because Plomeson had entered into a grazing lease with
a man who owned a horse; on occasion this horse had trespassed on the
neighbor's land. Plomeson and the neighbor ultimately agreed on a joint
fence project. They both provided cedar posts from cedar trees on their
properties, and both contributed hired hands to do the labor. The part-
time rancher, however, provided all of the wire. Thus the party with the
greater expected density of animals bore somewhat more than half the
costs.

Although Coase's parable implies that rules of cattle-trespass liability
would affect who pays for boundary fences, the most persuasive Shasta
County evidence indicates otherwise. Plomeson, who had pushed for passage of the Caton's Folly ordinance in 1973, asserted that in principle a
closure would reduce what he thereafter would be willing to contribute
toward boundary-fence costs.[24] Yet I found no evidence that the Caton's
Folly measure had influenced actual fence-cost splits within the territory
affected. None of the three landowners who owned land both inside and
outside Caton's Folly approached decisions on fence financing differently
in the two areas. Moreover, John Woodbury, a prime lobbyist for Caton's
Folly, admitted that the ordinance had not affected his own attitudes toward splitting fence costs. In the early 1970s Woodbury personally built a
five-strand barbed-wire fence around a twenty-acre field to be able to
offer his friends a place where they could graze their animals in May and
June. Woodbury thought he probably had built this fence after the closure
had gone into effect in 1973. He said that one reason his memory of the
exact year was hazy was that a closure would not affect his fencing decisions—a revealing statement coming from a closed-range activist.

24. In 1978 one of Plomeson's neighbors unilaterally replaced their common fence. By then
Plomeson had ceased to have livestock on his ranchette. Even though his neighbor arguably
owed him a bit of work on this particular line of fence, Plomeson stated that, had he been
asked in advance, he would have been willing to pay 20 to 40 percent of the costs of the
replacement fence. He would not have been willing to pay any more than that, he said,
because he knew that his ranchette had been placed in closed range. Although Plomeson
asserted that trespass law would have affected his willingness to pay for fencing, his assertion
should be discounted for several reasons. His fencebuilding neighbor in fact never asked
Plomeson to contribute anything, perhaps because the proportionality norm frees ranchette
owners without livestock from fencing costs, in both open and closed range. Moreover, even
before the adoption of the Caton's Folly ordinance, when the first fence on that particular
boundary had been installed, Plomeson had paid less than half its costs. Thus his basic view
that he owed only a minority of the fencework on that particular boundary never changed.
Nevertheless, Plomeson stands out as the only private landowner interviewed who volunteered that his legal rights as a landowner in closed range would enter his mind when he was
faced with a problem of splitting fence costs.

The proportionality norm, modified to incorporate focal points, is largely consistent with section 841's provisions on the sharing of fence costs. As mentioned, that statute only requires landowners to share fencing costs fifty-fifty in instances where the lands on *both* sides of the boundary have been enclosed. Because in the current era livestock owners are the principal enclosers of rural lands, the statute supports the standard norm that neighboring ranchers are to split fence costs evenly. Also consistent with the statute is the norm that owners of unfenced forests need not contribute to boundary-fence costs. Nevertheless, some customs of fence financing in Shasta County are inconsistent with section 841. For example, ranchers do not seek help on fence costs from owners of enclosed ranchettes. Moreover, section 841 never calls for the sharing of fence costs in unequal fractions, whereas the proportionality norm sometimes does produce such results.

Although no full-time cattleman was aware of section 841, it is of course conceivable that the statute had somehow contributed to the evolution of the norm of proportionality. There was no direct evidence that this had occurred, however. I regard it as more plausible in this instance that norms had influenced law than vice versa.

Does planting crops increase one's fencing obligations? The stated proportionality norm, which distributes fence burdens only according to the presence of livestock, asks nothing of landowners who have planted crops unusually vulnerable to trespass damage. Various scraps of field evidence support the normative irrelevance of the presence of crops. John Woodbury was outraged when his unfenced sixty-acre alfalfa field was repeatedly invaded by mountain cattle. The rancher Kevin O'Hara said that he felt a special responsibility to maintain his common fence with Owen Shellworth, because Shellworth, unlike himself, had irrigated pasture. Since O'Hara's cattle were more likely to break into Shellworth's relatively tasty lands than vice versa, O'Hara believed he had a moral obligation to do more work on their common fence. (Phil Ritchie, by contrast, the owner of an impressive irrigated pasture located within Caton's Folly, admitted to doing more than half the work of keeping his perimeter fences maintained.)

Whether Shasta County residents consider the vulnerability of crops relevant in trespass incidents is pertinent to the spirited debate in the legal literature about how people attribute moral responsibility for costs that arise from the interaction of incompatible activities. In "The Problem of Social Cost" Coase envisioned that, when a trespassing steer eats a farmer's alfalfa, the cowman's possession of the steer and the farmer's planting of the alfalfa are equally "causes" of the loss. Coase's critics later asserted that Coase's analysis failed to recognize the notions of causation embedded in ordinary moral analysis.[25] Richard Epstein, for example, would generally attribute causation to the agent who *acted,* and thus, because cattle move and crops don't, would presumptively regard the cattle owner as responsible for trespass damage to crops.[26] Epstein might see the content of Shasta County fencing norms as an affirmation of his analysis.

Utilitarian analysts would want growers of especially sensitive crops to have incentives to locate those crops in the safe places. The Shasta County fencing norms appear at first blush to ignore this consideration. This appearance, however, may be misleading. First, fencing-out norms, which put fencing burdens on cropgrowers, may indeed have prevailed in the American West (and possibly Shasta County) in the mid-nineteenth century.[27] Second, land-use patterns in Shasta County make it a poor setting for appraising the responsiveness of fence-financing norms to the vulnerability of a landowner's vegetation. Most owners of croplands in the Northeastern Sector deliberately allow livestock to enter those lands during part of the year. For example, after harvesting a hay crop, a hay farmer is likely to rent out his field to a stockman who will bring in animals to graze on the stubble. Because *pure* croplands are so rare in Shasta County, rural residents have almost no occasion to create norms to govern who should pay to fence them.

Procedural and Constitutive Norms: The Preference for Informality

When Shasta County landowners strike deals on how to share future fence costs, their negotiations are invariably informal. Despite the menu of offerings from the writers of legal formbooks, no rancher, and no attorney, could recall a written—much less a recorded—fencing contract between private landowners.[28] Indeed, they regard this degree of formality as unimaginable.

---

25. See, e.g., John Borgo, "Causal Paradigms in Tort Law," 8 *J. Legal Stud.* 419 (1979); Richard A. Epstein, "A Theory of Strict Liability," 2 *J. Legal Stud.* 151 (1973).

26. Richard A. Epstein, *Teacher's Manual* for Richard A. Epstein, Charles O. Gregory, and Harry Kalven, Jr., *Cases and Materials on Torts, 4th ed.* 5-1 (1984) (it is proper to say that cows trample corn, not that corn gets in the way of cows).

27. See infra Chapter 11, note 11 and accompanying text.

28. The one written fencing contract uncovered was an arrangement not between neighbors, but between the federal Bureau of Land Management and Kevin O'Hara, one of its grazing lessees. See infra Chapter 6, note 3.

When a major boundary-fence *construction* project is in the offing, the adjoining landowners may orally agree in advance how to share the costs. A few large ranchers also mentioned oral agreements under which a particular adjoiner would have exclusive future responsibility for *maintaining* a particular stretch of the common fence. They saw these long-term maintenance agreements as terminable at will. The long-term relationships in which they are embedded provide a system of social control that frees landowners from the hassle of negotiating detailed long-term contracts over fences.

Routine fence maintenance. Although oral arrangements for fence maintenance—both one-shot and long-term—are not unknown, a rancher is likely to make his seasonal inspections of perimeter fences without prior notification to his neighbors. Upon spotting a place where a wire has snapped or a fallen tree has pulled over some posts, the cowboy riding fence simply repairs it unilaterally. Thus Norman Wagoner, whose eight miles of fence adjoined the lands of only a handful of different neighbors, said he never coordinated annual fence repairs with them. When he would ride his fences every fall after the deer season, he would often find that his neighbor Dick Coombs had beaten him to repairing their common mile of fence.

The proportionality norm governs how neighbors should share maintenance duties over the long run. For two full-time ranchers, a fifty-fifty split is the proper long-term allocation of burdens, whereas a ranchette owner can freeload on a neighboring rancher's fence maintenance. Should a neighbor fail to perform his long-run share of maintenance duties, the injured adjoiner can employ the same remedies that trespass victims use. The first of these is mentally to enter a debit in the offender's interneighbor account, and then, if that proves insufficient, to escalate with truthful gossip and other forms of self-help.

Fence construction projects. More elaborate procedural norms govern the financing of new (and replacement) boundary fences. Because of the greater expense involved, a landowner is not permitted to undertake one of these projects unilaterally and then debit the noncontributing neighbor according to the proportionality norm. For major projects, in contrast to routine maintenance work, Shasta County norms indicate that one should contact one's neighbor in advance.[29] All the explicit arrangements to share construction costs that interviewees mentioned had been negoti-

29. Judges might be inclined to agree. See Megquier v. Bachelder, 112 Me. 340, 92 A. 187 (1914) (fence-viewer statute construed to require fencebuilder to notify viewers before undertaking project).

ated ex ante, and many respondents affirmed that this is the proper procedure. Because the norms governing the sharing of fencing costs are treated as binding, a neighbor is hardly free, however, to decline an appropriate ex ante request to share the costs of a fence construction project. Thus Mike Hassett, the owner of a fifteen-acre ranchette within Caton's Folly, said that if his neighbors unjustifiably refused to contribute to a fence construction project, he would undertake it anyway, and "get even with them some other way."

Shasta County norms forbid a neighbor from making cash payments to compensate an adjoining landowner for the time and effort the latter *personally* provided to a fence project. None of the dozens of informal fence pacts that were uncovered included payment for a neighbor's labor. In fencing disputes, as in trespass disputes, rural landowners in Shasta County regard cash transactions with neighbors as distasteful. Good neighbors should seek to maintain a cooperative ongoing relationship, as opposed to engaging in impersonal, arms' length dealings. The introduction of what is appropriately called "cold, hard cash" can signal distance and poison the atmosphere of a relationship.

In ordinary affairs among friends and neighbors, cash compensation seems to be permitted for out-of-pocket costs, but not for personal labor performed. When you invite guests to dinner, you wouldn't want them to pay cash as if they were at a restaurant; their friendly response would be to pay you back with a return dinner invitation. When a host and guest jointly arrange for the delivery of take-out food, the guest may be permitted to pay part of the food bill, but not to pay the host for the host's burden of washing dishes. Similarly, in Shasta County a neighbor can pay cash to defray part of a fencebuilder's materials bill (and the wages of any hired hand), but not to compensate the fencebuilder for his time and effort.

Because of the norm against paying cash for a neighbor's personal labor, adjoining landowners who agree to share fence costs usually identify certain in-kind contributions each will make. This makes a mutually undertaken boundary-fence project similar to an exchange of gifts, which helps maintain cooperative interneighbor relations. Suppose that application of the proportionality norm would call for two ranchers to split certain fencing costs fifty-fifty. As just noted, unless the labor were contracted out, one rancher could not take on the entire project and bill the other for half the cost of materials and labor. The two ranchers instead would be apt to adopt one of three varieties of in-kind splitting arrangements. In Shasta County, none of these three is common enough to be identified as the dominant approach, and one rancher in fact reported having personally used all three.

First, the two neighbors might handle the major improvements to their common stretch of boundary fence as a joint work project. In other words, they would split the materials bill fifty-fifty, and provide roughly equal amounts of in-kind labor.

Second, and perhaps more commonly, one neighbor may pay the entire materials bill (posts, wire, staples), while the other provides all the labor.[30] Because fence materials cost about as much as labor inputs do, this solution is regarded as effecting a fifty-fifty split. A labor/materials split of this sort often has clear practical advantages over a joint work project; for example, one rancher may have a hired hand available while the other does not.

Third, the neighboring ranchers may divide their common boundary into equally burdensome sections, and each take exclusive responsibility for building, and later maintaining, the fencing on one of the two sections.[31] Either an artificial monument (such as a special post) or a natural landmark (such as a creek) can function as the breakpoint.[32] Although law-library legal forms commonly invoke this system, it is unusual in Shasta County. The rancher and former supervisor Norman Wagoner had never even heard of the system, and no landowners reported having established an artificial midsection monument. In the two cases in which pairs of ranchers had agreed to divide fence responsibilities on a geographic basis, their common fencelines stretched over unusually rugged terrain and they had agreed on canyon bottoms as breakpoints. In choosing among the three cost-splitting arrangements, ranchers seem sensitive to utilitarian considerations. For example, the geographic-split solution was employed in the roughest terrain, where access for periodic maintenance was most difficult.

Remedial Norms: Self-Help Yet Again

Chapter 3 recounted how Shasta County residents mainly rely on informal self-help sanctions, such as gossip and mild forms of physical retal-

30. In all instances in which this method was reported to have been used, the rancher with the larger tract of land had provided the materials, no doubt to exploit scale efficiencies in purchasing and handling fence materials.

31. This is a time-honored technique. See, e.g., Osgood v. Names, 191 Iowa 1227, 184 N.W. 331 (1921) (defendant who breached oral promise to maintain a particular segment of boundary fence adjoining plaintiff's land can be held liable for death of plaintiff's cows who broke through that segment).

32. Two veteran ranchers told of hearing of an old custom under which each rancher would be exclusively responsible for repairing the stretches of common fence where the barbed wires had been attached to the post surfaces facing away from his lands. Neither knew of anyone who had actually followed this custom.

iation, to discipline a cattleman lax in controlling livestock. These same self-help sanctions undergird fence-financing norms, both substantive and procedural. The interviews turned up no examples of breaches of oral contracts to share the prospective costs of a major fence project. The following examples of informal remedial action therefore all involve either a refusal to agree to an appropriate ex ante fence-cost arrangement or, more commonly, a failure to perform one's share of routine fence maintenance.

When one adjoiner has failed to do his share of fence maintenance work, a pointed verbal request (implicitly backed by the threat of informal sanctions) is often enough to effect a correction. Thus after one of Tony Morton's cattle-owning neighbors hadn't laid a hand on their common fence for years, he lost patience and told her that it was her turn to do the repairs; his request jolted her into action. Bob Bosworth mentioned the possibility of a more formal threat: a registered letter to the uncooperative neighbor detailing failures to contribute appropriately to fence costs. Bosworth did not suggest what a rancher should do in case the letter failed to produce results, perhaps because he himself had never had a problem with a neighbor over fencing.

Yet it is again important to emphasize that the "fence subaccount" between two neighbors *is* a subaccount; someone who runs a deficit on fences can offset the deficit with a surplus in another subaccount. For example, Dennis Osborne forgave his neighbor for refusing to help out on boundary fencing because during Osborne's vacations the neighbor had helped keep an eye on Osborne's place. And mental accounts need only balance over the long term. For example, in 1967 Ted Plomeson unilaterally cleared the brush along one of his fences. A decade later his neighbor on that side unilaterally replaced the aging barbed-wire fence with a new four-strand version. Plomeson surmised that the neighbor remembered Plomeson's earlier service, and regarded the contributions as offsetting.

Owen Shellworth told of using more forceful self-help against a neighbor who had stinted on fencing obligations. The fence Shellworth shared with the Hunt estate fell into disrepair during the period when Frank Ellis was managing, and running hundreds of cattle on, Hunt estate pastures. After Shellworth shouldered a disproportionate share of the fence-repair work, he felt Ellis owed him something. Shellworth was already miffed at Ellis because Ellis had been slow in responding to Shellworth's request to borrow Ellis' D-8 Caterpillar bulldozer to scrape out a creekbed. Therefore, to recover what was due him on the fence, Shellworth took his truck to Ellis' ranch early one morning, "borrowed" the bulldozer without Ellis' consent, and used it for the creekbed job.

Fence-cost disputants in Shasta County rarely turn to third parties for help. The formal or informal appointment of fence viewers, a time-honored procedure that some states other than California still undergird by statute, is alien to Shasta County. Although public officials do receive complaints about loose livestock, they never hear specific complaints about adjoining landowners freeloading on fence expenditures.

The findings reported in the past two chapters pose a puzzle. If a closed-range ordinance has virtually no effect on who bears the cost of trespass damages and who pays for boundary fences, why do the residents of the Oak Run–Round Mountain area spend so much energy on proposed closures? More particularly, why did Frank Ellis reluctantly build a three-mile stretch of fence to prevent John Caton from supporting an ordinance to close the range at Oak Run? The next two chapters should help answer these questions.

5

×—×

Disputes Arising out of Highway Collisions Involving Livestock

After sundown on a December evening in 1980, Stan Schuster was driving a tractor-trailer eastbound on Gas Point Road in an open-range area southwest of Redding. Too late, his headlights lit up three Black Angus cattle standing in the roadway. Schuster's truck struck the cattle, veered off the pavement, and slammed into the trunk of a tree. Schuster's face was severely lacerated and his leg so badly crushed that it had to be amputated above the knee. The three cattle were destroyed, and the tractor nearly so.

Although Chapters 3 and 4 focused on disputes in which private law is largely irrelevant, it is far from true that private law *never* influences how residents in rural Shasta County resolve disputes. When, as in the Schuster accident, a vehicle collides with a domestic animal wandering on the highways of Shasta County, California tort law is likely to affect how the losses are borne.

One aspect of the vehicle-livestock collision story warrants emphasis at the outset. The ranchers of Shasta County believe, quite incorrectly, that the passage of a closed-range ordinance greatly increases a rancher's legal liabilities to a motorist who collides with a rancher's animals in the territory affected by the ordinance. As in the case of trespass law, most Shasta County cattlemen tend to view collision law in black-and-white terms. They believe a rancher in open range "has the rights" in a collision case. As many of them state it—almost as a proposition of natural law—a motorist who hits a bovine in open range "buys the cow." Consistently with this predilection for strict-liability rules, they think that the opposite rule prevails in closed range. In a closed area, as they see it, a cattleman must put up with any damage his animal may sustain in a highway collision and is liable, no questions asked, for any personal injuries or property damage the motorist has sustained.[1] These perceptions of the legal

---

1. In interviews, eight cattle owners and five county officials stated that the legal status of the range strictly determines the legal allocation of losses in collision cases. The only cattleman who suspected that negligence principles might apply was Norman Wagoner, a former mem-

impact of closures help explain the cattlemen's keen interest in closed-range petitions that come before the Board of Supervisors.

The Frequency of Vehicle-Livestock Collisions

To supplement and check interviewees' reports of collisions, an examination was made of California Highway Patrol (CHP) reports on vehicle-animal accidents occurring in unincorporated areas of Shasta County during 1978–1982.[2]

California Highway Patrol Accident Reports

The CHP is most likely to prepare a report on a highway accident if the accident occurred on one of the well-traveled highways that the CHP regularly patrols, or if the accident was serious enough to prompt a party, witness, or emergency-room staff member to call the CHP. Through interviews and other sources, I heard about four vehicle-livestock incidents that eventually resulted in lawsuits. The CHP had reports on all four. However, the agency turned out not to have reports on other, usually more minor, collisions, including one that resulted in an insurance claim for property damage.[3]

Despite their lack of inclusiveness, the CHP accident files provide the best available profile of vehicle-animal collisions in rural areas of Shasta County. In 1978–1982, the CHP reported 33 vehicle-animal collisions in unincorporated areas of Shasta County that resulted in human injury—that is, in at least a complaint of pain. (The great majority of CHP-reported livestock collisions involve only property damage, usually to both the vehicle and the animal.) Of the 33 injury accidents, 6 were caused by cattle, 6 by horses, 5 by dogs, and the remaining 16 by deer.

---

ber of the county Board of Supervisors. The animal control officer Brad Bogue was also a partial dissenter; he has tried to educate the cattlemen about California's fenced-lane statute (discussed infra, text at notes 33–36).

2. The CHP was able to provide a printout listing all "animal" accidents occurring in unincorporated areas of Shasta County between August 1978 (the earliest date for which data were available) and May 1982. The CHP database includes traffic accident reports prepared by all law-enforcement agencies in California. In rural areas CHP officers prepare virtually all included reports. The reporting system makes no use of over-the-counter submissions that parties involved in traffic accidents may unilaterally file after the fact. The CHP's accident coding system includes in the "animal"-accident category only incidents in which a vehicle had actually struck an animal. The printout therefore does not show incidents in which drivers had mishaps after successfully swerving to avoid animals. The CHP statistics presented in the text thus understate the perils that animals create on highways.

3. This was the Susie York fender-bender, recounted infra text accompanying note 36.

Thus the CHP data suggest that cattle and horses—the only animals with which closed-range ordinances deal—are less of a hazard than deer are.[4] This corresponds to the general perceptions of rural residents, many of whom spoke of daunting encounters with deer on the highway.[5]

Because the CHP files indicate the precise locations of all vehicle-livestock collisions, it was possible to tally separately those occurring during 1978–1982 in the Northeastern Sector. Within this six-hundred-square-mile sector of Shasta County extending northeastward from Redding,[6] the CHP reported 17 vehicle-livestock collisions during the four-year period. Four of the 17 involved horses, and the other 13, cattle (including 6 collisions involving animals belonging to traditionalists whom interviewees had identified as persons particularly careless in controlling their mountain cattle). Thirteen of the 17 collisions occurred after sundown. Of the 17, 1 resulted in human injury,[7] and 2 more in enough property damage to require the vehicle to be towed away. The horses and cattle struck in these collisions were less likely than the motorists to come out unscathed. In 8 of these 17 accident reports, the reporting CHP officer noted that the animal had been "killed" or "destroyed."

The busiest and best-patrolled road northeast of Redding is the fifty-mile stretch of State Highway 299 between Redding and Burney. This stretch includes a seven-mile segment of Highway 299 that falls within Caton's Folly, the only closed-range enclave in the Northeastern Sector.[8] Eleven of the 17 vehicle-livestock collisions reported occurred on Highway 299, but none within this seven-mile segment. There is some evidence that the passage of the Caton's Folly ordinance in 1973 may have reduced the subsequent frequency of livestock-induced traffic accidents

4. Horses and cattle caused only about 0.5 percent of total CHP-reported motorist-injury accidents in rural Shasta County in 1978–1982. The CHP printout revealed no instance in which a collision with an animal, wild or domestic, had caused a human fatality in Shasta County. The CHP's statewide data for 1972–1980 indicate an annual average of seven vehicle-animal collisions causing human fatalities, and six hundred causing nonfatal human injuries.

5. Vehicle-deer collisions are undoubtedly underreported in the CHP database. A deer collision is far less likely than a livestock collision to give rise to a third-party claim. A motorist who has hit a deer therefore has less reason to summon the CHP to the scene to prepare an accident report. A State Farm insurance adjuster who settles auto claims, including first-party collision-coverage claims, estimated that 90 percent of the vehicle-animal collisions in his files involved deer. This percentage is much higher than the CHP data would suggest.

6. In this context the Northeastern Sector is defined as the area bordered on the west by Deschutes Road (roughly the eastern limit of metropolitan Redding), on the south by State Highway 44, on the north by State Highway 299, and on the east by the longitude of the town of Burney.

7. A young woman suffered facial cuts when her vehicle struck a horse.

8. Figures 1.1 and 1.2 in Chapter 1 depict these locations.

occurring within it.[9] Nevertheless, the absence of CHP-detected collisions on this seven-mile stretch provides only weak support for the proposition that the passage of a closed-range ordinance can significantly improve highway safety. An animal owner concerned about liabilities to motorists in closed range would not even let his animals roam near such an area, yet 2 of the 11 vehicle-livestock collisions on Highway 299 in 1978–1982 occurred within one mile of Caton's Folly.

Collisions and Near Misses Not Reported to the CHP

Interviewees living in the Oak Run–Round Mountain area told of a number of widely known vehicle-livestock collisions that did not appear in the CHP files. Most of these occurred during 1978–1982, when Frank Ellis' herds often imperiled motorists in the Northeastern Sector. Ellis' stock caused at least four highway collisions during this period, only one of which appears in the CHP database as an "animal" accident.[10] Three ranchers also reported losing livestock in highway accidents before 1978, the start of the CHP report period.

Near misses are even more common. A motorist on minor roads in rural Shasta County often sees livestock on or beside the pavement. When changing pastures many cattlemen drive their herds on rural roadways. Two Oak Run residents separately told of "hair-raising experiences" and of being "run off the road" by herds being moved by Ellis' drovers. A few marginal operators deliberately allow their stock to graze the forage in road rights-of-way. Fences tend to prevent stray livestock from getting off a roadway once they are on it. Cattlemen therefore report that they pay particular attention to maintaining fences and closing gates near well-traveled ways. Al Levitt, the operator of the largest ranch in the Northeastern Sector, said he receives at least a dozen phone calls a year from neighbors who think, often incorrectly, that cattle out on the road are his. When a vehicle-livestock collision severely injures a motorist, as in the case of Stan Schuster, news of the event spreads among the county cattlemen like fire in dry chaparral.

9. See infra Chapter 6, text accompanying note 9. Because the CHP could not provide pre-1978 data, its database could not be used to examine over time the effect of the 1973 Caton's Folly closure on collision rates.

10. The Guthrie rear-ender, described infra text at note 44, was in the CHP files, but was not coded as an animal "accident" because no vehicle ever actually struck the pigs on the highway. See supra note 2.

The Role of Insurance

Rural residents may carry first-party (casualty) or third-party (liability) insurance for protection against losses arising out of highway accidents. Some motorists carry first-party collision coverage on their vehicles. Insurance companies also offer first-party policies on livestock. These coverages are called, quaintly enough, "inland-marine" riders. The insurance agents interviewed reported that ranchers rarely opt for inland-marine riders, except perhaps to protect against loss of a breeding bull or sheep (a particularly vulnerable animal).

In the early 1980s about 80 to 85 percent of California motorists carried liability insurance.[11] The typical auto liability policy would cover a motorist's liabilities, if any, for striking cattle on the highway. Because ordinary cattle have a value of only a few hundred dollars per head, an insured motorist might decide, however, not to refer a cattleman's claim to his liability insurer if the motorist thought the referral might result in a boost in his premiums. Some insurance companies vary their premiums according to a formula that discourages insureds from referring small claims to them.[12]

A cattleman is likely to have liability insurance that will cover, within policy limits, any damages he might owe a motorist who collides with his livestock. For the part-time cattleman, an ordinary homeowner's policy furnishes liability coverage. Cal Farm and the other insurance companies market to the major operators slightly more expensive "farm-ranch" policies that include liability protection. All cattlemen interviewed had liability policies, and some had umbrella coverages that provide protection against a claim of up to a million dollars. A rural judge stated, however, that a few marginal traditionalists decline to insure.

One of the arguments that cattlemen most often use when opposing closed-range ordinances is that a closure would cause Cal Farm and the other insurers to demand higher premiums for ranchers' liability cover-

---

11. *L.A. Times*, Nov. 23, 1986, p. 18, col. 4; *Peninsula Times Tribune*, June 28, 1984, p. A14, col. 1. Although Cal. Veh. Code §16020 nominally "required" motorists to have liability insurance in 1982, this statutory provision lacked teeth. Motorists had to show financial responsibility only *after* being involved in an accident that had caused either personal injury or property damage in excess of $500. This statutory requirement was stiffened somewhat in 1984. See King v. Meese, 43 Cal. 3d 1217, 1220–1221, 743 P.2d 889, 890–891, 240 Cal. Rptr. 829, 830–831 (1987).

12. State Farm, for example, provides its policyholders premium discounts of up to 10 percent for "accident-free" records during the prior six years, and may impose a surcharge of up to 50 percent for "chargeable accidents" in which State Farm paid out at least $200 for property damage.

age in the affected territories. In fact, the cattlemen greatly exaggerate how sensitive insurance companies are to minor legal distinctions. In setting premiums, Cal Farm not only doesn't distinguish between the open- and closed-range areas of Shasta County, it doesn't even distinguish between Shasta County and any other county in California. Cal Farm's liability-coverage premiums are utterly insensitive to local differences in both legal rules and accident rates.[13]

Even if an insurance company were to decide to vary its farm-ranch premiums by claims experience, it would be highly unlikely to conclude that the distinction between open- and closed-range areas was worth its attention. In 1978–1982 only two vehicle-livestock collisions in all of rural Shasta County resulted in severe personal injury.[14] Even if the tort law were to treat open-range collisions quite differently from closed-range collisions (which it does not), the amounts at stake would be unlikely to justify an insurer's administrative expense of creating different underwriting categories for ranges under varying legal regimes.

Because most motorists and cattlemen have liability coverage, insurance adjusters play a central role in the resolution of disputes arising out of vehicle-livestock collisions. In the animal-trespass context, where claiming and litigation are aberrational, rural residents could identify— or, to put it more bluntly, guess—the formal law's strict-liability rules better than insurance adjusters could.[15] In the vehicle-livestock collision context, the reverse is true. Here the formal law seems to cast a definite shadow. The evidence to follow will show that adjusters' comparative-negligence approach to collision disputes maps the law better than the cattlemen's strict-liability approach does.

Formal Law Applicable to Vehicle-Livestock Collisions

In American tort law, negligence (fault) is the basic principle for allocating the risk of loss from accidents. In general, the negligence approach imposes civil liability on an actor who has failed to exercise reasonable care under the circumstances and thereby caused harm to others. In certain types of accident cases, notably products liability actions, judges increasingly apply strict-liability rules, which allow recovery without proof of fault. Strict-liability rules are prominent, however, only in contexts

13. Interview with Ross Atkins, sales agent, Cal Farm Insurance Co., Anderson, Cal., Aug. 10, 1982.

14. These were the Schuster and Mollard accidents, discussed infra text accompanying notes 51–53.

15. See supra Chapter 3, text accompanying notes 38–42.

where the defendant is prima facie a much better cost-avoider than the plaintiff is.

The Common Law of Negligence

The Shasta County cattlemen believe that strict-liability rules apply in vehicle-livestock collision cases. All legal precedent on the issue indicates that the cattlemen's folklore on this subject is simply wrong. Highway collisions typically involve two or more moving objects, neither of whose owners is prima facie the obviously better avoider of the contact. Collision cases are thus particularly unlikely candidates for the judicial embrace of strict-liability rules.[16] In fact, courts and insurance adjusters in California consistently apply to vehicle-livestock collisions the same basic negligence principles that they apply to other types of traffic accidents.[17] Thus a cattleman whose carelessness has caused a collision is liable for the damages a non-negligent motorist has sustained. Conversely, a slain animal's owner, if he were himself free of negligence, can recover damages from a motorist whose careless driving killed the animal. These negligence rules formally prevail in *both* closed and open range.[18]

In closed range, where the cattlemen wrongly think that the law forces a stockman to "buy the car," legal precedents indicate that a plaintiff motorist must prove an animal owner's negligence in order to recover.[19] In a 1980 case arising out of a collision in a closed-range area of Shasta County, the motorist's attorney therefore rightly sought recovery from a horse owner on a negligence, not a strict-liability, theory.[20]

---

16. Cf. Pepper v. Bishop, 194 Cal. App. 2d 731, 15 Cal. Rptr. 346 (1961) (distinction between inanimate and self-propelled objects could help justify legislature's rejection of res ipsa loquitur in livestock-vehicle collision cases).

17. For an overview of the decisional law, see Note, "The California Law of Liability for Domestic Animals: A Review of Current Status," 11 *U.C.D. L. Rev.* 381, 391–395 (1978). See also Glanville L. Williams, *Liability for Animals* 378–392 (1939); Annots., 59 A.L.R.2d 1328 (1958); 20 A.L.R.2d 1053 (1951).

18. Special legal rules may govern the allocation of losses resulting from collisions between locomotives and livestock. See, e.g., Cal. Pub. Util. Code §7626 (West 1965) (railroad's duty to fence); Waters v. Moss, 12 Cal. 535 (1859); *Restatement (Second) of Torts,* §504 comment n (1977). Because there are no railroad tracks in the area northeast of Redding, this body of law is of no importance there.

19. See, e.g., Burnett v. Reyes, 118 Cal. App. 2d 878, 256 P.2d 91 (1953) (affirming judgment against plaintiff motorist who had failed to prove cattleman's negligence in collision in Kern County, a closed-range area). Two decisions that explicitly hold that a cattleman is not strictly liable in a vehicle-livestock collision are Reed v. Molnar, 67 Ohio St. 2d 76, 423 N.E.2d 140 (1981), and Vaclavicek v. Olejarz, 61 N.J. 581, 297 A.2d 3 (1972) (per curiam).

20. Mollard v. Knight, discussed infra text accompanying notes 52–53.

In open range, the relevant authorities similarly refute the cattlemen's folklore that "the motorist buys the cow."[21] All precedents call for the application of basic negligence principles to open-range accidents. For example, *Galeppi Bros., Inc. v. Bartlett,*[22] decided by a federal appellate court in 1941, squarely holds that in California a negligent cattleman is liable for injuries sustained by a motorist in an unfenced area of open range. In that case the motorist had struck a cow while driving on a federal highway in Lassen County, the county just east of Shasta. To support its holding, the *Galeppi Bros.* court cited an influential provision of the California Civil Code, section 1714, which states in broad terms that an actor is responsible for damage resulting from his negligence, that is, "his want of ordinary care or skill in the management of his property or person."[23] Dicta in several decisions of the California Courts of Appeal affirm the proposition that a negligent open-range cattleman[24] risks liability to motorists.[25] More recently, in two unreported decisions in 1982, a Justice Court judge in Shasta County applied basic negligence rules to two open-range collisions.[26]

21. Several western states have statutes that help cattlemen escape liability for collisions on unfenced highways. See, e.g., Nev. Rev. Stat. §568.360(1) (1986) (owner of livestock in open range has no duty to keep the animals off an unfenced highway); N.M. Stat. Ann. §66-7-363(c) (1978) (when a collision has occurred on an unfenced highway, the motorist can prevail only if able to prove that the "owner of livestock is guilty of specific negligence other than allowing his animals to range in said pasture"). California has no statute along these lines.

22. 120 F.2d 208 (9th Cir. 1941).

23. Cal. Civ. Code §1714 (West 1985).

24. An animal's owner is not the only person who may be liable for havoc it causes on a highway. For example, an agister who has been caring for someone else's animal, or the owner of land from which a lessee's cattle has escaped, may also be legally responsible. See, e.g., Davert v. Larson, 163 Cal. App. 3d 407, 209 Cal. Rptr. 445 (1985) (landowner may be liable for negligence); Stemmler v. Hamilton, 27 Am. Trial Law. Ass'n L. Rep. 209 (Madison County, Tex., Dist. Ct., Dec. 14, 1983) (motorist who suffered severe brain damage from collision with cow settled for $825,000 with owner of land from which cow escaped, and for an additional $6 million with the Gulf Oil Co., a long-term tenant that had negligently fenced the adjoining land through which the cow traveled). See also supra Chapter 3, note 20. In addition, a government may be liable for negligently designing or maintaining fencing along a highway. See Wisener v. State, 123 Ariz. 148, 598 P.2d 511 (1979) (state had wrongly been granted summary judgment in suit based on death of motorist killed in swerve to avoid cow on interstate highway).

25. Summers v. Parker, 119 Cal. App. 2d 214, 216, 259 P.2d 59, 60 (1953); Jackson v. Hardy, 70 Cal. App. 2d 6, 14, 160 P.2d 161, 165 (1945). (These two cases arose out of vehicle-livestock collisions in Ventura and Los Angeles counties, both closed-range jurisdictions). See also *Cal. Jur. 3d* Animals §66 (1973). Two of the Redding attorneys interviewed had researched this issue at the request of clients; both had concluded from authorities such as these that negligence rules govern open-range collisions.

26. See infra text accompanying notes 54–60.

To survive a motion to dismiss a lawsuit arising out of either an open-range or a closed-range collision, a motorist plaintiff must introduce direct evidence that the cattleman had negligently permitted the animal to go upon the highway. In 1931 the California Supreme Court made a short-lived effort to lower a motorist's evidentiary burdens when it held that the mere presence of a cattleman's animal on the highway suggests his negligence and therefore entitles a plaintiff motorist to invoke the common-law doctrine of res ipsa loquitur.[27] This doctrine has the procedural effect of ensuring that the issue of the cattleman's negligence reaches the jury even when the motorist fails to introduce direct evidence of the cattleman's negligence. The California Supreme Court's decision apparently ruffled some politically powerful feathers, and in 1933 the state legislature enacted a statute (still part of the Food and Agricultural Code) that bars a court from presuming an animal owner's negligence from the presence of his animal on a highway.[28]

California is a comparative-negligence state, and thus a plaintiff's contributory fault only reduces, and does not bar, his recovery from a negligent defendant.[29] Therefore, if both the cattleman and the motorist were to have been negligent, the formal law would entitle the cattleman to a partial recovery of the damage to the animal, and the motorist to a partial recovery for personal injuries and damage to the vehicle. According to California precedents these countervailing claims would not be set off against each other (at least if both parties had liability-insurance coverage).[30]

Statutes Relevant to the Issue of a Cattleman's Negligence

In many states the violation of a criminal statute or ordinance is negligence per se, that is, conclusive evidence of negligence.[31] In California,

---

27. Kenney v. Antonetti, 211 Cal. 336, 295 P. 341 (1931). This was hardly a radical ruling. About half the state courts that have faced the issue have held that the presence of a stray animal on the highway creates either an inference or presumption that the animal's possessor had been negligent. See Annot., 59 A.L.R.2d 1328 §6 (1958).

28. 1933 Cal. Stat. ch. 25, §423, p. 129. This statutory provision was amended in 1935 to forbid the "inference" as well as the "presumption" of negligence. 1935 Cal. Stat. ch. 265, p. 951. The amended statute is currently codified as Cal. Food & Agric. Code §16904 (West 1986). Pepper v. Bishop, 194 Cal. App. 2d 731, 15 Cal. Rptr. 346 (1961), rebuffed an amorphous constitutional challenge to this statutory denial of res ipsa loquitur.

29. Li v. Yellow Cab Co., 13 Cal.3d 804, 532 P.2d 1226, 119 Cal. Rptr. 858 (1975).

30. Jess v. Herrmann, 26 Cal.3d 131, 604 P.2d 208, 161 Cal. Rptr. 87 (1979).

31. See, e.g., Pigman v. Nott, 305 Minn. 512, 233 N.W.2d 287 (1975) (owner who violated statute against running animals at large held per se liable for damages sustained by motorist).

however, proof of a statutory violation only ensures that a judge must allow the jury to render a decision on the negligence issue.[32] A vehicle-livestock collision may bring a variety of different statutes into focus. For example, the motorist may have exceeded a speed limit and as a result have been unable to avoid a cow. On the issue of the cattleman's negligence, two specific legislative enactments are most likely to be pertinent: the California statute dealing with fenced lanes and Shasta County's closed-range ordinances.

The fenced-lane statute. Section 16902 of the California Food and Agricultural Code provides that an owner of livestock "shall not willfully or negligently" permit the livestock to go unaccompanied upon a public highway that is fenced on both sides.[33] This provision has been construed to apply to open-range areas as well as to closed.[34] Animals trapped within fenced lanes are hazardous both because they cannot readily escape and because a motorist who knows that a right-of-way is fenced may rely on the absence of livestock within it.

Section 16902's requirement that the cattleman be willful or negligent is peculiar because section 1714 of the California Civil Code, mentioned earlier, creates prima facie liability for willful or negligent conduct in *all* contexts. Perhaps because the fenced-lane statute is so specific and because its literal interpretation would make it redundant in light of section 1714, lawyers and law-enforcement officials in Shasta County tend to regard the mere presence of stray cattle in a fenced right-of-way as strong, if not conclusive, evidence of the cattle owner's negligence.[35]

My research uncovered six incidents in Shasta County in which livestock within a fenced lane had caused grief to motorists. Could one expect those who process collision disputes to learn of the relatively obscure section 16902? The Shasta County evidence on this score is unequivocal.

---

32. Satterlee v. Orange Glenn School Dist., 29 Cal. 2d 581, 177 P.2d 279 (1947).

33. The full text reads: "A person that owns or controls the possession of any livestock shall not willfully or negligently permit any of the livestock to stray upon, or remain unaccompanied by a person in charge or control of the livestock upon, a public highway, if both sides of the highway are adjoined by property which is separated from the highway by a fence, wall, hedge, sidewalk, curb, lawn, or building." Cal. Food & Agric. Code §16902 (West 1986).

34. See 16 Ops. Cal. Att'y Gen. 156, Opinion No. 50-142 (Nov. 16, 1950).

35. Animal Control Officer Brad Bogue interprets §16902 as making it "illegal" for someone to allow his cattle to stray upon a highway fenced on both sides. Bogue thus ignores the modifying phrase "willfully or negligently," and interprets the statute as making a cattleman strictly liable for collision damages his animals cause within a fenced right-of-way, regardless of whether the range is opened or closed. Judge George Knowlton rejected this strict-liability construction of the statute in Talmadge v. Cassidy, discussed infra text accompanying notes 58–60.

In all six of the resulting disputes, section 16902 was discovered and invoked on behalf of the motorist.

The most informally handled of the six disputes was Susie York's claim against Frank Ellis.[36] York's collision occurred on a fenced stretch of the Oak Run Road late one evening in 1979. While driving her Toyota, York dimmed her headlights for a passing car and was therefore unable to discern six of Ellis' cattle standing on the pavement ahead. Her vehicle struck a calf and suffered $1200 in damage. York asked Ellis to pay her auto repair bill. Ellis referred the claim to his insurance company and failed to counterclaim for the value of the dead calf. Ellis' insurer first denied liability because the collision had occurred in open range. Undeterred, York did a bit of lay research, learned of section 16902, and told Ellis' insurance adjuster about it. Eight weeks after York filed her claim the insurer settled for $800.

Closed-range ordinances. When a vehicle-livestock collision occurs in closed range, does that location bolster the motorist's case against the cattleman? As noted, most Shasta County cattlemen believe that this fact is decisive—that a closure changes the cattleman's liability for collision damages from none to strict. The law in action in Shasta County shows no such decisive impact because, as has been described, judges and insurance adjusters in Shasta County apply the same basic negligence principles to highway collisions in both open and closed range.

A formalist judge might even go so far as to hold that tort rules prevent a motorist from even introducing the fact that a collision occurred in closed range as evidence of the cattleman's negligence. The closed-range movement flowered in California long before the invention of the automobile. Its aim was to protect farmers from crop damage, not motorists from collision damage. A statutory violation is relevant in a tort case only if both the harm at issue is of a type the statute was designed to prevent and the plaintiff is in the class of persons the statute was designed to protect.[37]

Although formal legal analysis thus suggests that a closed-range ordinance should have no evidentiary weight in a collision case, the fact of a closure might in practice increase a motorist's chances of prevailing for a number of reasons. First, if a collision case were to be litigated, a trial judge might allow the motorist to introduce the fact that the collision had

36. The other five fenced-lane disputes are taken up later in this chapter. They include two civil lawsuits filed in Superior Court (*Schuster* and *Mollard*), one small claim (*Talmadge*), and two criminal prosecutions for misdemeanors (*Ellis* and *Whitlach*).

37. See William L. Prosser, *The Law of Torts* 192–197 (4th ed. 1971); Nunneley v. Edgar Hotel, 36 Cal. 2d 493, 497, 225 P.2d 497, 499 (1950). A third requirement is that the statutory violation be a cause-in-fact of the loss.

occurred in closed range as evidence that the cattleman had been negligent.[38] Although arguably inconsistent with formal doctrine, this judicial approach would, not wholly implausibly, treat the legislative decision to close the range in a particular territory as evidence that the enclosure of livestock was a cost-justified step in that territory. Second, a Shasta County ordinance makes it unlawful for a livestock owner, other than an owner of "livestock upon the open range," to permit his animals "to habitually trespass" on public property (such as a highway).[39] In cases where livestock have been "habitual" in their highway trespasses, this ordinance might be interpreted to make a cattleman prima facie negligent in closed-range areas, but not in open. Third, after an open-range collision, if the parties or their advisers were mistakenly to believe that "the motorist buys the cow" was the applicable rule, a motorist might refrain from claiming and a cattleman might resist offering payment. Fourth, if jurors were to share the cattlemen's belief that the open/closed range distinction should strictly determine the allocation of losses in collision cases, and were to know the type of legal range within which a collision had occurred, they might secretly nullify the judge's negligence instructions and substitute their own values.[40] For these four reasons, a closure may in fact somewhat increase motorists' prospects in collision cases, although certainly not by as much as the cattlemen's folklore would have it.[41]

38. The judge would thereby treat the closure as a circumstance relevant to how the trier-of-fact should resolve the negligence issues that arise out of a animal-vehicle collision. The logic could run as follows. Because cattlemen *perceive* a closed-range ordinance as greatly increasing their liabilities to motorists, a closure in fact reduces the number of animals that traditionalists run at large in and near closed areas. See infra Chapter 6, text accompanying notes 8–9. After a closure some motorists might observe this drop in the probability of encountering livestock on the highway. As a result reasonable motorists might drive faster in the affected territory. If some motorists were indeed to drive faster, that would increase the probability that any particular stray animal on the highway would cause a serious accident. This greater risk would in turn increase the social benefits a cattleman would generate by fencing in a particular animal.

39. Shasta County, Cal., Ordinance Code §3306c forbids anyone from permitting an animal "to habitually trespass on private or public property so as to damage or destroy any property or thing of value . . . , provided that this section shall not apply to livestock upon the open range." The attorney for the CHP patrolman Mollard invoked this ordinance after the closed-range collision described infra text accompanying notes 52–53, even though the facts of that case do not suggest that the defendant's horses had been habitually on the highway.

40. The Redding attorney Pete Schultz, who does defense work for insurance companies, predicted that a jury empaneled in Burney, a town in rural northeastern Shasta County, would have a pro-cattleman bias in a vehicle-livestock collision case. He thought that a jury in an urban area such as Sacramento would have a pro-motorist bias.

41. A closure does not seem to have much effect on a cattleman's risk of criminal prosecution. In Shasta County the few criminal actions prompted by livestock on the highway have been brought for violations of section 16902, the fenced-lane statute. This statute applies

The Settlement of Collision Disputes

The interviews and CHP files turned up for the 1978–1982 period ten livestock-vehicle collisions, mostly minor ones, in the Northeastern Sector. During the same period in other parts of rural Shasta County the CHP reported two collisions that had resulted in severe personal injury. Court records and interviews were used to determine what the parties involved in these dozen collisions did to resolve any disputes that may have followed. After at least six of the dozen collisions a victim either pursued an insurance claim or made some other formal demand. Indeed, in four of these six instances the claimant eventually filed a civil complaint to initiate litigation.

Compared with trespass and fence-finance disputes, which almost never result in litigation, collision disputes thus seem to be resolved relatively "legalistically." Can the theory of social control help explain why this is so? A synthesis of current law-and-economics and law-and-society scholarship suggests that the parties to a dispute are more likely to turn to legal rules and processes as they increase their subjective estimates of:

1. The intrinsic stakes (the amount by which the claimant's demand exceeds the defendant's offer).
2. The extrinsic stakes (the extent to which the outcome would implicate the economic, symbolic, or other welfare of the parties in contexts *other* than the current dispute).
3. The shallowness and shortness of their future relationship.
4. The probability that they can externalize the loss at issue to a third party, such as an insurance company.[42]

These variables suggest why formal claims are more likely to arise in Shasta County out of highway collisions than out of, say, arguments over the financing of boundary-fence repairs. First, when a collision has caused serious bodily injury to a motorist, the amount at stake far exceeds what is at stake in a fence-repair dispute. Second, fencing disputes arise between immediate neighbors; highway collisions, by contrast, often in-

---

identically in open and closed range. Two open-range prosecutions under it are State v. Ellis, 82 CR 026 (Central Valley Just. Ct., Cal.) (presence of Frank Ellis' pigs on the highway caused a rear-ender between motorists forced to brake suddenly); State v. Whitlach, 82 CR 324 (Central Valley Just. Ct., Cal.) (Oregonian's cattle had allegedly been frequently on the roads of the community of Central Valley). When animals stray, even habitually, onto highways that are *not* fenced, Shasta County law enforcement officials tend to respond with mediation, not prosecution. See supra Chapter 3, text at notes 33–35.

42. See infra Chapter 14, text at notes 63–67, for additional discussion of these variables.

volve strangers. Third, ranchers and motorists tend to carry liability insurance for highway collisions, but have no (and could get no) insurance against the risk that they would be sued for willful free-riding on neighbors' fencing expenditures.

A universe of a dozen collision incidents is of course usually too small to provide a statistically significant test of any theoretical proposition. It is nevertheless striking how powerfully the evidence from these incidents, marshaled below, supports the relevance of the four hypothesized determinants of the relative "legalism" of dispute resolution. For example, the four variables listed above successfully identify the types of accidents in which victims chose to lump their losses. The cattlemen Curtis McCall and Owen Shellworth separately told of instances in which they had slightly damaged their pickup trucks while trying to avoid hitting a neighbor's cow on the highway. Dispute-resolution theory suggests that these victims would be unlikely to submit claims because (1) the damages were minor, (2) the parties expected future dealings, and (3) the cattle owner might decline to refer a claim to his liability insurer out of a fear of an increase in premiums. And indeed, the two cattlemen-motorists both said that "of course" they had absorbed the damages to their pickup trucks.

By contrast, in each of the six collision incidents that eventually generated a victim claim, the disputants belonged to different subcultures. The cattlemen's antagonists in these six instances were three truckers, two ranchette owners who did not own cattle, and one CHP patrol officer. Five of these six incidents involved damage of at least $1000, and in four there was evidence that the losses were ultimately externalized in whole or part to insurance companies. These companies often play a central role in collision cases.

Insurance Claims

Six adjusters based in Shasta County were questioned about insurance claiming and settlement practices. Two of the adjusters were independent contractors; two were employed by Cal Farm, the dominant insurer of ranchers; and the remaining two were employees of State Farm, a leading automobile-insurance firm. The insurer-employed adjusters estimated that each of their offices (which serve several counties) processed on the order of twenty claims each year arising out of vehicle-livestock collisions.[43] Motorists, not cattlemen, initiate almost all claims, either by in-

---

43. This compares with the estimate of fewer than ten insurance claims a year arising out of trespass by livestock in Shasta County. See supra Chapter 3, text following note 64.

voking a first-party collision coverage against their own insurer, or by pressing a claim against the livestock owner, who may then, particularly if a large sum is involved, refer it to his liability insurer. A first-party insurer who has made a payment may also seek indemnification from a third-party insurer whose insured is primarily liable for the same loss. For example, when Joan Guthrie rear-ended a panel truck that had braked to avoid Frank Ellis' pigs, both vehicle owners obtained compensation under their collision coverages, and their first-party insurers pursued the matter with Ellis' liability insurer.[44]

A State Farm adjuster stated that his office rarely if ever saw original claims against motorists by ranchers who had lost animals in collisions. This adjuster did predict, however, that a cattleman who lost an animal would not hesitate to counterclaim against a motorist who had sought recovery for damage to a vehicle. Such a counterclaim was in fact pressed by the owner of the Black Angus cows that Stan Schuster killed on Gas Point Road.

The dynamics of insurance settlements in Shasta County seem generally similar to what H. Laurence Ross reported in *Settled Out of Court,* the leading study of auto-insurance adjusting.[45] Ross noted that insurance companies urge their adjusters to close files quickly. Adjusters in his sample settled about two claims per day.[46] To work at that rate, adjusters must economize on both factual and legal research. According to Ross, the formal law is therefore modified when it is actually applied. For example, he found that adjusters were apt to use comparative-negligence principles even in jurisdictions where contributory negligence was formally a complete defense, and to award something to almost all seriously injured claimants, even ones with highly dubious legal entitlements.[47]

Like the adjusters Ross describes, Shasta County adjusters try to avoid being legalistic with claimants. Their employers give them considerable discretion to reach settlements for amounts no greater than a few thousand dollars. In settling these minor claims, adjusters spend most of their efforts on fact-gathering, not legal research.

In a routine collision case it would be highly unusual for either the claimant or the adjuster to secure the services of an attorney. A veteran adjuster for Cal Farm, the company that writes liability policies for most Shasta County ranchers, could not recall a single livestock-vehicle case in

44. This incident also gave rise to the criminal case of State v. Ellis, supra note 41.
45. H. Laurence Ross, *Settled Out of Court* (rev. ed. 1980).
46. Id. at 134.
47. Id. at 122–135, 233–243.

which a claimant had been represented by a lawyer. The adjusters themselves know little or nothing about either the location of closed-range areas in Shasta County,[48] or fine points of collision law such as the existence of California's no-res-ipsa and fenced-lane statutes. As one State Farm adjuster said, "[The Company has] attorneys in Yuba City whom we can consult, but we don't do that if we can help it." Instead, at least when no more than a few thousand dollars is involved, the company adjusters reflexively apply rudimentary comparative-negligence principles. More often than not, the adjusters construe those principles as entitling a motorist damaged in an open-range collision to recover something from the cattleman's liability insurer.

Because most Shasta County ranchers accept the folklore that "the motorist buys the cow in open range," they think that insurance companies tend to knuckle under too easily to open-range claimants. Some Redding attorneys share this outlook. They believe that insurance companies sometimes pay off unmeritorious claimants in order either to save on defense costs or to avoid the additional liability that may arise out of a rejection of a good faith settlement offer.[49]

Paul Sampson, a State Farm adjuster who had helped investigate the Schuster accident, mentioned how thick that particular file was. When asked why it was thick, he responded that, because Schuster had lost a leg, the claim was a big one (over $100,000 of potential risk to State Farm), and that, as all adjusters know, the bigger the stakes, the thicker the file. Thereafter I began to refer to this simple, obviously correct proposition as "Sampson's Law": the quantity and quality of factual and legal research pertinent to a claim increases with the amount at stake.[50] Because most insurance claims are for small amounts, Sampson's Law accurately predicts that routine claims produce thin files; adjusters typically do no more than a barebones job of fact-finding, and not an iota of claim-specific legal research.

48. See supra Chapter 3, text accompanying notes 41–42.
49. Pete Schultz, the insurance defense lawyer, believes that insurers prefer quick settlements to avoid paying high defense costs. Another attorney emphasized the pressure that California law puts on liability insurers who decline settlement offers. In the face of his recommendation to the contrary, State Farm had agreed to settle Schuster's claim against its insured for the amount of the policy limit. He inferred that State Farm had done this because of Crisci v. Security Ins. Co., 66 Cal.2d 425, 426 P.2d 173, 58 Cal. Rptr. 13 (1967). Under that decision, a liability insurer that rejects a third-party claimant's offer to settle for an amount within the policy limit may be liable for the entire judgment that the claimant is ultimately awarded against the insured, *including* the excess (if any) over the policy limit.
50. This is not an original proposition. See H. Ross, supra note 45, at 90, 238.

Full Legal Processing: The Schuster and Mollard Cases

As stakes increase, the shadow of the law grows darker. When Susie York damaged a fender by striking Ellis' calf on the Oak Run Road, she pursued an insurance claim, but no government officials were notified and York carried out her own legal research. The Guthrie rear-ender caused by Ellis' pigs damaged two vehicles and led to some additional formal consequences—a California Highway Patrol report and the prosecution of Ellis for a criminal misdemeanor. Yet, as in the York incident, attorneys did not become involved in the ensuing insurance claims.

Major collisions are another matter. As noted, the CHP reports revealed only two vehicle-livestock collisions in unincorporated areas of Shasta County during the 1978–1982 period that resulted in "severe" personal injury. The two, involving the trucker Stan Schuster and the patrolman Alan Mollard, both occurred outside the Northeastern Sector. Both motorists eventually hired attorneys, who filed timely civil actions in the California Superior Court.

Schuster v. Judd. The collision that cost Schuster a leg occurred in legally open range at a place where Gas Point Road is fenced on both sides. The Black Angus cattle that Schuster's tractor-trailer rig struck had escaped through a gap in a barbed-wire fence at the common corner of two small ranches, one owned by the Blankenships, the other by the Judds. For years the Blankenships and the Judds had used a dead pine tree situated at this corner as a fence post. Three days before Schuster drove by, a severe storm had blown over the dead pine, pulling down the barbed wires stapled to the tree. Several Black Angus belonging to the Judds had escaped through this opening to make their way onto Gas Point Road and their fateful rendezvous with Schuster's truck.

In a complaint filed in Superior Court in Redding, Schuster's attorney, a member of a Bay Area personal-injury firm, sought over a million dollars to compensate Schuster for his amputated leg and severe facial lacerations.[51] The Blankenships and the Judds, each of whom had arguably been negligent both for using a dead tree as a fence post and for not inspecting their fences after the storm, were both eventually brought in as defendants. The Judds later counterclaimed against Schuster for the value of the three dead cattle. Schuster collected workers' compensation because he had sustained the injuries while driving on the job. The workers' compensation carrier joined the litigation to pursue its rights as a

51. Schuster v. Judd, No. 69531 (Super. Ct., Shasta County, Cal.) (complaint filed Mar. 27, 1981).

subrogee, as did the collision insurer who had paid out $7000 to the owner of the damaged tractor. State Farm and Hartford, the Judds' liability insurers, hired Redding and Sacramento attorneys to handle their defenses.

Eight months after Schuster's complaint was filed, and following some preliminary motions and a bit of discovery, the defendants' attorneys moved for summary judgment on the ground that there was no evidence that the defendants had been negligent. (They did not contend that cattlemen are never liable to motorists in open range.) Judge William Phelps denied this motion on March 12, 1982. The legal documents in the court file include citations to section 16902, the fenced-lane statute, and suggest that the fact that the Black Angus had been confined within a fenced right-of-way had been regarded by all as a strong point in the truck driver's favor. A month later State Farm and Hartford, through which the Judds had total liability coverage of $227,500, settled with Schuster for $225,000. The Blankenships, who had liability coverage of only $100,000, were then advised by their attorney to settle for $200,000, half of which would have to come out of their own pockets.

In 1982, when most of the field research for this book was conducted, the Board of Directors of the Shasta County Cattlemen's Association was abuzz over these developments. These settlements affronted the cattlemen's belief that a motorist always bears losses arising out of open-range collisions. The cattlemen were certain that the insurance companies and courts, because of either incompetence or gutlessness, had misconstrued the law.

Mollard v. Knight. The other "severe" personal injury accident listed in the California Highway Patrol printout was sustained by a CHP officer, Sergeant Alan Mollard. While driving on patrol late one night in March 1980 Mollard was alerted to a car theft. He saw the stolen vehicle and began a high-speed pursuit. The chase ended on Churn Creek Road in a closed-range area just south of Redding. There Mollard's patrol car struck two horses belonging to Leroy Knight. The horses had escaped from a fenced pasture and had wandered out onto the pavement at a place where it was fenced on both sides. The patrol car was totaled and Mollard suffered severe facial cuts.

Within two and a half months of Mollard's injury, his Redding attorney filed an action against Knight, the owner of the horses.[52] Although the collision had occurred in closed range, Mollard's attorney framed the

52. Mollard v. Knight, No. 66753 (Super. Ct., Shasta County, Cal.) (complaint filed June 5, 1980).

case as a negligence action, thereby rejecting the strict-liability approach that the cattlemen would have anticipated that he would use. The attorney eventually amended the complaint to assert that Knight had violated both the fenced-lane statute and the Shasta County ordinance that prohibits the habitual trespass of animals on public property.

The complaint demanded hundreds of thousands of dollars of compensation for Mollard and his wife. Asserting that Mollard had suffered special damages of over $50,000, the State Compensation Insurance Fund, which had paid workers' compensation to Mollard because he had been injured in the course of employment, joined the case to enforce its rights as a subrogee. One of the larger Redding law firms represented Knight's insurer. On July 22, 1981, a little over a year after the complaint had been filed, Mollard's attorney offered to settle with Knight's insurer for a total of $150,000. The court file of the case indicates that the matter was indeed settled for an undisclosed sum a few weeks later, just before the case was scheduled to go to trial. As in *Schuster v. Judd,* the litigation thus came to an end without much active involvement on the part of a Superior Court judge.[53]

The chronologies of the *Schuster* and *Mollard* disputes both support Sampson's Law. Each plaintiff had suffered facial scarring and other hard-to-value personal injuries. Each claimed a loss of over $100,000. Sampson's Law predicts that these uncertainties and high stakes would lead to the production of an unusually large amount of factual and legal research, and this did indeed occur. Compared with all other Shasta County disputes studied, fact-gathering was systematic and thorough.

A variety of different research teams helped thicken these two files. The Schuster and Mollard collisions educed by far the most elaborate of all the CHP accident reports on animal collisions. The defendants' insurance companies also assigned adjusters to interview witnesses and attorneys to research the legal issues. In addition, of the dozen vehicle-livestock collision cases studied, *Schuster* and *Mollard* were the only ones in which the claimants hired attorneys. These attorneys took the formal law seriously. Both teams of plaintiff attorneys found and emphasized section 16902, the fenced-lane statute. In *Schuster,* where the stakes were largest, the trucker's attorneys did the most library research; their briefs even cited a number of English cases involving a landowner's liability for damages stemming from the natural fall of a tree, one of the necessary antecedents of Schuster's mishap.

---

53. Judge Richard Eaton, for twenty-five years the presiding Superior Court judge in Shasta County, could not recall the trial of a single case arising from a highway collision involving livestock.

Two Small Claims: Clues to the
Symbolic Importance of Open Range

Few collisions result in losses large enough to enable a claimant to satisfy the Superior Court's jurisdictional requirements. In rural Shasta County smaller civil actions fall under the jurisdiction of tribunals called Justice Courts.[54] Many of these actions are filed as "small claims," that is, lawsuits in which the plaintiff is seeking to recover no more than $1500, and in which neither party can be represented by an attorney.[55] The Northeastern Sector of Shasta County falls within the jurisdiction of two Justice Courts: the Central Valley Justice Court (responsible for most of the sector, including the grasslands east of Redding) and the Burney Justice Court (responsible for the northernmost portion of the sector).

In an attempt to locate livestock-vehicle collision cases, I examined small claims filed during the prior eleven months in these two courts, quizzed court clerks and judges about these kinds of cases, and searched for the names of major modernist and traditionalist ranchers in the indexes of plaintiffs and defendants. In the Central Valley Justice Court these methods turned up no cases.[56] In the Burney Justice Court, however, they revealed two small claims stemming from vehicle-livestock collisions. Two traditionalist cattlemen had filed the claims, five days apart, against truckers who had collided with their cattle on Highway 299.[57]

The first of the small claims involved the death of a six-hundred-pound Hereford steer owned by the traditionalist Jim Talmadge. On the evening of October 23, 1981, Max Erskine was driving a log truck on Highway 299 near the bottom of the grade between Burney and the Hatchet Mountain summit. This stretch of road is fenced on both sides. While passing a slower vehicle, Erskine's truck struck Talmadge's steer. Talmadge had let the steer run at large on Hatchet Mountain. Because of cold autumn weather the animal had sought a lower elevation and had drifted down onto the roadway. Talmadge, aided by his fellow traditionalist Bob Moquet, filed a small claim to recover $378 from Tim Cassidy,

---

54. See Cal. Civ. Proc. Code §86(a)(1) (West 1982) (Justice Courts have jurisdiction when the plaintiff is demanding less than $15,000).

55. See Cal. Civ. Proc. Code §§116.2, 117.4 (West 1982). (Section 116.2 was amended in 1988 to raise the permitted maximum to $2500 by 1991. See West Supp. 1989.) The filing fee for a small claim is $6, an amount less than the fee for an ordinary civil action. See Cal. Civ. Proc. Code §117.14 (West Supp. 1989).

56. The judge who had sat on that bench for three and a half years could not recall any such cases, nor could the clerk who had handled civil filings there for the prior eleven years.

57. Judge Knowlton and the court clerk both reported vague recollections of prior small claims by animal owners against motorists.

the owner of the lumber truck.[58] Cassidy counterclaimed for $1015, the cost of repairing the truck's damaged bumper and grill.

In the second small-claim action, Roland Moquet, another traditionalist, sought to recover for the loss of a calf. The calf was killed the morning after the death of Talmadge's steer, on a part of Highway 299 where there was fencing along only one side. The calf had suddenly run across the highway in front of a flatbed truck being driven up the Hatchet summit grade by Bill Randall of Burney. Roland, Bob Moquet's brother, filed a small claim against Randall to recover $250.[59]

Judge George Knowlton, the sole judge of the Burney Justice Court, tried these two small claims in April 1982. After the trials Knowlton researched the legal issues himself. He correctly concluded that legal precedents called for the application of negligence principles to these open-range accidents. He also located the fenced-lane and no-res-ipsa provisions of the California Food and Agricultural Code. In July 1982 he released two written opinions, each a few paragraphs in length. He concluded that in neither case could he find negligence on the part of anyone and thus that the damages should lie where they had originally fallen. The traditionalists thus lost their claims for the value of the livestock, and the trucker Cassidy, his counterclaim for the damage to his truck. This result was particularly charitable to Talmadge, whose steer had not only been hit within a fenced lane but had also been seen wandering near Highway 299 for a full week before it had been struck.

Cattlemen rarely file lawsuits. If that is so, why had these traditionalists initiated small claims against the truckers? Although they were suing strangers from another subculture, a conducive condition, the sums they sought averaged barely over $300—an amount even a person of modest means would usually not take to court. The interviews and the court files both suggest that Talmadge, Moquet, and their traditionalist allies had large extrinsic stakes in these cases. They seem to have conspired to use the two small claims as a vehicle for obtaining a judicial affirmation of the folk principle that "the motorist buys the cow in open range." Because traditionalists repeatedly run cattle at large, this principle was of economic importance to them.

Moreover, the small claims carried a lot of symbolic freight for the traditionalists. A member of the Moquet clan (not formally trained in law) had presided over the Burney Justice Court as a justice of the peace through the mid-1970s. A few years later Governor Jerry Brown had

58. Talmadge v. Cassidy, No. 82-SC-87 (Justice Court, Burney, Cal., July 8, 1982).
59. Moquet v. Randall, No. 82-SC-83 (Justice Court, Burney, Cal., July 8, 1982).

appointed Judge Knowlton, a young Boalt graduate who had migrated to Shasta County from more urban parts of California, as the court's sole judge. In part because judges of the Justice Court are subject to competitive elections,[60] the two small-claim actions enabled the traditionalists to test and possibly shape the new judge's attitude toward the legitimacy and symbolic importance of the traditionalist mode of cattle husbandry in the Northeastern Sector foothills.

The narrative has produced a puzzle. The Shasta County cattlemen believe that motorists are strictly liable for collision losses in open range and that cattlemen are strictly liable in closed range. In fact, insurance companies and judges both consistently apply negligence principles to both open-range and closed-range collisions. Although the cattlemen may not know much negligence law, they are painfully aware that legal specialists regularly fail to honor their belief that "the motorist buys the cow in open range." For example, the modernist cattlemen knew of, and deplored, the large settlements that the trucker Schuster had won from ranchers' insurance companies. The traditionalists were furious at Judge Knowlton for not awarding damages to the owners of the mountain cattle that the truckers had killed in open range. Despite their awareness of these outcomes, the cattlemen continue to assert that the legal specialists who reach these results incorrectly interpret formal law. The next chapter, among other things, will explore why the cattlemen persist in thinking that the legal specialists, not they, are the ones ignorant of the governing legal rules.

60. See Cal. Elec. Code §25301 (West 1989); Cal. Gov't Code §71143 (West 1976).

6

━━

The Effects of Closed-Range Ordinances

Aclosure in Shasta County has one immediate and dramatic effect—
it prompts traditionalist cattlemen to drop their summer grazing
leases on unfenced tracts in and near the newly closed area. The cattlemen drop their leases because they perceive, incorrectly, that a closure
imposes important new costs on them. This chapter will compare the
cattlemen's view of the world with that of more informed observers. This
comparison will expose a notable flaw in the cattlemen's lens. The interesting questions are how this flaw came into being and why it continues
to exist.

How Shasta County cattlemen misperceive their legal risks when their
livestock run loose is a story that contains an important lesson for law-
and-economics theory. Such a narrative illustrates how complicating factors, particularly cognitive dissonance and the costs of obtaining obscure
legal information, may lead people to respond to legal changes in surprising ways.

How Cattlemen View the Legal Effects of a Closure

When asked why they strenuously oppose closed-range ordinances,
cattlemen virtually never respond with any mention of the fact that a
closure increases their legal liabilities in cattle-trespass cases. Most of
them are aware of that legal consequence, but they apparently regard it
as unmomentous. This is a sensible attitude for them to take. The monetary sums at stake in trespass incidents tend to be minor, and, more
important, the cattlemen recognize that, even in closed range, Shasta
County norms entitle a trespass victim to use self-help against the owner
of trespassing livestock.

When explaining their opposition to closures, the cattlemen instead
stress their fear of increased legal liabilities to motorists who might happen to collide with their cattle on the highway. As explained in Chapter
5, most cattlemen mistakenly think that a closure shifts the operative rule

in collision cases from "the motorist buys the cow" to "the cattleman compensates the motorist." In reality, insurance companies and courts apply the same basic comparative negligence rules to both open- and closed-range collisions.

The cattlemen share another relevant misperception that influences their behavior. This one involves their ability to shift risks. A rational actor saddled with new financial risks can ignore those risks to the extent that they can be sloughed onto third parties. The cattlemen of Shasta County might possibly be able to use three different markets to externalize any new costs that might attach to cattle ranching. The three are the market for cattle, the markets for factors used in cattle ranching, and the market for liability insurance. The cattlemen greatly underestimate how much the last of these markets enables them to externalize additional legal risks.

The Pricing of Cattle

Shasta County cattlemen correctly recognize that they cannot pass added operating costs forward to the feedlot operators who purchase their cattle. They know that the market for cattle is national, not local, and that they cannot influence prices within that market.

The Pricing of Grazing Leases

A traditionalist cattleman who leased unfenced summer pasture might hope to pass backward to his lessor at least part of any new costs arising out of a closed-range ordinance. He might anticipate that a closure that increased the costs of running cattle in a particular territory would shift downward stockmen's demand for grazing leases there, and thus cause grazing fees to fall.

The cattlemen recognize, however, that this second possible avenue for externalization is as futile as the first. Shasta County traditionalists know that the institutions that own and lease forests for summer range charge flat, non-negotiable grazing fees that are established without regard to whether a leasehold is in open or closed range.

The two major federal landlords, the Bureau of Land Management and the United States Forest Service, charge an unvarying cattle-grazing fee per animal unit month (AUM) on all their rangelands, not only throughout Shasta County, but throughout the western United States.[1]

1. See 43 U.S.C. §1905 (1983).

These agencies follow this policy even though federal rangelands vary not only in applicable tort regime but also in quality of forage, ruggedness of terrain, and alternative use.

Several corporations, such as the Roseburg Lumber Company and the clients of William Beatty & Associates, are significant suppliers of summer grazing leases in Superior California. These firms price their leases a bit more sensitively than federal agencies do. Although corporate grazing fees are also presented to cattlemen on a "take it or leave it" basis, these fees are commonly indexed to national beef prices and may also vary according to the quality of a rangeland's forage. The corporate lessors do not adjust their fees, however, from open to closed range.[2] They seem to regard that degree of fine-tuning as not worth its administrative costs. In no instance has a corporate landlord announced grazing-fee reductions after a closure.[3]

The Pricing of Liability Insurance

There remains a third and, as it happens, more promising market through which cattlemen might externalize costs arising from liabilities to motorists. Most cattlemen buy liability insurance. Insurers spread costs

2. An incident will illustrate the crudeness with which grazing fees are set. In the 1970s the Southern Pacific Land Company owned 360 acres of unfenced land in what became Caton's Folly. On December 1, 1973, Southern Pacific leased this land to the Kershaws for a flat annual fee of $55. During that year the Caton's Folly closure took effect, an event that could only be expected to drive down the value of the leasehold. When the lease came up for renewal, however, the company raised its annual fee to $100, a sum that the Kershaws agreed to pay.

3. Although institutional owners tend to set grazing fees by formula, they do sometimes vary the nonprice terms of their leases from site to site. For example, a closure conceivably might prompt the lessor of grazing land to insist on fencing, especially if the lessor thought the closure had increased its potential liability for trespasses and highway collisions that a lessee's cattle might cause. See supra Chapter 3, note 20; Chapter 5, note 24. An ambiguous incident illustrates the possibility of this sort of lessor response. In 1979 the Bureau of Land Management leased to Kevin O'Hara ten years of grazing rights on a quarter section of land. Now entirely surrounded by privately owned lands, this quarter section had remained in federal ownership because during the nineteenth century it had been the site of a way station for travelers on one of the few roads through the Northeastern Sector. The parcel then served as a commons on which the travelers stopping at the way station could graze their animals. As a condition for entering into the 1979 lease, the BLM insisted that O'Hara upgrade the existing perimeter fence on two sides of this quarter section and also build perimeter fence on the other two sides from scratch. O'Hara's son distinctly recalled that the BLM employee who helped him build this fence said that the BLM had insisted on its construction because the land lay within Caton's Folly, a closed-range area. The BLM area manager, however, asserted that the agency had insisted on the fencing only to protect the remains of the way station, an archaeological asset.

among insureds whenever they lump in the same premium category policyholders who pose different risks. Insurance categories tend to be
broad, not only because the law may prohibit certain forms of discrimination, but also because the refining of insurance categories increases an
insurer's administrative costs.[4] Cattlemen operating in a newly closed area
thus might plausibly hope that they could use their insurance companies
to shift to other insureds their (incorrectly anticipated) new risks of liability to motorists. This shift would be possible, for example, if Shasta
County liability insurers indiscriminately lumped open-range and closed-
range cattlemen together.

There is little correspondence between how insurance companies actually categorize policyholders in rural Shasta County and how the cattlemen anticipate that the companies will perform that task. State Farm and
Cal Farm, two of the major liability insurers, place great value on simplicity and therefore lump underwriting risks together in surprisingly
gross categories.

Cal Farm (which, according to its agents, is the insurer of 60 percent
of the farms in California) offers two types of policies, homeowner's and
farmowner's. An insured must buy a farmowner's policy if he owns over
twenty-five acres or is raising animals on a commercial basis. Cal Farm's
liability premiums for a farmowner's policy turn only on the number of
acres and the number of dwellings that the insured owns.

State Farm's basic distinction is between ordinary homeowners and
operators who make most of their income from agriculture. State Farm
requires agricultural operators to take out farm-ranch policies, as opposed to ordinary homeowner's policies, and charges them $10 a year
more for $100,000 in liability coverage.[5]

Because their rates would not vary with the answer received, Cal Farm
and State Farm do not require their insurance agents to ask an applicant

4. For discussion of how insurance companies classify risks, see Kenneth S. Abraham,
Distributing Risk: Insurance, Legal Theory, and Public Policy 64–100 (1986). See also Guido
Calabresi, *The Costs of Accidents* 47–50, 58–64 (1970).

5. In rural Shasta County the great bulk of a rural resident's property insurance premium
goes to pay for first-party coverage against casualty losses to buildings. Fire-fighting services
are much harder to provide in rural than in urban areas. The major variable that determines
State Farm's premium rates for farm-ranch policies is therefore the proximity of the insured's
buildings to a fire hydrant or fire station. In 1982, to obtain casualty coverage of $50,000 and
liability coverage of $100,000, a purchaser of an ordinary homeowner's policy in Shasta County
would pay State Farm $207 per year. A purchaser of a farm-ranch policy, if his farm buildings
were near a fire hydrant, would pay only a slightly higher sum, $217 per year, for the same
coverages. If his farm buildings were in the worst fire-protection district, however, the total
premium would be $376 per year.

how many and what kinds of farm animals he owns. Because these insurance companies do not even distinguish between, say, cattle ranchers and chicken ranchers, a cattleman applying for insurance is also obviously not asked whether he is a modernist who operates behind fence or a traditionalist who lets his cattle loose in the summer.

Nor do liability-insurance premiums vary with an insured's exact location. Cal Farm and State Farm both ignore, for example, how near a rancher is to a busy highway. Neither company distinguishes among different areas of rural Shasta County. Indeed, Cal Farm applies the same liability-insurance rate schedule throughout the state of California.

Insurers that decline to adjust liability premiums according to sizes or types of herds, modes of husbandry, and proximity to highways, would obviously also ignore legal trivia such as whether an insured landowner is located in open or closed range. Too few claim dollars turn on the type of legal range for it to be a viable actuarial category. Trespass-damage claims, for which a closure does increase a cattleman's formal liabilities, are rare and tend to involve paltry sums. As Stan Schuster's amputated leg illustrates, highway collisions can spark major claims, but a closure has little or no effect on legal entitlements in those instances. From an insurer's perspective, to vary premiums according to the type of legal range is to complicate the work of its sales agents unjustifiably. Closures simply have no effect on the classification of liability insurance risks.

Ranchers predict otherwise. The chief argument that the spokesmen for cattlemen make in public hearings on proposed closures is that a closure will increase cattlemen's liability-insurance costs and thus drive some of them out of the industry. For example, at the public hearing on the proposed Oak Run closure, the rancher Owen Shellworth said, "My neighbors [in Caton's Folly] where it's closed, they ask me, 'Why did we close it?' . . . The liability insurance [is] the first thing they think about."[6] In an interview Brand Inspector Bruce Jordan stated that closed-range ordinances tend to put traditionalist ranchers out of business by raising their insurance costs. The cattlemen's association president, Bob Bosworth, also predicted that insurance companies might respond to a closure by raising premiums in the affected area. This "insurance argument" is now a widely accepted part of the cattlemen's folklore.[7]

This argument is *slightly* more defensible than has just been implied.

---

6. When interviewed, Shellworth admitted that his insurer had not in fact raised his rates on account of the Caton's Folly closure.

7. A few cattlemen, such as the former supervisor Norman Wagoner, recognize that much evidence contradicts the folklore.

"Insurance costs" may rise even when an insurer does not hike its premiums for a given coverage. If a rancher were to believe (contrary to fact) that a closure would greatly increase his risk of liability for collisions, he could rationally anticipate two other kinds of increases in insurance costs. First, because insurance companies often do raise the liability-insurance premiums of the insureds against whom claims have recently been filed, a closure that prompted motorists to file more claims against a cattleman might eventually boost that cattleman's premiums. Second, if a cattleman were to view a closure as increasing the chances of a motorist's winning a mammoth claim against him, he would have to choose either to purchase additional liability-insurance coverage or to bear more uninsured risks. The Mortons, a ranching couple who had supported closing the range in their area, indeed predicted that they would have increased their liability coverage had the closure been adopted.

The cattlemen's "insurance argument," despite these grains of truth, remains greatly overblown. For example, insurance companies charge only minor amounts for added liability coverage. State Farm, for instance, charges $9 a year to increase liability coverage under a farm-ranch policy from $100,000 to $300,000. When the cattlemen make their insurance argument, however, they sound and act as if they believe something much less paltry is at stake.

The Allocative Effects of Closures

The crux of the matter is that Shasta County cattlemen perceive both that a closed-range ordinance will greatly increase their potential liabilities in collision cases and that these new risks cannot be externalized through insurance markets. That the cattlemen are in error on both scores does not prevent them from acting on their perceptions. A closed-range ordinance in fact deters the running of cattle at large because cattlemen see a closure as a source of major new costs.[8]

8. As Coase was the first to recognize, in a world without transactional frictions these costs would not be "new." In that world, if they were not protected by law, motorists and others endangered by loose cattle would have all along been paying cattlemen to take cost-justified steps to control livestock. Those payments would have sensitized cattlemen to the external costs of at-large grazing just as well as making the cattlemen liable for those costs would have. The Shasta County evidence shows the fancifulness of this story. For example, the zero-transaction-cost scenario wrongly assumes that cattlemen have perfect knowledge of collision law. In addition, there was no evidence that motorists or others had ever offered to pay Shasta County cattlemen to control at-large herds. The high costs of organizing the class of potential victims is a sufficient, if not necessarily the only, explanation for this inaction.

Closures Scare Away Traditionalist Cattlemen

Chapter 2 described several major political battles over enactment of closed-range ordinances in eastern Shasta County. These closures, when adopted, proved to intimidate the traditionalist cattlemen who had been operating in or near the affected territories.

The Shingletown-Viola closure. The Shingletown-Viola closure of 1966 was provoked by a traditionalist rancher with summer grazing leases on unfenced forests near Highway 44, a major entryway into Lassen National Park. This closure had immediate allocative effects of the exact sort that its proponents desired. According to Jim Cochran of William Beatty & Associates, the agent that handles grazing leases on most of the private forest lands in that area, the Shingletown-Viola closure caused traditionalist lessees to drop "all" their leases on not only the forests within the closed area but also for a distance of five miles around. Cochran believed that the traditionalists dropped the leases mainly because they thought that the closure had greatly increased their potential liabilities to motorists.

Caton's Folly. Like the Shingletown-Viola closure, the Caton's Folly closure of 1973 curtailed the operations of the traditionalists whose actions had provoked it.[9] Between 1968 and 1973 the traditionalist Ward Kearney and his co-venturer Dr. Arthur Cooley held the summer grazing lease on the United States Forest Service's twenty-five-square-mile Round Mountain allotment. In the early 1970s Kearney's aggressive grazing of Cooley's herds on this tract had swelled the number of stray mountain cattle near the hamlet of Round Mountain. When Steve Mattingly and the other antitraditionalists drafted the Caton's Folly closure petition in 1973, they targeted the area around the hamlet for closure.

In early 1974, a few months after the board had approved the Caton's

---

9. The Bureau of Land Management took aerial photographs of the southern and eastern portions of the Caton's Folly area in 1973, a few months before the Board of Supervisors approved that closure. The Forest Service photographed the same area in 1980. To go beyond interview data on allocative effects, I engaged a geobotanist, David Mouat, Ph.D., to examine these photographs with an eye to identifying changes in conditions both inside and outside the closed area. The aerial photographs, although taken at much too high an altitude to show fence structures, do reveal roads and basic vegetation patterns such as forest, brush cover, and grass. Aside from a few random changes in the degree of brush cover, Mouat could detect no evidence of changes in cattle operations either inside or outside Caton's Folly between 1973 and 1980. The number of stock tanks and stock ponds, for example, did not change. Signs of overgrazing were not visible from the air in either 1973 or 1980. Thus, although interviews conducted in 1982 turned out to indicate that Caton's Folly had put most traditionalists to flight a decade earlier, the consequences were too invisible to be corroborated from the air.

Folly closure, Cooley sold off all his livestock and left the cattle business. After 1973 neither he, Kearney, nor anyone else took out the lease on the Round Mountain allotment, a territory that one cattleman or another had leased in most years between 1942 and 1973. When Cooley was asked whether the closure had affected his decision to stop running cattle, he replied, "Oh, sure. . . . It had a very definite bearing." He added that a plunge in beef prices and a tightening of the federal tax rules applicable to cattle investors had also influenced his decision. But the closure had raised his apprehension of tort liability to motorists, especially because vehicles traveling on Highway 299 had struck his animals on several occasions. Prior to the closure, Cooley thought (probably on the advice of Kearney) that the applicable rule was that "the motorist buys the cow." As Cooley understood the law, the passage of Caton's Folly had shifted the legal advantage to motorists. Cooley considered relocating his herd from the Round Mountain allotment to more expensive fenced pasture, but he ultimately rejected this move as uneconomic.

Cooley observed that Kearney was "not a doctor" and therefore needn't be as concerned as Cooley was about tort liability to motorists. Yet, in a telephone interview, Kearney confirmed that Caton's Folly had also caused him to cease operations near Round Mountain. His policy is "to be sure it's open range" where he leases. Unlike Cooley, Kearney did continue to operate in the traditionalist style during the next decade. Kearney responded to Caton's Folly by shifting his summer range to leaseholds on private timber forests near Hatchet Mountain, an open-range area ten miles east of Round Mountain.

The traditionalist Bob Moquet's response to Caton's Folly was much like Kearney's. For many years prior to 1973 Moquet had leased unfenced forest lands in the Round Mountain area. After the closure, Moquet shifted his summer range to an open-range area on Little Hatchet Creek, near Kearney's new leasehold.

Caton's Folly did not put all traditionalists in its area immediately to flight, however. The perimeter of Caton's Folly took in the western part of Paul Totten's leasehold of some thirty square miles of the Roseburg Lumber Company's forest. Even after 1973, Totten renewed this lease annually and continued to run scores of mountain cattle on this unfenced domain. Totten kept up this leasehold until 1980, when Roseburg sought to almost double its grazing fees. And, as late as 1982, Jenny Larkham, a marginal operator with a small base ranch near Oak Run, was still regularly letting a few cattle loose to graze the sides of the roadways in the southern portion of Caton's Folly.

But these were exceptions. After Caton's Folly, residents of the Round

Mountain area noticed a thinning of the traditionalists' ranks. Several of the antitraditionalists who had lobbied for that ordinance asserted that it had had many of the consequences they had desired. The alfalfa farmer John Woodbury thought he had suffered fewer trespasses after the closure. Milt Quinn, an orchard owner, was "pretty sure" the ordinance had made a difference and noted that Ward Kearney was no longer running animals in the area. Phil Ritchie saw Moquet and Kearney's cattle less frequently after the closure; back in 1973 he had had the habit of keeping the gate across the driveway to his house area closed, but by 1982 his practice was to leave this gate open.

The threatened Oak Run closure. Doug Heinz's unsuccessful efforts in 1981–82 to close the area around Oak Run apparently had at least one major, if temporary, allocative effect. Heinz's campaign energized Supervisor John Caton into pressuring Ellis to build a barbed-wire fence along a three-mile stretch of the Oak Run Road that Ellis' loose livestock had made particularly perilous to drivers.[10] Ellis built this fence only weeks before the hearing at which the Board of Supervisors rejected Heinz's closure petition.

Why did Ellis ultimately decide to build this fence? Because he refused to be interviewed, one can do no better than speculate on his reasons. A first plausible reason would be to reduce his current tort liabilities to motorists. After he had become a big-time rancher, Ellis at some point asked his attorney to research whether precedent supported the cattlemen's belief that "the motorist buys the cow in open range." Ellis' attorney advised him, correctly, that this folklore does not jibe with legal reality, and that ordinary negligence rules apply. Therefore, when Ellis built this fence in what was still open range, he should have known that, among its other benefits, the fence would lessen his already existing risks of liability to motorists. Second, because Caton had threatened to support a closure if Ellis did not build the fence, to whatever extent that Ellis thought that a closure would further increase his tort liabilities, the fence promised to reduce his future risks. Third, once Caton had requested the fence, it came to symbolize the quality of Ellis' relations with both his neighbors and public officials. Ellis must have recognized that his refusal to fence would make ranchette owners, county politicians, and law-enforcement officials more antagonistic toward him. Thus his erection of the fence just prior to the public hearing was an overt signal of cooperation, just as his subsequent destruction of the same fence as a parting shot to Shasta County was an unmistakably hostile act.

10. See supra Chapter 2, text following note 12.

The Oak Run Road fence incident indicates several ways in which *pending* legislation may influence actors' behavior. To start with the obvious, an actor, when making a current decision, may take into account the probability of a bill's passage. Second, by publicizing an issue, a pending bill may prompt an actor to do what Ellis did—undertake more research on *current* law. Third, a legislator can do what Caton did: explicitly (or implicitly) use the threat of legislation as a club to induce an actor to change his current behavior. Fourth, the political debate over pending general legislation may end up focusing on certain specific cases (such as a fence along Oak Run Road), which become important symbols that alter the payoff structures of subsequent social interactions.

Modernist Cattlemen Go On As Before

Because modernist cattlemen manage their herds within fenced enclosures, they react much less than traditionalists do to the passage of a closed-range ordinance. Seven modernist cattlemen were asked what they would do differently if the Board of Supervisors were to throw the cattlemen's lands into closed range. "Not a thing," was the standard answer. Because most modernists vehemently opposed closures, this response might be somewhat self-serving; it denies that sponsors of a closure would achieve any instrumental gain, at least from them. When pressed, four modernists confessed that a closure might prompt them, out of fear of liability to motorists, to inspect their fences a bit more, to post more "No Trespassing" signs to keep out hunters and other potential fencecutters, and to check more often to see whether their gates were closed. They emphasized, however, that they were already in the habit of closing gates and monitoring fences.

Less hypothetical are the responses that modernist cattlemen have made to actual closures. Kevin O'Hara, who owned land within Caton's Folly at the time of that ordinance's passage, could not identify any influence the closure had had on his operations. In fact he had upgraded the fence around his land to make it stock-tight in 1972—a year before anyone could have anticipated the coming of Caton's Folly.

Curtis McCall, who knew his ranch straddled a boundary of Caton's Folly, was asked whether this bifurcated legal situation had caused him to vary his operations between the two areas. McCall responded with an emphatic "No," and added that the difference in legal regime had also had no effect on how he had shared fence costs with his neighbors.

Shellworth, a veteran modernist with a large ranch within Caton's Folly, did identify one tangible allocative effect of that closure. Buzzards

Roost Road, a paved but lightly traveled highway, runs between two of Shellworth's fenced pastures. Before Caton's Folly, Shellworth had occasionally allowed some of his cattle to graze within this fenced lane. After the ordinance was adopted, he stopped this practice because he saw a greater risk of liability to motorists. Thus, to the extent that he operated like a traditionalist, Shellworth acted like one: he responded as if a closure represented a real increase in the costs of at-large grazing.

The Distributive Consequences of Closures

A closure in Shasta County, although it has virtually no effect on legal outcomes, nevertheless has distributive consequences. These results stem from the traditionalists' perceptions that a closure is legally important, with the result that they tend to drop their summer grazing leases in and near affected areas.

A closure imposes significant economic costs on two groups. Owners of unfenced pastures in and around the closed area are deprived of grazing fees they would otherwise garner. The other losers are traditionalist cattlemen, such as Kearney and Moquet, who respond to a closure by shifting to other summer range; they presumably typically regard these substitutes as somewhat less satisfactory.

Who gains from a closure? Because these ordinances succeed in reducing the presence of loose livestock within the closed area, owners of ranchettes and other potential victims of mountain cattle face lesser risks of incurring uncompensated trespass losses. Standard economic theory suggests that these gains would be capitalized in the value of their lands. In this regard it may be significant that the ringleaders of the Caton's Folly and Oak Run closure movements, Steve Mattingly and Doug Heinz, both sold their land holdings within a few months of their greatest political efforts.[11]

The Symbolic Overtones of Closed-Range Battles

An understanding of the folklore that supports the cattlemen's "insurance argument" helps resolve the puzzle of why the politics of proposed

---

11. A private appraiser and a public property-tax assessor said, however, that they didn't take the legal status of range into account when appraising, apparently because they regard this legal variable as trivial. Perry Wiggen, a real estate broker who lived in the Northeastern Sector, theorized that a closure would raise the market value of ranchettes. He stated, however, that buyers don't ask about the legal status of the range and admitted that he himself didn't have a map that indicated the parts of the county that were closed.

closed-range ordinances are so heated. Once one appreciates that the cattlemen see the world through a flawed lens, one can appreciate both why traditionalists would bitterly oppose closed-range ordinances and why rural residents threatened by loose cattle would become activists in closed-range movements. The ultimate basis for their positions is identical: closures in Shasta County in fact deter at-large grazing.

Several subsidiary puzzles nevertheless remain. One is why modernist cattlemen eagerly ally themselves with the traditionalists in fighting closed-range petitions. Because modernists operate behind fences, they can't plausibly believe that closures will create major new risks for them or that insurance companies will dramatically raise their rates. As just observed, modernists in fact scarcely change their methods of husbandry after a closure. Why then do closures make them so genuinely hot and bothered? The second set of subpuzzles involves the evolution of the cattlemen's mistaken perceptions. Why did the cattlemen come to develop the beliefs that underlie their insurance-cost argument? How do they continue to maintain those beliefs in the face of a continuing flow of information that indicates that their beliefs are wrong?

Evidence of Cognitive Dissonance

The cattlemen resist absorbing information that is inconsistent with their folklore. As Chapter 5 recounted, Shasta County cattlemen repeatedly get reports that insurance companies and courts have not followed the adage that "the motorist buys the cow in open range." The cattlemen treat the receipt of these reports not as occasions for updating their beliefs about law but rather as occasions for railing about the incompetence of courts and insurance companies.

The cattlemen also resist assimilating information that indicates that insurance companies do not raise premiums after a closure. For instance, in a pro-closure speech at the hearing on the proposed Oak Run ordinance in February 1982, Doug Heinz attempted to puncture the cattlemen's insurance-cost argument. Heinz said that Oak Run landowners had been telling him that they had signed anticlosure petitions in order to keep their insurance premiums from going up. To show that this fear was unfounded, Heinz read from two letters written by State Farm and Cal Farm agents, both of whom affirmed that their companies do not vary liability premiums between open and closed range. Nevertheless, later in the same hearing Owen Shellworth, who knew that passage of the Caton's Folly ordinance had not led to a boost in his own liability-insurance premium, unblushingly reiterated the argument that a closure hikes cattlemen's insurance costs.

Concepts from social sciences other than economics provide possible solutions to these subsidiary puzzles. Political science, anthropology, and sociology furnish the notion of symbolic politics. Psychology furnishes the idea of cognitive dissonance. These concepts permit a political analysis that is richer, and much less tidy, than the variety that economists and public-choice theorists typically offer.

Symbolic Politics

Economic analysts tend not to put much stock in symbols. Symbolic victories, almost by definition, cannot have an appreciable impact on the victor's tangible wealth or chances of survival. Relatively humanistic social scientists, however, have long argued that the pursuit of symbolic gratification is an important feature of human life. Anyone inclined to dismiss this notion should ponder why Jews and others were so upset in 1985 when President Reagan announced plans to visit a cemetery where Nazi SS troopers were buried, why Vietnam War veterans cared a great deal about building a memorial in Washington, D.C., and why blacks expended scarce political capital to make the birthday of Martin Luther King, Jr., a national holiday.[12] The outcomes of these controversies seemed unlikely to affect the distribution or allocation of marketable resources, yet they nevertheless aroused great passion.

Joseph Gusfield, among others, has asserted that people may be interested in certain political outcomes because those outcomes will signal, in a psychologically important way, the relative status of various individuals within a society.[13] A person's sense of self-respect may turn in part on the respect authoritative institutional voices accord groups to which the person belongs. According to this view, battles over symbols are not simply preliminary skirmishes over more tangible political stakes, but are struggles over status rewards that are valued in and of themselves.

Some economists and public-choice theorists might dispute this last

12. On the last, see Derrick Bell, Jr., "A Holiday for Dr. King: The Significance of Symbols in the Black Freedom Struggle," 17 *U.C.D. L. Rev.* 433 (1984).

13. Joseph R. Gusfield, *Symbolic Crusade* 1–12, 166–188 (1963) (interpreting Prohibition as a symbolic struggle); John Griffiths, "Is Law Important?" 54 *N.Y.U. L. Rev.* 339, 355 (1979). Compare Murray Edelman's two books, *The Symbolic Uses of Politics* (1964) and *Politics as Symbolic Action* (1971), which seem to assert that politicians mostly employ symbolic acts to shape respondents' desires, not to mediate among persons whose desires arise independently from politics.

point. They might interpret symbolic struggles as tactical battles, best understood as parts of larger struggles over the material spoils of politics. This interpretation is often at least partially warranted. For example, an interest group might set up a battle over a symbol to obtain information about politicians or other interest groups. Symbolic victories may also change politically relevant perceptions, and thus bear material fruit at a later date. Visitors to a memorial for Vietnam War veterans, for example, might become more favorably disposed toward raising veterans' pensions. Nevertheless, it appears that symbolic victories can themselves bestow utility. The simplest explanation for the Shasta County cattlemen's opposition to a closed-range ordinance proposed for a rural area is that they regard a closure as a conspicuous kick in the teeth.

As Chapter 1 described, Shasta County has undergone rapid demographic and economic changes. The county population has increased ninefold over the past half century, and Redding is now big enough to meet the Census Bureau's definition of a Metropolitan Statistical Area. All cattlemen, both traditionalist and modernist, understandably see this urbanization as a threat to their relative status—economic, political, and social—in the county. A petition to close the range in a rural area of Shasta County, even if the closure would not have any predictable instrumental consequences, thus symbolizes a struggle between a traditional agrarian order and an emerging urban rival. For Shasta County cattlemen, a closure campaign is in significant part a struggle over official recognition of who has what place in the sun.

The Instrumental Masking of a Symbolic Struggle

The cattlemen never refer to, or perhaps even consciously recognize, the symbolic overtones of closed-range battles. They instead invariably invoke instrumental arguments, such as the insurance argument, that are objectively dubious. Interest groups seem to prefer to frame issues in instrumental, as opposed to symbolic, terms. A lobbyist, if unable to invoke the "public interest," will prefer to warn of threats to his clients' material well-being rather than to their egos. Thus Larry Brennan's petition against the Oak Run closure listed only instrumental reasons—that open range was needed to limit ranchers' liability, control predators, and so on.[14] Brennan's petition made no mention of another pertinent reason: that rural stockmen opposed the closure because they saw it as belittling them.

14. See supra Chapter 2, note 12 and accompanying text.

Another example from beyond Shasta County will underscore this tendency of interest groups to put an instrumental veil over a symbolic battle. The struggle over the Equal Rights Amendment was largely cast in terms of instrumental consequences. Opponents of the ERA sometimes invoked the specter of co-ed bathrooms, a result no court would read the amendment to require. ERA proponents emphasized the ending of sex discrimination of sorts that the Supreme Court had already thrown into doubt through its interpretations of the equal protection clause. Both sides were reluctant to acknowledge that the battle was mainly over whose rhetoric about women's roles would get symbolic blessing from governmental authorities.[15]

Individuals seem predisposed to suppress acknowledging that a political battle is about status symbols. To confess that these symbols are important is to admit insecurity about one's status. As a result, a person or a group of persons may develop and cling to "irrational" beliefs that provide a shield against having to confront their insecurities. Like members of any other social group, cattlemen do not want to see themselves as supplicants who need reassurance about their status from political actors. They understandably prefer to see themselves as rugged frontiersmen who, in the John Wayne tradition, are well beyond insult from politicians.

The Costs and Benefits of Cognitive Dissonance

A false folklore is advantageous to members of a social group when it does them little damage relative to the aid that it provides them. It is then, to quote a familiar phrase, a "useful myth." The disadvantage of a false belief is that it may lead to what in retrospect seems like a foolish decision. For example, because the cattlemen's folklore made them underestimate their liabilities to motorists in open range, some of them were underinsured. In recent years at least one couple, the Blankenships, paid dearly for this sort of error.[16] But it is also true that the cattlemen's false folklore rendered an important benefit. It provided ranchers with a sincere and face-saving instrumental argument with which to fight symbolically important battles. Since the Caton's Folly defeat in 1973, the ranchers have in fact won all major closure battles, thus obtaining repeated affirmations from the Board of Supervisors that the cattleman remains king in rural Shasta County.

15. See generally Deborah L. Rhode, "Equal Rights in Retrospect," 1 *L. & Inequality* 1, 5–8 (1983).

16. See supra Chapter 5, text accompanying note 51.

False folklores are perhaps usefully analyzed through a two-period model.[17] During the initial period, after a new topic suitable for folkloric treatment has just surfaced, the cognitive lenses that filter information are least flawed. At that stage, when deciding among folklores, members of a group subconsciously tend to reject those that would not be cost-justified. During the second period, however, after the folklore originally chosen has become ensconced, members' resistance to new and cognitively dissonant information can result in the continuation of a folklore that members would not at that point subconsciously adopt under first-period conditions. For example, once the cattlemen had subscribed to the notion that "the motorist buys the cow in open range," to admit later that this folklore was incorrect would threaten the authoritativeness of other aspects of their belief system. Currently, the Shasta County Cattlemen's Association not only does not hire attorneys to help members learn legal doctrine; it also in practice serves as a forum where the cattlemen reinforce and spread their incorrect folklore about collision law and insurance-company practices.

Markets for Information

Market forces often work to eliminate costly misinformation. This can happen in several ways. First, better-informed competitors may capture the markets of, or buy out, less-informed competitors. Second, those who have accurate information often can prosper by marketing it as such. To what extent could these sorts of market forces be expected to work in Shasta County to correct the cattlemen's false beliefs?

An initial point is that these market pressures are necessarily weak in the context of loose livestock in Shasta County. Too little is at stake. Particularly when their symbolic gains are factored in, the cattlemen's folklore rarely costs them much, if anything.

Market elimination of the misinformed cattlemen is highly unlikely. Most cattlemen love their work. In more technical terms, most obtain economic rents when pursuing their craft. To the extent that their folklore operates to reduce their financial returns, the loss is thus much more likely simply to reduce their rents than to drive them into a different line of work.

Market education of the misinformed is a possibility not so quickly dismissed. Here the key obstacles seem to be not only the strength of the

---

17. For a similar two-period model, see George A. Akerlof and William T. Dickens, "The Economic Consequences of Cognitive Dissonance," 72 *Am. Econ. Rev.* 307 (1982).

cattlemen's resistance to dissonant information but also the absence of any actor who would obtain major benefits from changing the cattlemen's beliefs. The cattlemen's major factual mistake is to underestimate their potential liabilities to motorists in open range. Liability insurers and owners of less risky types of summer rangeland therefore do have a slight incentive to instruct traditionalist cattlemen about the perils of running cattle at large. Accurate information is of course a public good. The private rewards of providing this public good, however, seem inadequate to induce its supply in the teeth of established contrary beliefs.

PART II

A Theory of Norms

7

×—×

The System of Social Control

The focus now shifts from the particular to the abstract. In general, the theory that follows is intended to aid in understanding why and how most people everywhere, like most residents of rural Shasta County, cooperate most, though hardly all, of the time. Who will deny that cooperation is ubiquitous? Would-be publishers of "good-news" newspapers have never found a market because human successes at interacting, particularly within close-knit communities, are far too common to be newsworthy.

More precisely, the theory offered is designed to illuminate in what social contexts and with what content informal norms emerge to help people achieve order without law. The analysis builds on the rapidly expanding interdisciplinary literature on cooperation. This body of work is now centered in disciplines, such as biology and economics, that start from the assumption that individuals are self-interested. Scholars in these fields have recognized that they must reconcile this unlovely starting assumption with the reality of ubiquitous cooperation. Sociobiologists are now seeking to understand why social insects such as ants and bees are able to live in communes, why birds figuratively and literally scratch each other's backs, and why animals of different species sometimes interact to mutual advantage. Similarly, social scientists are investigating why listeners send contributions to public radio, why business executives prize reputations for honest dealing, and why appointments committees at rival academic institutions are willing to exchange information on candidates for faculty positions. Much of the best work on cooperation draws on game theory, particularly that most famous of "noncooperative" games, the Prisoner's Dilemma.

This chapter immodestly begins the theoretical project by undertaking to develop a taxonomy of all methods through which individuals control themselves and one another. The goal of this endeavor is to illuminate the much larger social-control system within which the subsystem of informal enforcement of norms is embedded.[1]

---

1. Any taxonomy threatens to exaggerate cleavages among scattered phenomena. On the perils of taxonomic approaches, see John Griffiths, "The Division of Labor in Social Control," in 1 *Toward a General Theory of Social Control* 37 (Donald Black ed. 1984).

Table 7.1   A Tripartite Classification of Human Behavior

prosocial behavior	
	(a reward-triggering rule)
ordinary behavior	
	(a punishment-triggering rule)
antisocial behavior	

The task of dissecting the entire system of social control entails the development of a descriptive vocabulary that will be used throughout the remainder of the book. To start, a system of social control will be defined as consisting of *rules* of normatively appropriate human behavior. These rules are enforced through *sanctions,* the administration of which is itself governed by rules. The following taxonomy of the system of social control will distinguish between two types of sanctions, five controllers that administer sanctions and make rules, and five types of rules.[2]

Sanctions: Mixing Rewards and Punishments

Systems of social control typically employ both *rewards* and *punishments*—both carrots and sticks—to influence behavior.[3] In administering these positive and negative sanctions, enforcers usually apply rules that divide the universe of human behavior into three categories: (1) good behavior that is to be rewarded, (2) bad behavior that is to be punished, and (3) ordinary behavior that warrants no response.[4] Table 7.1, which illustrates a tripartite classification system of this sort, employs the standard sociological adjectives *prosocial* and *antisocial* to describe behavior that is out of the ordinary. Economists would use *goods* and (when

2. To compare the terminology that sociologists use, see generally sources in 1 & 2 *Toward a General Theory of Social Control* (Donald Black ed. 1984).

3. Rewards are goods, services, or obligations to which a person would assign a positive monetary value; punishments are goods, services, or obligations that a person would pay to be rid of. The distinction between punishments and rewards is well developed in behavioral psychology, where the two are sometimes referred to as positive and negative reinforcement. Sociologists, since Durkheim, have distinguished between penal and compensatory (restitutive) modes of social control. These are two different forms of punishment. What sociologists sometimes call therapeutic social control is a reward system; the person who seeks help from others is rewarded for recognizing and trying to remedy his plight. On these and other sociological distinctions, see Donald Black, *The Behavior of Law* 4–6 (1976).

4. For a fuller inquiry into the functions of these three categories, see Ellickson, "Alternatives to Zoning: Covenants, Nuisance Rules, and Fines as Land Use Controls," 40 *U. Chi. L. Rev.* 681, 728–733 (1973). See also Saul X. Levmore, "Waiting for Rescue: An Essay on the Evolution and Incentive Structure of Affirmative Obligations," 72 *Va. L. Rev.* 879 (1986); Donald Wittman, "Liability for Harm or Restitution for Benefit," 13 *J. Legal Stud.* 57 (1984).

Table 7.2 A Bifurcated Classification of Human Behavior

prosocial behavior	(reward/punishment switch-point rule)
antisocial behavior	

pressed) *bads* to describe these two extremes. Sociologists use the label *deviant* to describe people who act antisocially. There is no standard sociological label for people who act prosocially; these people will be referred to here as *surpassers*.

If the members of a social group wished to move behavior in a prosocial direction (upward in Table 7.1),[5] they conceivably could employ fewer than three normative classifications. For example, they could use a bifurcated system that dropped the ordinary-behavior category, and thus looked like the one in Table 7.2.[6] Or they could employ only punishments (rewards) as sanctions, and have a bifurcated system consisting of two categories: ordinary and punished (rewarded) behavior.

Finally, one could imagine a social-control system that placed all behavior in the same normative category and thus eliminated the need for the establishment of substantive rules whose role was to trigger changes in sanctions. For example, a society could establish an unachievable standard of perfect behavior for human conduct, and levy penalties on all behavior, with the penalties growing in magnitude as the deviation from perfection increased.

These unitary and bifurcated systems seem alien because in most social contexts people employ tripartite normative systems that make use of rewards, punishments, and no sanctions at all. Baseball fans, for example, cheer a shortstop's fielding gems, boo his errors, and sit on their hands when he handles a routine ground ball. Or suppose an automobile were to stall, block traffic in one of the two northbound lanes of a congested limited-access highway, and create a mile of backed-up vehicles. Most drivers would probably perceive that another motorist who stopped to

5. A utilitarian would not endorse the goal of eliminating all bads, however. When the sponsor of a bad activity is willing and able to compensate fully all persons damaged by it, it is often desirable to let the bad continue. See, e.g., Boomer v. Atlantic Cement Co., 26 N.Y.2d 219, 257 N.E.2d 870, 309 N.Y.S.2d 312 (1970) (although cement plant is a nuisance, neighbors should be limited to the remedy of damages).

6. Homans once (inaccurately) defined norms as rules of this character: "... [A] *norm* is a statement specifying how one or more persons are expected to behave in given circumstances, when reward may be expected to follow conformity to the norm and punishment, deviance from it." George C. Homans, *Social Behavior* 97 (rev. ed. 1974). Another of Homans' definitions of a norm is criticized infra note 15.

direct traffic would be acting prosocially, that motorists who quietly waited out the jam would be acting ordinarily, and that motorists who leaned on their horns while they waited would be acting antisocially. As both examples indicate, the rules used to evaluate day-to-day human behavior tend to be set so that the "ordinary" category encompasses most conduct that occurs. This approach has the advantage of reducing the costs of administering sanctions because that which is most common requires no response.[7]

Indeed, because behavior that ordinarily occurs typically warrants no punishment, the word *norm* is generally used in English in a potentially ambiguous way. *Norm* denotes both behavior that *is* normal, and behavior that people *should* mimic to avoid being punished. These two usages— one descriptive, one prescriptive—are potentially conflicting because almost everyone laments some features of the status quo. That the word *norm* has been able to maintain these two usages suggests that ordinary behavior is rarely regarded as antisocial behavior.

Five Controllers That Make Rules and Administer Sanctions

It is useful to distinguish between five *controllers* that may be sources of both rules of behavior and sanctions that back up those rules. The five consist of one first-party controller, one second-party controller, and three third-party controllers. An *actor* who imposes rules and sanctions on himself is exercising first-party control.[8] A promisee-enforced contract is a system of second-party control over the contingencies that the contract covers; the *person acted upon* administers rewards and punishments depending on whether the promisor adheres to the promised course of be-

---

7. The prevalence of tripartite systems is a clue that rulemakers are attuned to an overarching goal of minimizing costs, including administrative costs. For additional discussion of the tripartite approach, see infra Chapter 12, text accompanying notes 3–10.

8. The label *first-party* implies a self-control system arising from a person's atomistic reflections rather than from external socializing forces. In practice, socialization is apt to be a much more powerful source than reflection. Whatever the origin of self-enforced moral rules, there is broad agreement that the overall system of social control must depend vitally on achieving cooperation through self-enforcement. See, e.g., Thomas C. Schelling, *Micromotives and Macrobehavior* 128 (1978); Michael Taylor, *Anarchy and Cooperation* 7–8 (1976); John W. Thibaut and Harold H. Kelley, *The Social Psychology of Groups* 134–135 (1959); James Q. Wilson, "The Rediscovery of Character: Private Virtue and Public Policy," *Public Interest*, no. 81, at 3 (Fall 1985). Llewellyn thought that education, not law, was responsible for achieving the basic order in a society. See Karl Llewellyn, *The Bramble Bush* 107–118 (1951). He thus emphasized the combined roles of the self-control and informal-control systems.

havior. Third-party control differs from second-party control in that the rules are ones to which the actor may not have agreed; in addition, the sanctions may be administered by persons not involved in the primary interaction. Third-party controllers can be either nonhierarchically organized *social forces, organizations* (nongovernmental hierarchies), or *governments* (state hierarchies).

Controllers' Rules: Of Law and Norms

The rules that emanate from first-party controllers will be referred to as *personal ethics;* those from second-party controllers, as *contracts;*[9] those from social forces, as *norms;* those from organizations, as *organization rules;* and those from governments, as *law.*[10] (Although all of these will receive some attention, the emphasis will be on law and norms, the rules to which the Shasta County evidence is most relevant.)

Max Weber, surely one of the most impressive theorists of social control, applied a somewhat different taxonomy. Weber defined law as the rules enforced by bureaucrats who specialize in social-control activity.[11] Weber's approach strains ordinary language because it is insensitive to the identity of the controller who has made, or is enforcing, the rules. For example, employees of debt-collection agencies are specialized bureaucratic enforcers, but one ordinarily thinks of them as enforcers of contracts, not laws. Similarly, if the Catholic Church were to use specialized bureaucrats to enforce announced church policy, one would ordinarily view this not as the legal system in action but as something else—what is referred to here as organization control. The term *law* is used here as Donald Black uses it: to denote only governmental social control. The definition of a *government* is borrowed from Frank Michelman: a hierarchical organization that is widely regarded as having the legitimate au-

9. The term *contract* implies that both parties are voluntarily in association with one another. This term poorly describes instances in which one party is entirely dominant and able to dictate the other's behavior.

10. These definitions of law and norms correspond moderately well to current usage in American sociology. For example, Donald Black defines *law* as governmental social control. D. Black, *Behavior of Law,* supra note 3, at 2. Sociologists are still struggling with how to define *norms.* See George C. Homans, *The Human Group* 121–125 (1950); John Finley Scott, *The Internalization of Norms* 67–81 (1971); Jack P. Gibbs, "Norms: The Problem of Definition and Classification," 70 *Am. J. Sociology* 586 (1965). Some sociologists, particularly Continental ones, use *norm* to denote what is here referred to as a *rule.*

11. Max Weber, *Max Weber on Law in Economy and Society* 5 (Max Rheinstein ed. 1954); see also Anthony T. Kronman, *Max Weber* 28–31 (1983).

thority to inflict detriments on persons (within its geographically defined jurisdiction) who have not necessarily voluntarily submitted themselves to its authority.[12]

Ordinary human conduct will be referred to here as *primary behavior.* Social control activity (such as the administration of sanctions) carried out in response to (or in anticipation of) primary behavior, will be termed *secondary behavior.*[13] Rules govern secondary behavior as well as primary behavior, and an enforcer who improperly responds to another's primary behavior may himself suffer punishments. *Tertiary behavior* is social-control activity carried out in response to secondary behavior. This classification system could be extended tier by tier, in principle, to an infinite number of levels of social control.

These distinctions among different levels of behavior can contribute to a better understanding of how to prove the existence of a *rule.*[14] A guideline for human conduct is a *rule* only if the existence of the guideline actually influences the behavior either of those to whom it is addressed or of those who detect others breaching the guideline. The best, and always sufficient, evidence that a rule is operative is the routine (though not necessarily inevitable) administration of sanctions—whether rewards or punishments—upon people detected breaking the rule.[15] For example, the best evidence of a primary rule against dishonesty is a pattern of secondary behavior: the regular punishment of people discovered to be dishonest.[16] Conversely, the total absence of enforcement actions against

12. Frank I. Michelman, "States' Rights and States' Roles: Permutations of 'Sovereignty' in *National League of Cities v. Usery,*" 86 *Yale L.J.* 1165, 1167 (1977).

13. These adjectives also appear in H. L. A. Hart, *The Concept of Law* 89–96 (1961) (distinction between primary and secondary rules). The taxonomy of rules offered here differs from Hart's, however. See infra note 33.

14. Hart lucidly discusses how to prove the existence of rules in id. at 9–25. See also Emile Durkheim, *The Division of Labor in Society* 424–435 (George Simpson trans. 1933).

15. Compare Robert Axelrod, "An Evolutionary Approach to Norms," 80 *Am. Pol. Sci. Rev.* 1095, 1097 (1986): "A *norm* exists in a given social setting to the extent that individuals usually act in a certain way and are often punished when seen not to be acting in this way"; G. Homans, *Human Group,* supra note 10, at 123: "A norm, then, is an idea in the minds of the members of a group, an idea that can be put in the form of a statement specifying what the members or other men should do, ought to do, are expected to do, under given circumstances. . . . But even this definition is too broad and must be limited further. A statement of the kind described is a norm only if any departure of real behavior from the norm is followed by some punishment." These definitions show how estimable scholars of social control have tended to overemphasize the role of *negative* reinforcement and hence to slight the role of reward-triggering norms. But see id. at 297.

16. Rewards can also be used to create incentives for honesty. But if most people are honest most of the time, punishing the dishonest is likely to be administratively cheaper.

detected violators of a guideline is conclusive evidence that the guideline is not a rule.

An operative punishment-triggering rule may be so effective that it is never violated. There might then be no enforcement activity to observe to prove the rule's existence. In these situations other, less reliable, evidence may prove the existence of a rule.[17] For example, an observer may sometimes be justified in inferring primary rules from patterns of primary behavior. An alien who visited England could infer, without observing any enforcement activity, that there are rules that people should shake hands with their right hands, but drive on the left side of the road. Observing primary behavior is, however, a risky way of determining the rules that govern primary behavior, for false negatives and false positives are both possible. A false negative is most likely when detection of acts of deviancy is extremely difficult, but there is nevertheless an operative punishment-triggering rule that is regularly enforced against the few discovered deviants.[18] For example, if the Internal Revenue Service regularly treated proven income from tips as taxable income, that would be an operative rule even though IRS agents could rarely prove who had received tips. False positives are possible because not all behavior is normatively constrained. That people regularly sleep does not indicate that there is a rule that they should sleep. Only the regular punishment of detected nonsleepers, or the regular rewarding of sleepers, would provide ironclad evidence that rules govern the primary activity of sleeping.[19]

People often make aspirational statements about appropriate human conduct. These statements appear in statutes, in books of etiquette, in religious texts, in the adages of everyday speech, and so on. That aspirational statements support a rule is weak evidence that the rule is operative; this inference should be rejected, however, when evidence about patterns of primary or secondary behavior shows that people regularly flout the aspirational statement. What people do should be taken as more significant than what they say. For example, a criminal statute that prohibits unmarried adults from fornicating is not a rule as that term is used here if detected violators are not regularly punished. Similarly, Polonius'

17. A pattern of enforcement is thus a sufficient, but not a necessary, condition for the existence of a rule. But cf. J. Scott, supra note 10, at 72 (defining norms solely as patterns of sanctions).

18. Unlike deviants, surpassers typically have incentives to publicize their deeds. Unpunished closet deviance is therefore more common than unrewarded closet surpassing.

19. Cf. M. Weber, supra note 11, at 2–5 (comparing *conventions*—patterns of behavior whose violation will result in significant disapproval from others—with *customs*—regular patterns of behavior that lack this normative underpinning).

adage "Neither a borrower, nor a lender be"[20] suggests a normatively appropriate course of primary behavior, but patterns of both primary and secondary behavior show that it is not a rule in the United States today. Aspirational statements are likely to provide the best evidence of rules only when patterns of primary and secondary behavior are unknown. For example, because little is known of ancient times, the Ten Commandments, and equivalent aspirational statements in the sacred texts of other cultures, provide evidence of rules that prevailed in antiquity.

A rule can exist even though the people influenced by the rule are unable to articulate it in an aspirational statement. Children can learn to speak a language correctly without being able to recite any rules of grammar. Adults who daily honor a complex set of norms that govern dress would be startled if asked to lay out the main principles that constrain their choice of apparel. Rural residents of Shasta County had trouble articulating the norms that governed how they shared the costs of boundary fences. An observer of regular patterns of secondary (and, perhaps, primary) behavior may nevertheless be able to identify the content of unarticulated rules.

The existence of legal rules is usually easier to prove than is the existence of norms. Court dockets and police reports reveal efforts to enforce laws, and a law library contains most of the relevant (if often ambiguous) aspirational statements. Norms are harder to verify because their enforcement is highly decentralized and no particular individuals have special authority to proclaim norms. Still, the evidence presented in Chapter 3 was sufficient to support the conclusion that rural residents in Shasta County honor a norm that an owner of livestock is responsible for the conduct of his animals. The fact that many of the people interviewed said that a good neighbor would supervise his livestock was only weak evidence of this norm. That most of them did mind their animals said only a little more. The best evidence that this norm existed was that Shasta County residents regularly punished, with gossip and ultimately with violent self-help, ranchers who failed to control their cattle.

Controllers' Sanctions: Of State-Enforcement and Self-Help

The five controllers that provide rules of behavior—the actor himself, the person acted upon, social forces, nongovernmental organizations, and governments—also administer the rewards and punishments that are essential to the operation of a system of social control. The sanctions ad-

20. William Shakespeare, *Hamlet,* Act I, scene iii.

Table 7.3 Elements of a Comprehensive System of Social Control

Controller	Rules	Sanction	Combined System
1. *First-Party Control*			
Actor	personal ethics	self-sanction	self-control
2. *Second-Party Control*			
Person Acted Upon	contracts	personal self-help	promisee-enforced contracts
3. *Third-Party Control*			
Social Forces	norms	vicarious self-help	informal control
Organization	organization rules	organization enforcement	organization control
Government	law	state enforcement	legal system

ministered by these five controllers respectively will be referred to as (1) *self-sanctions,* (2) *personal self-help,* (3) *vicarious self-help,*[21] (4) *organization enforcement,* and (5) *state enforcement.*

Table 7.3 summarizes the terms for the various controllers' rules and sanctions and also supplies terms to describe a particular controller's combined system. As the table indicates, *informal control* is used here to describe the system of control that arises out of the operation of decentralized social forces. This locution enables the phrase *social control* to retain its conventional usage in sociology of denoting the global system that results from the work of all five controllers.[22]

The controller that makes a rule is commonly the controller that enforces it. This follows from the proposition that the best evidence of a rule is a pattern of regular enforcement. Nevertheless, different control-

21. *Self-help* literally denotes an individual's efforts to administer sanctions in his own behalf. This same compound word has also served, rather misleadingly, as the traditional legal and sociological label for sanctions administered by friends, relatives, gossips, vigilantes, and other nonhierarchical third-party enforcers. In deference to this semantic tradition, *self-help* is employed here to denote both methods of enforcement, and the adjectives *personal* and *vicarious* are applied to distinguish the second-party and third-party varieties.

22. See Morris Janowitz, "Sociological Theory and Social Control," 81 *Am. J. Sociology* 82 (1975) (incisive review of the evolution of the concept of social control).

lers can combine their efforts in countless ways to produce hybrid systems of social control. In particular, one controller can consciously enforce another controller's aspirational statements. Thus private citizens may become vigilantes who use self-help to enforce substantive legal rules.[23] Conversely, police officers may often apply norms and personal ethics, not "the book," in their everyday work.[24] When courts look to business custom to flesh out incomplete express contracts, the state is enforcing norms created by social forces.[25] A person who has "internalized" a social norm is by definition committed to self-enforcement of a rule of the informal-control system. An arbitrator who applies personal ethics in making an award may ultimately rely on the state to enforce the award.

Feedback loops may help to harmonize the rules of different controllers. For example, political forces may limit the deviation of law from norms, and, conversely, law may influence a citizenry's mores. As another example, one function of a contract may be to crystallize substantive entitlements that other sources had conferred in uncrystallized form. Chapter 14 will return to these feedback loops.

Five Types of Rules

One last taxonomy will complete the dissection of the social-control system. Five distinguishable types of rules of conduct apply to human behavior: (1) *substantive rules*, (2) *remedial rules*, (3) *procedural rules*, (4) *constitutive rules*, and (5) *controller-selecting rules*.[26] Each of the five controllers can make all five types of rules. For simplicity, however, only examples of governmental and informal rules—law and norms—will be used to illustrate the various types.

Substantive Rules

The core of a system of social control is its substantive rules. These define what primary conduct—that is, conduct unrelated to the making and enforcement of rules—is to be punished, rewarded, or left alone. A con-

---

23. See William M. Landes and Richard A. Posner, "The Private Enforcement of Law," 4 *J. Legal Stud.* 1 (1975).

24. See Donald Black, *The Manners and Customs of the Police* 180–186 (1980).

25. See Elizabeth Warren, "Trade Usage and Parties in the Trade: An Economic Rationale for an Inflexible Rule," 42 *U. Pitt. L. Rev.* 515 (1981).

26. Each of these types of rules can be subclassified into reward-triggering rules and punishment-triggering rules. See Table 7.1.

troller creates substantive rules by patterning its sanctions to encourage (or discourage) particular forms of primary behavior.

Remedial Rules

The substantive rules that trigger the administration of sanctions indicate only whether a reward or a punishment is to be dispensed when the trigger is tripped but say nothing about the nature and magnitude of the sanction to be administered. A system of social control therefore must include remedial rules that govern these questions.[27]

Remedial *laws* include the legal rules on remedies and other legal rules—such as rules of self-defense—that are more traditionally viewed as part of the substantive law.[28] Analogous remedial *norms* were found to exist in Shasta County. For example, a victim of a series of cattle trespasses is supposed to exhaust less drastic self-help measures before resorting to violence against the trespassing animals.[29]

Procedural Rules

Procedural rules govern how controllers are to obtain and weigh information before deciding whether to administer sanctions in particular instances. Codes of evidence and civil procedure contain basic procedural laws. An example of a procedural norm would be an informal rule on the quality of evidence an aggrieved person must have before being entitled to spread negative gossip about another's wrongdoing.

Constitutive Rules

Constitutive rules govern the internal structures of controllers. In the legal system, for example, constitutive rules determine the structure and interrelations of the various branches of government. The constitutive rules of the legal system are mostly governmental in source, but not invariably so. Current examples of operative constitutive norms at the fed-

27. Remedial rules constrain *all* forms of enforcement activity. For example, remedial rules constrain the tertiary behavior that is provoked by deviant or surpassing secondary behavior. Remedial rules also constrain enforcers' responses to breaches of procedural, constitutive, and controller-selecting rules.

28. The defense of self-defense recognized in the common law of battery is a remedial rule because it is applied to evaluate the propriety of a threatened person's response to another's prior (or anticipated) aggression.

29. See supra Chapter 3, text accompanying notes 54–58.

eral level are the practice of senatorial courtesy and the unwritten rule that the votes of four of the nine members of the Supreme Court are needed to grant a writ of certiorari.[30]

Constitutive rules also help structure the informal system of social control. For instance, constitutive norms may encourage members of a group not to be loners but rather to entangle themselves in the sorts of continuing relationships that help foster cooperative behavior.

The constitutive rules of organizations typically arise from a number of sources. Statutes often constrain the governance structures that the promoter of a new organization may use. Within these legal constraints the promoter drafts documents, such as articles of incorporation, that establish a governance structure. The constitutive rules of an organization often hold that its basic constitutive features cannot be amended without the unanimous consent of members. For example, each member of a homeowners' association typically has the right to veto a proposed reallocation of votes or assessments.[31] Constitutive rules of this nature are contracts, because each member expressly agrees to their content. Because unanimity is hard to achieve, the governing documents of organizations commonly authorize a supermajority of members, or perhaps even an elected board of directors, to change some rules that bind all members. Rules adopted in this fashion are organizational rules, not contracts, because dissenting members are coerced. For example, if the board of directors of a homeowners' association were to approve a by-law that governed when and where the general membership would hold its meetings, that constitutive rule should be viewed as an organizational rule, not as a contract among the organization's members.[32]

Controller-Selecting Rules

The crucial role of controller-selecting rules, the fifth and last category of rules, has gone little noticed.[33] In a society replete with governments, private organizations, social forces, contractual arrangements, and indi-

30. On the latter, see John Paul Stevens, "The Life Span of a Judge-Made Rule," 58 *N.Y.U. L. Rev.* 1, 10–21 (1983).

31. See Ellickson, "Cities and Homeowners Associations," 130 *U. Pa. L. Rev.* 1519, 1532 (1982).

32. See id. at 1529–1539.

33. H. L. A. Hart suggested that the operation of a legal system requires a variety of what he called "secondary rules." Some that he identified are analogous to what are here called constitutive and controller-selecting rules. See H. Hart, supra note 13, at 74–76, 89–94, 97–107. Yet Hart oddly asserted that only a legal system needs secondary rules. See id. at 113–114, 151.

viduals potentially capable of self-control, there must be rules that decide, for each domain of human activity, the division of social-control labor among the various controllers. Controller-selecting rules perform this function. They coordinate the social-control domains of, among others, the visible sovereigns that make and enforce laws and the invisible social forces that make and enforce norms.

All five controllers can make controller-selecting rules. When someone's personal ethics tell him to ignore a loss inflicted by another, he has selected the other party's self-control system as the sole source of social control. An arbitration contract is a second-party device for selecting a social-control system. A controller-selecting norm in rural Shasta County told rural residents to use norms and self-help to resolve cattle-trespass disputes, and not to refer those disputes to the legal system.

An example from academic life will illustrate the function of an organization's controller-selecting rules. Suppose a law student had allegedly plagiarized library sources during the preparation of a paper. The law school's staff would apply controller-selecting rules to determine where to find rules on what constitutes plagiarism and how plagiarists should be punished. These controller-selecting rules might point to the application of university standards and sanctions for plagiarism—an example of the use of contractual and/or organizational controls. If the law school relied entirely on a student's own individual conscience to control plagiarism, the school would be selecting the self-control system as the exclusive controller. If the school publicized the case among students and faculty, it would be choosing the informal enforcement of norms as the system of social control. Finally, if the copying violated a plagiarized author's legal rights in intellectual property, the law school might conceivably allocate the plagiarism dispute to the legal system for resolution.

Controller-selecting rules are somewhat similar to the choice-of-law and jurisdictional rules that courts use to decide, in a particular case, which government's law is to be applied and which government is to be responsible for imposing sanctions. Controller-selecting rules, however, address questions prior to the ones reached by choice-of-law and jurisdictional laws. They decide not *which* government's rules and enforcement powers are to be tapped but, rather, whether *any* government should have a say about the matter at hand. In short, an important function of controller-selecting rules is to limit the role of the legal system in human life.

When the controller-selecting rule of any controller disfavors the legal resolution of a dispute, that dispute is unlikely to enter the legal system. For example, if controller-selecting *norms* (informal rules) were to point away from governmental involvement in the settlement of a dispute, a party would be reluctant, because of likely informal sanctions, to knock on the courthouse door; similarly, if controller-selecting *laws* (government rules) were to deny the court jurisdiction over the matter—because, say, it was "nonjusticiable"—then a judge wouldn't let a knocking party in.

The Scope of a General Theory of Social Control

A general theory of social control would predict, on the basis of independent variables describing a society, the content of the society's rules— whether they be substantive, remedial, procedural, or controller-selecting.[34] Because a society's operative rules are best revealed by the characteristics of the events that regularly trigger enforcement activity, the general theory would predict which events would trigger sanctions, what the sanctions would be, how controllers would gather information, and which controller would administer a sanction in a given instance. To put forth even a rudimentary theory, an analyst would have to incorporate theories of the behavior of the five controllers. In other words, a general theory of social control requires subtheories of human nature, of market transactions, of social interactions, of organizations, and of governments. A theorist thus needs, just to get started, a command of psychology, economics, sociology, organization theory, and political science.

This is no small challenge. The goal of the remainder of this book is more modest. Its central purpose is to illuminate the workings of a particular subsystem—informal control—and to explore the intersection of that subsystem with the subsystem of law.

34. Because the theory of social control is so little developed, in their beginning ventures theorists would likely treat as exogenous independent variables the constitutive rules that determine group boundaries and controller structures. A more ambitious theory would make the content of constitutive rules endogenous.

8

✳—✳

Shortcomings of Current Theories of Social Control

In some situations, individuals are able to cooperate without governmental inducements to do so; in other situations, they need help from the state. Social scientists interested in human order have yet to develop a widely accepted theory of the interplay between informal social controls and the legal system. The law-and-economics and law-and-society schools each offer theoretical perspectives that are less than satisfactory.

Beyond Legal Centralism: A Critique of Law-and-Economics Theory

Law-and-economics scholars and other legal instrumentalists have tended to underappreciate the role that nonlegal systems play in achieving social order.[1] Their articles are full of law-centered discussions of conflicts—such as cattle-trespass disputes between farmers and ranchers—whose resolution is in fact largely beyond the influence of governmental rules. There are, of course, notable exceptions. Law-and-economics stalwarts such as Harold Demsetz and Richard Posner have understood that property rights may evolve in primitive societies without the involvement of a visible sovereign.[2] Several economists have emphasized that promisees can enforce express contracts without the help of the state.[3] Nonetheless, many scholars who work in law and economics still

1. This is hardly an original point. See, e.g., Lon L. Fuller, "Human Interaction and the Law," in *The Rule of Law* 171 (Robert Paul Wolff ed. 1971); John Griffiths, "Is Law Important?" 54 *N.Y.U. L. Rev.* 339 (1979).
2. See Harold Demsetz, "Toward a Theory of Property Rights," 57 *Am. Econ. Rev.* 347, 350–353 (Pap. & Proc. 1967) (development of fur trade led Labrador Indians to establish tradition of exclusive privileges to use hunting territories); Richard A. Posner, *The Economics of Justice* chs. 5–8 (1981) (economic analysis of order in preliterate societies). More explicit is Bruce L. Benson, "The Spontaneous Evolution of Commercial Law," 55 *S. Econ. J.* 644 (1989) (on medieval law among merchants).
3. See, e.g., Benjamin Klein and Keith B. Leffler, "The Role of Market Forces in Assuring Contractual Performance," 89 *J. Pol. Econ.* 615 (1981); Oliver E. Williamson, "Credible Com-

seem to regard the state as the dominant, perhaps even exclusive, controller.

The Legal-Centralist Tradition

Oliver Williamson has used the phrase *legal centralism* to describe the belief that governments are the chief sources of rules and enforcement efforts.[4] The quintessential legal centralist was Thomas Hobbes, who thought that in a society without a sovereign, all would be chaos. Without a Leviathan one would observe, in Hobbes's memorable words:

> . . . continual feare, and danger of violent death; And the life of man, solitary, poore, nasty, brutish, and short. . . . To this warre of every man against every man, this is also consequent; that nothing can be Unjust. The notions of Right and Wrong, Justice and Injustice have no place. Where there is no common Power, there is no Law; where no Law, no Injustice. . . . It is consequent also to the same condition, that there be no Propriety, no Dominion, no *Mine* and *Thine* distinct; but only that to be every mans that he can get; and for so long, as he can keep it. . . .[5]

Hobbes apparently saw no possibility that some nonlegal system of social control—such as the decentralized enforcement of norms—might bring about at least a modicum of order even under conditions of anarchy. (The term *anarchy* is used here in its root sense of a lack of government, rather than in its colloquial sense of a state of disorder. Only a legal centralist would equate the two.)

The seminal works in law and economics hew to the Hobbesian tradition of legal centralism. Ronald Coase's work is an interesting example. Throughout his scholarly career, Coase has emphasized the capacity of individuals to work out mutually advantageous arrangements without the aid of a central coordinator. Yet in his famous article "The Problem of Social Cost," Coase fell into a line of analysis that was wholly in the Hobbesian tradition. In analyzing the effect that changes in law might

---

mitments: Using Hostages to Support Exchange," 73 *Am. Econ. Rev.* 519 (1983). See also Richard Craswell, "Performance, Reliance, and One-Sided Information," 18 *J. Legal Stud.* 365, 367 (1989); Anthony T. Kronman, "Contract Law and the State of Nature," 1 *J.L. Econ. & Org.* 5 (1985).

4. Williamson, supra note 3, at 520, 537. Williamson himself is critical of legal centralism.

5. Thomas Hobbes, *Leviathan* 97–98 (Oxford Univ. Press ed. 1909); see also id. at 110–113 (only a state can force parties to abide by their covenants).

have on human interactions, Coase implicitly assumed that governments have a monopoly on rulemaking functions. In a representative passage Coase wrote: "It is always possible to modify by transactions on the market the initial *legal* delimitation of rights. And, of course, if such market transactions are costless, such a rearrangement of rights will always take place if it would lead to an increase in the value of production. . . ."[6] Even in the parts of his article where he took transaction costs into account, Coase failed to note that in some contexts initial rights might arise from norms generated through decentralized social processes, rather than from law.

In another of the classic works in law and economics, Guido Calabresi and A. Douglas Melamed similarly regarded "the state" as the sole source of social order:

> The first issue which must be faced by any legal system is one we call the problem of "entitlement." Whenever a state is presented with the conflicting interests of two or more people, or two or more groups of people, it must decide which side to favor. Absent such a decision, access to goods, services, and life itself will be decided on the basis of "might makes right"—whoever is stronger or shrewder will win. Hence the fundamental thing that the law does is to decide which of the conflicting parties will be entitled to prevail. . . .
>
> Having made its initial choice, society must enforce that choice. Simply setting the entitlement does not avoid the problem of "might makes right"; a minimum of state intervention is always necessary. Our conventional notions make this easy to comprehend with respect to private property. If Taney owns a cabbage patch and Marshall, who is bigger, wants a cabbage, he will get it unless the state intervenes. . . .[7]

In these passages Calabresi and Melamed lapsed into an extreme legal centralism that denied the possibility that controllers other than "the state" could generate and enforce entitlements.[8]

Economists have hardly been alone in exaggerating the state's role in

6. Ronald H. Coase, "The Problem of Social Cost," 3 *J.L. & Econ.* 1, 15 (1960) (emphasis added). Compare Ronald H. Coase, *The Firm, the Market, and the Law* 10 (1988) (an organization such as a commodity exchange is capable of creating "legal rules" because exchange members have repeat dealings and can expel deviants).

7. Guido Calabresi and A. Douglas Melamed, "Property Rules, Liability Rules, and Inalienability: One View of the Cathedral," 85 *Harv. L. Rev.* 1089, 1090–1091 (1972).

8. On the plausibility of Calabresi and Melamed's assertion that anarchic entitlements are highly correlated with a party's individual power, see infra Chapter 10, notes 23, 42.

making and enforcing rules of order. For example, Max Weber and Roscoe Pound both seemingly endorsed the dubious propositions that the state has, and should have, a monopoly on the use of violent force. In fact, as both those scholars recognized elsewhere in their writings, operative rules in human societies often authorize forceful private responses to provocative conduct.[9]

Perhaps because legal centralists overrate the role of law, they seem unduly prone to assume that actors know and honor legal rules. Economists know that information is costly, and a growing number emphasize that humans have cognitive limitations.[10] Yet in making assessments of the instrumental value of alternative legal approaches, respected law-and-economics scholars have assumed that drivers and pedestrians are fully aware of the substance of personal-injury law;[11] that, when purchasing a home appliance whose use may injure bystanders, consumers know enough products liability law to be able to assess the significance of a manufacturer's warranty provision that disclaims liability to bystanders;[12] and that people who set fires fully understand the rules of causation that courts apply when two fires, one natural and the other man-made, conjoin and do damage.[13]

---

9. Weber regarded the state as the supreme instrument of social control: ". . .[T]he modern state is a compulsory association which organizes domination. It has been successful in seeking to monopolize the legitimate use of physical force as a means of domination within a territory. . . . The right to use physical force is ascribed to other institutions or to individuals only to the extent to which the state permits it." Max Weber, *Essays in Sociology* 78, 83 (H. Gerth and C. Wright trans. 1958). In reality, no state has been able to prevent other controllers from using violence to enforce rules of behavior. See also Michael Taylor, *Anarchy and Cooperation* 4–5 (1976) (criticizing Weber's position). Pound's legal-centralist tendencies are revealed in the following passage: "It is a general principle that one who is or believes he is injured or deprived of what he is lawfully entitled to must apply to the state for help. Self-help is in conflict with the very idea of the social order. It subjects the weaker to risk of the arbitrary will or mistaken belief of the stronger. Hence the law in general forbids it." 5 Roscoe Pound, *Jurisprudence* §142, at 351–352 (1959). But see id. at 349, 352, 356 (acknowledging legal recognition of limited rights to exercise self-help). Cf. Robert Nozick, *Anarchy, State, and Utopia* 12–15, 26, 34–35, 88–89, 138–139 (1974) (even an ultraminimal state should sharply limit self-help because of danger that punishment will be wrongly inflicted).

10. See, e.g., George J. Stigler, "The Economics of Information," 69 *J. Pol. Econ.* 213 (1961); George A. Akerlof and William T. Dickens, "The Economic Consequences of Cognitive Dissonance," 72 *Am. Econ. Rev.* 307 (1982); sources cited infra Chapter 9, note 5.

11. A. Mitchell Polinsky, *An Introduction to Law and Economics* 39–52 (2d ed. 1989).

12. George L. Priest, "A Theory of the Consumer Product Warranty," 90 *Yale L.J.* 1297, 1350 (1981).

13. Steven Shavell, "An Analysis of Causation and the Scope of Liability in the Law of Torts," 9 *J. Legal Stud.* 463, 471, 495 (1980).

Some Evidence That Refutes Legal Centralism

As suggested already, many of the Shasta County findings cannot be squared with legal centralism. When adjoining landowners there decide to split the costs of boundary fences, they typically reach their solutions in total ignorance of their substantive legal rights. When resolving cattle-trespass disputes, virtually all rural residents apply a norm that an animal owner is responsible for the behavior of his livestock—even in situations where they know that a cattleman would not be legally liable for trespass damages. Although governmental rules and processes are often important in the resolution of disputes arising out of highway collisions between vehicles and livestock, most Shasta County residents badly misperceive the substantive law that applies to road accidents. Empiricists who have examined other social contexts have come up with analogous findings.

Substantive norms often supplant substantive laws. Law-and-society scholars have long known that in many contexts people look primarily to norms, not to law, to determine substantive entitlements. In a path-breaking study published in 1963, Stewart Macaulay found that norms of fair dealing constrained the behavior of Wisconsin business firms as much as substantive legal rules did.[14] H. Laurence Ross's study of how insurance adjusters settled claims arising from traffic accidents similarly found that the law in action differed substantially from the law on the books. Ross discovered, for example, that adjusters applied rules of comparative negligence even in jurisdictions where the formal law made contributory negligence a complete defense.[15]

Vilhelm Aubert investigated the impact of the Norwegian Housemaid Law of 1948.[16] That statute limited a maid's working hours to a maxi-

14. Stewart Macaulay, "Non-Contractual Relations in Business: A Preliminary Study," 28 *Am. Soc. Rev.* 55 (1963). Others have replicated Macaulay's general finding that norms and self-help are mainly what bring civility to business relations. See Sally Falk Moore, "Law and Social Change: The Semi-Autonomous Social Field as an Appropriate Subject of Study," 7 *L. & Soc'y Rev.* 719, 723–729 (1973) (study of "better" women's dress industry); Thomas M. Palay, "Comparative Institutional Economics: The Governance of Rail Freight Contracting," 13 *J. Legal Stud.* 265 (1984); James J. White, "Contract Law in Modern Commercial Transactions," 22 *Washburn L.J.* 1 (1982) (contract law did not influence how chemical companies allocated supply during shortages).
15. H. Laurence Ross, *Settled Out of Court* 240–241, 275–276 (rev. ed. 1980). This example, and some of the others that follow, indicate that norms (or perhaps self-enforced personal ethics) can influence the interactions of parties who are not members of a close-knit group.
16. Vilhelm Aubert, "Some Social Functions of Legislation," 10 *Acta Sociologica* 98 (1967).

mum of ten hours per day, gave maids entitlements to holidays and overtime pay, and imposed other labor standards on their employers. Although the ceiling of ten hours per working day was violated in about half the households studied, and the overtime pay provisions in almost 90 percent, Aubert found that no lawsuits had been brought under this statute within the first two years of its enactment. He concluded that a housemaid's basic mechanism for controlling employer abuse was a nonlegal one, namely, her power to exit the relationship by obtaining employment in another household.[17]

In a more recent study, Ross and Neil Littlefield found that a mass retailer of household appliances in Denver was significantly more solicitous of complaining customers than the law required.[18] For instance, the retailer would often refund a buyer's money without questions, even when it was not legally compelled to do so.

John Phillip Reid has described how norms brought about order in a virtually Hobbesian environment. In the mid-nineteenth century thousands of pioneers took the Overland Trail from Missouri to the West. Particularly in the mid-1840s, the situation on the trail was nearly anarchic; the identity of the national sovereign over much of the territory was disputed, and no government had law-enforcement agents in the area. According to Reid, travelers on the Overland Trail nonetheless demonstrated a strong respect for conventional norms of property. Those who lacked vital goods typically felt constrained to buy, not to take, what they needed from others.[19]

Laboratory evidence also casts doubt on legal centralism.[20] Elizabeth Hoffman and Matthew Spitzer fortuitously discovered the importance of substantive norms during their laboratory experiments on the dynamics of Coasean bargaining. In an early experiment Hoffman and Spitzer endowed their laboratory-game players with unequal initial monetary entitlements.[21] The game rules allowed the players to negotiate contracts

17. See also Note, "Alterations Needed: A Study of the Disjunction between the Legal Scheme and Chinatown Garment Workers," 36 *Stan. L. Rev.* 825 (1984) (garment workers do not invoke rights conferred under labor-standards legislation).

18. H. Laurence Ross and Neil O. Littlefield, "Complaint as a Problem Solving Mechanism," 12 *L. & Soc'y Rev.* 199 (1978).

19. John Phillip Reid, *Law for the Elephant: Property and Social Behavior on the Overland Trail* 339–340 (1980).

20. See, e.g., Leonard Berkowitz and Nigel Walker, "Law and Moral Judgments," 30 *Sociometry* 410 (1967) (actors' moral opinions are more strongly affected by the moral judgments of their peers than they are by the contents of formal law).

21. Elizabeth Hoffman and Matthew L. Spitzer, "The Coase Theorem: Some Experimental Tests," 25 *J.L. & Econ.* 73 (1982).

that would increase their joint monetary proceeds from the game. The contracts could include provisions for side payments. Hoffman and Spitzer expected to observe only Pareto superior contracts—that is, ones under which no party to the contract would come out monetarily worse off. In the two-person games, most players (especially those who knew that they would play against each other at least twice) were instead inclined to split equally the gross proceeds from a game, even when an equal split was Pareto inferior for one of them.[22] Intrigued by this result, Hoffman and Spitzer conducted another experiment from which they concluded that a set of informal norms—what they called "Lockean ethics"—helped govern when players were prone to equalize the gross proceeds.[23] In short, Hoffman and Spitzer tried to be sovereigns but found that norms (or conceivably personal ethics) often trumped their initial distributions of property rights.

The pervasiveness of self-help enforcement. Legal centralists regard governments as the chief enforcers of entitlements. The taxonomy of social-control systems summarized in Table 7.3 identified four other enforcement possibilities: self-sanction, personal self-help, vicarious self-help, and organization enforcement. As prior chapters have shown, self-help is rife in Shasta County. Ranchers who refuse to mind their cattle or to bear a proper share of boundary-fence costs risk the sting of negative gossip or some other relatively gentle form of neighbor retaliation, and rural residents are eventually willing to resort to violent self-help against the trespassing livestock of ranchers who have been repeatedly unmindful.

These findings also fit comfortably with what field researchers have found elsewhere. Sociologists have long been aware of the important role of gossip and ostracism.[24] Donald Black, who has gathered cross-cultural evidence on violent self-help, has asserted that much of what is ordinarily classified as crime is in fact retaliatory action aimed at achieving social control.[25]

22. See also Daniel Kahneman, Jack L. Knetsch, and Richard Thaler, "Fairness and the Assumptions of Economics," 59 *J. Business* S285, S288–S291 (1986). But see Glenn W. Harrison and Michael McKee, "Experimental Evaluation of the Coase Theorem," 28 *J.L. & Econ.* 653 (1985) (attributing some of Hoffman and Spitzer's results to the small size of the social surplus that players would obtain when moving to the joint maximum).

23. Elizabeth Hoffman and Matthew L. Spitzer, "Entitlements, Rights, and Fairness: An Experimental Examination of Subjects' Concepts of Distributive Justice," 14 *J. Legal Stud.* 259 (1985).

24. See Sally Engle Merry, "Rethinking Gossip and Scandal," in 1 *Toward a General Theory of Social Control* 271 (Donald Black ed. 1984).

25. Donald Black, "Crime as Social Control," 48 *Am. Soc. Rev.* 34 (1983). See also Sally Engle Merry, *Urban Danger: Life in a Neighborhood of Strangers* 178–186 (1981) (role of actual

Social scientists working outside of sociology increasingly appreciate the importance of self-help. Albert Hirschman has analyzed how people use the options of "exit," "voice," and "loyalty" to influence others around them.[26] Robert Axelrod has explored the game-theoretic strategy of Tit-for-Tat, a system of measured self-help that a person in a continuing relationship can use to induce cooperation from the other person in the relationship.[27]

The law itself explicitly authorizes self-help in many situations. Both tort and criminal law, for example, authorize a threatened person to use reasonable force to repel an assailant.[28] The legal-centralist assertion that the state monopolizes, or even aspires to monopolize, the use of force is patently false.[29]

The scantiness of legal knowledge. Ordinary people know little of the private substantive law applicable to decisions in everyday life.[30] Motorists may possibly learn that the failure to wear a seat belt is a misdemeanor, but only personal-injury lawyers are likely to know whether the tort law of their state makes an injured motorist's failure to wear a seat belt a defense in a civil action. First-year law students may complain that what they are encountering is boring, but never that it is old hat.

Surveys of popular knowledge of law relevant to ordinary household transactions, such as the leasing of housing or the purchase of consumer goods, invariably show that respondents have scant working knowledge of private law. For example, when interviewers asked some three hundred Austin households thirty yes-or-no questions about Texas civil law, "high-income Anglos" answered correctly an average of nineteen out of thirty, and "low-income Mexicans" thirteen out of thirty (a performance worse than chance).[31] Another survey revealed that a solid majority of Texas

---

and threatened violent retaliation in multiethnic urban neighborhood); Suzann R. Thomas-Buckle and Leonard G. Buckle, "Doing Unto Others: Disputes and Dispute Processing in an Urban American Neighborhood," in *Neighborhood Justice* 78, 79 (Roman Tomasic and Malcolm M. Feeley eds. 1982) ("In brief, what we found was reliance on self-help.").

26. Albert O. Hirschman, *Exit, Voice, and Loyalty* (1970).

27. Robert Axelrod, *The Evolution of Cooperation* (1984).

28. See, e.g., Kent Greenawalt, "Violence—Legal Justification and Moral Appraisal," 32 *Emory L.J.* 437, 448–466 (1983) (on criminal law rules on self-help).

29. It is more accurate to view the state as a major concentration of the privileged use of force, rather than as a monopolist thereof. See M. Taylor, supra note 9, at 4–5.

30. In some contexts a legal rule may influence the behavior of people ignorant of it. For example, if courts were to impose new tort liabilities on teenage drivers and insurance companies were to respond by increasing teenagers' liability premiums, fewer teenagers might drive even though none of them might know of the change in tort rules.

31. Martha Williams and Jay Hall, "Knowledge of the Law in Texas: Socioeconomic and Ethnic Differences," 7 *L. & Soc'y Rev.* 99, 113 (1972). See also Note, "Legal Knowledge of

patients in psychotherapy did not know that they were protected by a legal privilege of nondisclosure, perhaps because "[f]or 96% of the patients the therapist's ethics, not the state of the law, provided assurances of confidentiality."[32] In Vilhelm Aubert's study of the Norwegian Housemaid Law of 1948, mentioned earlier, housemaids and housewives were asked if they were aware of nine specific clauses in the statute, two of which it did not in fact contain. The respondents "recognized" the two fictitious clauses somewhat more frequently than the seven real ones.[33]

Highly educated specialists might be expected to have a somewhat better grasp of the private-law rules that impinge on their professional practices. Givelber, Bowers, and Blitch conducted a national survey of nearly three thousand therapists to measure knowledge of the California Supreme Court's 1975 *Tarasoff* decision that dealt with the tort duties of therapists when their patients have uttered threats against third parties.[34] They found that although 96 percent of California therapists and 87 percent of therapists in other states knew of the *Tarasoff* decision by name, the great majority wrongly construed it as imposing an absolute duty to warn, rather than a duty to warn only when a warning would be the reasonable response under the circumstances. Many of the therapists were (understandably) confused about whether a California Supreme Court decision could impose duties on therapists in other states.[35] Lest law professors be too quick to gloat, they should ask themselves how well they would perform if closely quizzed about their possible civil liabilities for photocopying copyrighted works for inclusion in class materials.[36]

The infrequent use of attorneys to resolve disputes. A person ignorant of legal rules can get help from an attorney. Yet even in the allegedly litigious United States, individuals who have nonbusiness problems are highly unlikely to turn to attorneys either to amplify their legal knowledge or to help pursue a claim. In Barbara Curran's nationwide sample of adults, one third had never used an attorney, and almost another third

Michigan Citizens," 71 *Mich. L. Rev.* 1463 (1973) (questionnaire respondents did better on criminal-law questions than on consumer-law questions).

32. Daniel W. Shuman and Myron S. Weiner, "The Privilege Study: An Empirical Examination of the Psychotherapist-Patient Privilege," 60 *N.C.L. Rev.* 893, 925 (1982).

33. Aubert, supra note 16, at 101.

34. Daniel J. Givelber, William J. Bowers, and Carolyn L. Blitch, "*Tarasoff*, Myth and Reality: An Empirical Study of Private Law in Action," 1984 *Wis. L. Rev.* 443.

35. Corporate executives regard products-liability litigation as a random influence that generates no clear signals. See George Eads and Peter Reuter, *Designing Safer Products: Corporate Responses to Product Liability Law and Regulation* 106–110 (Rand 1983). Given these executives' outlook, it is unlikely that they would bother to master the details of tort doctrine.

36. See infra Chapter 14, text at notes 68–86.

had used an attorney only once.[37] What prompts someone to take the unusual step of consulting an attorney in a nonbusiness context? Curran found that the most common impetus was not an interpersonal dispute but rather the transfer of property—that is, buying real estate, or planning or settling an estate.[38] A solid majority of American adults apparently go through their lives without ever hiring an attorney to help resolve a nonspousal dispute.[39] One of Curran's other survey results may help explain this finding. When asked to appraise the statement "Most lawyers charge more for their services than they are worth," 68 percent of the respondents replied that they agreed with it.[40]

The Civil Liability Research Project (CLRP) is the most ambitious empirical study of dispute-resolution practices in the United States.[41] The CLRP researchers have found that Americans are not reluctant to submit claims for compensation to other parties who they perceive have seriously wronged them. Of these claims, 68 percent result in the payment of some sort of compensation to the claimant.[42] Yet the CLRP data indicate that, even when a claim for over $1000 has been initially rejected, a claimant will employ an attorney to help resolve the dispute in only 10 to 20 percent of cases.[43] If personal-injury and alimony disputes were to be excluded from the sample, the frequency of attorney use would be much lower still.[44]

In short, most people know little private law and are not much bothered by their ignorance. Their experience tells them that the basic rules

37. Barbara A. Curran, *The Legal Needs of the Public* 186–194 (1977).

38. Id. at 196. About half of nonbusiness visits to attorneys involve these transactions. Marital matters are the third leading cause of the use of lawyers.

39. See Leon Mayhew and Albert J. Reiss, Jr., "The Social Organization of Legal Contacts," 34 *Am. Sociological Rev.* 309, 312 (1969) (61 percent of adults queried had never used an attorney in any nonproperty matter). Survey data indicate that about 20 percent of American adults have been parties in civil lawsuits (other than divorce cases). Marc Galanter, "Reading the Landscape of Disputes: What We Know and Don't Know (and Think We Know) about Our Allegedly Contentious and Litigious Society," 31 *UCLA L. Rev.* 4, 21 (1983). A study of an older, middle-class suburb of New York City found that during a twelve-month period, middle-class residents had initiated just one civil case against neighbors and social acquaintances (a suit by one youth to recover a $400 debt owed by another). The suburb had a population of 18,000. M. P. Baumgartner, "Social Control in Suburbia," in 2 *Toward a General Theory of Social Control* 79, 91–93 (Donald Black ed. 1984).

40. B. Curran, supra note 37, at 231.

41. See generally "Special Issue on Dispute Processing and Civil Litigation, Pt. 2, The Civil Litigation Research Project," 15 *L. & Soc'y Rev.* 485 (1980–81).

42. Richard E. Miller and Austin Sarat, "Grievances, Claims, and Disputes: Assessing the Adversary Culture," 15 *L. & Soc'y Rev.* 525, 537 (1980–81).

43. Id. at 546.

44. Id. at 537.

that govern ordinary interpersonal affairs are not in the law books anyway. This reality need not dispirit scholars who are inclined to use economic analysis to study social order. By shedding the legal-centralist tradition, law-and-economics scholars could make their work more relevant
than it has been. By realistically applying game theory, transaction-cost
economics, and similar tools, they may well be capable of developing a
robust theory of the division of social-control labor that is the envy of
other social scientists.

Beyond Exogenous Norms:
A Critique of Law-and-Society Theory

In contrast to the law-and-economics scholars, law-and-society scholars
have long been aware that norms and self-help play important roles in
coordinating human affairs. Perhaps because their vision of reality is so
rich, however, sociologists and their allies have been handicapped because
they do not agree on, and often don't show much interest in developing,
basic theoretical building blocks.[45] Anyone who widely reads in both law-
and-economics and law-and-society literature is bound to come away feeling that economists—although often disturbingly blind to realities—are
clearer, more scientific, and more successful in building on prior work.
The late Arthur Leff, who read extensively in both, saw law-and-economics as a desert and law-and-society as a swamp.[46] Just as aridity requires critical exposure, so does swampiness.

Sociological Theories of the Interaction of Law and Norms

Legal peripheralism and evidence that refutes it. Some sociologists are extreme legal peripheralists who dismiss the legal system as ineffectual. Legal peripheralism dates back at least to Tacitus, whose question "Quid
leges sine moribus?" (What are laws without morals?) continues to be
raised. This view was particularly popular a century ago, when the Social
Darwinist William Graham Sumner emphasized the role that "folkways"
played in achieving social order.[47]

45. See George C. Homans, *Coming to My Senses: The Autobiography of a Sociologist* 333–
348 (1984). See also sources cited infra note 78 (skeptics of possibility of positivist science).
46. Stanton Wheeler reported that Leff had used these metaphors in a casual conversation.
Compare Arthur Allen Leff, "Economic Analysis of Law: Some Realism about Nominalism,"
60 *Va. L. Rev.* 451, 468 (1974) (swampiness of holistic analysis).
47. William G. Sumner, *Folkways* 55 (1906). More recent examples of legal peripheralism
include Robert Bierstedt, *The Social Order* 223–224 (3d ed. 1970); Burton M. Leiser, *Custom,
Law, and Morality* (1969).

Extreme legal peripheralism is just as untenable as extreme legal centralism. Although law may often be overrated as an instrument of social engineering, it is not invariably toothless. For example, after the Russian Revolution the Communists who took over the state apparatus were eventually able to use law to alter (though hardly to transform totally) life in Moslem Central Asia.[48] In the United States, similarly, changes in federal civil rights law during the 1950s and 1960s helped undercut social traditions of racial segregation.[49]

Focused field studies of the impact of changes in private substantive law also refute extreme legal peripheralism. Chapter 6 described how the adoption of closed-range ordinances in Shasta County deters traditionalist ranchers from running their herds at large. Prior empirical studies have found, among other things, that the allocation of legal property rights in the intertidal zone affects labor productivity in the oyster industry,[50] that the structure of workers' compensation systems influences the frequency of workplace fatalities,[51] and that the content of medical malpractice law affects how claims are settled.[52] Most luminaries of the law-and-society movement currently embrace the sensible position that both law and norms can influence behavior.[53]

Theories of the division of social control labor. Because law-and-society scholars have appreciated that informal controls always supplement, and often supplant, the legal system, they have concerned themselves with the interplay between the legal system and less formal systems of social con-

48. Gregory J. Massell, *The Surrogate Proletariat* (1974); Gregory J. Massell, "Law as an Instrument of Revolutionary Change in a Traditional Milieu: The Case of Soviet Central Asia," 2 *L. & Soc'y Rev.* 179 (1968). Massell emphasized the failure of Soviet law to bring about rapid revolutionary change, but nevertheless identified some consequences of the legal intervention.

49. See James J. Heckman and Brooks S. Payner, "Determining the Impact of Federal Antidiscrimination Policy on the Economic Status of Blacks: A Study of South Carolina," 79 *Am. Econ. Rev.* 138 (1989) (fair employment act helped blacks obtain jobs in textile industry).

50. Richard J. Agnello and Lawrence P. Donnelley, "Property Rights and Efficiency in the Oyster Industry," 18 *J.L. & Econ.* 521 (1975).

51. James R. Chelius, "Liability for Industrial Accidents: A Comparison of Negligence and Strict Liability Systems," 5 *J. Legal Stud.* 293 (1976) (shift to workers' compensation reduced industrial accidents); Price V. Fishback, "Liability Rules and Accident Prevention in the Workplace: Empirical Evidence from the Early Twentieth Century," 16 *J. Legal Stud.* 305 (1987) (shift to workers' compensation increased fatalities in coal mining).

52. Patricia Munch Danzon and Lee A. Lillard, "Settlement Out of Court: The Disposition of Medical Malpractice Claims," 12 *J. Legal Stud.* 345 (1983).

53. See Donald Black, *The Behavior of Law* (1976); Lawrence M. Friedman, *The Legal System: A Social Science Perspective* 68–69 (1975); Robert L. Kidder, *Connecting Law and Society: An Introduction to Research and Theory* (1983); Richard Lempert and Joseph Sanders, *An Invitation to Law and Social Science: Desert, Disputes, and Distribution* (1986).

trol. Donald Black's *The Behavior of Law* is the most ambitious attempt to identify formally the variables that affect to what degree particular disputes fall within the shadow of the law.[54] John Griffiths and William Felstiner have also written insightfully about the division of social-control labor.[55] Stewart Macaulay, Ian Macneil, and others recognized (before any law-and-economics scholars did) that the presence of a continuing relationship increases the informality with which the parties to a contract resolve their disputes.[56] Law-and-society scholars would be the first to admit, however, that they are a long way from having a general theory of social control.

Theories of the Content of Norms

A key shortcoming of the law-and-society school has been its failure to develop a theory of the content of norms.[57] Why did the particular norms that prevail in Shasta County arise? Why do basic norms—such as honesty, promise keeping, and reciprocity—seem to emerge in most societies? Perhaps because they do not agree on a theory of human nature, sociologists and other law-and-society scholars have tended to treat observed norms as exogenous, rather than as dependent variables whose contents are to be explained.

Three theories of the substance of informal rules have gained some adherents. All three, however, are too flawed to have won general acceptance.

Functionalist sociology and anthropology. A supposedly outmoded theory, which nevertheless stubbornly refuses to die, holds that the norms

54. D. Black, supra note 53. Black's work is mostly focused on the content of controller-selecting rules, the subject of Chapter 14.

55. See Griffiths, supra note 1; John Griffiths, "The Division of Labor in Social Control," in 1 *Toward a General Theory of Social Control* 37 (Donald Black ed. 1984); William L. F. Felstiner, "The Logic of Mediation," in id. at 251; see also William L. F. Felstiner, Richard L. Abel, and Austin Sarat, "The Emergence and Transformation of Disputes: Naming, Blaming, Claiming . . .," 15 *L. & Soc'y Rev.* 631 (1980–81).

56. Macaulay, supra note 14; Ian R. Macneil, "The Many Futures of Contracts," 47 *S. Cal. L. Rev.* 691 (1974). The subsequent law-and-economics literature on self-enforced contracts, some of which is cited supra note 3, shows how transaction-cost economics can sharpen law-and-society insights.

57. See, e.g., George C. Homans, *Social Behavior* 2 (rev. ed. 1974) (in his major theoretical work, an eminent sociologist explicitly disclaims interest in content of norms); John Finley Scott, *The Internalization of Norms* 9 (1971) (noting the tendency of sociologists to treat norms as independent variables). The most impressive theoretical work on the content of norms is Edna Ullmann-Margalit, *The Emergence of Norms* (1977). It is notable that her inspirations were game theory and philosophy, not sociology.

of a social group serve to promote the group's survival and prosperity.[58] A crude version of this functionalist theory appeared a century ago in the work of the Social Darwinists.[59] The theory gained more academic respectability when less overtly political versions were espoused by the social anthropologists Bronislaw Malinowski and Alfred Radcliffe-Brown in the 1920s and 1930s[60] and by leading sociologists such as Robert Merton and Talcott Parsons in the 1950s.[61] In work published several generations earlier, Emile Durkheim and Eugen Ehrlich, two of the founders of the sociology of law, also exhibited pronounced functionalist tendencies.[62]

Chapter 10 will articulate a hypothesis that suggests that functionalists have been on the right track. Nevertheless, there can be no doubt that functionalists have tended to commit at least three types of analytic errors. First, functionalist thinking is apt to be circular. The analyst conclusively assumes that the norms observed are functional, and resorts to loose theories of group morale-building to explain brutal puberty rites and other bizarre practices. To escape charges of ex post rationalization, a functionalist must be able to predict the social-control practices that would be observed in an as yet unexamined setting.

Second and relatedly, functionalist sociologists and anthropologists have rarely been rigorous about how one judges whether a norm is functional for a group. Some social practices may be beneficial to some members of a group, but harmful to others. When a society conscripts its

58. The intellectual history of this idea is admirably surveyed in Donald T. Campbell, "On the Conflicts between Biological and Social Evolution and between Psychology and Moral Tradition," 30 *Am. Psychologist* 1103 (1975). A good introduction to the academic debate over functionalism is *System, Change, and Conflict* (Nicholas J. Demerath and Richard A. Peterson eds. 1967).

59. See, e.g., Walter Bagehot, *Physics and Politics* (1872); W. Sumner, supra note 47. The Social Darwinists have no sympathizers today. See Richard Hofstadter, *Social Darwinism in American Thought* (rev. ed. 1965); Edward O. Wilson, *On Human Nature* 208 (1978).

60. See, e.g., Bronislaw Malinowski, *Crime and Custom in Savage Society* (1926); Alfred R. Radcliffe-Brown, *Taboo* (1939). Homans has distinguished between these two scholars' forms of functionalism. See infra note 63.

61. Robert K. Merton, *Social Theory and Social Structure* 1–84 (rev. ed. 1957); Talcott Parsons, *The Social System* (1951). See also John W. Thibaut and Harold H. Kelley, *The Social Psychology of Groups* 135–142 (1959).

62. See Emile Durkheim, *The Division of Labor in Society* 49–229 (George Simpson trans. 1933) (on "The Function of the Division of Labor"); Eugen Ehrlich, *Fundamental Principles of the Sociology of Law* (W. Moll trans. 1936). Ehrlich believed that law is relatively unimportant and that social forces tend to produce the same norms in all human societies. Functionalist themes also pervade the work of more contemporary scholars. See, e.g., Ian R. Macneil, "Exchange Revisited: Individual Utility and Social Solidarity," 96 *Ethics* 567 (1986) (accepted patterns of exchange enhance social solidarity).

young adults to fight its wars, they may resent being sacrificed for the benefit of noncombatants. Economists have faced a similar analytic hurdle because one of their central terms, "efficiency," is potentially as ambiguous as "functionality." Economists have met this challenge by developing and debating a variety of definitions of efficiency, including the Pareto-superiority criterion, the Kaldor-Hicks criterion, and so on. Functionalists in other social sciences, by contrast, have been less likely to confront this ambiguity in their theory.

Third, and again relatedly, early functionalists had a tendency to consider a human group as a single organism whose "health" could be examined.[63] It was then easy for them to surmise that Darwinian evolutionary processes would help favor the survival of socially adaptive norms. In the following passage the libertarian scholar Friedrich Hayek lapsed into this sort of analysis:

> It is not only in his knowledge, but also in his aims and values, that man is the creature of civilization: in the last resort, it is the relevance of these individual wishes to the perpetuation of the group or the species that will determine whether they will persist or change. It is, of course, a mistake to believe that we can draw conclusions about what our values ought to be simply because we realize that they are a product of evolution. But we cannot reasonably doubt that these values are created and altered by the same evolutionary forces that have produced our intelligence. All that we can know is that the ultimate decision about what is good or bad will be made not by individual human wisdom, but by the decline of the groups that have adhered to the "wrong" beliefs.[64]

(Before nonlibertarian scholars dismiss these thoughts, they should be aware that both Lon Fuller and Thomas Schelling have also harbored suspiciously functionalist sentiments.)[65]

The difficulty with this sort of organic analysis is that evolutionary processes, as most biologists understand them, select either genes or in-

---

63. Homans called this version *societal functionalism.* He criticized this approach, which he associated with Radcliffe-Brown, for ignoring that social phenomena grow out of the behavior of individual actors. Homans was more approving of *individualistic functionalism,* which takes the individual as the basic unit of analysis. He identified Malinowski as a member of the latter school. G. Homans, *Coming to My Senses,* supra note 45, at 154–157.

64. Friedrich A. Hayek, *The Constitution of Liberty* 36 (Phoenix ed. 1978).

65. See Fuller, supra note 1, at 173; Thomas C. Schelling, *Micromotives and Macrobehavior* 124–133 (1978).

dividual organisms, not groups, for survival.[66] Assume, for example, that honesty is a functional norm in the sense that, if all the members of a group were consistently honest, they would each be better off than if everyone were consistently dishonest. Would the Darwinian struggle favor the survival of groups of honest persons? Not necessarily. A dishonest individual living in an environment of honest people might especially prosper, surrounded by easy marks. As a result, the Darwinian process would tend to select dishonest people for survival. In short, to support a Panglossian scenario of group evolutionary progress, functionalists could not rely simply on the biological theory of natural selection. Instead, they had to develop theories to explain how social-control systems would evolve within groups to prevent successful invasions by deviants who would subvert group welfare. The early functionalists were not aware of this missing theoretical link.[67]

Interest-group theories of norms. A second sociological theory, one less upbeat than functionalism, holds that members of powerful interest groups manipulate the content of norms to serve their own selfish interests. Traditional Marxist analysts, for example, see much of the normative baggage of a society as part of the false consciousness that deludes and hence pacifies the underclasses. Some neo-Marxist scholars, such as Isaac Balbus, and non-Marxist scholars, such as Howard Becker, also seem to have interest-group conceptions of norms.[68] In the eyes of interest-group theorists, the traditional use in English of male pronouns to describe hypothetical persons might be seen as evidence of men's efforts to subjugate women. Rational-actor theorists, by contrast, might view this same usage as a normatively neutral linguistic convention that solves, as well as does any other, what game theorists call a game of pure coordination.

Interest-group theorists would win more converts if they could identify the mechanisms through which well-placed interest groups might manipulate the norm-making process. One can readily understand how concentrated lobbies are able to influence the legal system. The informal-

66. See, e.g., Richard Dawkins, *The Selfish Gene* 8–12 (1976); Edward O. Wilson, *Sociobiology* 106–129 (1975). But see V. C. Wynne-Edwards, *Animal Dispersion in Relation to Social Behavior* (1962) (articulating a theory of group selection).

67. This book will not attempt a rigorous inquiry into how cooperation might evolve. See *infra* Chapter 13, text at notes 24–26. It therefore would be uncharitable to criticize the functionalists for their failures in this regard.

68. See Isaac D. Balbus, "Commodity Form and Legal Form: An Essay on the 'Relative Autonomy' of Law," 11 *L. & Soc'y Rev.* 571 (1976); Howard S. Becker, *Outsiders* 15–18, 147–163 (1963). Michael Taylor, "Structure, Culture, and Action in the Explanation of Social Change," 17 *Pol. & Soc'y* 115, 145–148 (1989), presents two examples, involving respectively the Christian church and British colonialists, that are consonant with interest-group theory.

control system, by contrast, is much more diffuse. Florists undoubtedly have had some success in promoting the tradition of Mother's Day gifts, and diamond merchants, the custom of diamond engagement rings. Nevertheless, norms seem generally resistant to deliberate influence. Totalitarian Communist regimes were not able to produce a "new man," Madison Avenue cannot convince most motorists to buckle their seat belts, and the right-to-life movement has little success in stemming the incidence of abortion. One weakness of the various interest-group theories is that they say little about when and how an interest group can control the content of norms.

A second shortcoming of the various interest-group theories is that they are seriously incomplete. Many fundamental social norms appear neutral in content. It is hard to see how common norms of honesty, reciprocity, promise keeping, and respect for the bodily integrity of others serve the interests of the strong at the expense of the weak. Some norms, such as norms of charity, at least facially help people who lack power. Interest-group analysts must amplify their theories so as to be able to explain norms that are distributively neutral or progressive.

Theories that some norms are genetically hard-wired. Over the past decade a handful of scholars, almost all located outside sociology, have explored the possibility that certain core substantive norms are hard-wired in the genetic material that humans carry.[69] The emergence of sociobiology—a discipline that seeks to reconcile the widespread phenomenon of cooperation among animals with the Darwinian theory of evolution—has helped to stimulate this line of inquiry.[70] As the theorists of hard-wired norms readily admit, their work to this point has been highly speculative.

A provocative article by Paul Rubin illustrates this type of scholarship.[71] Rubin hypothesized that evolutionary processes have shaped human ethics, and that tribes of hunter-gatherers had genetically influenced norms that were adapted to their situation. The rapid transition to modern mass society, Rubin speculated, has been too sudden for natural-selection processes to have updated the relevant genes. A hunter-gatherer

69. See George Edwin Pugh, *The Biological Origin of Human Values* (1977). See also Charles J. Lumsden and Edward O. Wilson, *Promethean Fire* (1983); A. Schotter, *The Economic Theory of Social Institutions* 160–164 (1981); Jack Hirshleifer, "Privacy: Its Origin, Function, and Future," 9 *J. Legal Stud.* 649 (1980).

70. E. Wilson, supra note 66, is the seminal work. For criticism of the approach, see, e.g., Philip Kitcher, *Vaulting Ambition: Sociobiology and the Quest for Human Nature* (1985).

71. Paul H. Rubin, "Evolved Ethics and Efficient Ethics," 3 *J. Econ. Behav. & Org.* 161 (1982).

tribe might be better off, for example, if it had a norm that required tribe members to provide aid to the sick and impoverished, because, in those societies, undeserving shirkers could readily be detected. This same norm of charity, suggested Rubin, might nonadaptively persist in anonymous mass societies, where shirking is harder to detect. This sort of analysis has yet to win many adherents, in part because, like functionalism, it seems to assume that the evolutionary process selects survivors at the level of the group, not of the individual.

The usual sociological approach: norms as exogenous givens. Most law-and-society scholars shy away from all theories of the content of norms. For example, in his justly famous study of contractual relations among Wisconsin business firms, Stewart Macaulay identified two principal norms that governed interfirm behavior: (1) "one ought to produce a good product and stand behind it"; and (2) "commitments are to be honored in almost all situations."[72] Essentially viewing people as rational actors who try to maximize their net gains,[73] Macaulay seemed to regard most of the behavior he observed as somehow adaptive. Yet he offered no explanation for the emergence of the particular norms he observed. Why had the business culture not generated norms of "caveat emptor" and "there is no such thing as a binding commitment"? Macaulay did not venture to say. He communicated the (important) message that controller-selecting norms can discourage actors from using the legal system, but did not offer a theory of the content of norms.

Similarly, in his book *The Human Group*, George Homans identified "a norm that is one of the world's commonest: if a man does a favor for you, you must do a roughly equivalent favor for him in return."[74] Homans drew on William Foote Whyte's *Street Corner Society*[75] to illustrate this norm of reciprocity. Whyte had studied the Norton Street gang, a group of young men of Italian descent living in a Boston slum. The Nortons believed in mutual aid but also in keeping accounts square. As Homans summarized it, the Nortons believe that "in bad times as in good, if you have a few extra dimes you are expected to give them to your friend when he asks for them. You give them to him because he is your friend; at the same time the gift creates an obligation in him. He must help you when you need it, and the balance of favors must be roughly equal. The

72. Macaulay, supra note 14, at 63. The contents of the norms that Macaulay found are examined infra Chapter 11, text at notes 15–21.
73. Macaulay, supra note 14, at 66.
74. George C. Homans, *The Human Group* 284 (1950).
75. William F. Whyte, *Street Corner Society: The Social Structure of an Italian Slum* (1943).

felt obligation is always present, and you will be rudely reminded of it if you fail to return a favor."[76] Although Homans stands out among sociologists for his clear-headedness, he nonetheless treats particular norms, even this the world's commonest, as exogenous facts of life.[77]

Just as microeconomists tend to take consumers' tastes as given and limit themselves to the study of market processes, so sociologists tend to work not on what norms are but on how norms are transmitted.[78] To shake this tradition, it is time to turn to an examination of the problem of cooperation and then to the articulation of a hypothesis about the content of norms.

76. G. Homans, *Human Group,* supra note 74, at 160.

77. See supra note 57 and accompanying text.

78. At the atheoretical extreme in sociology is the interpretivist position (arguably dominant among anthropologists during the 1980s) that a particular culture just is what it is, and, therefore, that an analyst can do no better than to acquire a local knowledge of the symbolic meaning of cultural practices. See, e.g., Clifford Geertz, *The Interpretation of Cultures* 3–54 (1973); see also Arthur A. Leff, "Law and," 87 *Yale L.J.* 989 (1978) (law professor's doubts about the possibility of positivist science). See generally Henry A. Walker and Bernard B. Cohen, "Scope Statements: Imperatives for Evaluating Theory," 50 *Am. Soc. Rev.* 288 (1985) (cleavage within sociology between scientists and interpretivists).

9

✕——✕

The Puzzle of Cooperation

Game theory provides a set of tools for the systematic dissection of the problem of human order. The advantage of game theory is that it forces its users to make explicit assumptions about human motivations and capabilities, and to identify the features of "games"—that is, interpersonal interactions—that are apt to influence conduct.[1]

The Rational-Actor Model

Game theorists adopt the rational-actor model that is currently dominant among social scientists of a positivist bent, especially those working in economics and public-choice theory.[2] The rational-actor model has two basic underlying tenets. It assumes, first, that each individual pursues self-interested goals and, second, that each individual rationally chooses among various means for achieving those goals.[3]

To be self-interested is not necessarily to act selfishly at every opportunity. A rational actor may choose to pass up a short-run gain to garner a long-run gain of greater present value. When rational-actor theorists ob-

---

1. Scholars from diverse fields have turned to game theory to sharpen their analyses of the phenomenon of cooperation. See, e.g., Robert Axelrod, *The Evolution of Cooperation* (1984) (political scientist); Russell Hardin, *Collective Action* (1982) (philosopher); John Maynard Smith, *Evolution and the Theory of Games* (1982) (biologist); Robert Sugden, *The Economics of Rights, Co-operation, and Welfare* (1986) (economist); Michael Taylor, *Anarchy and Cooperation* (1976) (philosopher); Edna Ullmann-Margalit, *The Emergence of Norms* (1977) (philosopher).

2. Social scientists in other disciplines commonly make use of the rational-actor model. See, e.g., George C. Homans, *Social Behavior* 15–50 (rev. ed. 1974); James Q. Wilson and Richard J. Herrnstein, *Crime and Human Nature* 41–66 (1985).

3. Jack Hirshleifer, "The Expanding Domain of Economics," 76 *Am. Econ. Rev.* 53, 54–62 (1985), succinctly presents the rational actor model and also summarizes criticisms of it. See also Ellickson, "Bringing Culture and Human Frailty to Rational Actors: A Critique of Classical Law and Economics," 65 *Chi.-Kent L. Rev.* 23 (1989). One of the model's most serious limitations is its failure to explain how people come to hold particular preferences. A plea for theory and research on this issue is Aaron Wildavsky, "Choosing Preferences by Constructing Institutions," 81 *Am. Pol. Sci. Rev.* 3 (1987).

serve ostensibly altruistic behavior they therefore tend to see it as part of a continuing, mutually beneficial pattern of exchange. Apart from interactions among kin, however, they tend to doubt the possibility of unalloyed altruism.[4]

The assumption that people are rational is a useful simplification that is known to be overdrawn. As Herbert Simon in particular has emphasized, people have limited cognitive capacities.[5] Some limitations in cognitive abilities are rather easily reconciled with the basic rational-actor model. For example, to assume people are rational does not presuppose that they endlessly calculate their every move. Because deliberation is time-consuming and endless innovation is risky, a rational actor may choose a course of action, not by calculating from scratch, but rather by drawing upon general cultural traditions, role models, or personal habits developed after trial-and-error experimentation.[6] These shorthand methods reduce decision-making costs, but actors who rely on them will tend to lag in adapting to changes in their surroundings.

In some contexts a person's perceptions seem to be distorted not by lack of cognitive capacity but rather by cracks in his lens. For example, in the face of much contrary evidence, Shasta County cattlemen adhered to the folklore that the "motorist buys the cow in open range." Psychologists theorize that cognitive dissonance may cause an individual to suppress information whose acceptance would make him feel foolish.[7] Similarly, Daniel Kahneman and Amos Tversky have assembled evidence that the framing of an outcome as a loss, as opposed to a forgone gain, has more effect on decision making than the rational-actor model would predict.[8]

The rational-actor model has drawn its heaviest fire from scholars who are suspicious of either reductionist theory or, at the extreme, the possibility of objective (positive) social science. Law-and-society scholars tend to be positivists, but they are also skeptical about model building. Al-

4. Howard Margolis, *Selfishness, Altruism, and Rationality* (1982), develops a somewhat less egocentric model of human behavior.

5. See, e.g., Herbert A. Simon, *Reason in Human Affairs* 3–35 (1983). See generally *Rational Choice: The Contrast between Economics and Psychology* (Robin M. Hogarth and Melvin W. Reder eds. 1986).

6. On the transmission of norms and culture, see Robert Boyd and Peter J. Richerson, *Culture and the Evolutionary Process* (1985); J. Maynard Smith, supra note 1, at 170–172.

7. See Elliot Aronson, *The Social Animal* 85–139 (2d ed. 1976); Leon Festinger, *A Theory of Cognitive Dissonance* (1957).

8. See, e.g., Amos Tversky and Daniel Kahneman, "Rational Choice and the Framing of Decisions," 59 *J. Business* S251 (no. 4, pt. 2, Oct. 1986); see also Jack L. Knetsch, "The Endowment Effect and Evidence of Non-Reversible Indifference Curves," 79 *Am. Econ. Rev.* 1277 (1989).

though something close to a rational-actor model has surfaced in the work of law-and-society stalwarts such as Stewart Macaulay and David Trubek,[9] most law-and-society scholars seem to regard it as too simple to have heuristic value. At the extreme among the nonpositivist critics are the Critical Legal scholars. Using more intuitive epistemologies, they assert that human nature and human tastes are highly contingent on historical circumstance. They would likely regard rational-actor theorists as fundamentally mistaken, for example, in taking the self-interestedness of individuals as a given.[10]

The subsequent analysis applies the rational-actor model and also makes considerable use of game theory. I am a positivist and am therefore interested in making and testing predictions. If a theory lacks assumptions about human motivations and decision-making processes, it cannot generate predictions. In my view, despite the undoubted simplicity of the rational-actor model, social scientists possess no technique with greater heuristic power.

The Vocabulary of Game Theory

Game theorists analyze interactions between two or more people ("games") in which the individual outcomes ("payoffs") for the people involved ("players") depend on their independent choices among plays. Some key variables in games are (1) the number of players, (2) the number of choices a player has available, (3) the patterns of payoffs under different conjunctions of player choices, and (4) the number of periods in which a game is to be played. Game theorists usually assume that the players

9. Stewart Macaulay, "Non-Contractual Relations in Business: A Preliminary Study," 28 *Am. Soc. Rev.* 55, 66 (1963); David M. Trubek, "Studying Courts in Contexts," 15 *Law & Soc'y Rev.* 485, 498–499 (1980–81).

10. See, e.g., Gerald E. Frug, "The City as a Legal Concept," 93 *Harv. L. Rev.* 1059, 1149–1150 (1980) ("We can transform society as much or as little as we want" in pursuit of the goal of empowering cities); Robert W. Gordon, "Historicism in Legal Scholarship," 90 *Yale L.J.* 1017, 1019–1020 (1981) (critics assert historical contingency of social life). See generally Steven H. Shiffrin, "Liberalism, Radicalism, and Legal Scholarship," 30 *UCLA L. Rev.* 1103, 1116–1119 (1983). There is a long tradition of opposition to the notion that human nature constrains human institutions in important ways. Karl Polanyi, for example, argued in a 1944 book that Adam Smith's "economic man" hardly existed before Smith wrote and is entirely a product of culture. *The Great Transformation* 44, 249–250 (1st Beacon paperback ed. 1957). But see, e.g., Edward O. Wilson, *On Human Nature* (1978); G. Homans, supra note 2, at 217: "Ours is the doctrine that 'human nature is the same the world over.'" On the long-standing tension between these opposing intellectual traditions, see Clifford Geertz, *The Interpretation of Cultures* 33–54 (1973); Thomas Sowell, *A Conflict of Visions* 18–39 (1987); infra Chapter 14, text accompanying notes 10–12.

know perfectly the matrix that shows the individual payoffs associated with different combinations of player choices, but that players cannot change those payoffs or communicate with each other except by making choices.

Game theory aspires to predict what players would choose to do in particular game situations. Because game theorists make use of the rational-actor model, they assume that players want to maximize their individual payoffs. Theorists call a choice "dominant" in a period of play if it would be in a player's self-interest for that period of play regardless of what the other player(s) were to choose to do.

The outcome of a game will be referred to here as "cooperative," or "welfare maximizing," when the players' choices have combined to deliver the largest total objective[11] payoff available, regardless of how individual players happen to share in that total.

In some games, those of pure coordination, the payoffs are structured such that the players have strong individual incentives to choose strategies that will conjoin to produce cooperative results. Every motorist, for example, recognizes that there will be gains from a convention that requires all to drive on the right (or left) side of the highway; every user of a language gains if there is a consensus about the meaning of given words. It is unremarkable that players reach cooperative outcomes in these sorts of games.[12]

The Prisoner's Dilemma

Theorists of cooperation therefore concentrate on more nettlesome situations in which rational players seem likely to make choices that will not conjoin to produce cooperative outcomes. The most famous game of this sort is the Prisoner's Dilemma. In a Prisoner's Dilemma the matrix of payoffs is structured so that the rational pursuit of self-interest seems destined to be an engine of Hobbesian impoverishment rather than of welfare production. Most analysts of cooperation assume that if players can achieve cooperative outcomes under the adverse circumstances of the Prisoner's Dilemma, they could certainly achieve cooperative outcomes under more favorable game conditions.[13]

11. See infra Chapter 10, text accompanying notes 14–22, for an explanation of the inclusion of this adjective.

12. On these games, see generally Thomas C. Schelling, *The Strategy of Conflict* 89–99 (1960); E. Ullmann-Margalit, supra note 1, at 74–133; David K. Lewis, *Convention* (1969).

13. See, e.g., *Rational Man and Irrational Society* (Brian Barry and Russell Hardin eds. 1982) and the sources in note 1 supra.

Table 9.1   An Illustrative Prisoner's Dilemma

| | | Player Two | |
		Cooperate	Defect
Player One	Cooperate	3, 3	0, 5
	Defect	5, 0	1, 1

Note: The payoffs to Player One are listed first.

Table 9.1 is based on a simple Prisoner's Dilemma set out in Robert Axelrod's important book on cooperation.[14] Two players play each other just once. Each has two choices, "Cooperate" or "Defect." The four cells in the matrix indicate the payoffs, in units of the prevailing currency, that would result from each possible conjunction of choices. Each cell contains two numbers, the first the payoff for Player One, and the second the payoff for Player Two. For example, if Player One were to Cooperate and Player Two were to Defect in this particular game, Player One would receive 0 and Player Two would receive 5. Observe that the cooperative, welfare-maximizing outcome is the upper-left quadrant, which is reached when both players Cooperate. The sum of the individual payoffs (6) is greater for that quadrant than for any other.

For a game to be a Prisoner's Dilemma, the pattern of payoffs must satisfy three conditions. First, Defecting must be the dominant choice for each player. Second, mutual decisions to Defect must produce individual payoffs for both players that are lower than the payoffs they each would have received had they both "irrationally" chosen to Cooperate. And third, the total payoff in the upper-left cell, which represents mutual Co-operation, must be larger than the total payoff in either the upper-right or the lower-left cells, which would be reached if one player Cooperated and the other Defected.[15]

Anyone who has not previously encountered the Prisoner's Dilemma

14. *The Evolution of Cooperation* 8 (1984). Readers already familiar with the Prisoner's Dilemma may prefer to skip to the next section. The phrase *Prisoner's Dilemma* came into use when early game theorists illustrated this type of game with an example in which two, separately confined, prisoners accused of a joint crime each had to decide whether or not to confess that they both were guilty.

15. When all conditions except this last one are met, the game is Specialized Labor. See infra text following note 16.

should spend a moment studying Table 9.1 to see that it indeed meets these devilish conditions. Imagine how Player One would analyze the situation. Because the game rules prevent the players from communicating prior to choosing what to do, Player One would not know whether Player Two was about to Cooperate or about to Defect. Suppose Player Two were about to Cooperate. According to the matrix of payoffs, Player One would gain 5 by Defecting, but only 3 by Cooperating; therefore an egoistic Player One would conclude that it would be wise to Defect if Player Two were about to Cooperate. Now suppose Player Two were about to Defect. In that case Player One would gain 1 by Defecting, but 0 by Cooperating. Thus, Player One would conclude that Defecting was his dominant choice; it would make him better off regardless of the choice Player Two was about to make. In Table 9.1 the payoffs and incentives are symmetrical, and Defecting would be Player Two's dominant choice as well. Mutual Defection, apparently the inexorable result of rational, self-interested play of the game, would produce payoffs of 1, 1, an outcome worse for both players than the 3, 3 results they would have obtained had both Cooperated. Because the total payoff of mutual Cooperation (6) is larger than the total payoff in either the upper-right or lower-left quadrants of the matrix (5), the third and final requirement for a Prisoner's Dilemma is satisfied.

Table 9.2 presents the structure of the Prisoner's Dilemma in simple algebraic terms. As an everyday example, imagine that the players in the Prisoner's Dilemma are adjoining landowners and that the game is over the construction of a boundary fence. To Cooperate in this example would be to contribute labor and materials to a cost-justified fence project; to Defect would be to fail to contribute. If the boundary-fence project situation were indeed structured like a Prisoner's Dilemma, the best result for either landowner would be for the other to build the fence as a solo project. Because $2B > A + D$ in a Prisoner's Dilemma, if both ad-

Table 9.2 An Algebraic Prisoner's Dilemma

| | | Player Two | |
		Cooperate	Defect
Player One	Cooperate	B, B	D, A
	Defect	A, D	C, C

Note: $A>B>C>D$ and $2B>A+D$.

Table 9.3 An Algebraic Version of the Specialized Labor Game

		Player Two	
		Work	Shirk
Player One	Work	B, B	D, A
	Shirk	A, E	C, C

Note: $A>B>C>D>E$, and $2B<A+D$.

joiners were to work together on a fence they would exploit economies of scale, perhaps of the type Robert Frost suggested in the poem "Mending Wall," that would not be exploited if one of them were to build it alone. In this example, a cooperative fence project would be better for each neighbor than no fence at all. For each neighbor Defection is, however, the dominant strategy, and the rational-actor model predicts that short-sighted neighbors would fail to build the fence.[16]

A Specialized-Labor Game

Another game, slightly different from the Prisoner's Dilemma, illustrates a common social situation that may also pose problems for egoists. Table 9.3 presents the game in algebraic form. Table 9.4 presents a numerical example, which can again be taken to involve the potential construction of a boundary fence. For reasons that will be apparent, this second game will be called "Specialized Labor."

Specialized Labor differs from the Prisoner's Dilemma in two respects. First, to reach the cooperative outcome the players must act *differently*. In this game the highest sum of payoffs is achieved when Player One Works and Player Two Shirks. In contrast to the Prisoner's Dilemma, joint-labor projects in Specialized Labor are welfare reducing. In the fence-building context, for example, one adjoining landowner would be able to build a boundary fence more cheaply than two could build it.

Second, in Specialized Labor the sum of the payoffs in the upper-right quadrant cannot be the same as the sum in the lower-left quadrant. In both Tables 9.3 and 9.4, the higher sum happens to be in the upper-right quadrant. This means that Player One has some special ability, not pos-

16. This example is highly unrealistic both because neighbors are typically situated in a continuing, not a one-time, relationship, and also because they usually have no trouble communicating with one another before making their choices.

Table 9.4 An Illustrative Specialized Labor Game

		Player Two	
		Build Fence	Shirk
Player One	Build Fence	3, 3	0, 7
	Shirk	7, −2	1, 1

sessed by Player Two, to act in a way that will maximize joint welfare. Inspired by Calabresi's notion of the "cheapest cost-avoider," let us call this specially capable person the "cheapest labor-provider." It is characteristic of a Specialized Labor game that a cheapest labor-provider is always present.[17]

Examination of Tables 9.3 and 9.4 will quickly reveal that Shirking is the dominant choice for each of the players in Specialized Labor. Mutual Shirking is a poor outcome. In Table 9.4, the resulting total payoff is 2, the lowest total for any quadrant. In Table 9.3, the resulting total is $2C$, which is stipulated to be less than $2B$ (the sum if both were to Work), which is in turn less than $A + D$ (the sum if only the cheapest labor-provider were to Work).

If transaction costs were zero and the players could negotiate in advance, it would be in their mutual interest in Specialized Labor situations to negotiate a contract obligating Player One to Work, permitting Player Two to Shirk, and obligating Player Two to make an appropriate side-payment to Player One.[18] In Table 9.3, the side-payment would have to be at least equal to $C - D$ (Player One's costs of Working), but could not exceed $A - C$ (Player Two's benefits from the Player One's Work). More concretely, in Table 9.4, the fence would cost Player One a net of 1 to build alone (1 − 0), and would confer benefits of 6 on Player Two (7 − 1). In that situation both parties would be better off if Player Two were to contract to pay Player One some sum between 1 and 6 to compensate Player One for building the fence as a solo project. If such contracting

17. One can readily imagine slight variations of this game. For example, the players could be equally skilled but still face disefficiencies of scale in returns to work. Or the cooperative outcome might be achievable only if the players performed slightly different tasks. These sorts of variations will not be analyzed.

18. For simplicity, the discussion assumes that the payoffs reflect how players both subjectively and objectively value outcomes. On this distinction, see infra Chapter 10, text at notes 14–18.

were impossible, the logic of game theory suggests that the players would simply miss out on these gains from trade.

The Source of Hope: Repeated Play

People who interact often expect that their current encounter will be but one incident in a series that will continue into the future. Game theorists call continuing relationships "iterated games," and each encounter a "period" of play. For each period a player has "choices." For an iterated game, however, a player can also adopt a "strategy," that is, a plan of action that determines the player's choices in all periods.

Theorists who have investigated repeated games have tended to focus on the iterated Prisoner's Dilemma, in part to see whether players can succeed in cooperating under relatively inauspicious circumstances.[19] The usual format involves two players who confront an identical, symmetric, Prisoner's Dilemma matrix period after period. The number of periods may be finite, have a finite expected value, or be infinite.

Thanks to Axelrod, the best-known strategy for the iterated Prisoner's Dilemma is Tit-for-Tat. A Tit-for-Tat player Cooperates in the first period and thereafter chooses the move that the other player chose for the previous period. Tit-for-Tat is thus never the first to Defect; in Axelrod's terminology, it is a "nice" strategy. A Tit-for-Tat player is not a patsy, however, because he immediately penalizes a Defection by the other player by Defecting himself in the next period.[20] A Tit-for-Tat player nevertheless bears no grudges; once he has squared accounts, he is willing to Cooperate thereafter as long as the other player also Cooperates.

Axelrod conducted several computer tournaments in which various strategies were paired against one another in a round-robin of iterated Prisoner's Dilemmas. In the tournaments the success of a strategy was measured according to the total payoffs it individually earned in its round-robin matches. Tit-for-Tat turned out to be the most successful of the strategies submitted, and much more successful than most of its competitors.[21] Nice strategies did best in Axelrod's tournaments because,

19. Much of this work involves complex mathematical modeling. See, e.g., Abraham Neyman, "Bounded Complexity Justifies Cooperation in the Finitely Repeated Prisoners' Dilemma," 19 *Econ. Lett.* 227 (1985); Ariel Rubinstein, "Finite Automata Play the Repeated Prisoner's Dilemma," 39 *J. Econ. Theory* 83 (1986).

20. An examination of Table 9.1 will reveal that a defection by Player One hurts Player Two regardless of the choice that Player Two makes.

21. R. Axelrod, supra note 1, at 30–43 and Appendix A.

when paired, they produced strings of mutually Cooperative outcomes. Moreover, by credibly threatening to punish Defections in later rounds, a Tit-for-Tat player encouraged Cooperation by forcing opponents to lower their estimates of the long-term gains associated with decisions to Defect. To show that his tournaments were not simply laboratory fun, Axelrod amassed anecdotal evidence that Tit-for-Tat strategies are frequently observed in practice. His most arresting example is that of British and German troops facing each other from opposing trenches in World War I, who often followed the Tit-for-Tat strategy of live and let live.[22]

Axelrod's work has obvious implications for students of informal systems of social control. As he presented it, Tit-for-Tat is a second-party system of social control. It is a strategy that is simple for a player to administer and for an opponent to recognize. In the language of behavioral psychology, a Tit-for-Tat strategy is a relentless system of operant conditioning. It promptly rewards cooperation and promptly punishes defections.

Tit-for-Tat, however, is operable only under a highly restrictive set of conditions. Axelrod's computer tournaments involved only two-player interactions and presented each player with only two choices per period. Payoffs were symmetrical and did not change from period to period.[23] A player had perfect knowledge of the history of each of his own dyadic matches but knew nothing of the outcomes of matches between others. A player's groupwide reputation was therefore never at stake.[24] In addition, Axelrod's basic format assumed players costlessly and perfectly administered their strategies. They could not, for example, accidentally "push the wrong button."[25]

Despite Axelrod's results, which provide hope that social and evolutionary processes may work to favor cooperative behavior, game theorists have not been able to deduce from plausible axioms that players in iterated Prisoner's Dilemmas will actually settle into a cooperative mode.

22. Id. at 73–87.

23. It is not clear that Tit-for-Tat would have fared as well if, for example, the payoffs in every fifth round had been tripled.

24. In this respect, Axelrod's tournament lacked a structural feature that is powerfully conducive to the evolution of cooperation. See infra Chapter 10, text accompanying notes 45–47.

25. On occasion, however, Axelrod has introduced into his computer tournaments the possibility of errors in perception. See R. Axelrod, supra note 1, at 182–183. A variety of ways of enriching the iterated Prisoner's Dilemma are discussed infra Chapter 12, text accompanying notes 39–48.

Indeed, most game theorists accept the "folk theorem" that asserts that any equilibrium, including an uncooperative one, can be stable as long as each player could do even worse.[26]

That a result cannot be deduced from axioms does not mean that it cannot be induced from observations. Evidence about how people actually behave suggests that the folk theorem is too pessimistic.[27] The next step is to articulate on the basis of field evidence a somewhat more upbeat hypothesis about the reality of social life.

26. See, e.g., Drew Fudenberg and Eric Maskin, "The Folk Theorem in Repeated Games with Discounting or with Incomplete Information," 54 *Econometrica* 533 (1986).

27. See infra Chapters 11–14. Robert Aumann, an esteemed game theorist, asserted in a talk at Stanford University on August 19, 1986, that he intuitively regarded the folk theorem as too gloomy.

10

✳ ✳ ✳

A Hypothesis of Welfare-Maximizing Norms

In uncovering the various Shasta County norms, I was struck that they seemed consistently utilitarian. Each appeared likely to enhance the aggregate welfare of rural residents. This inductive observation, coupled with supportive data from elsewhere, inspired the hypothesis that *members of a close-knit group develop and maintain norms whose content serves to maximize the aggregate welfare that members obtain in their workaday affairs with one another.*[1] (For brevity, hereafter this assertion will be referred to as "the hypothesis.") Stated more simply, the hypothesis predicts that members of tight social groups will informally encourage each other to engage in cooperative behavior.[2] It should be stressed that this proposition was *induced,* rather than deduced from an explicit model of social interactions.

Game theory makes possible a more rigorous and specific statement of the hypothesis. In the language of that framework, an initial, simplified version of the hypothesis predicts that when social conditions are close-knit, informal norms will encourage people in non-zero-sum situations to make choices that will conjoin to produce the maximum aggregate objective payoff.[3] Specifically, this means that norms will encourage people to Cooperate in Prisoner's Dilemma situations. Similarly, in Spe-

---

1. Other writers have advanced similar propositions but have not elaborated on them. See George Edwin Pugh, *The Biological Origin of Human Values* 362 (1977) (in small tribes norms of cooperative behavior will evolve); Edna Ullmann-Margalit, *The Emergence of Norms* 22, 60 (1977) (norms are likely to evolve to help people achieve cooperative outcomes in Prisoner's Dilemma situations); Warren F. Schwartz, Keith Baxter, and David Ryan, "The Duel: Can These Gentlemen Be Acting Efficiently?" 13 *J. Legal Stud.* 321, 329–332 (1984) (social conventions arise in part to help group members maximize the value of production).

2. In contexts where several competing norms could plausibly comport with welfare maximization, the hypothesis predicts only that members of a close-knit group would choose from among that set. See infra Chapter 11, text accompanying notes 22–72 (on whalers' norms).

3. This version is too simple because it ignores the desirability of economizing on transaction costs. The more precise, full-blown version of the hypothesis is presented infra text accompanying notes 20–22.

cialized Labor situations, at least when gains from Work are unambiguous and the transaction costs of contracting are significant, the hypothesis predicts that norms will encourage the cheaper labor-providers to Work, in part by encouraging Shirkers unilaterally to reward Workers who had previously helped them.

The general thrust of the hypothesis of welfare-maximizing norms is hardly novel. It can be seen as a restatement of several long-standing social-scientific theories of the dynamics of nonhierarchically organized groups. It crystallizes the central thrust of functionalist sociology and anthropology.[4] It echoes the thinking of Alexander Bickel, Lon Fuller, Friedrich Hayek, Thomas Schelling, and similar scholars who in diverse ways have kept alive the Burkean notion that decentralized social forces contribute importantly to social order.[5] By requiring that the social group be close-knit, the hypothesis brings to mind the law-and-society scholars' theme that continuing relationships help to civilize behavior. Finally, the hypothesis is in tune with much of the work by Axelrod and others on the evolution of cooperation.

For legal scholars, the hypothesis of welfare-maximizing norms may conjure up Richard Posner's controversial hypothesis that the common law evolves in a "wealth-maximizing" direction.[6] Although Posner consciously chose *wealth*, not *welfare*, to describe the maximand,[7] he and I both have in mind a noun that refers to all things and conditions that people value.[8] Because my hypothesis deals, however, with the content of norms (rules created by nonhierarchical social forces), its validity in no way depends on the validity of Posner's hypothesis about the content of judge-made law.

4. See supra Chapter 8, text accompanying notes 58–67.
5. See Alexander M. Bickel, *The Morality of Consent* 3–25 (1975); A. I. Ogus, "Law and Spontaneous Order: Hayek's Contribution to Legal Theory," 16 *J.L. & Soc'y* 393 (1989) (summarizing Hayek's voluminous writings); and sources cited supra Chapter 8, notes 64–65.
6. Posner concisely summarized his theory in Richard A. Posner, "A Reply to Some Recent Criticisms of the Efficiency Theory of the Common Law," 9 *Hofstra L. Rev.* 775, 775–777 (1981). See also William M. Landes and Richard A. Posner, *The Economic Structure of Tort Law* 1–24 (1987). A difficulty with Posner's thesis is that many recent common-law decisions have had an overtly redistributive cast.
7. See Richard A. Posner, "Utilitarianism, Economics, and Legal Theory," 8 *J. Legal Stud.* 103, 104–105, 119–136 (1979).
8. Posner regards nonmaterial pleasures as part of "wealth." See, e.g., id. at 120 (example of "a friendly game of bridge"). In some previously published articles upon which portions of this book are based, I employed the phrase *wealth maximizing*, not *welfare maximizing*. I decided to substitute *welfare* for *wealth* after discovering that some readers were prone to interpret *wealth* as a reference only to material advantages. *Welfare* is defined infra text accompanying notes 14–22.

Even though it echoes a variety of visions of social life, the hypothesis of welfare-maximizing norms runs counter to a diverse array of intellectual traditions. Because it implies that much order can emerge without law, it challenges Hobbes and the other legal centralists who have exaggerated the role of the Leviathan. The hypothesis also cannot be reconciled with the view of prominent scholars such as Jon Elster who regard many norms as dysfunctional.[9] The hypothesis is inconsistent, moreover, with Marxism and other ideologies that see norms as serving the narrow interests of some members of a group, presumably at the greater expense of other group members. It will appear reductionist to those who believe that nonutilitarian considerations such as corrective and distributive justice influence the content of workaday norms. Finally, it stands in opposition to the belief, currently ascendant in anthropology and many of the humanities, that norms are highly contingent and, to the extent that they can be rationalized at all, should be seen as mainly serving symbolic functions unrelated to people's perceptions of costs and benefits.[10]

Words of caution are immediately in order. The hypothesis of welfare-maximizing norms is not a blanket normative recommendation that social controllers use norms as rules. Such a sweeping interpretation would be unjustified for three important reasons. First, many social environments are not close-knit. The hypothesis does not predict that the norm-making process would lead to the evolution of cooperation in a transient social environment such as a singles bar at O'Hare Airport. Second, norms that add to the welfare of the members of a certain group commonly impoverish, to a greater extent, outsiders to that group. Examples are the norms of racial segregation in the Jim Crow era in the South, and norms of loyalty among the Gypsies or the Mafia.[11] Third, welfare max-

9. See Jon Elster, *The Cement of Society* 125–151 (1989), and Jon Elster, "Social Norms and Economic Theory," 3 *J. Econ. Persp.* 99 (1989). Elster's reluctance to develop a competing theory of the content of norms weakens what is otherwise a notable scholarly contribution.

10. Representative of this perspective in anthropology is Marshall Sahlins, *Culture and Practical Reason* (1976). Marvin Harris has been a leading opponent of the tide of interpretivism in anthropology. See *Cultural Materialism: The Struggle for a Science of Culture* (1979) (criticizing Sahlins at 233–257, 332–340).

11. "[Gypsies'] relations with [non-Gypsies] are of an opposite nature to their economic relations with each other. Economic relations between [Gypsies] are based on cooperation and mutual aid, and it is generally considered immoral to earn money from other [Gypsies]. [Non-Gypsies] are the only legitimate source of income and skill in extracting money from them is highly valued in [Gypsy] society." Anne Sutherland, *Gypsies: The Hidden American* 65 (1975). For discussion of the possible negative social consequences of cooperation at too parochial a level, see Robert Axelrod, *The Evolution of Cooperation* 180–181 (1984); E. Ullmann-Margalit, supra note 1, at 42–44.

imization is a goal of limited normative appeal. Because welfare is measured by objective values, not subjective utilities, even a utilitarian might
be uneasy about exclusive pursuit of it.[12] Moreover, many commentators
would accord significant, perhaps paramount, normative importance to
other social goals such as equality, corrective justice, or the protection of
fundamental individual liberties.[13]

Three key terms in the hypothesis require clarification: "welfare maximization," "workaday affairs," and "close-knit group." The following
discussion of those terms will reveal that the hypothesis can be asserted
in both a strong and a weak form, and that it is defended here only in its
weaker version.

Welfare Maximization

The hypothesis assumes that people by nature want more satisfactions.
To assume that people are inherently hungry for improvements in their
welfare, it must be stressed, is not to assume that people are relentlessly
materialistic. Even to hardened economists, "welfare" includes not only
commodities but also other outcomes that people might value as much or
more, such as parenthood, leisure, good health, high social status, and
close personal relationships.

To develop rules of behavior that will generate more welfare to share
in the aggregate, the members of a group must be able to agree on a
metric for appraising the costs and benefits of alternative arrangements.
The hypothesis is cast in terms of "welfare maximization," not "utility
maximization," to denote that norm-makers are forced to employ a potentially unreliable system of *objective* appraisals to determine whether or
not an outcome actually adds to shareable welfare. Why informal con-

12. See infra text accompanying notes 14–18.
13. Posner embraced wealth maximization as the governing normative principle for law-
makers in Posner, supra note 7. This triggered an avalanche of criticism, including Ronald M.
Dworkin, "Is Wealth a Value?" 9 *J. Legal Stud.* 191 (1980); Anthony T. Kronman, "Wealth
Maximization as a Normative Principle," 9 *J. Legal Stud.* 227 (1980); and "Symposium on
Efficiency as a Legal Concern," 8 *Hofstra L. Rev.* 485–770 (1980). Posner may since have back-
tracked. See Richard A. Posner, "The Ethics of Wealth Maximization: A Reply to Malloy," 36
Kan. L. Rev. 261, 263 n.6 (1988). But see Richard A. Posner, *The Problems of Jurisprudence*
356–392 (1990). Although few moral philosophers would identify adding to shareable pleasures as the only desideratum, it is hard to imagine that many would regard increasing human
satisfactions as morally irrelevant. See, for example, Donald Regan, *Utilitarianism and Cooperation* (1980), a normative analysis implicitly sympathetic to the enhancement of aggregate
welfare.

trollers are compelled to use a valuation system of this sort requires a bit of explanation.

The measurement of value is a fundamental issue in economics. Economists who are loyal to either the Pareto-superiority definition or the Kaldor-Hicks definition of efficiency believe that a *subjective* valuation system is the only trustworthy measure of value.[14] A subjective system allows each affected person to judge according to his own personal tastes the effects of an outcome on his welfare ("utility"). Some systems of social control are regularly responsive to subjective valuations. For example, a person who engages either in first-party control (the development of a personal ethics) or in second-party control (contracting with others) can read his own mind and apply his own subjective preferences.

In contrast, third-party controllers, because they cannot read the minds of others, must invariably rely on cruder, objective measures of the value of alternative outcomes.[15] In practice, lawmakers and other third-party controllers often look to market prices when valuing goods and services. They typically do this, for example, when conducting a cost-benefit analysis of a government policy or measuring damages in civil litigation.

Market prices are an inherently crude measure of value. For traded goods and services, prices promise to reveal accurately the subjective preferences of buyers and sellers at the margin, but are likely to misrepresent the subjective values of inframarginal buyers and sellers.[16] In the case of satisfactions that are not openly traded, such as good health and friendship, there are no market prices to observe. In addition, market prices are unlikely to reflect the third-party effects of transactions. To mitigate some of these shortcomings, a sophisticated system of objective valuation may attempt to estimate both the subjective valuations of typical inframarginal actors,[17] and the shadow prices of untraded goods and services. These sorts of adjustments can reduce, but not eliminate, the crudeness of the metric. In short, norm-makers and other third-party rulemakers cannot measure, much less maximize, "utility." The hypothesis predicts that in

14. On these definitions, see, e.g., Richard A. Posner, *Economic Analysis of Law* 11–15 (3d ed. 1986).

15. As a matter of personal ethics, you can aspire to do unto others as you would have them do unto you. Because norm-makers don't know your subjective preferences, they can only ask you to do unto others as you would want to have done unto you if you were an ordinary person.

16. See Ellickson, "Alternatives to Zoning: Covenants, Nuisance Rules, and Fines as Land Use Controls," 40 *U. Chi. L. Rev.* 681, 735–737 (1973).

17. Saul X. Levmore, "Self-Assessed Valuation Systems for Tort and Other Law," 68 *Va. L. Rev.* 771 (1982), explores some devices that might help induce the honest revelation of subjective preferences.

practice norm-makers do the best that utilitarians can do, which is to maximize *welfare*—the objective value of satisfactions of group members.[18]

As long as norm-makers live in a social environment orderly enough to enable people to enter into exchanges (a proviso discussed below), the norm-makers can obtain rough objective evidence of values by observing the terms of voluntary second-party exchanges between group members. The most visible of these are the market prices, in the prevailing currency, at which members exchange tradable goods and services. As relevant, though less readily visible, are the objective details of social exchanges that help reveal how much people value things that are not for sale. For example, the objective burden Dennis Osborne bore in taking on additional boundary-fence maintenance is a rough measure of how much he valued his neighbor's service of keeping an eye on his house while he was on vacation.[19] In a sketchy and inexact way, patterns of social exchange thus can help reveal how people value outcomes reached outside the marketplace.

Suppose that the members of a group were each to have full information about all prior explicit and implicit dyadic exchanges among members and were willing to use that information to measure welfare. In terms of game theory, this agreed-upon objective valuation system would enable observers of, and participants in, a game to assess the aggregate welfare associated with various foreseeable outcomes, to identify the cooperative outcome (the one with the highest aggregate objective payoff), and to measure the objective aggregate losses that would result if the players were to reach another outcome. This last measurement, the objective aggregate shortfall members would suffer were they to fail to exploit all potential gains from trade, identifies the *deadweight loss* arising from a failure to cooperate. The simplified version of the hypothesis of welfare-maximizing norms predicts that a group's norms will tend to direct members to choose actions that minimize the group's deadweight losses. In Prisoner's Dilemma situations this simplified version predicts, as mentioned, the existence of a substantive norm that each player should Cooperate. Operationally this would mean that an observer of a society would notice that detected Defections were regularly punished, that most players did Cooperate when placed in these game situations, and that the society was rife with aspirational statements about the virtues of Cooperation.

18. This is why the hypothesis is framed to predict "welfare-maximizing" norms, not "efficient" norms.
19. See supra Chapter 4, text following note 32.

This simplified version of the hypothesis is incomplete, however. Utilitarian actors would not simply concern themselves with minimizing deadweight losses. Even in close-knit settings, group members must incur transaction costs when using informal social controls to achieve cooperative outcomes. For example, it takes time and effort to detect wrongdoing, spread gossip, and administer self-help sanctions. If the members of a group wanted the largest objective pie to divide, they would therefore want their norms to work to *minimize the sum of deadweight losses and transaction costs they objectively incurred when interacting with one another.*[20] For example, they would want to engage in more enforcement activity to encourage cooperative behavior only if they expected that the marginal gains from the additional cooperation would exceed the marginal costs of the additional enforcement. Similarly, they would update their norms in response to new environmental conditions only if the gains from such a modification would exceed the transaction costs of effecting it.[21] The full-blown version of the hypothesis predicts that, under close-knit social conditions, this subtle calculus of cost minimization determines the workaday norms that govern such things as trade practices, sports etiquette, and relations among neighbors.[22]

Because this calculus explicitly incorporates transaction costs, it highlights the importance of nonsubstantive norms. By contrast, most theoretical discussions of cooperation emphasize only the need to make people act cooperatively in their primary behavior, the domain that substantive norms govern. This approach overlooks that a system of social control consists not only of substantive rules but also of rules—remedial, procedural, constitutive, and controller-selecting—that constrain secondary behavior, that is, the roles people play in the system of social control itself. A utilitarian would want these other rules to be welfare enhancing as

20. Major landmarks in the intellectual evolution of this particular calculus are Ronald H. Coase, "The Problem of Social Cost," 3 *J.L. & Econ.* 1 (1960); Guido Calabresi, *The Costs of Accidents* 26–31 (1970); and Frank I. Michelman, "Ethics, Economics, and the Law of Property," in *Ethics, Economics, and the Law* (Nomos XXIV) 3, 12 (J. Roland Pennock and John W. Chapman eds. 1982).

21. More specifically, a group's members may lose less from a cultural lag than they gain from the decision-cost savings they obtain from being able simply to mimic traditional practices. See Robert Boyd and Peter J. Richerson, *Culture and the Evolutionary Process* 14–16, 57–60, 80 (1985) (discussing the advantages of a cultural tradition of imitation and reviewing empirical evidence of lags in cultural responses to changed conditions).

22. When norm-makers regard a typical group member as risk-averse, they might also consider using norms to provide a degree of insurance against risks. A group that desires to provide informal insurance, however, is predicted to pursue that goal by means of foundational norms of pure charity, not by introducing an element of progressive redistribution into the content of its workaday norms. See infra text accompanying notes 28–34.

well. The hypothesis offered here predicts not only, for example, that the members of a close-knit society would tend to Cooperate in Prisoner's Dilemmas but also, on the unusual occasions that they had to punish Defectors, that they would tend to apply the least costly forms of punishment.

Workaday Affairs

A strong version of the hypothesis would predict that all norms of close-knit groups would be welfare maximizing in content. The hypothesis is asserted, however, only in a weak form that limits its scope to the norms that govern *workaday* matters. This modification means that the hypothesis does not apply to two sorts of *foundational* rules: (1) the ground rules that enable group members to engage in exchange; and (2) any *purely distributive* norms, such as norms of charity, that may exist. These refinements are necessary, respectively, to save the hypothesis from potential indeterminacy and to identify a possible weakness in its predictive power.

The Assumption of Exogenous Foundational
Rules That Enable Exchange

Only voluntary exchanges provide trustworthy evidence of objective values. To prevent coerced exchanges a society must develop ground rules that forbid threats to the person. These include rules against murder, maiming, and enslavement.

Personal property, whether held in a currency or in kind, is one of the most common mediums of exchange. A society can create a foundation of personal property in either of two basic ways. A Lockean system entitles a worker to own the fruits of individual labor. A communal system entitles each group member to some share of the group's joint output. After endowments of personal property have been bestowed in either of these ways, supplementary ground rules are needed to provide continuing protection to owners' property interests. For example, both Lockean and communal regimes must prohibit one member from intentionally stealing or vandalizing another member's distributed share.

It will be assumed here that a close-knit group invariably has exogenous foundational rules, legal or otherwise, that endow and secure basic rights in amounts ample to support voluntary exchange.[23] This assump-

---

23. Legal centralists such as Hobbes have been too quick to assume that foundational rules must be established by a state. Every person has an inherent endowment of brainpower and

tion is not unrealistic. In Shasta County, these ground rules were firmly in place. Indeed, all societies have rules—against murder, theft of personal property, and so on—along these lines.[24] For example, in each of the six highly diverse countries that Graeme Newman surveyed, over 97 percent of respondents stated that robbery should be illegal.[25]

As noted, the assumption of exogenous ground rules is necessary to save the hypothesis from a potential indeterminacy.[26] By establishing foundational entitlements in property, the ground rules enable exchanges that help reveal the objective value of traded and untraded goods, and hence provide a measurement of welfare that is essentially independent of the content of the workaday norms themselves.[27] Without this, there

---

musclepower, and also an instinct of self-preservation. Even in a state of nature, a person therefore naturally possesses some power to threaten self-help retaliation to deter others from attempting unconsented exchanges. Human instincts of *kin* preservation, moreover, could contribute importantly to the anarchic creation of property rights, because traditions of mutual family support would enable an individually weak person to draw on the resources of a larger kinship group. Because of these broad distributions of natural power, private property might spontaneously exist in a state of nature to an extent sufficient to support some voluntary trade. (See also Robert Sugden, *The Economics of Rights, Co-operation, and Welfare* 71–83 (1986); John Umbeck, "Might Makes Rights: A Theory of the Formation and Initial Distribution of Property Rights," 19 *Econ. Inquiry* 38 (1981).) Once the owners of informal property, either unanimously or as members of a faction, had coordinated to form a government, that government's laws might of course feed back to modify the foundational norms that had enabled the creation of the state. There is scant historical evidence about how the earliest governments came into being. Some evidence relevant to these fundamental questions might perhaps be provided by study of contemporary stateless societies and of lawless episodes such as the California Gold Rush.

24. See James Q. Wilson and Richard J. Herrnstein, *Crime and Human Nature* 22–23, 448–450 (1985). "...Certain acts are regarded as wrong by every society, preliterate as well as literate; among these 'universal crimes' are murder, theft, robbery, and incest." Id. at 22.

25. See Graeme Newman, *Comparative Deviance: Perception and Law in Six Cultures* 116 (1976).

26. Posner's critics have argued, quite correctly, that wealth maximization is an inoperable principle in the absence of some exogenous system for setting basic entitlements. See, e.g., Guido Calabresi, "About Law and Economics: A Letter to Ronald Dworkin," 8 *Hofstra L. Rev.* 553, 554–555 (1980); Jules L. Coleman, "Efficiency, Utility, and Wealth Maximization," 8 *Hofstra L. Rev.* 509, 524–526 (1980); Kronman, supra note 13, at 240. Posner has agreed with the logic of this criticism but has minimized its practical importance. Richard A. Posner, *The Economics of Justice* 111–112 (1981).

27. The theoretical possibility of an occasional indeterminacy remains. The content of even workaday rules can affect the value of one's possessions. For example, the market value of cattle may depend to some slight degree on cattle-trespass norms, yet the hypothesis supposes that norm-makers choose cattle-trespass norms partly on the basis of the market value of cattle. This circularity may in a few cases make the identification of a welfare-maximizing norm indeterminate. In the case of "workaday" norms, however, this risk is slight. For the

would be no exogenous metric by which to test the welfare-maximizing tendencies of rules. As a matter of logical necessity, the reach of the hypothesis thus must be narrowed to workaday affairs, that is, ordinary matters conducted on the stage that the ground rules have set.

Agnosticism about Norms of Pure Charity

Norms that support charity to non-kin—to the poor, for example—call for what seem to be pure wealth transfers.[28] Because the transfer process consumes resources and creates none, these norms might appear to run counter to the hypothesis.[29] This appearance may be misleading. Some analysts, for example, regard norms of charity as an informal social-insurance system that enhances welfare by spreading risks without generating the administrative costs of more formal social-insurance arrangements.[30] According to this view, potlatch gift-giving among Pacific Coast tribes, because it required reciprocation, was an implicit insurance system against poor salmon harvests.[31] Indeed, many scholars regard the conferral of a "gift" as obligating the donee to return the favor. According to this perspective, donors engage in gift-giving because it may work to their long-run advantage.[32]

The realities of charitable giving are much debated. Because the insurance and reciprocity theories of gifts may well be too simple, it is prudent to restate the hypothesis in a slightly weaker form: that, when members

---

implicit argument that potential indeterminacies fatally flaw all attempts at cost-benefit analysis, see Duncan Kennedy, "Cost-Benefit Analysis of Entitlement Problems: A Critique," 33 *Stan. L. Rev.* 387 (1981). Kennedy's arguments were countered in Richard Markovits, "Duncan's Do Nots: Cost-Benefit Analysis and the Determination of Legal Entitlements," 36 *Stan. L. Rev.* 1169 (1984). Among other criticisms, Markovits asserted that Kennedy vastly exaggerated the frequency of indeterminacy problems. Id. at 1172, 1188–1198.

28. As an empirical matter, giving gifts to kin seems more common than giving gifts to non-kin. See Robert L. Trivers, "The Evolution of Reciprocal Altruism," 46 *Q. Rev. Biology* 33 (1971). The analysis of norms here, and throughout the book, assumes that the interactions in question are among non-kin.

29. A rulemaker has no objective way of making an interpersonal comparison of the utility that a donor and donee would obtain from a good or service that might be transferred. Nevertheless, the balance of this paragraph assumes that makers of norms of charity may impute identical, risk-averse, utility functions to all members of their group.

30. See R. Posner, *Economics of Justice,* supra note 26, at 152–165.

31. See D. Bruce Johnsen, "The Formation and Protection of Property Rights among the Southern Kwakiutl Indians," 15 *J. Legal Stud.* 41 (1986). Compare Marvin Harris, *Cows, Pigs, Wars, and Witches: The Riddles of Culture* 111–130 (1974).

32. See sources cited infra Chapter 12, note 45. Theories of why gift-giving may be self-serving for a donor are summarized in Jack Hirshleifer, "The Expanding Domain of Economics," 76 *Am. Econ. Rev.* 53, 57–59 (1985).

of a close-knit group develop norms to govern workaday situations, the content of their norms is not influenced by distributive considerations. This leaves open the possibility that a group may develop norms of pure charity that are, in an informal system of social control, analogues of state taxation and welfare programs.[33]

As Mitch Polinsky has lucidly explained, broad tax and welfare programs are typically the cheapest and most precise ways through which a legal system can redistribute wealth. He therefore argues that efficiency considerations should primarily shape commonplace legal doctrine, such as tort and contract law.[34] The hypothesis I am proposing assumes that norm-makers in close-knit groups would subscribe to an unalloyed version of this principle, and would not allow redistributive considerations to influence the norms they developed for workaday situations. Even in its weakened form, the hypothesis thus predicts, for example, that a poor person would not be excused from a general social obligation to supervise cattle, and that a rich person would not, on account of his wealth, have greater fencing obligations. This is consistent with practice in Shasta County.

Close-Knit Group

The hypothesis predicts that welfare-maximizing norms emerge in close-knit settings but is agnostic about whether such norms can emerge in other social settings.[35] This qualification is necessary because an informal-control system may not be effective if the social conditions within a group do not provide members with information about norms and violations and also the power and enforcement opportunities needed to establish norms.[36] A group is *close-knit* when informal power is broadly distributed among group members and the information pertinent to in-

33. Michael Taylor, *Community, Anarchy, and Liberty* 104–129 (1982), conveniently marshals evidence of how stateless and utopian societies have attempted to achieve a more egalitarian distribution of wealth.

34. A. Mitchell Polinsky, *An Introduction to Law and Economics* 105–113 (1983).

35. Stated in continuous form, the hypothesis predicts that, the more close-knit a group is, the better it will be able to use its informal-control system to minimize the sum of transaction costs and deadweight losses. A nice illustration of degrees of close-knittedness is provided in Janet T. Landa, "A Theory of the Ethnically Homogenous Middleman Group: An Institutional Alternative to Contract Law," 10 *J. Legal Stud.* 349, 351–355 (1981). Landa predicted that Chinese middlemen in the rubber trade in Southeast Asia would use seven grades to rank the closeness of trading partners.

36. Not just an informal controller but every type of controller needs the sorts of information and power that are discussed in the text.

formal control circulates easily among them.[37] The vagueness of this definition is unavoidable; social environments are too rich to be described in terms of a few quantifiable variables. The residents of rural Shasta County are an example of a close-knit group, and the residents of a small, remote island are an example of an extremely close-knit group.[38]

Developments in game theory point to the structural conditions, such as repeat play, that are conducive to the emergence of cooperation. In the iterated Prisoner's Dilemma format that Axelrod and other game theorists commonly use, each player is given certain information, a dose of power, and, finally, some ready opportunities to exercise that power. These conferrals, which work to reduce the transaction costs of informal enforcement, appear to be the key conditions for the evolution of cooperation. For example, in Axelrod's computer tournaments involving iterated Prisoner's Dilemmas, "nice" strategies, such as Tit-for-Tat, prospered in comparison with less cooperative strategies.[39] In experiments involving human subjects Hoffman and Spitzer similarly found that iterated play powerfully enhanced cooperation.[40] From these sorts of game-theoretic findings, I take the inductive leap of identifying the central attributes of close-knittedness. Although not inspired by sociological theory, the results of this leap are unlikely to startle sociologists.[41]

Future Power to Administer Sanctions

The iterated Prisoner's Dilemma confers on each player an unmistakable power to levy self-help sanctions. This power arises from the conjunction of two features. First, the configuration of the payoff schedule in each

37. People who are not close-knit often cooperate because of the work of controllers other than informal enforcers. For example, a society may succeed in inculcating norms that each citizen subsequently enforces upon himself.

38. Life on remote islands is so cooperative that residents often find that they can dispense with a criminal justice system. See Lawrence M. Friedman, *American Law: An Introduction* 31–33 (1984) (discussing a study of Tristan da Cunha, an isolated island in the South Atlantic).

39. R. Axelrod, supra note 11, at 33, 43–44. (Axelrod's definitions of these terms are provided supra Chapter 9, text accompanying notes 19–22.) See also David M. Kreps, Paul Milgrom, John Roberts, and Robert Wilson, "Rational Cooperation in the Finitely Repeated Prisoner's Dilemma," 27 *J. Econ. Theory* 245 (1982).

40. Elizabeth Hoffman and Matthew Spitzer, "The Coase Theorem: Some Experimental Results," 25 *J.L. & Econ.* 73, 92–94 (1982).

41. The sociologist Sally Engle Merry, for example, identifies the essential prerequisites for effective social control as "close-knit and durable social networks" and "homogenous norms and values." *Urban Danger: Life in a Neighborhood of Strangers* 196 (1981). Implicit in the notion of durable social networks are both information exchange and the prospect of reciprocal power; implicit in the notion of homogenous values is agreement on how to appraise the objective consequences of actions.

period of play enables each player to make the other better (or worse) off. Second, the fact the game is iterated means the prospect of future retribution looms in all but the last period. Because neither player can unilaterally change the payoff schedules or terminate the game before its scheduled end, this universal allocation of power is inherent in the game.

When would analogous conditions of reciprocal and effective power exist in a social setting? First, each group member, or his reliable allies, would have to have some of the resources of power. The foundational entitlements that I have assumed satisfy this requirement. They ensure the protection of a member's bodily integrity and also guarantee that a member has a way of acquiring and holding personal property.[42] These basic assurances enable members to proceed with the task of creating workaday norms.[43]

To control others in a social setting, a group member must not only possess power but also have ready opportunities to exercise it. In social life, as in game theory, the prospect of unavoidable future encounters can provide these opportunities. The continuing relationship that law-and-society scholars assert abets cooperation is exactly analogous to iterated play in game theory. Both ensure a handy stream of self-help enforcement opportunities.[44] Iterated play not only decreases an enforcer's administra-

42. Sociological theory holds that inequality lessens cooperation. See, e.g., M. P. Baumgartner, "Social Control from Below," in 1 *Toward a General Theory of Social Control* 303, 334–336 (Donald Black ed. 1984); Donald Black, *The Behavior of Law* 11–36 (1976). Game theory suggests, however, that the members of a close-knit society need not necessarily have exactly equal countervailing power. To create incentives for cooperation, it is necessary that each member (and his allies) credibly have enough power ultimately to punish the worst possible misconduct, or reward the best possible heroism, of another member. In the anarchic American West, for example, the six-shooter could operate as an "equalizer" even though westerners varied greatly in their shooting ability and in their holdings of other resources of power. See Umbeck, supra note 23. On the difficulties of determining reciprocities in power, see Gary T. Schwartz, "The Vitality of Negligence and the Ethics of Strict Liability," 15 *Ga. L. Rev.* 963, 985–986 n.117, 990 n.137 (1981).

43. There is no reason for supposing that norms will evolve to serve the powerless. For example, cattle lack the innate power to control people, and legal and social systems confer scant power on cattle. As a result, human norms regarding cattle in Shasta County frequently are oblivious to the well-being of the cattle themselves. It is human welfare that human behavior tends to maximize.

44. Some types of relationships are better than others in this regard. As was noted in Chapter 3, sociologists distinguish between multiplex and simplex relationships. Two people have a multiplex relationship when they deal with each other along many different fronts. The prospect of a continuing multiplex relationship guarantees a rich menu of future opportunities to render self-help sanctions. In effect, a person who has enmeshed himself in a continuing multiplex relationship has given over a part of his future welfare as a hostage to the other person. See Oliver E. Williamson, "Credible Commitments: Using Hostages to Support Exchange," 73 *Am. Econ. Rev.* 519 (1983).

tive costs of applying sanctions but also increases his benefits. When relations are continuing, an enforcer will receive more personal benefits if
a particular sanctionee is induced to act more cooperatively in the future.

Information about the Past and Present

The prospect of repeat play by itself is not sufficient to induce cooperation. Players need information as well as effective power. In the absence
of adequate information, a continuing relationship among empowered
people may not be cooperative. Embezzlers, for example, exploit the ignorance of their steady employers.

The information requirements for cooperation are several. First, to
follow norms in current encounters, a person needs accurate objective
information about contemporary circumstances. In a two-person non-
zero-sum game, for example, the players cannot cooperate unless they can
forecast the aggregate payoffs that would result from the various combinations of their available choices. Similarly, to employ a Tit-for-Tat or
similar strategy in an iterated Prisoner's Dilemma game, a player must
have information about both the payoff structure in each prior period and
what opposing players chose to do during those periods. Without this
historical knowledge, an actor could not identify, or appraise the seriousness of, prior acts of deviancy and heroism, in order to calibrate his own
future responses correctly.[45]

Axelrod's computer tournaments did not allow for information networks, and thus a player never knew what an opponent had done when
interacting with others. In social life, by contrast, people must worry
about their reputations, because historical information can be shared.
Someone who Defects in the last period of play with a particular opponent must be concerned that others will learn about it. Many cultures
abet social control by encouraging their members to believe that enforcers
will know everything they have done. Omniscient (and omnipotent) gods
are common in religions. Many schoolchildren believe that their "permanent records" are far more complete than is actually the case. During
the past two decades, interest in the role of reputation has fittingly flowered among economists.[46]

As was just suggested, close-knit social groups in fact tend to contain

45. See Oliver Kim and Mark Walker, "The Free Rider Problem: Experimental Evidence,"
43 *Public Choice* 3, 15 (1984) (how anonymity spurs free-riding).
46. Two important early works were A. Michael Spence, *Market Signaling* (1974), and
George A. Akerlof, "The Market for 'Lemons': Quality Uncertainty and the Market Mechanism," 84 *Q.J. Econ.* 488 (1970).

cross-cutting webs of dyadic relationships, each of which may vary in intimacy and continuity. The existence of these networks contributes to informal control in several ways. First, these cross-cutting relationships help members maintain a gossip network through which to pass information about how particular members acted in the past in particular social interactions. Second, these interlinkages help members share information about previous consensual economic and social exchanges, and thus to develop the objective valuation system they need to assess the welfare-enhancing tendencies of various norms.[47] Third, because cross-cutting ties facilitate the identification and rewarding of "champions of the public," they enhance the possibility that a third-party Good Samaritan will exercise vicarious self-help to enforce norms.

The format of an Axelrod-type computer tournament is thus unrealistic in offsetting ways. On the one hand, it assumes that each player has *perfect* historical and current information about each dyadic relationship, whereas even intimate social relations are rarely so plain. On the other hand, it assumes that a player knows *nothing* outside of the histories of his own interactions. In close-knit groups, members actually use gossip to share an abundance of social information. Whether Axelrod's conditions were on balance too conducive, or too hostile, to the emergence of cooperation is still anyone's guess.

Implications

A close-knit group has been defined as a social network whose members have credible and reciprocal prospects for the application of power against one another and a good supply of information on past and present internal events. This definition suggests how sociological theory might be sharpened. The hypothesis predicts that departures from conditions of reciprocal power, ready sanctioning opportunities, and adequate information are likely to impair the emergence of welfare-maximizing norms. If these predictions were to be validated, analysts might call these departures "social imperfections," analogous to the "market imperfections" identified in traditional economic theory. Market imperfections—for example, externalities and imperfect competition—make it less likely that untrammeled market exchange will result in the efficient allocation of resources. Social imperfections make it less likely that people will engage in objectively beneficial social exchange. At bottom, economic and social imperfections both stem from the same source: the transaction costs that

47. See supra text accompanying notes 14–19.

may thwart people from exploiting opportunities to interact cooperatively. Either sort of imperfection opens up the possibility of useful state
intervention. Because governments are also imperfect, however, state interventions in both markets and informal-control systems may do more
harm than good.

The proffered definition of close-knittedness does not require the existence of certain social conditions that some observers might have anticipated. First, a particular group need not have an exclusive hold on a
particular member. As long as the conditions of requisite power and information are met in each instance, a person can be a member of several
close-knit groups simultaneously. For example, a person might be a member of a close-knit work force, a close-knit residential neighborhood, and
a close-knit religious group, even though the memberships do not overlap
at all.

Second, a group does not necessarily have to be small to be close-knit.
Since Tönnies, the sociological stereotype of close-knittedness has been
life in a rural village, a life often contrasted with the allegedly anomic life
in a mass urban setting.[48] A small population in practice tends to increase
quality of gossip, reciprocal power, and ease of enforcement; smallness is
therefore indeed highly correlated with close-knittedness. The definition
of close-knittedness assumes, however, that smallness per se makes no
difference apart from these correlated effects.[49]

Testing the Hypothesis

The hypothesis is in principle falsifiable. The variables that affect close-
knittedness—namely, reciprocity of power, future ease of exercising
power, and networks of information—are capable of measurement. For
example, if three black and three white fire fighters belonging to a ra-
cially polarized union were suddenly to be adrift in a well-stocked life-

48. Ferdinand Tönnies, *Community and Society* 43, 226–229 (Loomis trans. 1957) (in rural
areas one finds Gemeinschaft (real and organic association); in cities, Gesellschaft (imaginary
and mechanical association)). See also Louis Wirth, "Urbanism as a Way of Life," 44 *Am. J.
Soc.* 1 (1938) (urbanism weakens social ties). For criticism, and the counterthesis that urbanization allows the emergence of specialized subcultures, see Claude Fischer, *The Urban Experience* (1976); Claude Fischer, *To Dwell among Friends* (1982). There is evidence that outsiders
and newcomers to small, rural communities are more likely than longtime residents to use
the legal system. David M. Engel, "Cases, Conflict, and Accommodation: Patterns of Legal
Interaction in a Small Community," 1983 *Am. B. Found. Res. J.* 803, 819–821.

49. On the relevance of group size, see Mancur Olson, *The Logic of Collective Action* 53–65
(1965); Russell Hardin, *Collective Action* 38–49 (1982); Pamela E. Oliver and Gerald Marwell,
"The Paradox of Group Size in Collective Action," 53 *Am. Soc. Rev.* 1 (1988).

boat in the middle of the Pacific Ocean, as an objective matter the social environment of the six would have become close-knit and they would be predicted to cooperate.[50]

Norms are also identifiable. They are evidenced by patterns of sanctions, patterns of primary behavior, and aspirational statements.[51] In most contexts the objective costs and benefits of alternative norms are impossible to quantify with precision. Therefore, both norm-makers and analysts of norms must fall back on largely intuitive assessments of the utilitarian potential of alternative rules. This is the approach taken in the next four chapters, which analyze worldly examples that are plausibly supportive of the hypothesis.[52]

50. This statement assumes the continuing presence of foundational rules that forbid the firefighters from killing, maiming or imprisoning each other. For an account of actual lifeboat mores under conditions of deprivation, see A. W. Brian Simpson, *Cannibalism and the Common Law* (1984) (discussing Regina v. Dudley and Stephens, 14 Q.B. 273 (1884)).

51. See supra Chapter 7, text accompanying notes 14–20.

52. These chapters are organized according to the taxonomy of rules developed supra Chapter 7, text accompanying notes 26–33.

11

* * *

Substantive Norms:
Of Bees, Cattle, and Whales

The stuff of a civilization consists largely of its substantive norms. These norms identify the everyday behaviors that call for the informal administration of rewards and punishments. In a well-functioning civilization, these informal rules—which have no identifiable author, no apparent date of origin, no certainty of attention from historians—are among the most magnificent of cultural achievements.[1]

This chapter presents some concrete examples to provide intuitive support for the proposition that members of close-knit groups develop workaday substantive norms that are welfare maximizing.[2] To reiterate, a norm is welfare maximizing when it promises to minimize the members' objective sum of (1) transaction costs and (2) deadweight losses arising from failures to exploit potential gains from trade. The initial set of illustrative substantive norms is drawn from Shasta County. The focus then shifts to contract norms, particularly those uncovered by Stewart Macaulay in Wisconsin. The most extended treatment is reserved for a historical example: the informal substantive rules developed by whalers of the eighteenth and nineteenth centuries to govern the ownership of a whale that two or more ships had helped to capture. All these examples have been taken from social settings in which relationships were close-knit and ex-

1. What follows is similar in spirit to historical studies carried out by transaction-cost economists. See, e.g., Terry L. Anderson and P. J. Hill, "The Evolution of Property Rights: A Study of the American West," 18 *J.L. & Econ.* 163 (1975) (describing the informal emergence of exclusive rights to use federal rangelands in the Great Plains); Harold Demsetz, "Toward a Theory of Property Rights," 57 *Am. Econ. Rev.* 347 (Pap. & Proc. 1967) (finding adaptive evolution of property rights among Labrador Indians); Douglass C. North and Robert Paul Thomas, *The Rise of the Western World* (1973) (attributing the boom in Europe in and after the Middle Ages to the development of institutional arrangements and property rights that fostered productive economic effort).

2. A skeptic might question the representativeness of these case studies or deny their intuitive power. To allay such a skeptic, Chapter 15 will go beyond ex post explanation to put forward some ex ante predictions about the content of substantive norms in certain close-knit situations.

ogenous foundational rules had previously established a basis for exchange.

Shasta County Norms

The overarching substantive norm of the rural residents of Shasta County is that one should be a "good neighbor." This is a general call for cooperative behavior. Because this standard is so general, it is vulnerable to conflicting interpretations in a concrete case.[3] Perhaps as a result, Shasta County residents have developed narrower informal rules to govern certain ordinary interactions. The hypothesis asserts that welfare maximization is the most parsimonious explanation of the content of these workaday norms.

Cattle-Trespass Norms

A Shasta County norm holds an owner of livestock strictly responsible, irrespective of his negligence, for both intentional and accidental harms that his trespassing stock inflict on neighboring lands.[4] This norm poses two questions: first, why have rural residents made a stockman strictly liable, instead of limiting his liability only to instances in which he had been negligent? Second, if a strict-liability approach is to be employed, why does the Shasta County rule require the rancher, as opposed to the trespass victim, to bear trespass damages? After all, as Coase's parable demonstrated, both parties are capable of building fences to separate their incompatible activities.

The hypothesis predicts that, in a close-knit group, makers of tort norms strive to minimize the sum of members' transaction costs and deadweight losses arising from the risk of accidents.[5] To prevent deadweight losses, makers of tort norms should formulate rules that serve to induce individuals to exercise care as long as the marginal costs of additional care are exceeded by the marginal benefits (measured in reduced

3. Excessive generality also afflicts the common-law rule of neighborliness, "Sic utere tuo ut alienum non laedes" (use your own land in a such a manner as not to injure that of another).

4. This discussion addresses only the norm that governs a stockman's prima facie liability for trespass. A group's substantive norms applicable to accidents would, if fully developed, address *all* the substantive issues that arise in tort law—including, for example, causation, contribution among joint tortfeasors, and defenses based on the injured party's conduct.

5. Guido Calabresi, *The Costs of Accidents* 26–31 (1970), endorses a calculus somewhat richer than this as the appropriate target of torts policy.

accident costs) that the additional care brings about.[6] As in other contexts, transaction costs complicate matters. Welfare maximizers would incur transaction costs to fine-tune their incentives for care only as long as the benefits of further fine-tuning (measured in further reductions in dead-weight losses) would exceed the administrative costs of the additional fine-tuning.

Torts theorists usually start from the premise that strict-liability rules and negligence rules are equally effective at inducing cost-justified levels of care.[7] If so, a utilitarian would want to pick the liability rule that promised to minimize transaction costs. For Shasta County residents, a drawback of the negligence approach is that it would make a cattle-trespass incident the occasion for a detailed factual inquiry to determine whether or not the parties involved had failed to take cost-justified steps that might have prevented the (usually) minor damage that occurred. When norm-makers can confidently identify one of the parties to a common interaction as typically the cheaper cost-avoider in that situation, they can minimize transaction costs by making that party strictly responsible in that context.[8] Such a strict-liability rule greatly lessens the burden of fact-gathering in an individual case, although it is likely to call for more occasions for compensation than a negligence rule would.[9] In

6. This calculus echoes Learned Hand's famous definition of negligence as a failure to take a cost-justified safety step. See United States v. Carroll Towing Co., 159 F.2d 169, 173 (2d Cir. 1947).

7. A. Mitchell Polinsky, *An Introduction to Law and Economics* 39–52 (2d ed. 1989); Richard A. Posner, *Economic Analysis of Law* 160–165 (3d ed. 1986). These authors point out that the deterrent effects of the negligence calculus depend in part on whether it is applied to activity levels. Strict liability and negligence may also induce different levels of care when there are risks that adjudicators will misapply the governing standard (see John E. Calfee and Richard Craswell, "Some Effects of Uncertainty on Compliance with Legal Standards," 70 *Va. L. Rev.* 965 (1984)), or when actors find one of these rules easier to learn and apply than the other. These potential allocative differences between strict liability and negligence all arise from the transaction costs of administering rules.

8. The cheapest cost-avoider is the party in the best position to make a cost-benefit analysis between accident costs and accident prevention costs and to act on that analysis once it has been made. See G. Calabresi, supra note 5, at 139; Guido Calabresi and Jon T. Hirschoff, "Toward a Test for Strict Liability in Torts," 81 *Yale L.J.* 1055, 1060 (1972). The text assumes that norm-makers have an intuitive understanding of the Calabresian approach.

9. This trade-off between the simplicity of rules and the number of occasions for compensation has long been recognized. See R. Posner, supra note 7, at 528–529. Cf. Richard A. Posner, *The Economics of Justice* 199–203 (1981) (reasons why primitive societies would rely mostly on strict-liability rules). There has been a spirited academic debate over the relative efficiency of negligence and strict-liability rules in tort law. For the argument that ancient lawmakers essentially regarded the choice between these rules as a toss-up, see Saul X. Levmore, "Rethinking Comparative Law: Variety and Uniformity in Ancient and Modern Tort

Shasta County, an increase in the number of compensable events would be of little moment because, as Chapter 3 described, land-trespass disputes typically arise between neighbors who are already constantly adjusting their informal mental accounts with one another. In sum, a utilitarian calculus suggests that norm-makers should apply strict-liability rules to determine prima facie liabilities in cattle-trespass incidents.

The next issue is *who* should be made strictly responsible for damage to vegetation. Of the two characters in Coase's parable—the rancher and the farmer—Shasta County residents currently choose to burden the rancher. For this choice to be consistent with the welfare-maximization hypothesis, ranchers must be cheaper cost-avoiders of unintentional trespasses by their livestock than trespass victims are. For two reasons, this is highly plausible. First, as ex-urbanites have increasingly established ranchettes in rural Shasta County, typical residents have become less and less knowledgeable about how to fend off bovine animals. Cattlemen are currently much more familiar than ranchette owners with barbed-wire fencing, the most cost-justified means for controlling livestock. Second, a cattleman can act on his own to fence in his herd. By contrast, the potential victims of loose cattle are numerous. Motorists, a large and diffuse group whose members arguably benefit the most from cattle control, have particular difficulty mobilizing themselves for collective action. The current Shasta County norm therefore appears correctly to identify the rancher, not the farmer, as prima facie the cheaper avoider of costs posed by stray cattle. This norm, which is consistent with the ancient English common-law rule on cattle trespass, is thus offered as a datum in support of the hypothesis that norms evolve in a welfare-maximizing direction.[10]

The hypothesis is also invoked, more boldly, to predict that, if historians were able to gather evidence on the subject, they would discover that during the mid-nineteenth century Shasta County norms did *not* make livestock owners strictly responsible for unintentional cattle-trespass damages. During the early history of the state of California, irrigated pastures and ranchettes were rare, at-large cattle numerous, and motorized vehicles unknown. In addition, a century ago most rural residents were accustomed to handling livestock. Especially prior to the invention

---

Law," 61 *Tulane L. Rev.* 235 (1986). The hypothesis of welfare-maximizing norms suggests that the observed content of accident norms within close-knit groups could help analysts identify in which contexts strict-liability rules or negligence rules would be the more utilitarian approach in tort law.

10. See also William M. Landes and Richard A. Posner, *The Economic Structure of Tort Law* 110–111 (1987) (economic analysis of legal rules of fencing-out and fencing-in).

of barbed wire in 1874, the fencing of rangelands was rarely cost-justified. In those days an isolated grower of field crops in Shasta County, as one of the few persons at risk from at-large cattle, would have been prima facie the cheaper avoider of livestock damage to crops. The hypothesis predicts that, to avoid the expense of a detailed negligence-rule inquiry, nineteenth-century Shasta County norms would therefore have placed the risk of an accidental trespass on the farmer who had failed to fence the animals out.[11]

Norms That Determine Who Pays for Boundary Fencing

As Chapter 4 described, a Shasta County rancher who proposes to build or improve an objectively cost-justified boundary fence, after telling the adjoining owner about the proposal, is entitled to build the fence and then informally bill an appropriate share to the noncontributing neighbor. The fraction of the construction costs the nonbuilder owes is roughly equal to his fraction of the total livestock that the two landowners run in the vicinity of the new fence. Any unpaid debt is registered in informal interneighbor accounts. When a debtor lags in squaring informal accounts, Shasta County norms entitle the creditor to get even through measured self-help.

A norm that forces a landowner to disgorge his objective benefits from another's prepublicized boundary fence project promises to contribute to the aggregate welfare of rural residents of Shasta County. First, this norm reduces the transaction costs neighbors incur when dickering over boundary-fence improvements. If a fencebuilder were to have no informal right to restitution, this bilateral monopoly situation would be fraught with incentives for strategic behavior. The proportionality norm sharply truncates the range of permissible bargaining positions, and

---

11. My search for evidence of the content of nineteenth-century trespass norms proved to be unavailing. Evidence about the norms that prevailed during a prior time is inherently difficult to obtain. Old diaries, letters, and newspaper stories may contain aspirational statements, descriptions of practices, and accounts of self-help enforcement. References to custom in judicial opinions, some of which are presented in the whaling example later in this chapter, may also be a fruitful source. During the past century in the western United States, there has been a sharp increase in ranchers' *legal* liabilities for cattle trespass. See supra Chapter 3, text accompanying notes 7–35. On the nineteenth-century legislative politics surrounding this issue, see J. Orin Oliphant, *On the Cattle Ranges of the Oregon Country* 319–337 (1968); Kenneth R. Vogel, "The Coase Theorem and Cattle Trespass Law," 16 *J. Legal Stud.* 149, 161–180 (1987). My analysis supposes that this legal change accompanied, was responsive to, or triggered a change in norms, but does not choose among these competing temporal sequences. On the feedback loops that may interconnect legal and informal control systems, see infra Chapter 14, text at notes 59–62.

hence promises to expedite transactions. Second, the norm discourages fence-construction proposals that are not objectively cost-justified. Allocating costs in proportion to the presence of livestock is a rough-and-ready method to allocate costs in proportion to objective benefits conferred.[12] This formula discourages foolish fence projects because, when a would-be fencebuilder has ordinary tastes, it tends to make his personal cost-benefit ratio equal to the social cost-benefit ratio.

Steven Cheung discovered the existence of an analogous norm among orchard owners in rural Washington state. Each orchard owner there is informally obligated to provide bees in proportion to his number of orchard trees.[13] Cheung concluded that it is administratively cheaper for a cluster of orchardmen to provide the public good of pollination by means of this unwritten social contract rather than by means of express contracts.[14] The Shasta County fencing norms suggest that even in two-party situations, where express contracting is far easier, unwritten social contracts may also establish some default duties to supply public goods.

The Shasta County norms that allocate boundary-fence costs make heavy use of focal-point solutions, such as fifty-fifty and all-or-nothing. Although focal-point solutions reduce the precision of production incentives, they save transaction costs when they obviate the need for exact calculations. According to the hypothesis, Shasta County residents employ focal-point divisions of fence costs because the resulting administrative savings outweigh the deadweight losses stemming from the imprecision in incentives.

Macaulay's Contract Norms

Stewart Macaulay's study of relations among close-knit Wisconsin businessmen turned up two prominent contract norms.[15] The first, that "com-

---

12. It should be reemphasized that the benefits a party receives from a boundary fence depend in part on the allocation of the risk of loss from cattle trespass. Because Shasta County cattlemen are today informally liable for cattle-trespass damages, cattlemen, and not their neighbors, currently obtain most of the benefits of fences. Conversely, if cropgrowers indeed bore trespass risks during the nineteenth century, fence-cost norms are then predicted to have placed greater financial burdens on owners of at-risk crops.

13. Steven N. S. Cheung, "The Fable of the Bees: An Economic Investigation," 16 *J.L. & Econ.* 11, 30 (1973).

14. Cheung did not comment on the total number of hives that all orchard owners put together were informally required to provide. The hypothesis supposes that this aggregate number would be roughly the cost-justified amount. Some limitations on the informal-control system's capacity to provide public goods are discussed infra Chapter 14, text accompanying notes 32–67.

15. See Stewart Macaulay, "Non-Contractual Relations in Business: A Preliminary Study," 28 *Am. Soc. Rev.* 55, 63 (1963).

mitments are to be honored in almost all situations," is unquestionably welfare enhancing.[16] A norm requiring the performance of executory promises enables traders to go beyond simple barter. In the absence of this norm parties might conceivably be able to secure future performance by means of clumsy security devices such as hostages and bonds, but only at the expense of high transaction costs.[17] Members of a close-knit group benefit from a general norm that exposes those who break promises to informal sanctions because this norm relieves bargainers of the administrative hassle of making transaction-specific guarantees of future performance.

The general principle that "commitments are to be honored" is of course too broad, and thus Macaulay was right to qualify it with the phrase "in almost all situations." Impossibility, duress, lack of capacity, and other conditions provide legal excuses for the breaking of promises. Cogent utilitarian rationales for these legal doctrines have been developed.[18] The hypothesis predicts that the norms of close-knit groups would excuse the breaking of promises in a somewhat analogous set of contexts.

The second contract norm that Macaulay identified was that "one ought to produce a good product and stand behind it." This implied-warranty norm is also plausibly welfare enhancing for buyers and sellers in the aggregate. This norm puts the risk of product defects on the seller, the party typically better informed about product characteristics and in the better position to control them, and forces the seller to speak up if it prefers that the risk be allocated in another way. Informal implied warranties of fitness are thus predicted to be found among close-knit buyers and sellers not only in Wisconsin, where Macaulay observed them, but also in Patagonia, Timbuktu, or wherever.

16. Rules requiring the keeping of promises have been identified as part of the minimum natural law of a society. H. L. A. Hart, *The Concept of Law* 192–193 (1961). It has also been argued that a disposition to honor commitments enhances a person's chances of survival. Robert A. Frank, "If *Homo Economicus* Could Choose His Own Utility Function, Would He Want One with a Conscience?" 77 *Am. Econ. Rev.* 593 (1987). Numerous field studies have uncovered norms that require promises to be kept. See, e.g., Cheung, supra note 13, at 29; David M. Engel, "The Oven Bird's Song: Insiders, Outsiders, and Personal Injuries in an American Community," 18 *L. & Soc. Rev.* 551, 577–579 (1984). But see Fred Korn and Shulamit R. Dektor Korn, "Where People Don't Promise," 93 *Ethics* 445 (1983) (asserting that natives of the Tonga Islands don't expect promises to be kept).

17. See Anthony T. Kronman, "Contract Law and the State of Nature," 1 *J.L. Econ. & Org.* 5 (1985).

18. See Robert Cooter and Thomas Ulen, *Law and Economics* ch. 7 (1988); R. Posner, *Economic Analysis,* supra note 7, at ch. 4.

Another common contract norm, arguably a corollary of both of Macaulay's norms, forbids barterers from lying about what they are trading. Falsehoods threaten to decrease welfare because they are likely to increase others' costs of eventually obtaining accurate information. Honesty is so essential to the smooth operation of a system of communication that all close-knit societies can be expected to endeavor to make their members internalize, and hence self-enforce, norms against lying.[19] Of course a no-fraud norm, like any broadly stated rule, is ambiguous around the edges. Norms may tolerate white lies, practical joking, and the puffing of products.[20] By hypothesis, however, these exceptions would not permit misinformation that would be welfare threatening. The "entertaining deceivers" that anthropologists delight in finding are thus predicted not to be allowed to practice truly costly deceptions.[21]

Whaling Norms

The practices of high-seas whalers in the pre-steamship era powerfully illustrate how nonhierarchical groups can create welfare-maximizing substantive norms. Especially during the period from 1750 to 1870, whales were an extraordinarily valuable source of oil, bone, and other products.[22] Whalers therefore had powerful incentives to develop rules

19. Except for a few dissident anthropologists, virtually all observers assume the universality of norms against lying. See, e.g., Sissela Bok, *Lying: Moral Choice in Public and Private Life* (1978) (moral philosophers in wide variety of societies condemn lying); David K. Lewis, *Convention* 177–195 (1969); John Finley Scott, *The Internalization of Norms* 119–121 (1971) ("ubiquitous and strong" norm of honesty); Donald T. Campbell, "On the Conflicts between Biological and Social Evolution and between Psychology and Moral Tradition," 30 *Am. Psychologist* 1103, 1118–1119 (1975) ("dishonesty is regularly among the sins" deplored in ancient societies).

20. See, e.g., Clifford Geertz, "Suq: The Bazaar Economy in Sefrou," in Clifford Geertz, Hildred Geertz, and Lawrence Rosen, *Meaning and Order in Moroccan Society* 123, 212 (1979). Nevertheless, reputations for honesty are highly valued at the Moroccan bazaar, and "lying . . . is . . . in many ways the premier sin" in Islam. Id. at 204–205, 211.

21. On entertaining deceivers, see, e.g., Myrdene Anderson, "Cultural Concatenation of Deceit and Secrecy," in *Deception: Perspectives on Human and Nonhuman Deceit* 323, 343 (Robert W. Mitchell and Nicholas S. Thompson eds. 1986) (Saami of Lapland); Michael Gilsenan, "Lying, Honor, and Contradiction," in *Transaction and Meaning: Directions in the Anthropology of Exchange and Symbolic Behavior* 191 (Bruce Kapferer ed. 1976) (Lebanese). A cross-cultural study of permissible practical joking would provide a good test of the hypothesis.

22. Century-old judicial opinions valued single whales (of unreported species) captured in the Sea of Okhotsk, located north of Japan, at over $2000. Swift v. Gifford, 23 Fed. Cas. 558 (D. Mass. 1872) (No. 13,696) ($3000); Taber v. Jenny, 23 Fed. Cas. 605 (D. Mass. 1856) (No. 13,720) ($2350). In that era, mean family income in the United States was on the order of $600 to $800 per year. See supra Chapter 1, note 34.

for peaceably resolving rival claims to the ownership of a whale. In *Moby-Dick*, Herman Melville explains why these norms were needed:

> It frequently happens that when several ships are cruising in company, a whale may be struck by one vessel, then escape, and be finally killed and captured by another vessel.... [Or], after a weary and perilous chase and capture of a whale, the body may get loose from the ship by reason of a violent storm; and drifting far away to leeward, be retaken by a second whaler, who, in a calm, snugly tows it alongside, without risk of life or line. Thus the most vexatious and violent disputes would often arise between the fishermen, were there not some written, universal, undisputed law applicable to all cases.
>   ...[T]he American fishermen have been their own legislators and lawyers in this matter.[23]

Melville's last sentence might prompt the inference that whalers had some sort of hierarchical trade association that established rules governing the ownership of contested whales. There is no evidence, however, that this was so. Anglo-American whaling norms seem to have emerged spontaneously over time, not from decrees handed down by either organizational or governmental authorities.[24] In fact whalers' norms not only did not mimic law; they *created* law. In the dozen reported Anglo-American cases in which ownership of a whale carcass was contested, judges regarded themselves as bound to honor whalers' usages that had been proved at trial.[25]

The Whaling Industry

At first blush it might be thought that high-seas whalers would have been too dispersed to constitute a close-knit social group. During the industry's peak in the nineteenth century, for example, whaling ships from ports in

---

23. Herman Melville, *Moby-Dick* ch. 89 (1851) (Penguin Eng. Lib. ed. 1972, at pp. 504–505).

24. Melville asserts that the only formal whaling code was one legislatively decreed in Holland in 1695. Id. at 505. He does not describe the contents of this code, and the Anglo-American judicial decisions on whale ownership make no mention of it.

25. See, e.g., Addison & Sons v. Row, 3 Paton 339 (1794); Swift v. Gifford, 23 Fed. Cas. 558 (D. Mass. 1872) (No. 13,696); see generally Oliver Wendell Holmes, Jr., *The Common Law* 212 (1881). But cf. Taber v. Jenny, 23 Fed. Cas. 605 (D. Mass. 1856) (No. 13,720) (holding for plaintiff on the basis of general common law regarding abandoned property, despite defendant's (doubtful) assertion that the usage was otherwise).

several nations were hunting their prey in remote seas of every ocean. The international whaling community was a tight one, however, primarily because whaling ships commonly encountered one another at sea, and because whalers' home and layover ports were few, intimate, and socially interlinked. The scant evidence available suggests that whalers' norms of capture were internationally binding.[26]

The Greenland fishery was the first important international whaling ground. The Dutch were the leaders there around 1700, but they later encountered increasing competition from French, British, and United States whaling vessels. After 1800, ships from the two English-speaking nations became dominant both in Greenland and elsewhere, and by the mid-1800s the United States, a fledgling international power, had emerged as the preeminent whaling nation.[27]

American whalers were concentrated in a handful of small ports in southern New England. Nantucket, the dominant North American whaling port in the eighteenth century, was home to over half the New England whaling fleet in 1774.[28] During the 1820s, New Bedford supplanted Nantucket as the leading American whaling center and berthed half the whaling ships in the United States in 1857.[29] Life within these specialized ports centered on the whaling trade. Because of its remote island location and strong Quaker influence, Nantucket was a particularly close-knit community. "There is no finer example in history of communal enterprise than the Nantucket Whale Fishery. The inhabitants were uniquely situated for united effort. . . . Through intermarriage they were generally related to one another, and in fact were more like a large

26. A dictum in Fennings v. Lord Grenville, 1 Taunt. 241, 127 Eng. Rep. 825, 828 (Ct. Comm. Pleas 1808), asserts that the fast-fish "usage in Greenland is regarded as binding on persons of all nations." The loneliness of the high seas encouraged whalers from different countries to collaborate with one another. Melville, in Chapter 81 of *Moby-Dick*, provides a fictional account of a mid-Pacific meeting in which the *Jungfrau* of Bremen hailed the *Pequod* of Nantucket in order to obtain lamp oil. An actual high-seas trade between British and New England ships is described infra note 35.

27. See Clifford W. Ashley, *The Yankee Whaler* 23–29 (1938); Elmo Paul Hohman, *The American Whaleman: A Study of Life and Labor in the Whaling Industry* 5–6, 20–22 (1928). The United States industry peaked in about 1846, when its whaling fleet consisted of over 700 vessels. At that same time the combined whaling fleets of all other nations totaled 230 ships. Edouard A. Stackpole, *The Sea Hunters: The New England Whalemen during Two Centuries, 1635–1835* 473 (1953).

28. E. Stackpole, supra note 27, at 53–54. Edward Byers, *The Nation of Nantucket: Society and Politics in an Early American Commercial Center, 1660–1820* (1987), provides a comprehensive history of early Nantucket.

29. E. Hohman, supra note 27, at 9.

family than a civic community. . . . [T]he people were so law-abiding that
there was little or no government in evidence on the Island."[30] Many
Nantucketers shifted to New Bedford when it emerged as the leading
whaling center. There whaling also became a "neighborhood affair."[31]

The captains who commanded whaling ships occupied pivotal positions in the development and enforcement of whaling norms. Two captains based in the same small whaling port were unquestionably in a
close-knit group, and would be vulnerable, for example, to gossip about
misconduct at sea. Moreover, the captains' social circles tended to extend
well beyond their home ports. Migrants from Nantucket, the world's
wellspring of whaling talent, became influential not only in other New
England ports but also in foreign whaling nations. By 1812, for example,
149 different Nantucketers had commanded British whaling ships.[32]

Even whalers sailing from distant ports tended to socialize at sea. In
Moby-Dick, Melville portrays eight meetings between the *Pequod* and
other whaling vessels and devotes a chapter to the "gam."[33] A gam was a
friendly meeting between the officers of two whaling ships that had encountered each other at sea. Typically, the two captains would meet for
several hours on one ship, and the two chief mates on the other. One
reason for the gam was to obtain whaling intelligence. ("Have ye seen the
White Whale?") In addition, whaling ships might be on the high seas for
three or four years at a stretch. More than most seamen, whalers were
eager to pass on letters to or from home[34] and to trade to replenish supplies.[35] Although the gam was hardly a mandatory ritual among whalers,
only they, and no other seamen, engaged in the practice.[36]

Whalers also congregated in specialized layover ports. When the Pa-

---

30. C. Ashley, supra note 27, at 31.

31. Id. at 99. In developing the hypothesis of welfare-maximizing norms, I have treated
social conditions as largely exogenous. See supra Chapter 7, note 34. A more ambitious theory
might attempt to attribute the close-knittedness of the whalers' home ports to their recognition that a tight land-based social structure would abet cooperation at sea. See also infra
Chapter 13, text accompanying notes 9–26.

32. C. Ashley, supra note 27, at 26. See generally E. Stackpole, supra note 27, at 133–144,
390.

33. H. Melville, supra note 23, ch. 53, pp. 340–344.

34. Id. at 341; E. Hohman, supra note 27, at 87.

35. See, e.g., E. Keble Chatterton, *Whalers and Whaling* 111 (1926) (quoting the 1836 journal
of Samuel Joy, a New England whaling captain: "I got an anchor from an English ship for 40
lbs tobacco and a steering oar. . . .").

36. "So then, we see that of all ships separately sailing the sea, the whalers have most
reason to be sociable—and they are so." H. Melville, supra note 23, at 342. See also C. Ashley,
supra note 27, at 103–104; E. Hohman, supra note 27, at 16; Samuel Eliot Morison, *The
Maritime History of Massachusetts 1783–1860* 325 (1921).

cific fisheries developed, for instance, the Maui port of Lahaina emerged as a whalers' hangout in the Hawaiian Islands.

Hypothetical Whaling Norms

These close-knit whalers recognized that they needed norms to govern the ownership of whales that one ship had helped to kill, but that another ship had ultimately seized. To reduce deadweight losses, the whalers might have set a whaling ship's fraction of ownership to equal its fractional contribution to a capture. For example, a ship that had objectively contributed one-quarter the total value of work would be entitled to a one-quarter share. In the absence of this rule, opportunistic ships might decline to contribute cost-justified but underrewarded work.

This approach is too simple, however, because utilitarian whalers would also be concerned with the transaction costs associated with their rules. They would tend to prefer, for example, bright-line rules to fuzzy standards that would prolong disputes. Finding a cost-minimizing solution to whaling disputes is vexing because there is no ready measure of the relative value of separate contributions to a joint harvest. Any fine-tuning of incentives aimed at reducing deadweight losses is therefore certain to increase transaction costs.[37]

In no fishery did whalers adopt as norms any of a variety of rules that are transparently poor candidates for minimizing the sum of deadweight losses and transaction costs. An easily administered rule would be one that made the actual possession of a whale carcass normatively decisive. According to this rule, if Ship A had a live whale on a line, Ship B would be entitled to attach a stronger line and pull the whale in. A possession-decides rule of this sort might lead to serious deadweight losses, however, because it would encourage a ship to sit back like a vulture, freeload on others' efforts in the early stages of a hunt, and move in late in the chase. Whalers never used this norm.

Equally perverse would be a rule that a whale should belong entirely to the ship whose crew killed it. Besides risking ambiguities about the cause of a whale's demise, this rule would create inadequate incentives for whalers both to inflict nonmortal wounds and to harvest dead whales that had been lost or abandoned by the ships that had slain them.

---

37. This discussion assumes that welfare-maximizing whalers would ignore the risk that their actions might excessively deplete the stocks of whales. This assumption will be examined infra text following note 71.

To reward early participation in a hunt, whalers might have developed a norm that the first ship to lower a boat to pursue a whale had an exclusive right to capture so long as it remained in fresh pursuit. This particular rule would create numerous other difficulties, however. In addition to creating the potential for disputes over which ship had lowered a boat first, this rule would create strong incentives for the premature launch of boats and might work to bestow an exclusive opportunity to capture on a party less able than others to exploit that opportunity.[38]

Somewhat more responsive to incentive issues would be a rule that a whale belongs to a ship whose crew first obtained a "reasonable prospect" of capturing it and thereafter remained in fresh pursuit.[39] This rule would reward good performance during the early stages of a hunt, and would also free up lost or abandoned whales to later takers. A reasonable-prospect standard, however, is by far the most ambiguous of those yet mentioned, invites high transaction costs, and, like the other rules so far discussed, was not employed by whalers.

Actual Whaling Norms

Whalers developed an array of informal rules more utilitarian than any of the fanciful ones just presented. Evidence of the details of actual whaling norms is fragmentary. The best sources are the court reports in which evidence of usages was admitted, especially when the contesting whalers agreed on the usage and only disputed its application.[40] Seamen's journals, literary works such as *Moby-Dick,* and historical accounts provide additional glimpses of the rules in use.

38. According to John R. Bockstoce, *Whales, Ice, and Men: The History of Whaling in the Western Arctic* 61 (1986), whalers in the western Arctic had informally agreed to defer to the first boat in the water, but tended to ignore this agreement when whales were scarce. Bockstoce's authority for this proposition is thin. He apparently relies on William Fish Williams, "The Voyage of the *Florence,* 1873–1874," in *One Whaling Family* 368 (H. Williams ed. 1964), an old man's remembrance of a whaling voyage taken at age fifteen. The incident that prompted Williams' mention of this practice was one in which the whalers who deferred to another ship's lowered boats were "too far off to take any interest in the affair." More probative would have been an incident in which a ship nearer to a whale had deferred to a prior lowering by a more distant ship.

39. In his dissent in the staple Property casebook decision, Pierson v. Post, 3 Cai. R. 175, 2 Am. Dec. 264 (Sup. Ct. N.Y. 1805), Judge Livingston argued that a fox hunter with a "reasonable prospect of taking" his prey should prevail over the actual taker.

40. See Hogarth v. Jackson, 1 Moody & M. 58 (1827) (parties agreed that the fast-fish rule prevailed in the Greenland fishery); Swift v. Gifford, 23 Fed. Cas. 558 (D. Mass. 1872) (No. 13,696) (parties stipulated that New England whalers honored the first-iron rule).

Whaling norms were not tidy, and were certainly less tidy than Melville asserted in *Moby-Dick*.[41] Whalers developed three basic norms, each of which was adapted to its particular context. As will be evident, each of the three norms was sensitive to the goal of avoiding deadweight losses; each not only rewarded the ship whose crew had sunk the first harpoon but also enabled others to harvest dead or wounded whales that had seemingly been abandoned by prior hunters. All three norms were also sensitive to the problem of transaction costs. In particular, norms that bestowed on a whaling ship an exclusive right to capture tended to be shaped so as to provide relatively clear starting and ending points for the time period of that entitlement.

The fast-fish, loose-fish rule. Prior to 1800, the British whalers operating in the Greenland fishery established the norm that a claimant owned a whale, dead or alive, so long as the whale was fast—that is, physically connected by line or other device to the claimant's boat or ship.[42] This fast-fish rule was well suited to this fishery, because the prey hunted off Greenland was the right whale.[43] Right whales, compared with the sperm whales that later became American whalers' preferred prey, are both slow swimmers and feeble antagonists.[44] The British hunted them from sturdy whaling boats. Upon nearing a quarry, a harpooner would throw a harpoon with line attached. The trailing end of the line was tied to the boat.[45] So long as the harpoon both held fast to the whale and also remained connected by the line to the boat, the fast-fish norm entitled the harpooning boat to an exclusive claim of ownership superior to that of any sub-

41. See H. Melville, supra note 23, ch. 89.

42. Addison & Sons v. Row, 3 Paton 339 (1794); Hogarth v. Jackson, 1 Moody & M. 58 (1827). In Chapter 89 of *Moby-Dick*, Melville identified the fast-fish, loose-fish distinction as the governing principle among American whalers. Melville also noted at several points, however, that an American whaler who had merely placed a waif (a small, flagged pole) on a dead whale owned it so long as he evinced an intent and an ability to return. See H. Melville, supra note 23, at 500, 505. The evident tension between these two rules drew no comment from Melville.

43. The ambiguous term *right whale* is used here to refer to a family of closely related species of baleen whales. The two most commonly hunted species were the Biscayan right whale and the Greenland right whale (or bowhead).

44. Gordon Jackson, *The British Whaling Trade* 3–11 (1978); C. Ashley, supra note 27, at 65; E. Hohman, supra note 27, at 180. Some whaling crews, "though intelligent and courageous enough in offering battle to the Greenland or Right whale, would perhaps—either from professional inexperience, or incompetency, or timidity, decline a contest with the Sperm whale...." H. Melville, supra note 23, at 279. Needless to say, Melville's fictional and ferocious Moby-Dick was a sperm whale.

45. See C. Ashley, supra note 27, at 93.

sequent harpooner. If the whale happened to break free, either dead or alive, it was then regarded as a "loose fish" and was again up for grabs. Although whalers might occasionally dispute whether a whale had indeed been fast,[46] the fast-fish rule usually provided sharp beginning and ending points for a whaler's exclusive entitlement to capture and thus promised to limit the transaction costs involved in dispute resolution.

The fast-fish rule created incentives well adapted to the Britishers' situation in Greenland. Because right whales are slow and docile, a whale on a line was not likely to capsize the harpooning boat, break the line, or sound to such a depth that the boatmen had to relinquish the line. Thus the fast-fish rule was in practice highly likely to reward the first harpooner, who had performed the hardest part of the hunt, as opposed to free-riders waiting in the wings. Not uncommonly, however, a right whale sinks shortly after death, an event that requires the boatmen to cut their lines.[47] After a few days the sunken whale bloats and resurfaces. At that point the fast-fish rule entitled a subsequent finder to seize the carcass as a loose fish, a utilitarian result because the ship that had killed the whale might be far distant by then. In sum, the fast-fish rule was a bright-line rule that created incentives for both first pursuers of live whales and final takers of lost dead whales.

The iron-holds-the-whale rule. In fisheries where the more vigorous sperm whales predominated, whalers tended to shift away from the fast-fish rule. The evidence on whalers' practices is too fragmentary to allow any confident assertion about when and where this occurred. The fast-fish rule's main competitor—the rule that "iron holds the whale"—also provided incentives for whalers to perform the hardest part of the hunt. Stated in its broadest form, this norm conferred an exclusive right to capture upon a whaler who had first affixed a harpoon, lance, or other whaling weapon to the body of the whale. The iron-holds-the-whale rule differed from the fast-fish rule in that the weapon did not have to be connected by line or other means to the claimant. The norm-makers had to create a termination point for the exclusive right to capture, however, because it would be foolish for a Moby Dick to belong to an Ahab who had sunk an ineffectual harpoon days or years before. Whalers therefore allowed an iron to hold a whale only during the time that the claimant remained in fresh pursuit of the iron-bearing animal. In some contexts,

46. See Hogarth v. Jackson, 1 Moody & M. 58 (1827) (whale merely entangled in a line is fast).

47. E. Hohman, supra note 27, at 165n. H. Melville, supra note 23, at 468, asserted that twenty slain right whales sink for every sperm whale that does.

the iron-affixing claimant also had to assert the claim before a subsequent taker had begun to "cut in" (strip the blubber from) the carcass.[48]

American whalers tended to adopt the iron-holds-the-whale rule wherever it was a utilitarian response to how and what they hunted.[49] Following Native American practices, some early New England seamen employed devices called drogues to catch whales. A drogue was a wooden float, perhaps two feet square, to which the trailing end of a harpoon line was attached. The drogue was thrown overboard from a whaling boat after the harpoon on the leading end of the line had been cast into the whale. This technique served both to tire the animal and to mark its location, thus setting up the final kill.[50] Because a whale towing a drogue was not physically connected to the harpooning boat, the fast-fish rule provided no protection to the crew that had attached the drogue. By contrast, the iron-holds-the-whale rule, coupled with a fresh-pursuit requirement, created incentives suitable for drogue fishing.[51]

The latter rule had particular advantages to whalers hunting sperm whales. Because sperm whales swim faster, dive deeper, and fight more viciously than right whales do, they were more suitable targets for drogue fishing. New Englanders eventually did learn how to hunt sperm whales

48. Although the phrase *fresh pursuit* does not appear in whaling lore, it nicely expresses the notion that the crew of the first ship to affix an iron had rights only so long as it both intended to take the whale and also had a good chance of accomplishing that feat.

49. "The parties filed a written stipulation that witnesses of competent experience would testify, that, during the whole time of memory of the eldest masters of whaling ships, the usage had been uniform in the whole fishery of Nantucket and New Bedford that a whale belonged to the vessel whose iron first remained in it, provided claim was made before cutting in." Swift v. Gifford, 23 Fed. Cas. 558, 558 (D. Mass. 1872) (No. 13,696). The *Swift* opinion also cited Bourne v. Ashley, 3 Fed. Cas. 1002 (D. Mass. 1863) (No. 1698), to the effect that the usage of the first iron had been proved to exist as far back as 1800. *Swift* held that this usage was a reasonable one and was applicable to a dispute over a whale caught in the sea of Okhotsk, located east of Siberia and north of Japan. It is highly doubtful, however, that the usage of the first iron was as universal among New Englanders as the parties had stipulated in *Swift*. The *Swift* opinion itself mentioned British cases that described other usages in effect among the international community of whalers in the Greenland and mid-Pacific fisheries. See also H. Melville, supra note 23, at 505, for the irreconcilable assertion that American whalers honored the fast-fish rule.

50. See C. Ashley, supra note 27, at 89–93; H. Melville, supra note 23, at 495. The barrels used to slow the great white shark in the film *Jaws* (Universal 1975) are the modern equivalents of drogues.

51. In Aberdeen Arctic Co. v. Sutter, 4 Macq. 355, 3 Eng. Ruling Cas. 93 (1862), the defendant had seized in the Greenland fishery a whale that the plaintiff's Eskimo employees had fettered with a drogue but not captured. The court held for the defendant because the plaintiff had failed to prove any exception to the fast-fish usage, which was well established in the Greenland fishery.

with harpoons attached by lines to boats.[52] The vigor of the sperm whale compared with that of the right whale, however, increased the chance that the line would not hold or would have to be cut to save the boat. A "fastness" requirement would thus materially reduce the incentives of competing boatmen to make the first strike. The iron-holds-the-whale rule, by contrast, was a relatively bright-line way of rewarding whoever won the race to accomplish the major feat of sinking the first harpoon into a sperm whale. It also rewarded the persistent and skillful because it conferred its benefits only so long as fresh pursuit was maintained.

Most important, sperm whales, unlike right whales, are social animals that tend to swim in schools.[53] To maximize the total catch, whalers' norms had to encourage boatmen who had discovered a school to kill or mortally wound as many animals as quickly as possible, without pausing to secure the stricken whales to the mother ship.[54] Fettering whales with drogues was an adaptive technology in these situations. The haste that the schooling of whales prompted among hunters also fostered the related usage that a waif holds a whale. A waif is a pole with a small flag atop. Planting a waif into a dead whale came to signify that the whaler who had planted the waif was claiming the whale, was nearby, and intended to return soon. When those conditions were met, the usages of American whalers in the Pacific allowed a waif to hold a whale.[55] Because a ship might lose track of a whale it had harpooned or waifed, whaling norms could not allow a whaling craft to hold a whale forever. When a mere harpoon (or lance) had been attached, and thus it was not certain that the harpooning party had ever fully controlled the whale, the harpooning party had to be in fresh pursuit and also had to assert the claim before a subsequent taker had begun the process of cutting in.[56] On the

52. C. Ashley, supra note 27, at 65–66, 92–93.

53. Id. at 75; H. Melville, supra note 23, ch. 88.

54. In two instances in the Galápagos fishery, single ships came upon schools of sperm whales and single-handedly killed ten or more in one day. E. Stackpole, supra note 27, at 401.

55. In two cases arising in the Sea of Okhotsk the defendants had slaughtered whales that the plaintiffs had waifed and anchored on the previous day. The plaintiffs prevailed in both. See Bartlett v. Budd, 2 Fed. Cas. 966 (D. Mass. 1868) (No. 1075) (plaintiff, who had proved the usage that a waif holds a whale, was independently entitled to recover as a matter of property law); Taber v. Jenny, 23 Fed. Cas. 605 (D. Mass. 1856) (No. 13,720) (plaintiff, who had a high probability of retaking the whale, should prevail as a matter of property law over defendant, who should have known from the appearance of the whale that it had been killed within the previous twelve hours).

56. See Heppingstone v. Mammen, 2 Hawaii 707, 712 (1863); Swift v. Gifford, 23 Fed. Cas. 558, 558–559 (D. Mass. 1872) (No. 13,696). E. Hohman, supra note 27, at 166, asserted, without citing authority, that a subsequent taker of a sperm whale bearing whaling iron also had to give the owner of the iron a reasonable length of time to retake the whale. Cutting in was a

other hand, when a waif, anchor, or other evidence of certain prior control had been planted, the planting party had to be given a reasonable period of time to retake the whale, and hence might prevail even after the subsequent taker had completed cutting in.[57]

Because the iron-holds-the-whale usage required determinations of the freshness of pursuit and sometimes of the reasonableness of the time period elapsed, it was inherently more ambiguous than the fast-fish norm was. By hypothesis, this is why the whalers who pursued right whales off Greenland preferred the fast-fish rule. The rule that iron holds the whale, however, provided better-tailored incentives in situations where drogues were the best whaling technology and where whales tended to swim in schools. In these contexts, according to the hypothesis, whalers switched to iron holds the whale because that rule's advantages in reducing deadweight losses outweighed its transaction-cost disadvantages.

Rules that split ownership. In a few contexts whaling norms called for the value of the carcass to be split between the first harpooner and the ultimate seizer.[58] An English decision enforced a practice arising in the fishery around the Galápagos Islands that a whaler who had fettered a sperm whale with a drogue was entitled to share the spoils fifty-fifty with the ultimate taker of the carcass.[59] The court offered no explanation for the different norm that had arisen there, although it seemed aware that sperm whales were often found in large schools in that fishery. The utilitarian division of labor in harvesting a school of whales is different than

---

laborious process that involved the whole crew. It could not be begun until after the crew had chained the whale to the ship and rigged up special slaughtering equipment. See H. Melville, supra note 23, chs. 66–67; E. Hohman, supra note 27, at 167. Hohman stated that if the first vessel to have attached a harpoon or lance were to come upon a subsequent taker who had justifiably begun to cut in, the first vessel remained entitled to any blubber still in the water. Id. at 166.

57. See Bartlett v. Budd, 2 Fed. Cas. 966 (D. Mass. 1868) (No. 1075) (defendant had cut in on the day after the plaintiff's crew had killed, anchored, and waifed the whale); see also E. Hohman, supra note 27, at 166 ("Thus a carcass containing the 'waif' of a vessel believed to be in the general vicinity was never disturbed by another whaler.").

58. A fact-specific example of this solution is Heppingstone v. Mammen, 2 Hawaii 707 (1863), where the court split a whale fifty-fifty between the owner of the first iron and the ultimate taker. The crew of the *Oregon* had badly wounded the whale in an initial attack but had been on the brink of losing it when it was caught and killed by the crew of the *Richmond*. The *Richmond* then surrendered the carcass to the *Oregon*, whose captain refused the *Richmond*'s request for a half share. In light of the uncertainty that the *Oregon* would have retaken the whale, the court rendered the Solomonic solution that the *Richmond*'s captain had proposed.

59. Fennings v. Lord Grenville, 1 Taunt. 241, 127 Eng. Rep. 825 (Ct. Comm. Pleas 1808).

that for hunting a single whale. The first whaling ship to come upon a large school should fetter as many animals as possible with drogues and leave to later-arriving ships the task of capturing and killing the encumbered animals.[60] The Galápagos norm enabled this division of labor. It also split ownership fifty-fifty, a focal-point solution that is administratively simple and tends to help foster a spirit of cooperation.[61]

Better documented is the New England coastal tradition of splitting a beached or floating dead whale between its killer and the person who finally finds it. The best known of the U.S. judicial decisions on whales, *Ghen v. Rich,*[62] involved a dispute over the ownership of a dead finback whale beached in eastern Cape Cod. Because finback whales are exceptionally fast swimmers, whalers of the late nineteenth century slew them from afar with bomb-lances. A finback whale killed in this way immediately sank to the bottom and typically washed up on shore some days later. The plaintiff in *Ghen* had killed a finback whale with a bomb-lance. When the whale later washed up on the beach, a stranger found it and sold it to the defendant tryworks. The trial judge held a hearing that convinced him that there existed a usage on the far reaches of Cape Cod that entitled the bomb-lancer to have the carcass of the dead animal, provided in the usual case that the lancer pay a small amount (a "reasonable salvage") to the stranger who had found the carcass on the beach. As was typical in whaling litigation, the court deferred to this norm and held the tryworks liable for damages, reasoning: "Unless it is sustained, this branch of industry must necessarily cease, for no person would engage in it if the fruits of his labor could be appropriated by any chance finder.... That the rule works well in practice is shown by the extent of the industry which has grown up under it, and the general acquiescence of a whole community interested to dispute it."[63]

The norm enforced in *Ghen* divided ownership of a beached finback whale roughly according to the opportunity costs of the labor that the whaler and beach-finder had expended. It thus ingeniously enabled dis-

---

60. In *Fennings* the plaintiff had in fact left the drogued whale in order to pursue another.

61. The act of splitting benefits (or burdens) in precisely equal fractions among members of a group is a weak signal that the members are of equal status, a message that itself tends to promote mutual respect and future cooperation. A fifty-fifty split between two parties promotes solidarity better than, say, a sixty-forty split does. This may be one reason why friends who dine together at a restaurant commonly pay equal shares of the check when their consumption has been roughly equal, and why modern law tends to split property acquired during marriage equally between spouses. See generally infra Chapter 13, text at notes 9–17.

62. 8 F. 159 (D. Mass. 1881).

63. Id. at 162.

tant and unsupervised specialized laborers with complementary skills to coordinate with one another by implicit social contract. According to the hypothesis, the remote location and small population of the far reaches of Cape Cod provided social conditions conducive to the evolution of this utilitarian solution. Local fishermen who engaged in offshore whaling apparently were able to use their informal social networks to control beachcombers who were not formally connected to the whaling industry.[64]

The choice between entitling the ultimate seizer to a preestablished fraction of the whale, such as the half awarded in the Galápagos, or to a "reasonable reward," as on Cape Cod, is a typical rule/standard conundrum. "Reasonableness" standards allow consideration of the exact relative contributions of the claimants. Compared with rules, however, standards are more likely to provoke disputes about proper application. The hypothesis supposes that norm-makers, seeing that rules better reduce transaction costs and that standards better reduce deadweight losses, develop workaday norms with an eye on minimizing *total* costs.[65]

Whaling Norms and Whaling Law

The example of the high-seas whalers illustrates, contrary to the legal-centralist view, that informal social networks are capable of creating rules that establish property rights. Whalers had little use for law or litigation. The five reported American cases resolving the ownership of whales at sea all arose out of the Sea of Okhotsk. With the exception of an 1872 decision[66] in which the year of the whale's capture was not indicated, all involved whales that were caught during the years 1852 to 1862. The lack of litigation over whale ownership prior to that period is remarkable for

64. Two centuries before *Ghen* New Englanders had enacted ordinances that dealt with an analogous problem. The seventeenth-century hunters of right whales in the near-shore Gulf Stream were better at killing them than at gaining control of their corpses. In 1688 the Plymouth Colony had rules requiring whalers to place identification marks on their lances and specifying how many shillings a finder who towed a dead whale ashore was to receive from the lancer. See George Francis Dow, *Whale Ships and Whaling* 9–10 (1925). Long Island laws of the same period called for the killer and the finder of a dead whale at sea to split it equally, and also entitled the finder of a whale carcass on a beach to receive a reward. Id. at 15.

65. The seminal works on choices between legal rules and standards are Isaac Ehrlich and Richard A. Posner, "An Economic Analysis of Legal Rulemaking," 3 *J. Legal Stud.* 257 (1974), and Duncan Kennedy, "Form and Substance in Private Law Adjudication," 89 *Harv. L. Rev.* 1685, 1687–1688 (1976). See also Colin S. Diver, "The Optimal Precision of Administrative Rules," 93 *Yale L.J.* 65 (1983).

66. Swift v. Gifford, 23 Fed. Cas. 558 (D. Mass. 1872)(No. 13,696).

two reasons. First, it suggests that for more than a century American whalers were able to resolve their disputes without any guidance from American courts. Second, whalers succeeded in doing this during a time period in which all British decisions on whale ownership supported norms other than the iron-holds-the-whale rule that the Americans were increasingly adopting.

Why litigation burst forth from incidents in the Sea of Okhotsk in the 1850s is unclear. One possibility is suggested by the fact that most of the whales found in that vicinity were bowheads, a relatively passive species.[67] For these baleen whales it may have been utilitarian for whalers to revert from the first-iron rule to the fast-fish rule. American whalers, accustomed to hunting sperm whales in the Pacific, may have had trouble making this switch.

A more straightforward explanation is that by the time this spate of litigation occurred the New England whaling community had become less close-knit. The American whaling industry had begun to decline during the 1850s and was then decimated during the Civil War, when several of these cases were being litigated.[68] The deviant whalers involved in the litigated cases, seeing themselves nearing their last periods of play, may have decided to defect. In two of the five reported cases arising out of the Sea of Okhotsk (*Swift* and *Bourne*), the opposing parties even operated out of the same port, New Bedford. When the whalers' social networks began to unravel, apparently even their informal headquarters was affected.

Were Whalers' Norms Welfare Maximizing?

Ex post explanations are less persuasive than successful ex ante predictions. An analyst armed with the hypothesis of welfare-maximizing norms would be unlikely to succeed in predicting the precise substantive whaling norms that would develop in a particular fishery. Information about costs and benefits is inevitably fuzzy, both to the norm-makers themselves and to analysts.[69] However, an analyst could confidently identify a large set of substantive norms that would *not* be observed, such as, in the whaling case, "possession decides," "the first boat in the water," or

---

67. J. Bockstoce, supra note 38, at 28–29.

68. E. Hohman, supra note 27, at 290–292, 302.

69. Compare Saul Levmore, "Variety and Uniformity in the Treatment of the Good-Faith Purchaser," 16 *J. Legal Stud.* 43 (1987) (predicting that, although all legal systems will easily decide that it is appropriate to deter theft, they will come up with a variety of solutions to the much more challenging problem of whether the original owner of stolen property should prevail over a good-faith purchaser of that property).

"a reasonable prospect of capture." The content of the three basic norms that the whalers did develop tends to support the hypothesis; all three were consistently sensitive to both production incentives and transaction costs and were adapted in utilitarian fashion to conditions prevailing in different fisheries.

Any ex post explanation risks being too pat, and this one is no exception. A critic might challenge the offered utilitarian interpretation on a number of grounds. First, the evidence suggests that whalers might have been wise to use the first-iron rule for sperm whales and the fast-fish rule for right whales. They did not, and instead varied their rules according to the location of the fishery, not according to species. Perhaps whalers anticipated that species-specific rules would engender more administrative complications than their fishery-specific rules did. Because there are dozens of whale species other than sperm and right whales, it may have been simplest to apply to all species in a fishery the rule of capture best suited to the most commercially valuable species found there. In addition, a cruising whaling ship had to have its boats and harpoons at the ready.[70] This necessity of prearming may have limited the whalers' ability to vary their capture techniques according to species.[71]

Second, a critic could assert that the whalers' norms were too short-sighted to be welfare maximizing. By abetting cooperation among small clusters of competing hunters, the norms aggravated the risk that whalers in the aggregate would engage in overwhaling. The nineteenth-century whalers in fact depleted their fisheries so rapidly that they were steadily impelled to fish in ever more remote seas. Had they developed norms that set quotas on catches, or that protected young or female whales, they might have been able to keep whaling stocks at levels that would have supported sustainable yields.

The rejoinders to this second criticism point up some general shortcomings of the informal system of social control in comparison with other social-control systems. Establishment of an appropriate quota system for whale fishing requires both a sophisticated scientific understanding of whale breeding and also an international system for monitoring worldwide catches. For a technically difficult and administratively complicated task such as this, a hierarchical organization, such as a formal trade association or a legal system, would likely outperform the diffuse social forces that make norms.[72] Whalers who recognized the risk of overfishing thus could rationally ignore that risk when making norms on

70. E. Chatterton, supra note 35, at 140.
71. I am grateful to Richard Craswell for this idea.
72. See infra Chapter 14, text at note 67.

the ground that norm-makers could make no cost-justified contribution to its solution.

Whalers might rationally have risked overwhaling for another reason. Even though overwhaling may not have been welfare maximizing from a global perspective, the rapid depletion of whaling stocks may well have been in the interest of the club of whalers centered in southern New England. From their parochial perspective, grabbing as many of the world's whales as quickly as possible was a plausibly welfare-maximizing strategy. These New Englanders might have feared entry into whaling by mariners based in the southern United States, Japan, or other ports that could prove to be beyond their control. Given this risk of hostile entry, New Englanders might have concluded that a quick kill was more advantageous for them than creating norms to stem the depletion of world whaling stocks. The whaling saga is thus a reminder that norms that enrich one group's members may impoverish, to a greater extent, those outside the group.

12

✳ ✳ ✳

Remedial Norms: Of Carrots and Sticks

All systems of social control require rules on remedies. Although re- medial rules indirectly *influence* everyday conduct (primary behav- ior), they *apply* only to the conduct of enforcers (secondary behavior). When an enforcer violates a remedial rule, the enforcer is himself subject to sanctions administered at the tertiary level of social control. If those tertiary-level enforcers were to misbehave, they would be subject to sanc- tions administered at the fourth level, and so on.[1]

It is hardly news that remedial rules pervade all areas of substantive law. Less familiar are the remedial rules that social groups develop to constrain enforcers other than the state. For example, when a group chooses self-help as its instrument of control, it must regulate the use of this high-risk technique. A person who exercises self-control is also guided by remedial rules; someone who has internalized the substantive norm of honesty will look to internalized remedial rules to determine *how much* guilt he should feel after telling a lie.

This chapter addresses the rules that constrain informal third-party en- forcers. The hypothesis predicts, as in other contexts, that remedial norms among the close-knit serve to minimize the sum of members' transaction costs and deadweight losses. The initial step toward remedial efficiency is accomplished through the adoption of substantive rules that divide human actions into three categories: deviant actions that should be punished, sur- passing actions that should be rewarded, and ordinary actions that warrant no response.[2] A second cluster of remedial questions centers on the *type* of remedy to be used when a punishment (or reward) is deemed appropriate. I will focus here on alternative forms of punishment. The legal system punishes by means of stigmatization, monetary penalties, incarceration, and other devices. Norm-makers also have an elaborate range of punish- ments, and tend to make utilitarian choices from among this array. Third,

1. See supra Chapter 7, text accompanying note 13.
2. Because the patterned administration of remedies creates substantive rules, what fol- lows will be closely related to some of the discussion in Chapter 11.

having chosen a particular type of remedy, enforcers must next determine how severe a dose to administer. If a system of informal control were to make a deviant liable for damages, for example, it would have to have rules on measuring damages. An enforcer who mismeasured remedies would himself be deserving of punishment, as when parents who underdiscipline (or overdiscipline) their children lose status among their adult friends. An informal system for measuring damages is needed generally to calibrate self-help, and particularly to enable people to follow an Even-Up strategy, an approach to workaday affairs that is outlined below.

How Enforcers Mix Punishments, Rewards, and Inaction

Economists primarily focus on the production of "goods" and "services," that is, human outputs that command positive prices. In a market economy, social control of productive activity is largely achieved through contracts, a mechanism that motivates producers via bargained-for rewards. Other mechanisms, such as norms and laws, may supplement the market by conferring noncontractual rewards on surpassers.

Less studied in economics are "bads" and "disservices," human actions that are welfare reducing in the aggregate. In contexts in which the members of a group can readily bribe deviants to stop their damaging actions, contracts could indeed control bads. For at least two reasons, however, a society is unlikely to rely much on voluntary contracting—or indeed on any system of rewards—to suppress bad behavior. First, a policy of bribing deviants to stop their antisocial activity would put more resources in the hands of people whose comparative advantage was the reduction of aggregate welfare. This would likely violate principles of distributive justice. Second, as was discussed in Chapter 7, by using the tripartite approach of punishing bad behavior, rewarding good behavior, and leaving ordinary behavior alone, a social group can greatly reduce the number of occasions in which sanctioning is needed and thereby economize on transaction costs.

In reality, social groups do typically turn to the coercive force of punishments, legal or informal, to deter the production of bads and disservices. The study of punishment is less the province of economists than it is of lawyers, who are specialists in state force; of sociologists, who are specialists in informal social controls; and of psychologists, who are specialists in guilt. Game theory also illuminates methods of suppressing bads and disservices. Problems of human coordination can be represented as non-zero-sum games. The two specific non-zero-sum games described in Chapter 9—the Prisoner's Dilemma and Specialized Labor—are predicted to give rise to different standard informal sanctions. Informal enforcers are predicted to tend to use punishments (such as negative gossip) to penalize Defections in Prisoner's Dilemmas and rewards (such as positive gossip) to compensate Work in Specialized Labor situations.

Punishment for Failure to Perform Routine Work

A coordination problem in which the cooperative outcome is reached when all players provide identical labor (that is, when there is no cheapest labor-provider) is best modeled as a Prisoner's Dilemma. An occasion for a round of applause is a situation of this sort.[3] In these contexts the hypothesis predicts that close-knit groups will generate a norm that all members should contribute, without prospect of reward, to producing this particular public good.[4] The reasoning behind this prediction is as follows: Because members of close-knit groups can be expected to succeed in applying norms to escape from Prisoner's Dilemmas, there will be many more acts of Cooperation than acts of Defection; it will therefore be cheaper to punish Defectors than to reward Cooperators. When most applaud, it is administratively easier to punish the few nonapplauders than to reward the many applauders. The Golden Rule and Kant's Categorical Imperative are broad aspirational statements that urge unrewarded cooperation in Prisoner's Dilemma situations.[5]

Shasta County residents currently use punishment-triggering rules to induce ranchers to supervise their cattle. Why don't they instead reward cattlemen who exercise care? For the reasons just presented, close-knit groups can induce *ordinary* care more cheaply through sticks than through carrots.[6] This can be seen by looking at a simplified model of a close-knit society. Assume that such a society were to exist in two time periods, one formative and the other mature. If the hypothesis is correct,

3. Applause is not primary behavior; it is a reward administered at the secondary level of social control. Routine volunteer activities, such as the provision of labor to help monitor controlled burns in Shasta County or of snacks during halftimes at youth soccer games, are examples of routinely provided work at the primary level.

4. To economists, a *pure public good* is an activity whose benefits are universally available and nonrivalrously consumed. (Activities that bestow benefits unevenly are impure public goods.) The term *public good* is misleading in some contexts, because, contrary to the analysis in the text, it implies that a supplier of the good in question should invariably be rewarded.

5. Religions other than Christianity also endorse the Golden Rule. See Sissela Bok, *Lying: Moral Choice in Public and Private Life* 93n (1978) (Judaism and Confucianism).

6. Formative Anglo-American tort-law decisions defined negligence as a lack of "ordinary" care. See, e.g., Brown v. Kendall, 60 Mass. (6 Cush.) 292 (1850) ("ordinary care"); Vaughan v. Menlove, 3 Bing. (N.C.) 468, 132 Eng. Rep. 490 (C.P. 1837) (behavior of a person of "ordinary prudence").

during the formative period the society would develop and enforce norms to reduce the costs of accidents. During this initial stage these norms might be enforced by means of any imaginable combination of rewards for care and punishments for lack of care. Whatever the initial mix of sanctions, by the time the society had matured, the informal-control system would have molded most ordinary behavior into appropriately careful behavior. And, once behaving with appropriate care had become normal (though not necessarily universal), it would be administratively cheaper to punish the relatively rare instances of carelessness (or of the occurrence of accidents) than to reward careful behavior (or the nonoccurrence of accidents). In its mature stage, then, a welfare-maximizing society would generally rely on punishments to induce ordinary care.

Similarly, ranchers in Shasta County are expected to shoulder their share of producing routine local public goods, such as construction of boundary fencing and supervision of controlled burns. Because these work projects draw on skills that an ordinary rancher has, they are best modeled as Prisoner's Dilemmas.[7] The gossip mills of rural Shasta County are consequently more rife with negative gossip about free-riders (such as Frank Ellis) who shirk ordinary responsibilities than with positive gossip about ranchers who perform in the ordinary way. As another illustration, recall that Stephen Cheung found among orchardmen in Washington a custom that one should provide bees in proportion to one's trees. Cheung comments that "[o]ne failing to comply would be rated as a 'bad neighbor,' it is said, and could expect a number of inconveniences imposed on him by other orchard owners."[8] Washington orchardmen apparently informally punish those who fall below the bee standard, rather than informally rewarding those who meet it.

Rewards for Performing Unusual Work

Other public-goods problems are better modeled as Specialized Labor games. This is true when players have asymmetric abilities to provide

7. Each rancher, regardless of his subjective personal abilities, is required to meet the objective standard of what an ordinary rancher would do under the circumstances. This approach frees social controllers from inquiring into the exact abilities a particular party has. Negligence law has followed this approach since Vaughan v. Menlove, 3 Bing. (N.C.) 468, 132 Eng. Rep. 490 (C.P. 1837). This ordinary-person standard operates as a stick that goads people to acquire ordinary skills. Carrots are dangled to encourage people to acquire extraordinary skills, however. Because above-normal conduct, by definition, is relatively rare, it is administratively cheaper to reward cheapest labor-providers who have exhibited exceptional skills, knowledge, or daring than to punish those who have not.

8. Steven N. S. Cheung, "The Fable of the Bees: An Economic Investigation," 16 *J.L. & Econ.* 11, 30 (1973).

valuable work and the largest total payoff occurs when only the cheapest labor-provider works.[9] These situations require norms more sophisticated than the Golden Rule, because identical conduct is not desired from all.[10] From a static perspective, it might seem wise for members of a close-knit group to punish cheapest labor-providers who Shirk rather than to reward ones who Work; if cooperation (here, Work) were indeed rife among the close-knit, this approach would give rise to fewer occasions for sanctioning. From a dynamic perspective, however, a policy of punishing cheapest labor-providers would discourage people from pursuing desirable activities such as acquiring extraordinary skills and seeking out encountering situations in which they could act as heroic rescuers. This accounts for the assertion that close-knit societies tend to use rewards to induce Work in Specialized Labor situations.

In most Specialized Labor situations in a market economy, cooperative outcomes are reached through contractual exchange. The Shirker who would benefit from another's Work promises in advance to make explicit financial rewards to the Worker. Transaction costs, however, preclude the use of markets in a variety of situations where Work would be welfare enhancing. For example, a person in peril, such as a drowning swimmer, may lack the time, knowledge, or capacity to negotiate a Work contract with a would-be rescuer. In other contexts, specialized labor might benefit a numerous and diffuse group of persons, each of whom would be tempted to free-ride on others' contracts for that labor.

In Specialized Labor situations where norms would be a more economical device than contracts, the hypothesis predicts that members of close-knit groups will provide informal rewards to induce Work. More concretely, informal enforcers can be expected to confer high social status on leaders, role models, heroic rescuers, and other surpassing performers who provide services that are difficult to arrange by express agreement. Indeed, in rural Shasta County, the highest social status seemed reserved for ranchers, such as Dick Coombs, who by word and deed were most unswervingly committed to being good neighbors.

Choosing among Types of Self-Help Punishments

The homily "Two wrongs don't make a right" teaches that an enforcer who is entitled to administer some form of punishment is nevertheless constrained in choice of punishments. Remedial norms attempt to avoid

9. See supra Chapter 9, text accompanying notes 17–18.
10. Philosophers have long been aware of this point. See Edna Ullmann-Margalit, *The Emergence of Norms* 54 (1977).

"two wrongs" results. These norms govern both the permitted types of informal remedies, and also the sequence in which an informal enforcer should apply these remedies.

Informal Damages, Informal Injunctions

The standard remedy of a private-law litigant is an award of damages. In the domain of life governed by informal control, the analogue of an award of damages is an informal adjustment of mental accounts: the moral debtor is informally held to "owe," and is required eventually to repay, the moral creditor an appropriate amount. (The calculation of this amount will be taken up shortly.) Like the legal system, however, the informal control system does not rely entirely on compensatory forms of redress. For a variety of reasons, a grievant may see an entitlement to compensatory relief as inadequate. First, when the malefactor lacks the assets to make good on the debt, an award of informal damages is all but meaningless. Second, when a grievant is protected only with damages, anyone willing to pay the collectively set price can disrupt the grievant's world.[11]

Because of these shortcomings in compensatory relief, social-control systems develop rules to govern the availability of more extraordinary remedies. In a legal system, the usual extraordinary remedy is the injunction, which orders or forbids certain future actions. In a system of informal enforcement, the closest equivalent to the injunction is a freighted warning to the deviant. Many such warnings are partially veiled. A landowner who complains to a cattle owner about past trespasses is usually not only seeking to remedy those past events but also implicitly warning that any future trespasses will trigger increasingly harsh responses. Although a grievant's warning may sometimes spell out the dire consequences that deviants will suffer if they fail to comply, these consequences often remain vague. When informal injunctions are explicit, they are likely to incorporate the familiar phrase "or else."

To be worth more than an informal award of compensatory damages, an informal injunction must be backed with extra force—what Calabresi and Melamed call a "kicker."[12] Unlike law enforcers, informal enforcers cannot credibly use the threat of incarceration to undergird an informal

11. To prevent this sort of disruption, a social-control system must protect an entitlement with a property rule, that is, a rule that prohibits the disruption. See Guido Calabresi and A. Douglas Melamed, "Property Rules, Liability Rules, and Inalienability: One View of the Cathedral," 85 *Harv. L. Rev.* 1089, 1106–1110, 1124–1127 (1972).

12. Id. at 1126 & n.70.

injunction, because kidnapping is apt both to trigger a feud and to result in a criminal prosecution. Unable to employ incarceration, informal enforcers resort to the threat, or use, of measured violence. Indeed, according to Donald Black, a good portion of crime is actually undertaken to exercise social control.[13] In practice, then, remedial norms commonly entitle a grievant to issue an appropriately tailored injunction and to back it up with a threat of illegal self-help violence.

To be consistent with the hypothesis, remedial norms would permit the extraordinary remedy of the informal injunction only in contexts in which an ordinary person would regard an informal award of damages as inadequate. For example, when a person lacked the assets to repay an informal debt, remedial norms would be somewhat more accepting of threats of bodily violence. Similarly, an owner seeking to protect unique property would have readier recourse to an informal injunction than would an owner of fungible property.[14]

The Sequencing of Remedial Steps

Remedial norms require that an informal grievant exhaust, in sequence, a specified order of self-help measures.[15] When the grievant's remedy is limited to informal damages, as it usually is, remedial norms generally call for a grievant to proceed, until satisfied, by: (1) providing the deviant with notice of the informal debt, thereby enabling the deviant to resolve the matter voluntarily by means of a side-payment; (2) circulating truth-

---

13. See Donald Black, "Crime as Social Control," 48 *Am. Soc. Rev.* 34 (1983). The Shasta County field study turned up no evidence of remedial use of bodily violence to a deviant. This appears to be the ultimate self-help sanction. Some cultures have developed elaborate remedial norms to govern self-help mayhem. See Warren F. Schwartz, Keith Baxter, and David Ryan, "The Duel: Can These Gentlemen Be Acting Efficiently?" 13 *J. Legal Stud.* 321 (1984). Newspapers occasionally report escalating feuds between neighbors that have culminated in fatal gunfire. See Michael Norman, "Suburban Feud's End: One Dead and One Jailed," *N.Y. Times*, Oct. 11, 1984, p. B1, col. 1 (neighbors' feud snowballed in Long Island suburb, ending in death); "Feud over Goats Ends with Fatal Shooting," *S.F. Chron.*, Mar. 26, 1987, p. 28, col. 5 (landowner in rural Tehama County who had been a victim of trespassing goats slew neighbor who owned the goats).

14. The Shasta County field work turned up one instance of a possible injunction to protect unique property: Frank Ellis, an unreliable source, asserted that Doug Heinz had threatened to kill Ellis' cattle to protect the Heinz homestead from trespass. Heinz denied making this threat, however. See supra Chapter 2, text accompanying note 10.

15. A deviant's debt might have arisen in a variety of ways. For example, he might have been the sole Defector in a Prisoner's Dilemma situation or have failed to make a side-payment to compensate the grievant after the grievant had Worked in a Specialized Labor game.

ful negative gossip about the deviant's unpaid debt; and (3) physically seizing or destroying a measured amount of the deviant's assets.[16] According to the hypothesis, this pattern of escalating steps is designed to minimize the costs of effective deterrence. The basic logic of the system is transparent: the remedial devices most likely to be costly in and of themselves are not made available until less costly approaches have been tried without success.

Notice and gossip. Chapter 3 described the norms in Shasta County that govern responses to cattle trespass. These illustrate the proper sequence for exhausting informal remedies. When a rancher's cattle have escaped and caused harm, a victim's appropriate initial response is to notify the rancher of the event. Notice enables the cattleman to render an apology, a remedy sufficient to reestablish equilibrium after a de minimis trespass. After a serious trespass, however, the owner of the wayward livestock may have to make a gift to square the informal ledger.[17]

When a cattleman has failed to square accounts after proper notice, remedial norms entitle a trespass victim to increase the pressure by circulating truthful negative gossip about the cattleman's misconduct. The lash of negative gossip helps prompt its target to square accounts because a person's opportunities typically depend to a significant degree on reputation.[18] As a remedial measure, talk is cheap. Because lines of communication are already established, members of a close-knit group can

---

16. In some contexts remedial norms may eventually allow a grievant to take more extraordinary steps, such as bringing in a third party to help resolve the dispute or inflicting bodily harm on the deviant. Some trespass victims in Shasta County did complain to public officials. More commonly, however, they first resorted to measured self-help violence to property. On this choice, compare Sally Engle Merry, *Urban Danger: Life in a Neighborhood of Strangers* 178 (1981) (lower middle-class urbanites regard violent retaliation as more appropriate than calling the police), with M. P. Baumgartner, *The Moral Order of a Suburb* 80–82 (1988) (upper middle-class suburbanites rarely call officials, but even more rarely resort to violence).

17. As Chapter 13 will discuss, constitutive norms commonly call for informal debtors to make compensatory side-payments to neighbors in kind, not in cash.

18. Sociologists and anthropologists have repeatedly stressed the role of reputation and the power of gossip. See generally Sally Engle Merry, "Rethinking Gossip and Scandal," in 1 *Toward a General Theory of Social Control* 271 (Donald Black ed. 1984). Pertinent case studies include David M. Engel, "Cases, Conflict, and Accommodation: Patterns of Legal Interaction in a Small Community," 1983 *Am. Bar Found. Res. J.* 803, 825, 857–858; S. Merry, *Urban Danger,* supra note 16, at 186–188; Sally Falk Moore, "Law and Social Change: The Semi-Autonomous Social Field as an Appropriate Subject of Study," 7 *L. & Soc'y Rev.* 719, 729 (1973) (role of reputation in "better" women's dress industry). Economists and business scholars also acknowledge the importance of reputations. See, e.g., David M. Kreps, "Corporate Culture and Economic Theory," in *Perspectives on Positive Political Theory* 90 (James E. Alt and Kenneth A. Shepsle eds. 1990).

quickly spread negative gossip. Truthful negative gossip is also a less risky remedy than, say, the seizure of the deviant's assets, because the target of the gossip is less likely to mistake the remedial step as unprovoked aggression. Victims who retaliate with gossip are of course tightly constrained by the remedial norm that gossip must be truthful. This general principle is important enough to have earned a spot in the Ten Commandments: "Thou shalt not bear false witness against thy neighbour."[19]

Forceful destructions and seizures in Shasta County. Verbal remedies are too mild to discipline persistent Shasta County deviants such as Frank Ellis. Shasta County norms therefore entitle trespass victims who have exhausted the devices of notice and negative gossip, or for whom those remedial actions would obviously be fruitless,[20] to destroy or seize a measured amount of the deviant's property. These forceful forms of self-help are used more sparingly than verbal ones because they involve larger costs to victims and pose greater risks of further escalation. The most galling way to suffer a loss of property, all else equal, is to lose it to an intentional taker or destroyer. Consider a book in one's collection. The loss of this book to a thief or vandal is likely to be more upsetting than its loss through accident. Moreover, losing property already in one's possession tends to be more grievous than losing a prospect that an objective observer would regard as having equal value. These evaluative reactions may be partly a matter of human instinct.[21]

Remedial norms govern whether a destruction or seizure should be carried out openly or surreptitiously. When the person whose goods are subject to dispossession would be likely to agree on the amount of his prior informal debt, an enforcer who engages in a forceful dispossession should do so openly to publicize the extent to which he has squared accounts through self-help.[22] An enforcer is likely to be permitted to carry out a forceful dispossession on the sly, however, when the dispossessed

19. Exodus 20:16. See also Merry, "Law and Social Change," supra note 18, at 276; Arthur J. Vidich and Joseph Bensman, *Small Town in Mass Society* 36 (rev. ed. 1968) (the "most despised person in the community" is one who maliciously spreads false gossip).

20. For example, because outsiders are not vulnerable to adverse gossip, insiders need not exhaust that remedy against them. As a result, grievants are permitted to turn to violence against outsiders more quickly than against insiders. See Jonathan Rieder, "The Social Organization of Vengeance," in 1 *Toward a General Theory of Social Control* 131, 153–157 (Donald Black ed. 1984).

21. See Ellickson, "Bringing Culture and Human Frailty to Rational Actors: A Critique of Classical Law and Economics," 65 *Chi.-Kent L. Rev.* 23, 35–40 (1989) (on Tversky and Kahneman's prospect theory). Evolutionary processes might possibly select for a human tendency to retaliate against an intentional taker of possessions.

22. See also infra Chapter 13, text accompanying note 6.

party would be likely to underestimate the amount of his informal debt. A debtor who undervalues his debt may wrongly regard an objectively justified remedial action as excessive. In such an instance, protecting the anonymity of the rightful dispossessor helps reduce the risk of subsequent feuding.

Although both destructions and seizures deprive the dispossessed party of property, these two self-help remedies vary in their cost-effectiveness. A retaliatory destruction has an obvious disadvantage: it damages an asset—imposing a deadweight loss on group members as a whole. Application of the remedy of an eye for an eye, for example, brings about the loss of a second eye. If the loser of the first eye were instead to seize money or goods, that dire consequence would be avoided.[23] As a result, one might always expect norm-makers to prefer forceful seizures over forceful destructions. The field evidence reviewed below, however, does not support this generalization.

The major disadvantage of a seizure, as opposed to a destruction, is that someone who loses property to an intentional taker is more likely to interpret the event as an act of initial aggression than as an exercise in self-help. For example, when Owen Shellworth "borrowed" Frank Ellis' bulldozer to collect the fence debt Ellis informally owed him, Ellis might have mistakenly thought Shellworth was stealing the bulldozer, and gone after him with a shotgun. If Shellworth had only vandalized the bulldozer, it is more certain that Ellis would have understood the event as an enforcer's attempt to exercise informal control.

Many informal remedies commonly used in Shasta County create deadweight losses of a sort that unmistakably signal that the enforcer was seeking only to exercise self-help.[24] Consider the remedial norm that entitles a victim of repeated, unredressed trespasses to herd the offending livestock to a place inconvenient for the stock owner. When applied, this remedy requires both the trespass victim and the cattle owner to engage in offsetting—and hence unproductive—cattle driving. Nevertheless, the

---

23. If group members were to give weight to the policy goal of compensating losses (perhaps on loss-spreading grounds), they would have yet another reason for preferring a retaliatory seizure to a retaliatory destruction. The hypothesis supposes, however, that risk-distribution goals do not influence the content of workaday norms. See supra Chapter 10, note 22.

24. Analogous signals are employed in urban settings. See Suzann R. Thomas-Buckle and Leonard G. Buckle, "Doing Unto Others: Disputes and Dispute Processing in an Urban Neighborhood," in *Neighborhood Justice* 78, 86–87 (Roman Tomasic and Malcolm M. Feeley eds. 1982) (an appropriate informal punishment for repeated misparking is the spray-painting oᶠ graffiti on the vehicle).

remedy is ingenious in that it can be interpreted only as someone's effort to exercise social control.

Cattle-trespass victims who have exhausted milder remedies are also entitled to inflict a measured amount of mayhem on invading livestock. In Shasta County I learned of several instances of retaliatory wounding of animals.[25] Of these, Tony Morton's remedial destruction was the most creative. After exhausting lesser self-help remedies, Morton surreptitiously castrated a bull that had repeatedly trespassed. Because castration saps a bull's ferocity, Morton's revenge served as a permanent injunction against its future trespassing.

Why aren't victims permitted to slaughter trespassing stock for meat, a sanction that often would avoid some of the waste that arises from wounding? A partial answer is that a stockman might misinterpret the slaughter of his animals as rustling, which in cattle country is one of the most serious acts of initial aggression. The Morton incident points up two other potential advantages of a destruction as opposed to a seizure. First, the amount of a destruction can be calibrated to equal the debt; a seizure, by contrast, presents an all-or-nothing choice. Second, an informal enforcer concerned about avoiding or terminating a feud wants to be able to act surreptitiously, and a destruction is usually easier than a seizure to cover up. If Morton had taken the bull, for example, his neighbor might later have seen the bull in one of Morton's fields.

The field study in Shasta County turned up only one instance of the self-help _seizure_ of trespassing cattle. Doug Heinz resorted to this remedy after his repeated verbal complaints to Frank Ellis had proved fruitless.[26] Ellis later discovered the cattle in Heinz' possession and insisted on their return. Heinz complied with Ellis' demand, perhaps in part to eliminate ambiguity about his reason for taking the cattle. (The elaborate procedural constraints on the exercise of the ancient legal remedy of "distraining cattle damage feasant," found in statutes such as California's Estray Act, seem partly designed to reduce the risk of ambiguity about the purpose of a seizure.)[27] Because Heinz returned the animals to Ellis before

25. See supra Chapter 3, text following note 58.
26. See supra Chapter 3, text accompanying notes 65–66.
27. See supra Chapter 3, note 29 and accompanying text. A defendant is more likely to accede to an adverse judgment when a neutral third party has rendered that judgment. As a result, risks of escalation and feuding among disputants are likely to be lower after a legal judgment than after a private seizure of uncertain motivation. Because of its greater neutrality, a legal system can employ the remedy of damages, which ultimately functions as a forcible seizure, as its standard private remedy. Conversely, modern legal systems almost never make use of the forcible destructions that are prominent in informal-control systems. See also Rich-

receiving compensation for his costs of pasturing them, he signaled that he lacked backbone as an informal enforcer. This encouraged Ellis, ever the bully, to renege on his promise of later paying pasturage to Heinz. Heinz' mishandling of his self-help remedies eventually led him to escalate with a lawsuit to recover the pasturage Ellis owed him.

Exhaustion of remedies in other social environments. Investigators of other close-knit societies have turned up complex systems of remedial norms. James Acheson found that the lobstermen of Maine, for example, have informally divided their fishing grounds into exclusive territories. When an interloper sets lobster traps in someone else's territory, the first remedial step is a warning:

> The violator is usually warned, sometimes by verbal threats and abuse, but usually by surreptitious molestation of lobstering gear. Two half-hitches of rope may be tied around the spindle of the buoy, or legal-sized lobsters may be taken out and the doors of the traps left open. Fishermen have been known to leave threatening notes in bottles inside the offending traps, and one colorful islander carves a representation of female genitalia in the styrofoam buoys. Most interlopers move their gear when warned in these ways.[28]

When a warning does not suffice, lobstermen are entitled to move on to stiffer remedial actions. Acheson makes no mention of the device of negative gossip, perhaps because the lobstermen either do not share membership in a close-knit group with the interloper or are unable to identify him. Lobstermen instead jump immediately to the use of force. Like ranchers in Shasta County, they tend to prefer anonymous forceful destructions to forceful seizures:

> If the violations persist, the traps are destroyed. Fishermen have destroyed traps by "carving them up a little" with a chain saw or by smashing them with sledge hammers. When such traps are pulled [out of the water], the owner has little doubt as to what has happened. Usually, however, the offending traps are cut off: they are pulled, the buoy toggles and warp line are cut, and the trap is pushed into deep water, where there is little chance of finding it.[29]

---

ard A. Posner, *The Economics of Justice* 192–193 (1981) (contrasting current tort remedies with remedies in use in primitive societies).

28. James M. Acheson, *The Lobster Gangs of Maine* 74 (1988).

29. Id.

This last move can be seen as a more severe version of the cattle-trespass victim's act of herding stock to a remote location. Observe that a Maine lobsterman does not seize a trespasser's traps for personal use; that remedial step might be misinterpreted. As Acheson notes:

> The norms [of territoriality] are ... widely obeyed, and although the entire coast is patrolled by only a few wardens, there is little trouble. Fishermen are very careful to punish intruders in ways that will not provoke a massive, violent response. According to one fisherman, "The trick to driving a man [out of the area] is to cut off just one or two traps at a time." This harassment makes it unprofitable to fish an area but does not challenge a man to open warfare, since he can only guess who cut his traps.[30]

This pattern of gradual escalation of force against unresponsive deviants pervades a wide variety of social-control systems. Criminal-law systems are harsher on repeat offenders, and so are organizations. The leaders of the kibbutzim of Israel gradually escalate the forcefulness of their organizational responses against antisocial members—from informal negative gossip, to official rebuke at a group meeting, to the ultimate punishment of expulsion.[31] Schools and universities similarly tend to levy increasing sanctions against students who have posed repeated disciplinary problems. Indeed, even animals, when they engage in contests against one another, slowly escalate the aggressiveness of their acts.[32]

Measuring Damages in a System of Norms

An informal system of social control requires rules on the measurement of damage that are at least as elaborate as those found in a legal system. First, there must be rules to measure the magnitude of the informal debts that arise from primary behavior. Rules of this sort determine how large a voluntary side-payment the deviant has to make to meet the pledge, "I'll make it up to you." Second, because compensation is often provided in the form of conferrals of goods or services, rules are needed for the valuation of these in-kind transfers. For example, to what extent does one's service of keeping an eye on a neighbor's house during the neigh-

30. Id. at 75.
31. See Melford E. Spiro, *Kibbutz: Adventure in Utopia* 101–103 (rev. ed. 1970); see also Richard Schwartz, "Social Factors in the Development of Legal Control: A Case Study of Two Israeli Settlements," 63 *Yale L.J.* 471, 489 (1954).
32. See John Maynard Smith, *Evolution and the Theory of Games* 149 (1982).

bor's vacations compensate for one's failure to share in maintaining the common boundary fence? Third, a victim informally privileged to resort to self-help force needs a valuation system to determine how much of the deviant's assets to destroy or seize. Was Tony Morton privileged to castrate a bull that had repeatedly trespassed? Although makers of remedial norms might set the quantum of forfeitable assets to equal the amount of the outstanding debt, they might also, for example, raise the forfeitable amount for deterrence reasons.

Informal rules on these issues can help members of a close-knit group achieve cooperative outcomes. First, as will be shown, the proper calibration of remedies can encourage cooperative primary behavior. Second, the presence of rules on remedies helps people settle their disputes. If a victim and a grievant valuated informal damages differently they would have difficulty squaring their interpersonal accounts. If the victim's estimate of damages exceeded the deviant's estimate, the victim might forcefully retaliate after the deviant had made an "inadequate" payment. The deviant might in turn retaliate against the grievant's "unjustified" use of force, and a continuing feud would ensue.[33] Conversely, if the deviant's valuation of his debt exceeded the victim's, a continuing cycle of reciprocated gift-giving might result. Either of these failures to achieve equilibrium would be administratively costly and, in the case of feuds, might ultimately result in violent destruction.[34]

Game theory helps to reveal how utilitarian norm-makers calculate the size of informal debts that arise out of primary behavior. The Prisoner's Dilemma can be used to illustrate the measure of damages for the violation of standards of behavior that apply to all actors (as the basic rules of tort law do). The Specialized Labor game can be used to illustrate the measure of the rewards that cheapest labor-providers are to receive when

---

33. For a description of perhaps the most notorious feud in the United States, in which twelve people died over the course of as many years, see Altina L. Waller, *Feud: Hatfields, McCoys, and Social Change in Appalachia, 1860–1900* (1988). The risk of differences in valuation may explain why remedial norms often support, after the exhaustion of lesser remedies, *anonymous* acts of measured destruction. See supra text accompanying note 22.

34. Because damage awards are based on the losses that an ordinary member of the group would suffer, unusually sensitive persons are likely to regard informal damage awards as undercompensatory. To illustrate, someone unusually squeamish about the presence of cattle might regard as inadequate the informal compensation to which victims of breaches of cattle-supervision norms are entitled. The upshot is that a hypersensitive person must bear the burden of arranging for special preventive measures to protect himself. This is analogous to the way in which nuisance law treats the issue of hypersensitivity. See Ellickson, "Alternatives to Zoning: Covenants, Nuisance Rules, and Fines as Land Use Controls," 40 *U. Chi. L. Rev.* 681, 751–757 (1973).

Table 12.1   The Results of $(B - D)$ Punishments for Defections in Prisoner's
Dilemma Games

		Player Two	
		Cooperate	Defect
Player One	Cooperate	B, B	$B, A - (B - D)$
	Defect	$A - (B - D), B$	C, C

Note: $A>B>C>D$, and, because it is a Prisoner's Dilemma, $2B>A+D$.

they perform surpassing work (the problem of unjust enrichment in contract law). The analysis will identify a utilitarian formula for damages,
termed the *liquidated-Kantian formula,* that is identical in both contexts.
This formula works to bestow on the player who has alone chosen to
Cooperate or Work an amount equal to the objective costs he incurred
because the other player failed to choose the same course of action. This
simple measure of damages will be shown to provide incentives for cooperative primary play in most contexts.[35]

The Debit for a Defection in a Prisoner's Dilemma

In the simple Prisoner's Dilemma in Table 9.1, if Player One were to
Cooperate and Player Two were to Defect, Player One's payoff would be
reduced from 3 to 0 by Player Two's failure to emulate his cooperative
behavior. According to the test just proposed, Player One's damages
therefore should be set equal to 3. In an informal system of social control,
Player Two would mentally enter a credit of that amount in favor of
Player One, and Player One would conversely mentally enter that amount
of debit for Player Two.

In the algebraic Prisoner's Dilemma in Table 9.2, the liquidated-Kantian formula indicates that the damages due after the "tort" of Defection
should be set at $B - D$. If certain to be forthcoming, this measure of
damages would reduce the payoffs of a sole defector by $B - D$, and
increase the payoffs of a sole cooperator by a like amount. These alterations would convert the objective payoffs in the Prisoner's Dilemma in
Table 9.2 to those in Table 12.1.

35. The discussion in the text is limited to the measurement of compensation in some
specific two-person games; it does not explore whether the results can be extended to other
sorts of games.

The dominant strategy for both players in Table 12.1 is Cooperation. Because the matrix is symmetrical, Player One's situation need only be examined to show that this is so. If Player Two were about to Defect, Player One would be better off Cooperating because $B > C$. If Player Two were about to Cooperate, Player One would be better off Cooperating if $B > A - (B - D)$. This equation can be transposed to $2B > A + D$, which was stipulated as true for a Prisoner's Dilemma. Therefore, when remedial rules calculate the informal debt for a unilateral Defection at $B - D$, and a Cooperator's collection of that debt is certain, rational actors will Cooperate in Prisoner's Dilemma games.

The utilitarian advantage of the liquidated-Kantian formula is not simply that it creates incentives for proper play. The formula also makes use of information, namely, the magnitudes of B and D, that both players want to gather before making their choice among plays. That no new appraisals are needed during the enforcement stage promises to reduce transaction costs.

The Credit for Work in a Specialized Labor Game

An algebraic form of the Specialized Labor game was introduced in Table 9.3. In this game, $B - D$ is also prima facie a welfare-maximizing measure of the reward that a Shirker should pay to a cheapest labor-provider who has Worked. Recall that the welfare-maximizing outcome occurs in this game when the cheapest labor-provider Works and the other player Shirks. If the rightful Shirker were certain to compensate the cheapest labor-provider with a reward of $B - D$ for Working, the payoffs in Table 9.3 would be transformed into those in Table 12.2.

In Table 12.2, Player Two's dominant strategy is to Shirk, the choice a welfare-maximizing group would want him to make. This is true because if Player One were about to Shirk, Player Two, preferring C to E,

Table 12.2   The Results of $(B - D)$ Credits for Work in Specialized Labor Games

| | | Player Two | |
		Work	Shirk
Player One	Work	B, B	$B, A - (B - D)$
	Shirk	A, E	C, C

Note: $A>B>C>D>E$, and, because it is a Specialized Labor game, $A+D>2B$.

would also opt to Shirk. And if Player One (the cheapest labor-provider) were about to Work, Player Two would prefer to Shirk if $A - (B - D) > B$. This equation transposes to $A + D > 2B$, which was stipulated to be true for a Specialized Labor game. Player One, anticipating that Player Two would decide to Shirk, would choose to Work, because $B > C$. Thus, if the liquidated-Kantian formula, $B - D$, were employed to measure the reward for specialized labor, and if it were certain that the benefited Shirker would pay this amount to the Worker, rational actors would have incentives to achieve cooperative outcomes in Specialized Labor games. As in the Prisoner's Dilemma, the $B - D$ measure has the advantage of making use of information that players would want to gather before choosing their primary plays.[36]

Other damage formulas that might be constructed from the existing entries in the game matrix would create less precise incentives. For example, remedial norms might entitle a Worker to a reward of $C - D$, that is, *restitution* of the out-of-pocket costs of being the sole Worker. This damage formula, however, would, when Player Two could be expected to Shirk, make the cheapest labor-provider no more than indifferent to the choice of Working or Shirking; Player One would net C either way. Alternatively, the remedial rule might require Player Two to *disgorge* $A - C$, his benefits from Player One's decision to Work. The problem with this measure is that it creates the wrong incentives for Player Two. Player Two would net B if he also Worked, but a lesser amount, C, if he Shirked. Because Work by both players does not lead to the cooperative outcome in a Specialized Labor game, remedial rules should not encourage that result.

The liquidated-Kantian measure of rewards for Work, by contrast, has the splendid feature of conferring on both players some of the net benefits of a cooperative outcome in a Specialized Labor game.[37] As indicated in the prior discussion of Table 12.2, when $B - D$ is the measure of the reward, Player Two's dominant strategy is to Shirk. Player One then has net gains from Working, because $B > C$. That Player Two ends up with net gains after rewarding Player One with $B - D$ requires a bit of proof.

36. On the related debate among contracts scholars over the relative merits of the reliance and expectation measures of damages, see Robert Cooter and Melvin Aron Eisenberg, "Damages for Breach of Contract," 73 *Calif. L. Rev.* 1432 (1985); Charles J. Goetz and Robert E. Scott, "Enforcing Promises: An Examination of the Basis of Contract," 89 *Yale L.J.* 1261 (1980).

37. Compare William M. Landes and Richard A. Posner, "Salvors, Finders, Good Samaritans, and Other Rescuers: An Economic Study of Law and Altruism," 7 *J. Legal. Stud.* 83 (1978), discussing measures of rewards to salvors at sea.

Player Two would have net benefits if $C < A - (B - D)$. This equation transposes to $B + C < A + D$. Because it was stipulated that $2B < A + D$, and because $B > C$, then $B + C < A + D$.

Measurement of Damages in Practice

The hypothesis thus suggests that norm-makers will be inclined to take a liquidated-Kantian approach to the measure of damages in both Prisoner's Dilemma and Specialized Labor games. Of course, the problem of setting damages is more complex than has been admitted. Some adjustments to the $B - D$ measure might serve to reduce the sum of transaction costs and deadweight losses. Norm-makers might, for example, entitle informal enforcers to charge interest, that is, to convert past damages to present value. Although this adjustment would improve the accuracy of incentives for cooperation, utilitarians might still reject it because in some contexts present values are hard to calculate and might prove to be a fertile source of disagreements. Similarly, if enforcement is less than certain, a sum greater than $B - D$ might be needed to create proper incentives.

In addition, because cognitive capacities are limited, remedial norms may allow, indeed even require, roughness in the calculation of informal debt. In light of the transaction costs of computing damages, norm-makers might apply formulas simpler than liquidated Kantianism. A rule that de minimis damages are to be ignored (that is, assessed at zero), for example, could gain more in transaction-cost savings than it lost in the dilution of incentives. The rural residents of Shasta County, though sensitive to the need for care in the measurement of damages, were certainly not sticklers about balancing ledgers. They only roughly repaid debts (or avenged the nonpayment of debts) arising from cattle trespasses and defaults on fencing obligations. Like the Maine lobstermen, when they used violent self-help, they applied it in crude, though definitely not indiscriminate, amounts. For example, they were careful to shoot at wayward cattle with buckshot, not bullets. When Shellworth took Ellis' bulldozer, he kept it temporarily, not permanently.[38] By analogy, a patron leaving a restaurant might ponder the choice between leaving no tip and leaving a 15 percent tip, but hardly the choice between a 14 and 15 percent tip. This utilitarian roughness of social practice makes more difficult any attempt at field testing of the prediction that the underlying remedial formula is liquidated Kantianism.

---

38. See supra Chapter 4, text following note 32.

Even-Up: A Strategy for Cooperative
Members of a Close-Knit Group

The inquiry into the measurement of damages for the breach of norms suggests ways in which game theorists could enrich their study of non-zero-sum games. The most influential analysts of cooperation, such as Robert Axelrod, have investigated an iterated Prisoner's Dilemma involving continuing, identical encounters between two persons who each know only the history of their own dyadic relationship. This game structure provides each player with sufficient information and power to exercise self-help against the other. As Chapters 9 and 10 discussed, the iterated Prisoner's Dilemma is therefore a useful, if simplistic, first approximation of life in a close-knit social group. Axelrod and others have shown the power of the elementary strategy of Tit-for-Tat to induce cooperative play in this artificial setting.

In a move toward realism, let us add three complications to the iterated Prisoner's Dilemma.[39] First, instead of repeating the same type of game each round, let us insert games other than the Prisoner's Dilemma in some innings. A simple initial complication, explored below, would allow the random use in different innings of two types of games: Prisoner's Dilemma games such as that in Table 9.2, and Specialized Labor games such as that in Table 9.3. Second and relatedly, let us allow the magnitudes of the payoffs for a particular type of game to vary from inning to inning. For example, in one Prisoner's Dilemma out of five, the entries in each box in the payoff matrix might be increased twentyfold.[40] Third, let us empower a player unilaterally to make an unexplained side-payment between rounds, perhaps to retire debts incurred in prior rounds.[41]

If all three complexities were added, what strategy would be the logical extension of Axelrod's Tit-for-Tat? Tentatively, several strategic enrichments would seem necessary. First, because stakes are allowed to vary from inning to inning, a player would need an accounting system to keep track of the magnitude of imbalances that had arisen from past play. The liquidated-Kantian measure of damages (the $B - D$ formula) can serve as the basis for such an accounting system. Second, a player's strategy

---

39. Axelrod himself canvassed a variety of possible enrichments in Robert Axelrod and Douglas Dion, "The Further Evolution of Cooperation," 242 *Science* 1385 (1988). Also instructive is Jack Hirshleifer and Juan Carlos Martinez Coll, "What Strategies Can Support the Evolutionary Emergence of Cooperation?" 32 *J. Conflict Resolution* 367 (1988).

40. This change would render the simple strategy of Tit-for-Tat inoperable.

41. Because the game is being structured to reveal the potential role of norms, these side-payments are envisioned as unilateral, not as part of a spot bilateral contractual exchange.

should include the tactic of making unilateral side-payments to correct past mistakes and to repay outstanding debts. If both players' strategies called for making these payments, players could avoid the deadweight losses that arise when creditors are forced to act uncooperatively to square accounts.

These elements provide the basis for an "Even-Up" strategy that seems likely to be individually and collectively welfare maximizing for members of close-knit groups. An Even-Up player would keep a running mental account of how he stood with each other member of the group. After each dyadic interaction (inning of play), he would make an appropriate entry in his account with the player whom he had just played. If both players had just Cooperated (or both had just Defected) in a Prisoner's Dilemma, for example, no change in entries would be appropriate. However, if Player One had just Cooperated and Player Two had just Defected, and if they were both Even-Up players, they would record that Player Two owed Player One a new informal debt of $B - D$. Similarly, in a Specialized Labor game, after Player One had Worked and Player Two had Shirked, they would record an identical increase of $B - D$ in debt.

When deciding what to do in an upcoming round with another player, an Even-Up player would examine the current balance in his dyadic account with that player. The Even-Up player would observe the following rules:

1. If the balance in the mental account were zero, or only trivially different from zero, the Even-Up player would choose the strategy that intersected with the objectively cooperative (welfare-maximizing) outcome. Under these circumstances, for example, an Even-Up player would Cooperate in Prisoner's Dilemma situations, and, in Specialized Labor games, Work only when he was the cheapest labor-provider.

2. If the Even-Up player were currently to owe the other player more than a de minimis amount, the Even-Up player would immediately make a unilateral side-payment to the other player to square their account at zero. Then, the Even-Up player would proceed to cooperate as under rule 1.

3. Except as noted in rule 4, if the Even-Up player were to conclude that the other player owed him more than a de minimis amount, he would exercise self-help by Defecting in a Prisoner's Dilemma game and Shirking in a Specialized Labor game when he was the cheapest labor-provider.

4. To reduce the risk of cycles of escalating retaliatory action, an Even-Up player would only employ self-help if the magnitude of an effective sanction (the measure $B - D$) would be less than twice the current debt owed. This rule of thumb is designed to ensure that the sanctioning process brings balances in mental accounts closer to, not further from, zero.[42]

In a formal series of iterated Prisoner's Dilemmas involving more than de minimis stakes, Even-Up would function identically to Tit-for-Tat. Even-Up is a "nice" strategy that is never the first to defect. When wronged, it is immediately willing to administer measured punishments until informal accounts are again squared.

Because Even-Up and the triply enriched iterated game are more life-like, they offer a number of heuristic advantages over Tit-for-Tat and the Prisoner's Dilemma. The enriched game presents players with a sequence of widely varying game matrixes. Even-Up makes a bow to the reality of transaction costs because an Even-Up player lets a minor imbalance persist. Even-Up allows a player to atone for a past error, whether intentional or negligent, through the making of a unilateral side-payment; in the standard iterated Prisoner's Dilemma, by contrast, a single error may lead to an endless echo of reprisals. In sum, Even-Up is a strategy more suited than Tit-for-Tat to the variegated, transaction-cost laden, mistake-filled world in which we live.

Many Shasta County residents appear to follow something like an Even-Up strategy. Their live-and-let-live approach calls for them to put up with minor matters.[43] As we have seen, when a nontrivial loss arises from a failure to supervise cattle or contribute to boundary-fence maintenance, residents mentally adjust interneighbor accounts and then usually repay the debt (or, conversely, avenge its nonpayment) in a measured way. For example, a ranchette owner in Shasta County used the phrase

42. As an illustration, suppose that Player Two currently owed Player One a debt of 3, and that the players faced a round structured as a Prisoner's Dilemma. Player One, acting on the assumption that Player Two would Cooperate in the next round, would himself choose to Defect in that round only if $B - D$ were less than 6. If $B - D$ were greater than 6, Player One's sanction might throw the account further out of balance than it had been before.

43. But compare Edward C. Banfield, *The Moral Basis of a Backward Society* 121 (1958): "Peasants [in southern Italy] sometimes exchange labor or make each other small loans of bread or cash, but they do so from self-interest, not from charity or fellow-feeling. No one expects help from another if the other stands to lose by helping. The peasant who works for another keeps a careful record of his hours. Even trivial favors create an obligation and must be repaid. When a visiting social scientist said he planned to leave the key to his house with a neighbor for a few days while he was away, his landlord pointed out that such a thing would be foolish. 'You would needlessly create an obligation which you would have to repay.'"

"get even" in predicting how he would respond to a neighbor's refusal to share appropriately in the costs of a boundary fence.[44]

More generally, the familiarity of the phrase "get even," the biblical remedy of an eye for an eye, the norm of reciprocity that George Homans calls one of the world's most common, anthropologists' findings of gift exchange, friends' tendencies to alternate in hosting social events—all these hint at the pervasiveness of something like an Even-Up approach to social interactions.[45]

It is tautologically true that if *all* members of a close-knit society were Even-Up players, they would apply welfare-maximizing norms to Prisoner's Dilemma and Specialized Labor interactions. Because Even-Up players are "nice" people when accounts are square, they Cooperate in Prisoner's Dilemma situations and Work in Specialized Labor situations. When another's Work has helped them, or when they have mistakenly Defected, they immediately make an appropriate side-payment to square accounts.

Game theorists are beginning to explore the dynamic evolution of social groups when members can enter, exit, and change their strategies. The hypothesis of welfare-maximizing norms implies that evolutionary processes within close-knit groups would favor the selection of strategies, such as Even-Up, that encourage cooperative primary play and also contain mechanisms for punishing deviants and rewarding surpassers. For the hypothesis to remain credible, game theorists would have to show that a group consisting entirely or mostly of Even-Up players would be an evolutionary stable society, that is, one in which a new entrant would not find an uncooperative strategy to be more lucrative than Even-Up.[46] Sim-

44. See supra Chapter 4, text following note 29. Inspired in part by this incident, I was initially tempted to use "Get-Even" as the label for what I now call the Even-Up strategy. Carol Rose convinced me, however, that "get even" misleadingly connotes an element of vengefulness that is often not felt by those who use this strategy.

45. Leading sociological works that are in tune with this sort of "exchange theory" are Peter M. Blau, *Exchange and Power in Social Life* (1964); George C. Homans, *Social Behavior* 217–221 (rev. ed. 1974). Sources on gifts and other exchanges in preliterate societies include Marcel Mauss, *The Gift: Forms and Functions of Exchange in Archaic Societies* (Ian Cunnison trans. 1954); Marshall Sahlins, *Stone Age Economics* 185–230 (1972); Michael Taylor, *Community, Anarchy, and Liberty* 65–94 (1982). The viewing of social interactions as a form of self-interested exchange of course offends commentators who believe that this perception may itself undermine feelings of community. See, e.g., Richard M. Titmuss, *The Gift Relationship* 239 (1971). The prevalence of masking devices, such as in-kind gift exchanges, suggests that norm-makers often share Titmuss' concern. See also infra Chapter 13, text accompanying notes 14–17.

46. The notion of an evolutionarily stable society was first developed in J. Maynard Smith, supra note 32, at 10. According to some analysts of multiperson Prisoner's Dilemmas, both

ilarly, they would also have to show that evolutionary forces would initially enable Even-Up players to survive entry into close-knit groups dominated by players using other strategies.

Axelrod's research on the evolution of strategies came to the conclusion that, under specified conditions, clusters of players using Tit-for-Tat and similar "nice" strategies can successfully invade hostile environments, become more and more numerous, and resist subsequent invasion by deviants.[47] Cooperative players tend to prosper not only because they interact well with one another but also because they are as successful as anyone at avoiding endless feuds with players who do not employ nice strategies. Whether Even-Up players would do as well under a richer set of game conditions is a question only experimental game theorists can answer.[48]

---

cooperators and deviants may be able to exist in fixed proportions at equilibrium. See id. at 11–17; Thomas Schelling, *Micromotives and Macrobehavior* 226–229 (1978). If the great majority of players living in a mixed society of this sort were to adopt a strategy similar to Even-Up, the hypothesis of welfare-maximizing norms would possess predictive power, even though deviancy would also be common.

47. See Robert Axelrod, *The Evolution of Cooperation* 55–69, 88–105 (1984). See also Robert Sugden, *The Economics of Rights, Co-operation, and Welfare* 115–121 (1986).

48. Social groups that include both cooperative and uncooperative players are analyzed in Donald Regan, *Utilitarianism and Co-operation* 124–189 (1980) (primarily normative analysis), and T. Schelling, supra note 46, at 217–243 (positive analysis).

13
* * *

Procedural and Constitutive Norms:
Of Gossip, Ritual, and Hero Worship

Procedural norms govern a member's duties to transmit, to other members of the group, information whose circulation would help minimize internal disputing. Constitutive norms govern a member's obligations to sustain the group as an effective institution of informal control. Within close-knit groups, both types of norms are predicted to be shaped so as to enhance the objective welfare, tangible and intangible, of group members.

Procedural Norms

The hypothesis predicts that procedural norms will call for the transmission of information whenever the expected value of that transmission, measured in reduction of deadweight losses, is likely to exceed the costs of effecting the transmission. Utilitarian procedural norms help members both to avoid disputes and to resolve disputes quickly and amicably. In Shasta County, rural residents had informal duties to communicate before disputes arose, while disputes were ongoing, and after disputes had been settled. They also had duties to sustain the group's general bank of information about members' reputations.

Dispute-Specific Information

A person about to undertake a primary action may have an informal duty to warn those whom he is about to affect, so that they can either adjust their affairs or attempt to persuade him to adjust his. In rural Shasta County, a rancher who intends to build or replace a boundary fence must notify his neighbor in advance to safeguard his entitlement to recover a share of the fence costs from that neighbor.[1] This norm encourages ex

1. See supra Chapter 4, text accompanying note 29.

ante bargaining over how a boundary fence should be built, or, indeed, whether it should be built at all, hence reducing the risk of a deadweight loss. There may also be duties to warn of unexpected omissions; for example, a professor who is going to miss a class is informally obligated to tell the students in advance so that they can mitigate the damages that would stem from fruitless attendance.

Other procedural norms deal with information transfer after a dispute has arisen. A legal system's procedural rules identify authoritative decision makers and ensure the expeditious presentation of claims, defenses, and evidence both to that decision maker and to the other parties involved. Systems of social control that lack judges or other authoritative decision makers have analogous, if much cruder, rules of pleading and evidence.

It is usually cheapest for two people to settle a dispute between themselves, because this approach eliminates the burden of educating an additional outside decision maker about the facts. Procedural norms therefore tend to require a grievant to complain first to the party whose actions gave rise to the grievance, and to give that party adequate opportunity to make amends.[2] Partly for this reason, children tend to ostracize as a tattletale a child who too quickly reports a playground squabble to an adult. In Shasta County, a victim of trespass by a neighbor's cattle is initially required to report the trespass to the neighbor, but to no one else.[3] In a legal system, by contrast, a plaintiff's complaint is filed not only with the other party but also in a court.

When an informal complaint does not result in a settlement, a grievant's subsequent remedies are also tailored to minimize the costs of passing information. The Shasta County norms that authorize forceful remedial sanctions designate the grievant, rather than a third party, as the preferred enforcer. In all discovered instances in Shasta County in which informal force was applied to trespassing livestock, for example, the trespass victim himself applied it.[4] The transaction-cost advantage of second-party enforcement is, again, that no third party need go through the process of appraising the justness of the underlying grievance.

In some contexts informal third-party enforcement may be more utilitarian than second-party enforcement, however. Bringing in a neutral

---

2. These norms function in part as controller-selecting norms, because they direct disputants to use second-party self-help rather than some system of third-party control.
3. See supra Chapter 3, text preceding note 47.
4. See supra Chapter 3, text following note 58.

third party as a mediator or arbitrator may break a deadlock, help prevent a feud, or provide the cheapest credible source of enforcement.[5] In Shasta County I found one important type of third-party enforcement—the general circulation of negative gossip about deviants. Procedural norms encourage third parties to transmit this truthful remedial gossip to those in the best position to make use of it.

When a notorious informal debt has been repaid, the party who has been made whole bears an informal duty to tell others that accounts have been squared. This affirmative duty to gossip about remedial successes helps ensure that others will not overpunish former debtors who have "paid their dues." That Shasta County residents knew about each other's (often criminal) acts of self-help against Frank Ellis' cattle is evidence that they were bound by a norm to publicize their remedial acts. In a case where an enforcer would have good reason to fear that an appropriate sanction would set off a feud, however, a justified enforcer may be entitled to keep his remedial acts anonymous, that is, to report to neighbors only that some unknown vigilante has taken corrective steps.[6]

General Reputational Information

The residents of rural Shasta County gossip all the time. Indeed, any close-knit group is likely to have procedural norms that ask members to help spread truthful information about the prior prosocial or antisocial behavior of other members.[7] By facilitating the flow of reputational information, these norms deter future uncooperative behavior by increasing an actor's estimates of the probability that informal enforcers would eventually catch up with him.

Because informal groups are not hierarchies, they lack official sets of records.[8] Instead, members mostly circulate relevant historical informa-

5. See supra Chapter 12, note 27; infra Chapter 14, text accompanying notes 46–49.

6. See also supra Chapter 12, text following note 22.

7. Jeffrey A. Kurland and Stephen J. Beckerman, "Optimal Foraging and Hominid Evolution: Labor and Reciprocity," 87 *Amer. Anthropologist* 73 (1985), advances the thesis that the development of reciprocal information exchange about food sources was a key step in human social evolution. Similarly, information exchange about prospects and perils created by other humans would also promote survival.

8. In contexts where oral communication and human memories are likely to be highly fallible, a group is apt to assign record-keeping responsibilities to a hierarchy. In a school, for example, the central staff has the task of recording pupils' grades and disciplinary problems. Ancient Egyptian history suggests that one of the state's earliest functions was the keeping of

tion by word of mouth and store it in their memories. Some members may specialize in the transmission and storage of social-control information, however. Those who do this—doyens, yentas, social insiders—must be informally rewarded, perhaps with higher social status. In this way and others, procedural norms help supply the information requirements of an informal system of social control.

Constitutive Norms

By informally joining together as a cooperative club of enforcers, individuals can achieve a much higher degree of social control than they could achieve if they were to live in isolation. In a social environment where enforcement is likely to be all for one and one for all, the prospect of third-party enforcement makes deviants and surpassers much more likely to behave cooperatively. Constitutive norms are the informal rules that help glue an informal group together.[9]

Membership Rules and Rituals of Solidarity

Some constitutive norms serve to define and identify a group's membership. Current members can prosper by attracting entrants whose arrival would increase possibilities for mutually advantageous exchange within the group. Norms that establish initiation standards and rituals provide screening devices that may help ensure that new members will honor the group's norms. In contexts where members might not otherwise recognize each other, constitutive rules governing dress, speech, or etiquette may aid identification.[10]

Because a fly-by-night member might exploit a group by acting selfishly immediately after joining, the constitutive norms of a group may require a member to give "hostages"—the term some economists use to denote assurances against opportunism. Consider, for example, a business

---

land titles. John P. Powelson, *The Story of Land: A World History of Land Tenure and Agrarian Reform* 17 (1988).

9. As two astute observers have noted, ". . . it is no accident that social life is arranged so as to minimize the occurrence of one-shot prisoner's dilemmas." "Epilogue," *Rational Man and Irrational Society* 367, 385 (Brian Barry and Russell Hardin eds. 1982). Constitutive norms do much of this arranging.

10. But see Jon Elster, "Social Norms and Economic Theory," 3 *J. Econ. Perspectives* 99, 108–109 (1989) (skeptical assessment of functionalist explanations of norms of etiquette).

executive who moves to a new city. The executive may quickly be able to obtain the trust of other local executives by enmeshing himself in the activities of an "appropriate" club. In joining the club, the executive hands over as hostages both the entry fee[11] and a major part of his social life.

Hierarchical organizations often have formalized symbols and rituals, such as insignia, songs, and periodic meetings. In addition to giving members a means for identifying one another, these may also provide continuing tests of allegiance if a member's willingness (or unwillingness) to embrace group symbols accurately signals depth of loyalty.

Like a hierarchy, a nonhierarchical group can develop constitutive norms that support a set of symbols. When the cattlemen of Shasta County assembled at a public hearing to oppose the Heinz closure petition, for example, they came wearing cowboy hats.[12] Many ranchers also signal their mutual allegiance by hanging, say, a rifle or a picture of John Wayne on their living-room wall. As Chapter 6 discussed, the best explanation for the cattlemen's furious opposition to proposed closed-range ordinances was their determination to preserve an open-range legal regime that to them signified that the cattleman was still king of the county. A group also may make use of negative symbols. For the rural residents of Shasta County, Frank Ellis, the most egregious deviant, came to personify the evils of a lack of neighborliness.[13]

According to the hypothesis, norm-makers would respond—although often not consciously—to the cost-effectiveness of alternative symbols and rituals. For example, a group could be expected to continue to honor its traditional symbols not only because of inertia but also because a symbol is likely to improve with age. In many contexts the selection of a symbol is a game of pure coordination to which there are many equally good solutions. If the members of a group would gain from adopting a flag, for example, it is likely that numerous different flag designs would serve them equally well. In such a context the hypothesis predicts the emergence of some symbol, but cannot forecast its exact content.

Constitutive norms can enhance group solidarity by structuring dealings in a way that requires members continually to reaffirm their ongoing

---

11. Technically, because the entry fee is a sunk cost, the hostage is the cost of paying a similar fee at another club.

12. See supra Chapter 2, text preceding note 13.

13. One theory of deviancy, dating from Durkheim, holds that deviants provide a target around which others can organize and obtain solidarity. See Kai T. Erikson, *Wayward Puritans: A Study in the Sociology of Deviance* 3–29 (1966); Stanton Wheeler, "Deviant Behavior," in *Sociology: An Introduction* 647, 656–657 (Neil J. Smelser ed., 2d ed. 1973).

trust. A prime example is the implicit Shasta County norm that directs neighbors to use in-kind transfers, not cash payments, to retire informal debts. Because money is the most tradable of goods, in-kind transfers seem inefficient at first blush. Norm-makers recognize, however, that there is an important symbolic difference between market and gift exchange.[14] A cash transaction, cold and impersonal, is the standard form of exchange among strangers. A constitutive norm favoring in-kind transfers ("gifts") repeatedly puts members through the ritual of signaling that they are in solidarity, rather than at arm's length.[15] This reinforces mutual expectations of continuing cooperative interactions.

In Shasta County a neighbor who unilaterally mends a boundary fence therefore expects not a check from the benefited neighbor but a return of the favor the next time fence repairs roll around. A rancher who has given volunteer help at a controlled burn of brush similarly expects in-kind reciprocation. When one ranchette owner's goat ate his neighbor's tomatoes, the goat's owner responded by helping to replant the tomatoes, not by sending a check. These sorts of responsive gifts not only redress debts but also send a much-valued message of personal trust.[16]

Urban professionals are bound by norms that similarly favor in-kind transfers. Dinner guests, for example, commonly bring their host a gift such as a bottle of wine. But no dinner guest would, instead of bringing wine, arrive and say, "Here's twenty dollars. I've learned in an Economics course that you'd undoubtedly prefer this to the usual bottle of wine." The tender of cash would signal that the guest thought of the dinner not as an occasion among friends but as an occasion at a restaurant, where diners have a merely commercial relationship with those who serve them.

For related reasons, close-knit groups are likely to have constitutive norms that forbid a member from being too explicit in identifying the instrumental value of social exchange within the group. When returning

14. This point is explored in Robert H. Frank, *Choosing the Right Pond: Human Behavior and the Quest for Status* 192–213 (1985) (chapter entitled "Why Do Ethical Systems Try to Limit the Role of Money"); Steven Kelman, *What Price Incentives? Economists and the Environment* 69–77 (1981) (asserting that putting a price on something tends to cheapen it); Margaret Jane Radin, "Market-Inalienability," 100 *Harv. L. Rev.* 1849 (1987).

15. See Jack L. Carr and Janet T. Landa, "The Economics of Symbols, Clan Names, and Religion," 12 *J. Legal Stud.* 135 (1983); Janet T. Landa, "The Enigma of the *Kula Ring*: Gift-Exchanges and Primitive Law and Order," 3 *Int. Rev. of L. & Econ.* 137 (1983) (ritualistic exchange of necklaces and armshells in Melanesia); Ian R. Macneil, "Exchange Revisited: Individual Utility and Social Solidarity," 96 *Ethics* 567 (1986) (advancing thesis that accepted patterns of exchange enhance social solidarity). See also sources cited supra Chapter 12, note 45.

16. See also supra Chapter 3, text accompanying note 64.

a dinner invitation, a host should leave unsaid any motivation to square accounts. A professor who responds to a colleague's request for comments on a draft should not say, "Now you owe me one." Fellow-feeling seems more likely to arise when members are seen to act out of friendship, not out of a need to scratch each other's backs. Close friends have such a long future ahead of them that they need not worry about minor imbalances in the reciprocated favors between them. Therefore, a person who mentions that accounts have fallen a bit out of balance indicates either a lack of intimacy or some skepticism about future solidarity.[17]

Diffuse But Credible Rewards for Third-Party Enforcers

In accord with Hobbes' *Leviathan* and Mancur Olson's *Logic of Collective Action*,[18] many analysts assume that a general populace cannot achieve public order in the absence of a central authority capable of applying coercive sanctions. Except in quite small groups, it is thought, incentives to free-ride prevent the emergence of spontaneous self-help enforcement. If they can maintain close-knittedness, however, even thousands of people can achieve public order without aid of a hierarchy. On isolated islands that have virtually no formal government, for example, residents have experienced little crime.[19] In ways that are poorly understood, constitutive and other norms emerge to provide the glue that makes possible a surprising degree of order without law.

The key to this process is the "altruistic" enforcement of norms by uninvolved third parties. Examples of champions of the public are easy to find. Consider this letter to the editor published in the *New York Times* under the heading "Hero of the Metropolis":

> To the Editor:
> Who says New York is a tough, heartless city? Certainly not this lady from Boone, N.C.!
> On Sunday morning, Oct. 18, a young hero named Eric Zimmerman saw a hooligan taking my wallet out of my zipped-up handbag; chased, tackled and wrestled him to the ground; retrieved my wallet and then returned it to me. This brave soul received cuts, scrapes and bruises and loss of his eyeglasses—all for a perfect stranger.

17. See Arthur J. Vidach and Joseph Bensman, *Small Town in Mass Society* 34 (rev. ed. 1968) (small-town norm against "openly confronting others with unbalanced accounts").
18. Mancur Olson, *The Logic of Collective Action* (1965).
19. See supra Chapter 10, note 38; Chapter 11, text accompanying note 30. See also infra Chapter 14, note 40 (preliterate cultures).

People like Eric Zimmerman restore a lot of faith in this lady from Boone. In my town, ol' Daniel would be proud!

Beverly A. Rosen
Boone, N.C.[20]

To reconcile Beverly Rosen's rescue with the assumption of self-interested behavior, one must suppose that Eric Zimmerman and other heroic suppliers of public goods anticipate receiving rewards. A first possibility is that internalized norms motivate altruistic enforcement activity. According to this view, bystanders would feel guilty if they were to fail to act, or would be flush with self-satisfaction after having acted as enforcers.[21]

A second possibility is that seemingly altruistic enforcers are motivated by incentives supplied by third parties. For example, a heroic rescuer such as Eric Zimmerman might anticipate that his deeds would result in personal acclaim. As was noted earlier, to the extent that third-party incentives are necessary to motivate enforcers, in principle these incentives must be provided at an infinite regress of levels. Thus there must be incentives for Beverly A. Rosen of Boone, North Carolina, to reward Eric Zimmerman with a glowing letter, incentives for the editor of the *Times'* letters to the editor to recognize that this vignette was worthy of publicity, and so on.

That the third-party enforcement of norms requires a potentially infinite regress of levels of social control seems, at first blush, destructive of the possibility of informal cooperation.[22] It is possible, however, that the multitude of levels of social control may enhance prospects for cooperation. Perhaps the *perception,* or better yet the existence, of a few virtuous leaders or other committed third-party enforcers at the highest level of social control creates incentives for cooperative activity that cascade down and ultimately produce welfare-maximizing primary behavior. It may be notable in this regard that the architects of religious thought have long recognized that the threat of an omniscient and omnipotent deity operating at an ultimate level of social control is, if credible, a wondrously powerful instrument for fostering cooperation. The perceived presence within a group of a critical mass of self-disciplined elders or other good

20. *N.Y. Times,* Nov. 10, 1987, p. 30, col. 5. Copyright © 1987 by The New York Times Company. Reprinted by permission.

21. Robert Sugden, *The Economics of Rights, Co-operation, and Welfare* 145–161 (1986), explores this possibility.

22. This difficulty is emphasized in Elster, supra note 10, at 105.

citizens, known to be committed to the cause of cooperation, might be as effective as a deity.[23]

Art and literature can serve to sustain the many layers of incentives that are necessary to support the altruistic enforcement of norms. In prior eras, Odysseus, El Cid, and Lancelot were model heroic avengers; more recently we have Rambo and the Karate Kid. Popular culture not only reinforces first-party preferences to enforce norms altruistically; it also tells third parties that it is appropriate to reward enforcers after the fact. Superman elicits admiration from Lois Lane; Batman, from Vicki Vail. These particular exemplars are of course cultural icons not of close-knit groups but of mass populations. The broad appeal of these cultural figures may stem from the ease with which a reader or viewer can see that the heroes' doings hold valuable lessons for behavior within smaller groups.

According to the hypothesis, close-knit nonhierarchical groups can achieve much of the internal order that legal centralists have classically regarded as the job of a Leviathan. Because the hypothesis was induced, not deduced, no rigorous effort will be made here to explain the mechanics that underlie spontaneous cooperation. The definition of close-knittedness developed in Chapter 10, however, implies that the mechanism at work depends on group members' having both continuing reciprocal power over one another and also a bank of shared information. Constitutive and procedural norms are what support these structural prerequisites of informal order.[24]

Game theorists with the daring to investigate deductively the dynamics of multi-inning, multiperson games have been seeking to identify mechanisms that create general social pressures toward cooperation.[25] The

23. James M. Acheson, *The Lobster Gangs of Maine* 58–63 (1988), describes in one social context the elevated status of leaders and their special role in the enforcement of norms.

24. A chicken-and-egg problem arises at this point. Constitutive norms, which establish the identity and duties of group members, help keep a group close-knit. However, close-knittedness is what enables a group to generate utilitarian constitutive norms in the first place. How then might a close-knit group first get going? One possibility is that the tightness of a group's social structure and the welfare-enhancing features of its norms are linked symbiotically, and gradually feed synergistically on one another. See Edna Ullmann-Margalit, *The Emergence of Norms* 105–106 (1977). Another possibility is that kinship groups, for whom cooperation is widely understood to have a biological base, provide nuclei around which larger cooperative societies can gel. See supra Chapter 10, note 23.

25. See R. Sugden, supra note 21, at 132–138; Robert Axelrod, "An Evolutionary Approach to Norms," 80 *Am. Pol. Sci. Rev.* 1095, 1100–1102 (1986) (referring to norms supporting enforcement as "metanorms"); Dilip Abreu, "On the Theory of Infinitely Repeated Games with Discounting," 56 *Econometrica* 383 (1988); David Hirshleifer and Eric Rasmusen, "Cooperation in a Repeated Prisoner's Dilemma with Ostracism," 12 *J. Econ. Behav. & Org.* 87 (1989).

widespread adoption of the Even-Up strategy described in Chapter 12, for example, might be sufficient to provide incentives for the diffuse enforcement of norms.[26] In any event, the empirical reality, evidenced in Shasta County and elsewhere, is that there can be much order without law.

26. Cooperative members of a group require a system for calculating how much each of them should reward a Good Samaritan who has assumed an unusual burden of enforcement. To use the notation in Thomas Schelling, *Micromotives and Macrobehavior* 217–243 (1978), suppose that there are n members of a close-knit group, of whom k are cooperators who play Even-Up strategies. The rest are opportunists. Suppose also that a reward of size x is necessary to induce a cheapest labor-provider to act as a third-party enforcer. Under these conditions, the Even-Up players have two polar ways of calculating how much each of them should reward an enforcer after his unusually good deed. The first method, which puts on the heroic enforcer the risk of free-riding by opportunists, calls for each cooperative member to give him a reward of x/n. The second method, which lifts the risk of free-riding from the enforcer and spreads it among the group of Even-Up players, increases the reward from each member to x/k. Under the first of these approaches, the champion of the public is entitled to enter an informal credit of x/n against each of the free-riders; under the second approach, each of the k Even-Up players is entitled to enter a tiny credit, $(x/k - x/n)/(n - k)$, against each free-rider. In practice, when choosing among these two approaches and other, less precise, alternatives, utilitarians would consider both the transaction costs inherent in the accounting measures and the risk of deadweight losses that would arise if enforcement incentives were inadequate.

14
* * *

Controller-Selecting Norms:
Of Contracts, Custom, and Photocopies

Chapter 7 introduced the five basic controllers: the self, express contracts, informal social forces, hierarchical private organizations, and the state. Each of these controllers is capable of both generating and enforcing rules. Controller-selecting norms are the informal rules through which nonhierarchical groups seek to apportion tasks among these various sources of social control.

The relative merit of different controllers is an overarching topic in social science. Here lie such crucial questions as the division of functions between the state and the private sector, the respective role of contracts and firms in industrial organization, and the interplay between collective (third-party) moral systems and first-party personal ethics.[1]

Feedback loops often serve to bring the work products of different controllers into congruence. For example, personal ethics, norms, and laws are all likely to include a rule that speakers should be honest. Nonetheless, different controllers not infrequently come up with conflicting rules. In open-range areas of Shasta County, for example, ranchers who let their cattle stray were not *legally* liable, but were *informally* liable, for trespass damages. When the rules of controllers vary in this way, controller-selecting norms, by directing disputants to use a particular source of rules, determine ultimate obligations.

In Shasta County, controller-selecting norms led rural residents to keep cattle-trespass and boundary-fence disputes within the informal control system. A rural resident who violated these norms, for example, by taking a squabble over fencing obligations into the legal system, risked ostracism for being unduly litigious. By contrast, other controller-selecting norms in Shasta County permitted grievants to litigate highway-collision and water disputes. Why did Shasta County norms select different

---

1. An insightful overview of choice among contractual, elite, and traditional rules can be found in Robert C. Clark, "Contracts, Elites, and Traditions in the Making of Corporate Law," 89 *Colum. L. Rev.* 1703 (1989), an article much in tune with this book.

Table 14.1   Altruism as an Escape from a Prisoner's Dilemma

		Player Two	
		Cooperate	Defect
Player One	Cooperate	6, 6	5, 5
	Defect	5, 5	2, 2

controllers in these instances? The hypothesis predicts that the controller-selecting norms of close-knit societies serve to induce members to choose among controllers in a manner that minimizes the sum of members' deadweight losses and transaction costs.

The Many Escapes from the Prisoner's Dilemma

All five controllers can potentially steer people to act in a welfare-maximizing way. For example, each controller may be able to induce both players to Cooperate in a two-person Prisoner's Dilemma. In essence, the various controllers achieve this result by changing the matrix of game payoffs in a manner that shifts each player's dominant choice away from Defection.[2]

The first-party system of social control consists of the enforcement of a personal ethic upon oneself.[3] Suppose a person were to honor a personal ethic of altruism requiring him to love his neighbors as much as himself. That ethic would compel him to choose plays with an eye to maximizing the total objective payoff for all players. In other words, an altruistic player would sum all payoffs in each quadrant and insert the total as his new individual payoff for that quadrant. If applied by both players in the Prisoner's Dilemma depicted in Table 9.1, the ethic of altruism would convert the payoffs to those shown in Table 14.1. In the game in Table 14.1, both players would regard Cooperation as the dominant strategy, because it would bring the largest personal payoff regardless of what the other player chose to do.[4]

The second-party system of social control—the bilateral contract—

2. See generally Jack Hirshleifer, "Evolutionary Models in Economics and Law: Cooperation versus Conflict Strategies," 4 Research in L. & Econ. 1, 20–38 (1982) ("Escapes, Mainly from the Prisoner's Dilemma").

3. See Table 7.3, which lays out the taxonomy of the overall system of social control.

4. See generally Michael Taylor, Anarchy and Cooperation 69–83 (1976) (effect of altruism on the Prisoner's Dilemma).

provides a simple escape from the Prisoner's Dilemma. If players were able to communicate and negotiate at no cost, they could enter into an express executory contract that required both to Cooperate and created transaction-specific mechanisms, such as hostages, to secure these executory obligations. Because mutual Cooperation produces the highest total payoff, achieving it would generate gains from trade for the players to split. (To bar this ready escape, the rules of the standard Prisoner's Dilemma prohibit the players from communicating in advance of play.)

Each of the third-party enforcers—social forces, private organizations, and governments—can impose sanctions to influence players' choices. For example, a sovereign can impose criminal or civil penalties on players who have chosen to Defect. A player aware that a sanction might follow a particular choice would appropriately adjust the payoffs associated with that choice. If large and certain enough, a sanction could therefore make Cooperation the dominant strategy for a rational actor who, in the absence of that sanction, would be tempted to Defect. More concretely, a third-party enforcer who applied with certainty a liquidated-Kantian measure of damages would create incentives for cooperative play in both Prisoner's Dilemma and Specialized Labor games.[5]

Utilitarian Choice among Controllers

To minimize their total costs, members of a group must pay attention to a variety of considerations when selecting a controller. First, some controllers are more likely than others to succeed at utilitarian rulemaking. For example, in many contexts, contracts are more utilitarian than norms, and norms in turn are more utilitarian than legal rules. Everything else being equal, it is advantageous for a group to refer a coordination problem to the controller most likely to resolve it according to welfare-maximizing rules.

Second, choice among controllers is complicated by the fact that the work of any controller gives rise to certain associated transaction costs. For example, it is laborious to negotiate contracts, inculcate norms, and levy legal penalties. When developing controller-selecting norms, utilitarians would be alert to the comparative advantages of the various controllers on this score.[6] When one controller would be the most promising

---

5. See supra Chapter 12, text accompanying notes 35–37.

6. For a useful discussion of the comparative advantages of alternative institutions, see Neil Komesar, "In Search of a General Approach to Legal Analysis: A Comparative Institutional Alternative," 79 *Mich. L. Rev.* 1350 (1981).

source of rules but another would be the cheapest enforcer of rules, controller-selecting rules might designate a hybrid form of social control.[7] For instance, negative gossip, a cheaply administered informal sanction, may become accepted as the preferred method for punishing the breach of express contracts.[8]

Third and relatedly, utilitarians would be sensitive to exploiting scale efficiencies in the operation of controllers. A social group that ceased enforcing norms, for instance, would lose solidarity, thereby jeopardizing its future capacity to function as an informal controller. Shasta County neighbors thus may use norms instead of contracts to apportion routine fence-maintenance burdens, not only to save the transaction costs of using express contracts, but also to limit the number of (symbolically unfriendly) arm's length transactions that weaken their group.

Last, because the process of applying controller-selecting norms itself entails transaction costs, welfare-maximizing norm-makers would recognize the advantage of rules that identified the "jurisdictions" of the various controllers in a manner that most people would find simple to follow.[9] To illustrate, rules that always allowed a grievant to sue a neighbor for loss of water, but never for cattle-trespass damages, would simplify the subject-matter jurisdictions of controllers.

The Merits of Self-Control, Contracts, and Organizations

The Shasta County evidence is most relevant to the question of how people choose between governments and nonhierarchical social forces as controllers. The interplay between law and norms therefore will be examined in some detail below. The other three controllers are predominant in many social contexts, however, and warrant brief attention.

Self-Control

To what extent can an individual be expected to control himself? James Q. Wilson and Richard J. Herrnstein have encapsulated three views of human nature that have figured importantly in social science and political

7. See supra Chapter 7, text accompanying notes 23–25.

8. Compare Oliver Williamson, *Markets and Hierarchies* 37–38 (1975) (the "atmosphere" of transactional modes influences people's preferences among them).

9. If its Latin roots are taken literally, *jurisdiction* means where the "law speaks." The text discusses not only the domain of law but also the domains of nonlegal rules, to which the word *jurisdiction* is technically inapplicable.

theory.[10] The first, "Man the Calculator," is the view of Hobbes and Bentham. It is reflected in the economist's usual assumption of self-interested, rational action. Believing that only external constraints can keep people from acting opportunistically, analysts who embrace this rational-actor model tend to be skeptical of the power of a self-enforced personal ethics.

Wilson and Herrnstein associate a second view, "Man the Naturally Good," with Rousseau. Members of this camp believe that a person must be socialized to be selfish.[11] This optimism might incline these sorts of thinkers to accept the proposition that a Buddha or a Kant could single-handedly develop and follow a set of personal ethics.

Wilson and Herrnstein themselves clearly prefer a third view of human nature, "Man the Social Animal." They identify Aristotle as its progenitor.[12] Analysts embracing this more sociological view would doubt that a person's ethics can arise in any important way out of asocial contemplation.[13] They would be sympathetic, however, to the notion that a person's enforcement upon himself of norms that his parents, teachers, and others have inculcated can function as an important means of social control.

The Aristotelian view is easiest to reconcile with human experience. After a comprehensive review of the causes of crime, Wilson and Herrnstein conclude that Rousseau was "hopelessly romantic" about natural human inclinations.[14] Rational-actor analysts, for their part, have a conception of human motivation that is too sterile and asocial. What except self-enforcement can explain donations to public radio?[15]

Ian Macneil has provided a vivid, two-sided example of the altruistic self-enforcement of norms, even among strangers:

> My wife and I recently saw a poignant illustration of the intense strength of the reciprocity norm while eating lunch in a small park

10. James Q. Wilson and Richard J. Herrnstein, *Crime and Human Nature* 514–525 (1985).

11. See generally Jean Jacques Rousseau, *The Social Contract and Discourses* (G. D. H. Cole trans. 1973).

12. See generally Aristotle, *Politics* (Ernest Barker trans. 1952).

13. Social psychologists consider social forces an important influence on how a person develops a self-concept. See Erik H. Erikson, "Identity, Psychosocial," 7 *Int'l Encyc. Social Sci.* 61 (1968); Muzafer Sherif, "Self Concept," 14 id. 150.

14. J. Wilson and R. Herrnstein, supra note 10, at 520.

15. Economic analyses of charitable giving include Bruce Robert Kingma, "An Accurate Measurement of the Crowd-out Effect, Income Effect, and Price Effect for Charitable Contributions," 97 *J. Pol. Econ.* 1197 (1989) (on giving to public radio); Joel M. Guttman, "A Non-Cournot Model of Voluntary Collective Action," 54 *Economica* 1 (1987).

outside a McDonald's restaurant in Chicago. An elderly derelict was digging through the many trash barrels, salvaging and ravenously gobbling down the bits of sandwiches and other food left by the more affluent. A young woman, watching this, quietly went over and handed him her own unopened lunch. She turned and walked away. Instead of eating the lunch, he began digging away in the small bundle of his belongings, pulled out a pretty scarf he had salvaged from somewhere, and started to follow her to make a reciprocal gift. But she, young and swift, and perhaps somewhat embarrassed by her own generosity, walked away too fast for him to catch her. Here was someone about as isolated from his society as one can be who nevertheless felt intensely the need to reciprocate, even though the other person clearly never dreamed of such reciprocation.[16]

This vignette, and many others like it, demand that rational-actor analysts pay attention to the force of conscience.

Norm-makers often recognize the possibility of self-discipline. "Live and let live" is a rule that, when applicable, selects an actor's conscience as the sole controller. In a passage remarkably consistent with the present analysis, Georg Simmel suggested long ago why a social group might adopt this particular controller-selecting rule:

> In the morality of the individual, society creates for itself an organ which is not only more fundamentally operative than law and custom, but which also spares society the different sorts of cost involved in these institutions. Hence the tendency of society to satisfy its demands as cheaply as possible results in appeals to "good conscience," through which the individual pays to himself the wages of his righteousness, which otherwise would probably have to be assured to him in some way through law or custom.[17]

The degree of reliance on self-control can be expected to vary according to social circumstances. A close-knit group that can cheaply and unfailingly inculcate uniform norms into children and other new arrivals can be expected to use this device more than a diverse group would. If the members of a group were to place a high value on individual self-

16. Ian R. Macneil, "Values in Contract: Internal and External," 78 *Nw. U.L. Rev.* 340, 349 n.27 (1983).

17. Georg Simmel, "The Number of Members as Determining the Sociological Form of the Group, I," 8 *Am. J. Sociology* 1, 19 n.1 (1902). Simmel, it should be noted, failed to mention the process costs of inculcating good consciences.

realization, they would be concerned about the stultifying effects of the systematic inculcation of norms. Communitarians, however, might regard a process of intensive socialization as a worthy means to a desirable end—the creation of an atmosphere of fellow-feeling.[18]

Contracts as Social Controls

A society's norms and laws provide the default rules that govern human behavior within it. Although these standard obligations are sometimes called a "social contract," that phrase is misleading because these third-party rules are binding on unconsenting individuals. True contracts are second-party rules that two or more parties negotiate in order to establish variations in, or crystallizations of, the default package of third-party rules. The great advantage of contracting, compared with third-party social controls, is that contracts give force to individuals' *subjective* valuations of outcomes, as opposed to the impersonal objective valuations that third-party controllers are forced to employ.[19] Contracts thus enable parties to exploit gains from trade that third-party controllers might not even know are available. No system of social control is better at reducing deadweight losses.

Contracts, however, have a major drawback: the transaction costs of arranging and enforcing them. Because of these costs, members of a group may find it more welfare maximizing to honor the default rules that third parties have set.[20] This is especially true in contexts where labor skills are relatively uniform. For example, adjoining ranchers in Shasta County find it cheaper to honor the norm that divides boundary-fence maintenance burdens fifty-fifty than to negotiate over the matter. A cattleman would be ridiculed if he were to initiate formal negotiations to establish a written fence-maintenance pact.[21] A cattleman's duties to contribute labor to a controlled burn are also socially created, as are the bee-keeping obligations of Cheung's Washington orchardmen. These sorts of informal obligations evoke Henry Maine's well-known vision of a society arranged by status, rather than by contract.[22]

18. See, e.g., Richard M. Titmuss, *The Gift Relationship* 239 (1971).

19. See supra Chapter 10, text accompanying notes 14–18.

20. In the rare instances in which neither law nor norms are in force, small groups of people may use contracts to create standard obligations. See John Umbeck, "A Theory of Contract Choice and the California Gold Rush," 20 *J.L. & Econ.* 421 (1977).

21. See supra Chapter 4, text accompanying note 28.

22. Henry Maine, *Ancient Law* 164–165 (1864).

A practice of reciprocated, norm-driven work may leave individuals with uneven levels of benefits and burdens, however, especially when the individuals vary in their situations, knowledge, and skills. When labor is specialized in this way, utilitarians' controller-selecting norms would tend to ask members to hire workers by express contract. Contracts are better than informal social forces at systematically rewarding those who have gone to the trouble of acquiring special skills. Labor markets also pair skilled workers and jobs with a sensitivity to subjective costs and benefits that norms cannot come close to duplicating.

A norm is likely to impose an informal duty to work, however, when high transaction costs obviate the use of contracts. In certain Specialized Labor situations a cheapest labor-provider can greatly enhance objective welfare by Working.[23] A suburban teenager, who is not bound by any social obligation to mow a neighbor's lawn, nevertheless has a moral duty to rescue a neighbor's baby drowning in a puddle. Although a suburbanite can readily contract for lawn-mowing services, a drowning baby has neither the time nor the capacity to contract for a rescue.

The transaction costs of contracting tend to be lower when the contracting parties have continued dealings with each other. A continuing relationship fosters informal trust because it facilitates monitoring and enables the ready administration of self-help sanctions.[24] When parties are *intimately* close-knit, however, contracting may not be in their interest. The arm's length negotiation of a contract can pollute the atmosphere of a close relationship by implying that the parties don't trust each other enough to rely on informal exchange.[25] This sort of atmospheric critique of market exchange runs through the work of writers from Karl Marx to Karl Polanyi to Richard Titmuss.[26] Although there is some basis for this critique of contractual relations, these authors often seem blind to the many benefits of contracting.[27] Historical evidence suggests that explicit markets are an unmatched engine for the enhancement of human wel-

23. See supra Chapter 9, text accompanying note 18.

24. See, e.g., Benjamin Klein and Keith B. Leffler, "The Role of Market Forces in Assuring Contractual Performance," 89 *J. Pol. Econ.* 615 (1981).

25. See supra Chapter 13, text accompanying notes 14–17.

26. See, e.g., Karl Polanyi, *The Great Transformation* 163–177 (1957) (labor markets interfere with organic social organization); R. Titmuss, supra note 18, at 198 (payments for blood donations sap altruism). A useful review of the competing outlooks is Albert O. Hirschman, "Rival Interpretations of Market Society: Civilizing, Destructive, or Feeble," 20 *J. Econ. Lit.* 1463 (1982).

27. See Samuel L. Popkin, *The Rational Peasant: The Political Economy of Rural Society in Vietnam* 1–31 (1979) (criticizing Polanyi and other "moral economists").

fare, especially among persons who are not intimates.[28] In contexts where explicit market exchange would be the least-cost means for members of a close-knit group to obtain gains from trade, their controller-selecting norms are predicted to direct them to resort to contracts.

Private Organizations as Controllers

Organizational rules were not important in the slice of Shasta County I examined, but in many other contexts they play a central role. Business firms have work rules. Part of the job of the Dean of Students is to keep the undergraduates in line. Baseball executives and umpires are key disciplinarians of players; in 1989 Commissioner Bart Giamatti's handling of the Pete Rose case drew roughly as much press as did the trial of Ollie North, which was going on at the same time.

The exploding field of organization theory deals with how business executives mix two particular instruments of social control: the contract and the firm.[29] Whether to monitor agents internally by means of a firm's hierarchy or externally by means of contracts is just one aspect of the larger question of choice among social-control systems. Most organization theorists anticipate that business executives will choose among instruments of control in an economizing way,[30] a prediction that is in accord with the hypothesis. Because these theorists have been primarily interested in how people coordinate to supply marketable goods and services, however, they have had little to say about the relative merits of organizations as makers and enforcers of rules in spheres outside the business sector.

An informal group often has acknowledged leaders to whom controller-selecting norms ask disputants to turn for mediation or arbitration. For instance, norms may require siblings to take unresolved disputes to their parents; gang members, to the leader of the pack. The victims of Frank Ellis' marauding cattle once complained to the Shasta County Cattlemen's Association, and the county Board of Supervisors also sometimes made efforts to slough social-control responsibilities onto that or-

28. When they vote with their feet, people provide a crude indication of how they assess the overall merits of market and nonmarket economies. For example, the net flow of migrants from East Germany to West Germany during 1989 can be taken to signal, among other things, the migrants' relative preference for a market economy.

29. The watershed article on this topic is Ronald H. Coase, "The Nature of the Firm," 4 *Econometrica* (n.s.) 386 (1937). A more recent landmark is O. Williamson, supra note 8.

30. See, e.g., Oliver E. Williamson, *The Economic Institutions of Capitalism* 1 (1985).

ganization.[31] The field of alternative dispute resolution includes within its purview these semihierarchical systems, which lie in the middle ground between informal control and organization control.

The Choice between Law and Norms

Members of close-knit groups are hypothesized to employ and mix informal and legal systems of social control in a manner that minimizes members' total costs.[32] If the hypothesis is correct, the content of controller-selecting norms will reflect general expectations about the comparative efficiencies of social forces and the state in generating and enforcing rules.[33] In addition, when deciding what controller to select to handle a specific dispute, group members will pay heed to the features of that dispute—its subject matter, gravity, parties, and so on—that would tend to make it appropriate for one controller or another. Because of the ever-present threat of transaction costs, norm-makers may trade off precision in the selection of controllers for simplicity in the definition of controllers' jurisdictions.

Relative Competence at Reducing Deadweight Losses

A rational utilitarian would be more willing to confer rulemaking functions upon the state if the state had a comparative advantage over norm-makers in generating rules supportive of cooperative outcomes.[34]

Some general advantages of government-made rules. An especially valuable function of government is to supply laws designed to override the parochial norms of close-knit subgroups within it. A norm of "honor among thieves" may well be welfare maximizing for thieves, but welfare diminishing for society at large. Whalers' norms of the nineteenth century maximized the immediate catch of whales, but resulted in overfish-

31. See supra Chapter 2, text accompanying note 14.

32. Compare Donald Black, *The Behavior of Law* (1976), an ambitious, multifaceted inquiry into the independent variables that influence the importance of law in the overall system of social control.

33. To simplify the exposition, this section assumes that members of a close-knit group have only two instruments—informal control and legal control—by which to achieve cooperative outcomes.

34. Owen M. Fiss, "The Death of the Law?" 72 *Cornell L. Rev.* 1, 2, 15 (1986), argues that judges and other government officials have a special role in articulating group values. The text assumes that norm-makers do not regard state officials as inherently better than informal leaders—such as Dr. Martin Luther King, Jr., the columnist George Will, and Shasta County's Dick Coombs—at articulating values.

ing. A communitarian's dream of numerous small autonomous communities might end up as a nightmare of constant strife between neighboring groups. The state's strength and territorial breadth give it an unmatched capacity to control the antisocial tendencies of subgroups. If feasible, even-handed state policing against parochial norms would confer a reciprocity of advantage on all state residents. In a healthy political system, a state would therefore tend to punish actors who have hurt the larger society by honoring a group's parochial norms. A few groups, of course, such as teenage gangs, Gypsies, and organized criminals, might refuse to submit to these state efforts, perhaps out of the sense that their net advantage would lie in a policy of evasion and defiance. The members of most informal groups, however, can be expected to recognize the legitimacy of even-handed state policies to counter parochialism. In part because of the threat of state punishment of parochial behavior, mainstream groups might be inclined to develop controller-selecting norms that asked members to submit to the enforcement of laws that preempted their parochial norms. For example, norms among modern-day whalers are predicted to support the quotas on catches that are established through international conventions.

Some branches of government may be more likely than others to adopt welfare-maximizing rules. Richard Posner believes, for example, that judge-made law tends to be efficiency enhancing and that legislation tends to be efficiency reducing.[35] If the members of close-knit groups were to agree with Posner, they would be more tolerant of legal claims based on common-law doctrine than of claims based on statutes. Neighbors thus might be more accepting of a private land-use lawsuit based on a nuisance theory than of one based on building-code requirements.

Some general advantages of informal rules. By hypothesis, the more close-knit a group, the more successful it will be at generating and enforcing utilitarian norms to govern internal disputes.[36] A close-knit group's members will often regard their norms as superior to governing laws, both because distant lawmakers may be less informed than norm-makers and also because selfish interest groups can generally manipulate laws more easily than norms. For these reasons, a close-knit group capable of generating a relatively reliable and cheap system of informal social control is

---

35. See, e.g., Richard A. Posner, *Economic Analysis of Law* 495–499 (3d ed. 1986).

36. This is a staple among law-and-society scholars. See, e.g., D. Black, supra note 32, at 107–109 (1976); Richard Schwartz, "Social Factors in the Development of Legal Control: A Case Study of Two Israeli Settlements," 63 *Yale L.J.* 471 (1954).

predicted to have controller-selecting norms that discourage members from taking intermember disputes into the legal system.

In rural Shasta County, residents strongly favored the informal resolution of internal disputes. As Norman Wagoner, the cattleman who had served on the Board of Supervisors, put it, "Being good neighbors means no lawsuits."[37] Rural Shasta County is by no means atypical in its lawlessness. As James Acheson has described, the lobstermen of Maine also have rules against resort to the legal system:

> Fishermen feel strongly that the law should be kept at bay and that people should handle their own problems. Any fisherman who goes to the police about trap cutting not only looks ineffectual and ridiculous but is somewhat of a threat. When a man's traps are missing, taking the law into his own hands is not only more effective but also maintains his standing among fellow fishermen.[38]

Significantly, the reluctance to use law is not limited to remote rural areas. Stewart Macaulay found it among Wisconsin executives: "One businessman said that customers had better not rely on legal rights or threaten to bring a breach of contract law suit against him since he 'would not be treated like a criminal and would fight back with every means available.'"[39]

Groups with large or transitory memberships are usually not close-knit and cannot rely as much on informal social control. As a result, resort to the legal system tends to be tolerated more in industrialized than in preindustrial cultures,[40] and more in large cities than in small towns.[41] Law also plays a lesser role in Japan's relatively homogenous society than it does in the United States.[42]

37. See generally supra Chapter 3, text accompanying notes 54–68.

38. James M. Acheson, *The Lobster Gangs of Maine* 75 (1988).

39. Stewart Macaulay, "Non-Contractual Relations in Business: A Preliminary Inquiry," 28 *Am. Soc. Rev.* 55, 64 (1963).

40. Band- and village-based cultures have been able to create order without a state apparatus. See Marvin Harris, *Culture, People, Nature: An Introduction to General Anthropology* 355–372 (2d ed. 1975); Susan Reynolds, *Kingdoms and Communities in Western Europe, 900–1300* 15, 38 (1984) (unwritten custom served as main source of rules).

41. David M. Engel, "Cases, Conflict, and Accommodation: Patterns of Legal Interaction in a Small Community," 1983 *Am. Bar Found. Res. J.* 803, 816–821, 851–856. See also supra Chapter 10, note 48.

42. See Takeyoshi Kawashima, "Dispute Resolution in Contemporary Japan," in *Law in Japan* 41 (Arthur Taylor von Mehren ed. 1963); but compare J. Mark Ramseyer and Minoru Nakazato, "The Rational Litigant: Settlement Amounts and Verdict Rates in Japan," 18 *J. Legal Stud.* 263 (1989).

When citizens believe that their government is illegitimate, they will be particularly reluctant to refer disputes to it. For example, when judges are known to be corrupt, a close-knit group's norms are more likely to tend to condemn a member who takes another to court. When outsiders control a group's legal system, the group's controller-selecting norms are apt to preclude use of that system altogether; after the Soviet Communists seized legal control of Moslem central Asia, the Moslems responded by directing disputes away from the Communist legal system.[43]

Relative Competence at Reducing Transaction Costs

The operation of any system of social control entails process costs—such as those involved in circulating information, administering sanctions, and maintaining system institutions. The controller-selecting norms of close-knit groups are predicted to be sensitive to the relative competence of informal and legal systems in carrying out these administrative tasks.

The ways through which people learn norms and legal rules, for example, vary in their costliness. Norms are often obscure because they must be inferred from diffuse practices. As a result a legal system may have a comparative advantage in promulgating clear rules; indeed, one of the legal system's useful functions may be to crystallize informal rules.[44] Only specialists, however, are likely to have ready access to the official documents in which legal rules are set out. As legal realists have convincingly shown, moreover, legal doctrine is not determinate in many instances. Thus people may choose against law, or drastically simplify it in action, in order to avoid the administrative costs of finding the law or learning its technicalities.

In general, parties involved in informal control are apt to be able to complete fact-finding much faster than legal specialists can. Informal justice is often same-day justice. When all participants are close-knit, informal fact-finders are also more likely to be astute appraisers of the credibility of witnesses. Legal systems are likely to be better, however, at gathering expert testimony and ensuring the neutrality of fact-finders.

The state has two distinct, sometimes decisive, advantages as an administrator. First, the enforcement of group values is a public good that, because of risks of free-riding, tends to be undersupplied.[45] A state can

---

43. See Gregory J. Massell, "Law as an Instrument of Revolutionary Change in a Traditional Milieu: The Case of Soviet Central Asia," 2 *L. & Soc'y Rev.* 179, 208–211 (1968).

44. See Karl N. Llewellyn, "What Price Contract?—An Essay in Perspective," 40 *Yale L.J.* 704, 722 n.45 (1931).

45. See supra Chapter 13, text accompanying notes 18–26.

prevent free-riding by compelling payment of taxes, the revenues from which are used to hire police officers, judges, and other specialized enforcers. As social imperfections rise, a group's members are increasingly likely to regard law enforcement as more cost-justified than informal enforcement. For example, city dwellers rely on government more than small-town residents do, in part because informal enforcement is chancier in cities.

Second, informal enforcement is perilous when the parties to a dispute are likely to disagree on who owes what to whom. Then the exercise of self-help may lead to a feud—an endless echo of reciprocal, and possibly escalating, sanctions.[46] A party who believes he has been victimized by a *legal* decision against him, by contrast, is more likely to acquiesce in it because of the court's overwhelming power, comparative neutrality, and relative anonymity.[47]

The risk that informal control will escalate has led even libertarians such as Robert Nozick to endorse the prevailing scholarly view that government should have a monopoly in the application of forceful sanctions.[48] Members of close-knit groups are not nearly as statist as the scholars. In Shasta County, feuds are rare because remedial norms strictly regulate self-help by calling for the punishment of persons who respond with excessive force.[49] Aware that their informal-control system is unlikely to spiral out of control, rural residents countenance forceful self-help in appropriate circumstances.

Both the legal system and the informal-control system may be characterized by efficiencies (or disefficiencies) of scale in administration. Once an informal-control system has been established among neighbors, for example, their marginal costs of referring additional disputes to it may be lower than before. Conversely, once the state has assumed a major role in social control, even more state control may be utilitarian. If police officers have begun to walk on street patrol to deter violent crime, they can readily be assigned to an antigraffiti campaign as well.

If efficiencies of scale in social-control subsystems were large and continuous, people might conceivably regard *both* a tiny state and a massive state as preferable to a middle-sized state, on the ground that giving major roles to both legal and informal systems would be wastefully duplicative. Some anarchist writers, such as Pyotr Kropotkin, have criticized

46. See supra Chapter 12, note 33 and accompanying text.
47. But see Melvin Aron Eisenberg, "Private Ordering through Negotiation: Dispute-Settlement and Rulemaking," 89 *Harv. L. Rev.* 637, 659–660 (1976) (bringing in a stranger as a judge tends to drive disputants farther apart).
48. Robert Nozick, *Anarchy, State, and Utopia* 26, 88–89, 138–139 (1974).
49. See supra Chapter 3, text accompanying notes 54–58.

the modern trend toward more state control for this reason.[50] They worry that people will eventually not be willing to bear the transaction costs of maintaining two elaborate, and potentially redundant, systems of social control. They see the rise of the legal system as permanently crowding out the more spontaneous, and to them more desirable, system of informal control. In the same vein, Michael Taylor believes that state provision of social insurance causes private mutual aid to wither, perhaps at an accelerating rate as role models for altruistic behavior become scarcer.[51] Although future empirical work may provide support for this concern in some contexts, in Shasta County and elsewhere people continue to maintain both informal and legal systems of social control and to mix them in sophisticated ways. This is a clue that in practice, efficiency-of-scale considerations do not force a populace to choose between the polar solutions of the night-watchman state and the totalitarian state.

Mixing the Informal and Legal Systems

A hybrid system of social control is in place when one controller enforces another's rules.[52] Because one controller may be the best rulemaker while another is the most efficient enforcer, utilitarians' controller-selecting norms would reward, with a greater volume of business, a controller that enforced another's better rules.

The law's use of custom as a source of rules. In practice, judges often self-consciously enforce "custom," the legal label for informal rules.[53] As Chapter 11 described, when resolving lawsuits over the ownership of dead whales, judges looked to whalers' customs to determine property rights. During the nineteenth century especially, custom was an important determinant of the standard of care in accident cases.[54] In both its original broad outlines and its current substantive details, the Uniform Commercial Code frequently gives legal status to the usages of merchants.[55]

---

50. Pyotr Kropotkin, *Mutual Aid: A Factor of Evolution* 227–228 (1914).

51. Michael Taylor, *Anarchy and Cooperation* 134–140 (1976). See also Donald Black, *The Manners and Customs of the Police* 196–199 (1980).

52. See supra Chapter 7, text accompanying notes 23–25.

53. Early English law borrowed unashamedly from custom. See Carleton Kemp Allen, *Law in the Making* 67–160 (7th ed. 1964). Clark, supra note 1, at 1726–1740, provides a rich discussion of the pros and cons of adherence to traditional rules.

54. See, e.g., Titus v. Bradford, B. & K. R.R., 136 Pa. 618, 626–627, 20 A. 517, 518 (1890).

55. See, e.g., Uniform Commercial Code §1-102(2)(b) (1988) (one underlying purpose of the UCC is "to permit the continued expansion of commercial practices through custom, usage and agreement of the parties"); id., §1-205(5) ("applicable usage of trade" is to be used in interpreting an agreement). See generally Zipporah Batshaw Wiseman, "The Limits of

A utilitarian judge would be wise to apply customary rules in contexts where those rules are more likely than legal rules to be welfare maximizing in content. According to the hypothesis, a close-knit group acting in contexts where it was unable to impose losses on outsiders would be a reliable source of utilitarian customs. If the hypothesis is sound, a utilitarian judge could confidently defer, for example, to the customs of merchants engaged in repeat dealings, but not necessarily to the customary treatment of pedestrians by motorists.[56]

Custom may "lag," as Judge Learned Hand rightly noted when rejecting an asserted customary standard of care in *The T. J. Hooper*.[57] Lags occur because people can rationally choose to reduce decision-making costs by imitating prevailing customs and not paying close attention to the advent of new information and technologies.[58] Because courts are also imperfect, however, a utilitarian judge should trump custom with a legal rule only when there is reason to think that judges have a comparative advantage in identifying a welfare-maximizing practice.

A utilitarian lawmaker would be sensitive not only to the substantive advantages of alternative informal and legal rules but also to their relative transaction costs. A good reason to base commercial law on commercial custom, for example, is that merchants already have a sense of their own customs but might have to hire attorneys to learn law. Conversely, in a society with a welter of dispute-engendering informal land-transfer practices, lawmakers might be wise to establish and enforce uniform formalities for those transactions.

Informal enforcement of legal rules. Persons who are not law-enforcement bureaucrats sometimes self-consciously choose to enforce legal rules. Vigilantism of this sort tends to become more prevalent as a state weakens. A police strike brings out informal enforcers of law. When sheriffs were outmanned in the American West, frontiersmen carried six-shooters to assist in the self-help enforcement of law.

Scholars have disputed the degree to which members of an informal group are likely to enforce laws that differ from the group's norms.[59]

Vision: Karl Llewellyn and the Merchant Rules," 100 *Harv. L. Rev.* 465, 492–538 (1987); Note, "Commercial Law and the American *Volk*: A Note on Llewellyn's German Sources for the Uniform Commercial Code," 97 *Yale L.J.* 156 (1987).

56. R. Posner, supra note 35, at 152–154, discusses when a legal system should recognize compliance with custom as a defense in a negligence action.

57. 60 F.2d 737, 740 (2d Cir. 1932).

58. See supra Chapter 10, note 21.

59. See generally supra Chapter 8, text accompanying notes 47–53. Sociologists often assert that the symbolic mantle of law tends to strengthen *congruent* norms. But see Stewart Macau-

Legal peripheralists argue that informal groups systematically reject intrusive laws.[60] Legal centralists offer the opposite thesis that, presumably
because informal enforcers are prone to select the state's rules, norms
generally tend to converge toward law.[61] Neither of these extreme positions is consistent with the evidence. On the one hand, for example, the
passage of a closed-range ordinance in Shasta County has little effect on
the informal resolution of cattle-trespass and fence-maintenance disputes
there. On the other hand, it is highly plausible that the civil rights acts of
the 1960s helped to weaken norms of racial segregation in the South.[62]
Although it seems clear that law sometimes affects social mores, not much
is known about when and how these feedback loops operate.

The Influence of Dispute Characteristics
on Controller Selection

To maximize welfare, a group's controller-selecting rules must be sensitive not only to the relative general competencies of informal and legal
institutions but also to the suitability of referring particular types of disputes to one or the other of these controllers. Four characteristics of a
dispute are likely to influence the identity of the controller to which it is
assigned.[63]

First, as law-and-society scholars have long emphasized, the nature of
the relationship between two disputants significantly influences how they
are supposed to resolve their disputes. Two individuals in a continuing
multiplex relationship typically possess reciprocal power and also good
information about each other's past behavior. Social groups therefore
strongly encourage intimates to use the informal-control system. Controller-selecting norms are more tolerant of litigation when it is brought
against strangers.[64] The social-distance variable helps explain why controller-selecting norms permitted Shasta County residents to take high-

---

lay, "Elegant Models, Empirical Pictures, and the Complexities of Contract," 11 *L. & Soc'y
Rev.* 507, 520–521 (1977) (noting the paucity of evidence supporting this assertion).

60. See Richard D. Schwartz, Book Review, 34 *J. Legal Educ.* 736, 738–739 (1984); sources
cited supra Chapter 8, note 47.

61. See, e.g., Ramseyer and Nakazato, supra note 42, at 285–289.

62. For evidence that these laws affected employment practices, see source cited supra
Chapter 8, note 49.

63. The following discussion revisits issues taken up supra Chapter 5, text accompanying
notes 42–60.

64. See, e.g., D. Black, supra note 32, at 40–46 (1976); Richard Lempert and Joseph Sanders, *An Invitation to Law and Social Science* 235 (1986).

way-collision disputes, but not fence-maintenance disputes, into the legal arena.

Second, the size of the stakes matters.[65] The greater the stakes, the more likely it is that the exercise of informal remedies will trigger a violent feud. When stakes are small, a grievant is less likely to regard the relatively high administrative costs of the legal system to be worthwhile.[66] For these reasons, the greater the damage from a livestock-vehicle collision, the more likely Shasta County residents were to take it to court. They also tended not to legalize cattle-trespass disputes, which typically involve small stakes, but said they would be willing to legalize water-rights disputes, on which much more is apt to ride.

Third, the substantive content of a dispute matters for several reasons. Legal and informal-control systems vary in their ability to handle technical complexity. Governments (and other hierarchical controllers) tend to be better at obtaining and responding to expert advice. Because fence-cost disputes typically involve simple facts and technologies, controller-selecting norms in Shasta County tend to relegate such conflicts to informal resolution. Groundwater supply networks, by contrast, are difficult to observe and for sensible management may require technically intricate rules involving return flows, allocation during shortage, and so on. Because the technical complexity of water issues usually overtaxes the norm-making skills of neighboring households, the legal system is likely to have major comparative advantages in the resolution of water disputes.[67] Government rulemaking is particularly unlikely to be welfare enhancing, however, in the many spheres of activity in which well-placed rent seekers can obtain legislation that aids them at the greater expense of the politically weak. In these spheres, people are predicted to recognize the relative incompetence of the political process and, therefore, to tend to choose norms over law. For example, as will be shown below, professors have chosen to trump the federal statutes that excessively protect publishers from the photocopying of copyrighted material for classroom use.

65. Both the intrinsic and extrinsic aspects of a dispute influence its magnitude. See supra Chapter 5, text preceding note 42.

66. Marc Galanter, "Reading the Landscape of Disputes: What We Know and Don't Know (and Think We Know) about Our Allegedly Contentious and Litigious Society," 31 *UCLA L. Rev.* 4, 20 (1983). For related reasons, large legal claims are more likely to go to trial than small ones. See Patricia Munch Danzon and Lee A. Lillard, "Settlement Out of Court: The Disposition of Medical Malpractice Claims," 12 *J. Legal Stud.* 345, 362–367 (1983); W. Kip Viscusi, "The Determinants of the Disposition of Product Liability Claims and Compensation for Bodily Injury," 15 *J. Legal Stud.* 321, 331–332 (1986).

67. If sophisticated agribusiness firms were to control most of the land in a particular territory, however, their hydrologists might be better than lawmakers at devising water norms.

Fourth, all else equal, the members of a group can be expected to choose the controller that best enables them to externalize costs to outsiders. From the members' perspective, a failure to exploit an opportunity for externalization is a deadweight loss. When a state does a poor job of policing the socially wasteful practices of organized-crime families, members of those groups may regard it as welfare maximizing to decide their internal disputes according to their selfishly insular norms. Conversely, in other legal contexts a self-interested group may turn to the legal system partly because it enables them to shift costs to taxpayers, insurance companies, or others. When the costs of legal services to the poor are borne by taxpayers, impoverished individuals can be expected to resort more frequently to the legal system. Similarly, Shasta County residents are likely to sue over vehicle-livestock collisions, but not over boundary-fence costs, in part because their liability insurance covers the former but not the latter. Within a viable marriage, personal-injury litigation between spouses is likely only when an insurance company will pick up the tab. As these examples illustrate, willingness to use law depends not only on the comparative institutional competence of the legal system in general but also on the specific features of particular disputes.

The Lawlessness of Academic Photocopying

Because academic institutions seem to be disproportionately populated with legal centralists, it is fitting to develop in some depth an example that suggests that professors can reject law just as emphatically as the cattlemen of Shasta County do.

Current federal law appears to place severe restrictions on an instructor's photoduplication of copyrighted material for inclusion in class readings. When copies are made without the consent of the copyright owner, the legal question is whether the copying is a "fair use."[68] This has traditionally been, and remains, a murky area of law. During the drafting of the Copyright Act of 1976, at the urging of congressional committee members, representatives of publishers, authors, and educational institutions agreed to a set of "Guidelines" for classroom copying. These Guidelines were included in the House Report on the bill that amended the

---

68. 17 U.S.C. §107 (1988) (explicitly stating that "multiple copies for classroom use" may be a fair use in a particular case). See generally William W. Fisher, "Reconstructing the Fair Use Doctrine," 101 *Harv. L. Rev.* 1661 (1988).

act.[69] Although originally privately drafted, the Guidelines are widely interpreted as stating authoritative law.[70]

The Guidelines are tough. Suppose an instructor were to photocopy for classroom distribution, year after year and without consent, an article such as Ronald H. Coase's "The Problem of Social Cost." This practice would arguably violate the Guidelines for three distinct reasons.[71] First, Coase's article exceeds the Guideline standard for "brevity," which imposes a ceiling of 2500 words for a work of this sort. Second, the repeated copying would violate the standard for "spontaneity," because it would not be "unreasonable to expect a timely reply to a request for permission." Third, the Guidelines explicitly state that "Copying shall not . . . be repeated with respect to the same item by the same teacher from term to term." When willful infringement has been proved, the Copyright Act authorizes a judge to award a copyright owner a civil penalty of up to $100,000 plus attorney fees.[72] Because university officials on some campuses periodically circulate copies of the Guidelines to faculty members, a copyright owner might well be able to prove that an infringer was, if not a knowing violator of the Guidelines, at least willfully inattentive to them.[73]

Indeed, the Association of American Publishers (AAP) has helped sponsor a number of the test cases brought by copyright owners to enforce the Guidelines against duplicators of class materials. In the best known of these, *Addison-Wesley Publishing v. New York University,*[74] the defendants were a university, nine professors, and an off-campus com-

69. See H.R. Rep. No. 1476, 94th Cong., 1st sess. 65–70 (1976), reprinted in 1976 *U.S. Code Cong. & Ad. News* 5678–5683. The Guidelines are also included in the "Historical Note" to 17 U.S.C.A. §107 (1988).

70. Marcus v. Rowley, 695 F.2d 1171, 1178–1179 (9th Cir. 1983); Melville B. Nimmer, 1 *Nimmer on Copyright* §13.05 [E][3][a] (1985). The Guidelines were honored in the settlement in Addison-Wesley Publishing v. New York University, infra note 74.

71. The Guidelines themselves profess to set the minimum, not the maximum, standard of fair use. Nevertheless, there is reason to believe that some judges would construe them as setting the maximum. See sources in note 70.

72. 17 U.S.C. §§504(c)(2), 505 (1988). Prior to 1988, the ceiling was $50,000.

73. A covering memo circulated in 1987 at Stanford University read in part, "The Provost's Office periodically reminds the faculty and staff members engaged in teaching and research that we must be aware of and abide by the law." Stanford University Memo to Members of the Faculty and Academic Staff, from James N. Rosse, Provost, on "Copyright: Copies of Printed Material for Teaching and Research," November 1987.

74. 82 Civ. 8333 (S.D.N.Y. April 7, 1983) (*1983 Copyright Law Decisions* (CCH) ¶25,544), analyzed in Note, "Fair Use of the Guidelines for Classroom Copying?: An Examination of the Addison-Wesley Settlement," 11 *Rutgers Computer & Tech. L.J.* 111 (1985).

mercial copy center. The parties ultimately entered into a settlement agreement. In the publicized portions of the agreement, the copy center and the university pledged to honor the Guidelines in the future.[75] In 1989, a group of eight publishers followed up with a highly publicized suit against Kinko's, a leading chain of commercial copy centers, alleging copyright violations in the making of photocopied anthologies for university courses.[76]

Despite this daunting legal backdrop, there is abundant, if unsystematic, evidence that university instructors engage in rampant unconsented photocopying when preparing class materials. Law professors I have questioned almost invariably admit to the unconstrained copying of articles for class use, although most note that they would decline to duplicate major portions of books. The people who manage duplicating rooms within law schools also confess that they make no effort to enforce legal constraints on copying; they instead expect professors to police themselves. At my behest, several commercial copy centers located just off a campus duplicated, no questions asked, multiple copies of an original photocopied from an article in a professional journal. I have overheard a staff member of a copy center tell a patron that copyright laws prevented him from photocopying more than 10 percent of a book presented as a hardcopy original; the patron then asked whether he himself could use the copy center's equipment to accomplish that task and was told that he could. These bits of evidence support the AAP's contention that copyright violations on campuses are "widespread, flagrant, and egregious."[77]

In short, professors' substantive norms seem to permit the unconsented copying for class use, year after year, of articles and minor portions of books. Professors apparently allow this informal rule to trump copyright law. The instructors' norm of reciprocal fair use enables them to economize on two sorts of transaction costs. First, a norm permitting unconstrained minor copying relieves professors of the task of learning the

75. See Stacy E. Palmer, "Publishers Withdraw Lawsuit Charging NYU and Professors with Copyright Infringement: University Will Step Up Its Efforts to Control Photocopying," *Chron. Higher Educ.,* Apr. 20, 1983, at A1, col. 3.

76. Judith Axler Turner, "Eight Publishers Charge Copyright Violation, Sue Copying Chain," *Chron. Higher Educ.,* May 3, 1989, at A1, col. 4.

77. Statement of Allan Wittman, chairman of the AAP copyright committee, quoted in *Chron. Higher Educ.,* Jan. 5, 1983, at 26, col. 1. Although the AAP has yet to assemble data on the issue, its officials remain "absolutely" convinced that rampant violations continue. Telephone interview with the AAP's Carole Risher, July 17, 1989. See also Sheldon Elliot Steinbach, "Photocopying Copyrighted Course Materials: Doesn't Anyone Remember the NYU Case?" 50 *West's Educ. L. Rep.* 317 (1989).

mind-numbing intricacies of fair-use doctrine. Second, liberal copying rights spare academics from the transaction costs of both writing and responding to letters of consent. Although this may seem like a minor matter, it often is not. For example, an instructor who during a summer had put together a set of several dozen copyrighted readings for a fall class might have to delay sending the materials for duplication until the last of the permission letters had arrived. In practice, this might prove harrowing. In a case study in which 23 permission letters had been sent to publishers, only 17 publishers had responded in any way within six months of the mailing.[78]

Moreover, professors can sense that on copyright issues Congress will be more responsive to the intense lobbying of publishers than to the pleas of professors and universities about transaction-cost barriers to the enrichment of university course materials. As a result, professors are likely to reason that replacing copyright law with their own copying norms would not only enhance their welfare but also be a principled act of subversion of special-interest legislation.[79] It should be stressed that the professors' decision to reject copyright law is made with only a dim awareness of the substance of that law; most professors, certainly most law professors, would flunk if quizzed on the details of legal restrictions on copying for classroom use. What professors are aware of is not the specifics of the law but rather the unlikelihood that Congress would enact welfare-enhancing rules in this context.

The choices professors make among rules of intellectual property are undoubtedly somewhat more complex than has just been suggested. If a creator of intellectual property (or a purveyor of publishing services) cannot capture the full value of his labor, there may be a suboptimal amount of publishing. Professors have a sound basis for anticipating, however, that the liberal, unconsented copying of articles and chapters would result in few deadweight losses of this sort. In practice, authors of academic articles and monographs (as distinguished from books) are not much motivated by royalties and other payments from publishers.[80] Even the academic journals with the largest circulations seldom pay honoraria to the

78. Gail Paulus Sorenson, "Impact of the Copyright Law on College Teaching," 12 *J. College & Univ. L.* 509, 516 (1986).

79. See id. at 537 (AAP position threatens to "impede effective education and knowledge production").

80. Academic cultures provide significant indirect rewards to successful scholars. These include promotions in rank, raises in salary, and advancements in social status. These diffusely administered systems serve to stimulate the production of new ideas, without at the same time conferring monopolies on creators in the way that the copyright system does.

authors whose articles they accept. In addition, most authors of academic articles happily mail reprints to colleagues at no charge. Compilers of law-school casebooks and class materials have found that academic authors and academic publishers routinely grant, at no charge, permission to reprint short excerpts.[81] It appears that most academic authors are so eager for readers to know and cite their work that they usually regard a royalty of zero or even less as perfectly acceptable. For them small-scale copying is not a misappropriation but a service. Because academic norms favor the free exchange of information, a professor gauche enough to charge another for a reprint or for permission to duplicate an article for a seminar would immediately become the target of a whispering campaign.

Impressionistic evidence suggests that professors' substantive norms *do* disallow the copying of major portions of books for classroom use; such copying would significantly diminish authors' royalty income. For example, although academic norms permit an instructor to copy, for student use, articles from professional journals, they do not permit the reproduction of, say, the first half of a commercial coursebook. As a result, an author victimized by another's major copying would be entitled to circulate negative gossip about the offender. In an extreme case, professors' controller-selecting norms might even entitle the victim to use the legal system to vindicate rights under the Copyright Act.

Nonetheless, there appears to be no published report of a case in which a college professor had sued another for duplicating copyrighted work for classroom use.[82] About a third of a million people teach in institutions of higher education in the United States. At first blush, this professorate might appear to be too sizable and uncohesive to support norms on copying. Professors operate, however, in social networks more close-knit than an outsider might imagine. Instructors in higher education are divided into disciplines, each of which has a highly developed information network including journals, annual meetings, and so on. Serious violations of copying norms would be hard to cover up because the incriminating evidence would be available both in stores and in the hands of numerous

---

81. Each year Professor Gary T. Schwartz of the UCLA Law School writes for permission from the authors of the articles he includes in his class materials. He reports that no author has ever either declined him permission or charged him a penny. When preparing a casebook on land-use regulation, I found that authors and academic presses routinely granted at no charge my requests to reprint short portions of copyrighted books and articles.

82. Of course, one reason publishers sue more often is that their stakes are greater than those of authors. Notably, in a case in which a public school teacher sued another for unpermitted copying of a cake-decorating booklet, the author-plaintiff was also the publisher. Marcus v. Rowley, 695 F.2d 1171, 1173 (9th Cir. 1983).

students. As a result, the members of a discipline have considerable ability to administer informal punishments, such as adverse gossip, against deviants who have either excessively copied or excessively enforced their copyrights.

The interests of publishers are different from those of professors and authors. Unlike academic authors, publishers—especially commercial presses[83]—depend on sales revenues for survival. Whether unconstrained copying is injurious to publishers is unclear, however. Stan Liebowitz has argued that copying does not harm journal publishers because publishers can indirectly appropriate revenues from copy users, for example, by charging more for library subscriptions.[84] But the AAP's continuing legal campaign against copying suggests that commercial publishers may have made a different assessment of where their interests lie.

In any event, professors' norms are hypothesized to be welfare maximizing only for professors themselves. Academics are predicted to show unwavering concern for publishers only in contexts in which the welfare of publishers would be linked to their own.[85] Because of campus ties, for example, professors might be more solicitous of university presses and bookstores than of commercial counterparts. So long as professors have little reason to anticipate a shortage of publishing houses in general, professors' reluctance to copy large portions of books is most plausibly interpreted as stemming mainly from their solicitude for author-professors' royalty incomes, not from their concern about the revenues received by commercial publishers and booksellers.

In the two leading test cases concerning copying for classroom use, the plaintiffs were commercial publishers and the prime defendant, an off-campus commercial photocopy center.[86] That this is the most legalized of photocopy relationships is consistent with the hypothesis: of all the par-

83. There is evidence that commercial publishing companies are more likely than university presses or professional associations to charge fees for permission to copy for classroom use. See Sorenson, supra note 78, at 516–517.

84. S. J. Liebowitz, "Copying and Indirect Appropriability: Photocopying of Journals," 93 *J. Pol. Econ.* 945, 947–950 (1985). See also Stanley M. Besen and Sheila Nataraj Kirby, "Private Copying, Appropriability, and Optimal Copying Royalties," 32 *J.L. & Econ.* 255, 280 (1989) ("where either the cost of copying is low or originals are expensive to produce, the producer may be better off not imposing a royalty").

85. These professorial norms may be parochial and therefore not welfare maximizing for society as a whole. Utilitarian policy initiatives on the copying problem might include government taxes on the sale of photocopying equipment and annual sales of blanket licenses by consortia of publishers to consortia of universities. See Sorenson, supra note 78, at 536–537. These sorts of initiatives are beyond the competencies of norm-makers.

86. The eight publishers who brought the *Kinko's* lawsuit in 1989 joined neither universities nor professors as defendants. See Turner, supra note 76. Those sorts of associated parties were included as named defendants in *Addison-Wesley,* however.

ties involved in off-campus photocopying controversies, commercial publishers and commercial copy centers have the most remote relationship. Publishers cannot punish the copy centers by withdrawing business, because they have too little of it to withdraw; for their part, the copy centers, because they buy few books, cannot informally retaliate against a publisher's overzealous enforcement of the Guidelines. When the frailness of social linkages saps the potential for informal control, parties' controller-selecting norms are apt to tolerate litigation. The relevance of social distance is underscored by the fact that in its most recent test case the AAP declined to sue *university*-run copy centers for infringement of copyrights. Publishers are rightly skittish about initiating welfare-threatening litigation against the employers of the persons on whom many of their book sales depend. As the publishers no doubt recognize, professors, like the residents of rural Shasta County, know how to get even.

PART III

The Future of Norms

15

Testing the Content of Norms

The hypothesis that close-knit groups generate norms that maximize the objective welfare of group members was induced from scattered observations in Shasta County and elsewhere. A more formal analysis would have included an attempt to deduce the same hypothesis from explicit axioms. A dip into the highly mathematical theory of noncooperative games quickly convinced me that I would have to leave that sort of undertaking to others. Part II therefore argued only that a wide variety of norms are intuitively consistent with the hypothesis. But it can be argued that this method is not always convincing, both because the examples chosen may be unrepresentatively Panglossian, and because intuitive reactions vary.

This chapter responds to these anticipated criticisms. It begins by discussing two well-known counterexamples from Italy and Uganda that might be put forth to illustrate that close-knit groups are capable of generating norms that *reduce* the welfare of their members. The discussion of these counterexamples itself indicates how after-the-fact analysis of a case study can fail to convince. The successful ex ante prediction of what will be found in an unexamined social environment tends to be more persuasive than the ex post rationalization of known evidence. The balance of this chapter, therefore, employs the hypothesis to generate specific and falsifiable predictions about the content of norms that apply to land-related disputes in the contemporary United States.

Counterevidence?

Social scientists sometimes report uncovering norms that they regard as unmistakably welfare reducing. Two of the better-known examples are Colin Turnbull's work on the Ik of northern Uganda and Edward Banfield's study of the norms of peasants in Montegrano, a southern Italian

267

village.[1] On close examination, however, these two studies are less threatening to the hypothesis than first impressions would suggest.

Turnbull found an unsettling pattern of inhumanity among the Ik, a once-nomadic tribe with a few thousand members. Ik parents were at best indifferent to the welfare of their children after infancy. The Ik also took delight in others' suffering: "... [M]en would watch a child with eager anticipation as it crawled toward the fire, then burst into gay and happy laughter as it plunged a skinny hand into the coals.... Anyone falling down was good for a laugh too, particularly if he was old or weak or blind."[2]

Banfield found no horrors as graphic as these, but concluded that the Italian peasants he studied were practitioners of what he called "amoral familialism," a moral code that asked its adherents to "[m]aximize the material, short-run advantage of the nuclear family; assume all others will do likewise."[3] According to Banfield, this attitude hindered cooperation among families and helped keep the villagers mired in poverty.

Both of these studies drew fire immediately after they appeared. Turnbull's critics chastised him for failing to stress that when he was studying the Ik the tribe members were literally starving to death as a result of external events. A few years before Turnbull's visit the government of Uganda had turned the Ik's traditional hunting ground into a national park, forcing the tribe to attempt to survive by farming in a nearby drought-plagued area. Previously cooperative in hunting, the Ik became increasingly inhumane as they starved.[4] Rather than undermining the hypothesis, the tragic story of the Ik thus actually supports the hypothesis' stress on close-knittedness: cooperation among the Ik withered only as their prospects for continuing relationships ebbed.[5]

Reviewers similarly disputed Banfield's interpretation of life in the southern Italian village. Some suggested that the evidence Banfield pre-

---

1. Colin M. Turnbull, *The Mountain People* (1972); Edward C. Banfield, *The Moral Basis of a Backward Society* (1958). Jon Elster cites these two studies, as well as a number of others, in his attack on functionalist theories of norms. See Jon Elster, "Social Norms and Economic Theory," 3 *J. Econ. Perspectives* 99, 110-113 (1989).

2. C. Turnbull, supra note 1, at 112–113.

3. E. Banfield, supra note 1, at 85.

4. C. Turnbull, supra note 1, briefly presented these facts at 24–26, but did not emphasize them in his analysis.

5. Similar criticisms of Turnbull's *The Mountain People* appear in Peter Singer, *The Expanding Circle* 24–26 (1981); James A. Knight, "On the Ik and Anthropology: A Further Note," 17 *Current Anthropology* 777 (1976) (what Turnbull observed is typical of human behavior under conditions of semi-starvation); "More Thoughts on the Ik and Anthropology," 16 *Current Anthropology* 343-358 (1975).

sented could be read as showing that the people of Montegrano, as a group, had adapted as well as possible to an unpromising environment.[6] Further, Banfield's own evidence often contradicted his thesis of amoral familialism. He observed, for example, that "relations among neighbors are generally good."[7] And while recognizing that the villagers had powerful norms of reciprocity in the granting of favors, he condemned this because "they do so from self-interest, not from charity or fellow-feeling."[8] Banfield's findings of cooperation among neighbors and the reciprocation of favors are consistent with the hypothesis, which of course does not predict what Banfield apparently chose as the earmark of a well-ordered society—the absence of self-interested motivation.

More generally, anthropologists have sometimes attempted to puncture the balloon of Panglossianism by describing how members of some primitive societies believe in magic, engage in brutal rites, and so forth. Members of the Dani tribal group in Western New Guinea, for example, cut a finger from the hand of each of a man's close female relatives after he dies.[9] Although a few anthropologists, notably Marvin Harris,[10] are adept at coming up with utilitarian explanations for seemingly bizarre practices, this sort of functionalism is currently out of favor in anthropology. The hypothesis nevertheless predicts that, if they became better educated in science, members of a preliterate tribe would tend to abandon old practices that their new knowledge had revealed to be welfare reducing.[11] A tribe that used to turn to rain dancing during droughts thus is predicted to phase out that ritual after tribe members learn more meteorology. Tribes are predicted to abandon dangerous puberty rites after members obtain better medical information. As tribe members become more familiar with science in general, the status of their magicians and

6. See Thomas McCorkle, Book Review, 61 *Am. Anthropologist* 133 (1959); William Muraskin, "The Moral Basis of a Backward Sociologist: Edward Banfield, the Italians, and the Italian-Americans," 79 *Am. J. Soc.* 1484 (1974).

7. E. Banfield, supra note 1, at 122.

8. Id. at 121.

9. Richard A. Barrett, *Culture and Conduct: An Excursion in Anthropology* 5–6 (1984).

10. See, e.g., *Cannibals and Kings: The Origins of Culture* (1977); *Cows, Pigs, Wars, and Witches: The Riddles of Culture* (1974).

11. Members of the Algonquian tribes in Canada, for example, did discard their religious belief that a slain animal spontaneously regenerates itself after this belief had stimulated overhunting of valuable forest animals. Various perspectives on this example are discussed in Robert A. Brightman, "Conservation and Resource Depletion: The Case of the Boreal Forest Algonquians," in *The Question of the Commons: The Culture and Ecology of Communal Resources* 121, 130–133 (Bonnie J. McCay and James M. Acheson eds. 1987). The updating of norms is likely to lag, of course, because rational actors are rightly reluctant to abandon long-standing customs. See supra Chapter 10, note 21.

witch doctors should fall. As a more contemporary example, faith in astrology should correlate negatively with knowledge of astronomy. These propositions are potentially falsifiable.

Some Predicted Property Norms

Relations among adjoining landowners, co-owners of land, and residential landlords and tenants all provide domestic contexts for testing the hypothesis. Although a complex body of property law formally applies to each of these relationships, the theory developed in Part II predicts that close-knit parties would largely ignore these legal doctrines and instead apply informal norms whose content would maximize their mutual objective welfare. Evidence showing that these relationships are relatively legalistic, or that the operative informal rules vary significantly from those that will be outlined, would weaken the claim that the hypothesis has heuristic value.[12]

Relations among Adjoining Landowners

It is widely believed that urbanization weakens social ties, and hence informal cooperation, among neighbors.[13] If so, residents of urban areas might be predicted to be generally more inclined than the rural landowners in Shasta County to look to the complex common-law rules that formally apply to disputes between adjoining landowners.[14] The analysis in Chapter 14 nevertheless suggests that adjoining city homeowners would

12. An investigator can falsify the existence of a predicted norm with evidence that (1) close-knit participants do not punish persons who they know have violated the norm, (2) ordinary behavior is not in accord with the norm, or (3) group members' aspirational statements are inconsistent with the norm. See supra Chapter 7, text accompanying notes 14–20.

13. For several reasons, a group of urban neighbors is likely to be somewhat less close-knit than a group of rural neighbors. An urban area offers a richer set of socializing opportunities. By diffusing social networks, urbanization is thus likely to weaken the neighborhood gossip channels that are an important element of informal-control systems. In addition, an urban resident who is the target of neighborhood ostracism can turn to alternative social circles more readily than a rural resident can. Although urbanization thereby weakens the third-party control of groups of neighbors, the informal power of *immediately adjoining* neighbors remains strong for reasons to be explained in the text. On urbanization generally, see sources supra Chapter 10, note 48.

14. "Adjoining Landowners" is a chapter heading in both *American Jurisprudence 2d* and *Corpus Juris Secundum*, the two encyclopedias of American law. See 1 *Am. Jur. 2d* Adjoining Landowners §§1–136 (1962); 2 *C.J.S.* Adjoining Landowners §§1–74 (1972). A scholarly analysis of the general problem is Stewart E. Sterk, "Neighbors in American Land Law," 87 *Colum. L. Rev.* 55, 69–88 (1987) (stressing the bilateral monopoly aspect).

be just as unlikely to resolve their disputes through law. Most homeowners live in one house long enough to anticipate complex continuing relationships with their immediate neighbors. Even when they are not friends in a social sense, adjoining homeowners are likely to interact on a variety of issues, such as fencing, trees, drainage, security, noise, and street parking. They can easily discern when one of them has violated a norm of neighborliness and, because of their continuing interactions, can readily even up unbalanced accounts. Under these conditions, people are predicted to govern their general affairs by means of informal social control rather than the legal system.[15]

Boundary fences. As a first concrete example, consider the issue of how two adjoining homeowners should divide the expense of a common boundary fence. Many states have statutes that nominally govern the sharing of these fence costs; the common law of restitution may also formally apply.[16] Boundary fences, however, typically involve only small stakes. Materials for a simple boundary fence between two urban or suburban lots will likely cost somewhere in the hundreds, not thousands, of dollars, and many homeowners are capable of erecting the fencing themselves. In addition, going through the legal system almost never enables a pair of neighbors to externalize fencing expenses to a third party such as an insurance company. In light of these conditions, adjoining suburban homeowners are predicted not to consult legal rules before arranging for boundary fence work. If quizzed, practicing attorneys are predicted to report that clients simply do not come to them with questions about these legal rules.

Although it is more difficult to forecast the content of the informal fencing norms that adjoining homeowners apply, I predict that these are similar to the fencing norms observed in Shasta County.[17] If so, if one neighbor were to propose in advance to the other that the two share the

15. Although this assertion takes the form of an ex ante prediction, I should confess my awareness of some evidence on the subject. A valuable field study on dispute processing among neighbors is M. P. Baumgartner, *The Moral Order of a Suburb* (1988). Baumgartner analyzed conflicts among unrelated acquaintances in an older middle-class suburb outside New York City. She found that aggrieved parties rarely resorted to the legal system but instead adopted nonconfrontational strategies such as avoidance, ostracism, conciliation, and secret complaining. On neighbor interactions in higher density settings, see Sally Engle Merry, *Urban Danger: Life in a Neighborhood of Strangers* (1981); Leonard G. Buckle and Suzann R. Thomas-Buckle, "Doing Unto Others: Disputes and Dispute Processing in an Urban American Neighborhood," in *Neighborhood Justice: Assessment of an Emerging Idea* 78 (Roman Tomasic and Malcolm M. Feeley eds. 1982) (urban neighbors rely on self-help).

16. See supra Chapter 4, notes 4–12 and accompanying text.

17. See supra Chapter 4, text accompanying notes 19–32.

costs of an objectively cost-justified fence, the latter would be informally obligated to bear that fraction of total costs that would equal his fraction of total objective benefits. Focal-point solutions, such as fifty-fifty splits, should be common. To maintain the solidarity of the neighbor relationship, an informal fencing debt is likely to be discharged in kind—through the subsequent return of reciprocating favors or through the provision of fencing materials—rather than through cash compensation for the labor of the neighbor who erected the fence. A neighbor is also predicted, however, not to be obligated to share in the costs of a fence that was put up without prior warning or the need for which was created by the fencebuilder's subnormal activities (such as the harboring of a vicious dog).

Trees that block views. As a second concrete problem, suppose that a typical shade tree situated in the backyard of an urban homeowner's downhill lot were to grow to block the ocean view from the living-room windows of another homeowner's uphill house. Because an ocean view is objectively worth far more than a treetop, the hypothesis predicts the existence of a substantive norm entitling the uphill homeowner to obtain the removal of the offending branches. Homeowners are predicted to reach this result without any arm's length bargaining and without any investigation of the formal law on the subject.[18]

The next issue is to what extent, if at all, the uphill owner would be indebted to the neighbor who removed the offending treetop.[19] Because the topography of lots is so varied, neighbors usually have asymmetric capacities to provide welfare-enhancing tree-cutting services. In a Specialized Labor situation of this sort, an uphill owner whose view is reopened is predicted to incur an informal obligation to provide restitution to the downhill owner who trimmed the tree.[20] Again, because immedi-

18. See supra Chapter 14, text accompanying note 25 (intimately close-knit parties often prefer to create duties through norms rather than through contracts). In modern subdivisions, restrictive covenants may govern the issue of trees that block views. A promising topic for research within these subdivisions is the extent to which controller-selecting norms require neighbors to resolve tree disputes according to the terms of the covenants rather than according to informal norms.

19. In Calabresi-Melamed terms, this is the question of whether the downhill owner, who decidedly should not possess the bargaining power that property-rule protection would confer, should nevertheless be protected by a liability rule. See Guido Calabresi and A. Douglas Melamed, "Property Rules, Liability Rules, and Inalienability: One View of the Cathedral," 85 *Harv. L. Rev.* 1089 (1972).

20. In Specialized Labor situations, the hypothesis predicts that close-knit groups will generate norms that call for compensation of Workers who confer special benefits. See supra Chapter 12, text accompanying notes 9–10.

ate neighbors would want to avoid impersonal cash transfers for labor, an uphill owner can be expected to provide this restitution in kind, perhaps by personally hiring the tree-trimmer who performs the work.

Solar access. Third, consider a homeowner's rights to solar access, a problem that in some jurisdictions is governed by a complex body of law. California, for example, has an elaborate statute designed to protect an installed solar collector from the shade of a subsequently planted tree.[21] Nevertheless, because they typically have continuing relationships, adjoining homeowners are predicted to resolve most solar-access issues without reference to these legal provisions. Indeed, neighbors are predicted to punish informally any homeowner who invokes the law of solar rights.[22]

Solar collectors are rare and shading risks can usually be minimized through adroit siting of solar equipment. As a result, solar issues should be governed by the general utilitarian norm that holds that those who carry out hypersensitive land uses are the cheapest avoiders of damages resulting from those special vulnerabilities.[23] If so, a tree owner would not have any informal obligation to avoid shading a neighbor's collector. A tree owner might comply with a solar neighbor's request to trim, of course, especially if he expected the neighbor to render informal compensation for that service.[24]

Relations among Concurrent Owners of Land

Most of the tens of millions of parcels of real estate in the United States are owned by two or more persons. These co-owners typically employ one of the standard common-law forms of concurrent ownership.[25] The

21. See Cal. Pub. Res. Code §§25980–25986 (West 1986) (Solar Shade Control Act).

22. More specifically, neighbors are predicted to have imposed social sanctions on the homeowners who sought legal relief from ordinary shading in Prah v. Maretti, 108 Wis. 2d 223, 321 N.W.2d 182 (1982), and Sher v. Leiderman, 181 Cal. App. 3d 867, 226 Cal. Rptr. 698 (1986).

23. Nuisance law embraces this rule. See Ellickson, "Alternatives to Zoning: Covenants, Nuisance Rules, and Fines as Land Use Controls," 40 *U. Chi. L. Rev.* 681, 751–757 (1973).

24. A field investigator might therefore have difficulty distinguishing situations in which a tree owner is protected by a property rule (predicted for the solar-collector case) and situations in which a tree owner is protected only by a liability rule (predicted for the ocean-view case).

25. A study of 1620 deeds recorded in 1959–60 in five urban California counties found that 60 percent of the grantees were married couples taking title as joint tenants. Yale B. Griffith, "Community Property in Joint Tenancy Form," 14 *Stan. L. Rev.* 87, 88 n.4 (1961); see also N. William Hines, "Real Property Joint Tenancies: Law, Fact, and Fancy," 51 *Iowa L. Rev.* 582, 585–591 (1966) (52 percent of Iowa land transfers between 1954 and 1964 created joint tenancies).

most important of these are the joint tenancy, under which the share of a deceased co-owner automatically passes on his death to the surviving co-owner(s), and the tenancy in common, under which a decedent's fractional interest passes at his death to his heirs or devisees.

Concurrent owners may share the benefits and burdens of their common land disproportionately. For example, friends who are co-owners of a ski-resort condominium unit may not occupy the unit in the same proportion that they have made contributions to the unit's purchase and upkeep. If perturbed by these inequalities, co-owners might refer to the set of common-law rules that formally determine the rights and duties of concurrent owners.[26]

The theory of norms developed in this work predicts, however, that these co-owners will rarely consult law. People willing to acquire land together tend to be intimates—spouses, blood relatives, lifelong friends. The expense of consulting lawyers makes going to law a negative-sum game. Because co-owners tend to be intimate, they can usually be expected to rely on informal rules and self-help sanctions to keep each other in line.

Anticipating future difficulties over sharing, co-owners may prepare a contract governing their relationship. Co-investors whose relationship is single-strandedly financial can be expected to be most likely to do this; spouses and close relatives, the least likely. When co-owners do write up a contract, the hypothesis forecasts that they will bargain from starting positions set by informal norms, not by the formal law of concurrent owners. When a divorce, death, or falling out severs the relationship among concurrent owners, they can no longer rely on the informal-control system. Litigation that does occur among concurrent owners is therefore predicted typically to involve parties who lack the prospect of a continuing relationship.[27]

26. See sources in Jesse Dukeminier and James E. Krier, *Property* 321–324 (2d ed. 1988); Lawrence Berger, "An Analysis of the Economic Relations between Cotenants," 21 *Ariz. L. Rev.* 1015 (1979).

27. As a simple test of this proposition, I read the twenty cases listed under the keynote "Tenancy in Common, §29, Repairs & Improvements" in West's Ninth Decennial Digest, which canvassed all appellate cases reported in the West system between 1976 to 1986. Despite the keynote's heading, some of these cases in fact involved joint tenancies, not tenancies in common. In eighteen of the twenty cases, the parties disputing the crediting of repairs and improvements to common property had either recently been, or were at the same time, terminating their legal relationship by means of divorce or partition proceedings. (The two remaining cases involved, respectively, the co-owners of a right-of-way, and an instance in which the state of the title to the property at issue was incredibly muddled.) Although appellate cases are not necessarily representative of disputes in general, the results of this exercise are consistent with the notion that co-owners with an ongoing relationship are disinclined to use lawyers.

The substantive norms of concurrent owners are generally predicted to be similar to the fencing norms observed in Shasta County. If so, a co-owner's fraction of total objective burdens of property ownership would be informally set to equal the fraction of the total objective benefits from the property that he received.[28] (Roughly, to each according to the objective value of his inputs.) This formula has the virtue of stimulating individual co-owners to propose objectively cost-justified contributions to the common land. To encourage joint projects, however, norms are predicted to require a co-owner who is contemplating an improvement to notify the other co-owners in advance of the project.[29] Should they refuse to go along with an objectively cost-justified project, however, the improving co-owner is predicted to be entitled to proceed with the improvement and to claim an informal credit against the noncontributors.[30]

The strict accounting of past inputs and outputs, however, would be transactionally costly and signal a lack of trust. Because co-owners tend to have more intimate relationships than do adjoining landowners, they are likely to be especially interested in maintaining symbols of relational solidarity. Hence, concurrent owners can be expected to turn to rough focal-point solutions even more often than Shasta County fence-builders do.

Relations between Landlords and Residential Tenants

Landlord-tenant relationships generate far more litigation than do neighbor and co-owner relationships. The theory offers an explanation for why landlords and tenants are relatively prone to turn to law, but also predicts that they will tend to refrain from doing so until near the end of a leasehold.

Most absentee landlords have only single-stranded relationships with their residential tenants. The single strand is severed when the tenancy ends. When the end approaches, the parties have no prospect of a continuing relationship through which each can informally control the other. At that juncture, they are likely to turn to the legal system to settle a dispute over, for example, unpaid rent or the return of a security deposit. A landlord who rents out units in a small building in which he himself

28. See supra Chapter 4, text accompanying notes 19–27.

29. Shasta County fencebuilding norms call for notice under analogous circumstances. See supra Chapter 4, text accompanying note 29.

30. Common-law doctrine sometimes denies credit to a co-owner who has unilaterally made an objectively cost-justified improvement. See J. Dukeminier and J. Krier, supra note 26, at 322. The legal problem is analyzed in Saul X. Levmore, "Explaining Restitution," 71 Va. L. Rev. 65, 83–84 (1985).

resides, however, often has multistranded relationships with tenants. Resident landlords are predicted to resolve disputes with tenants more informally than absentee landlords do.

End-game relations. A crisis in a landlord-tenant relationship most commonly develops when a tenant has failed to pay rent but still remains in possession. Even though these sorts of disputes involve small monetary sums, they tend to be resolved through the legal system. All states have statutes that forbid a landlord from using self-help to oust a tenant. The statutes instead require the landlord to initiate a summary eviction action, a legal proceeding that usually takes no more than a few months to complete. A landlord who wins judgment in a summary action can obtain a court order directing a government officer, such as the local sheriff, to remove the nonpaying tenant from possession.

That the state has attempted to monopolize the process of removing tenants is unremarkable, because the state often attempts to squeeze out rival forms of social control. What *is* notable is that, in this context, both landlords and tenants largely defer to the state's exercise of power. Landlords seem to appreciate that a tenant threatened with physical ouster from his dwelling is likely to defend his territory with force. Tenant violence is less likely when the tenant has been given an opportunity to justify his nonpayment of rent to a third party and, if that justification fails, is ousted not by the landlord directly but by agents representing the overwhelming force of the state.[31] Landlords, recognizing that the state indeed often has a comparative advantage as a controller of doomed landlord-tenant relationships, apparently eject nonpaying tenants more commonly by means of a lawful eviction procedure than by self-help ouster.

Mid-game relations. The theory anticipates, however, that a landlord and tenant are unlikely to be legalistic when they anticipate that their relationship will continue for a significant interval. In such cases, both should recognize the comparative advantage of informal control. Many residential tenancies are month to month. This arrangement provides each side with the option of rapid exit. The exercise of an exit option by one side typically imposes costs on the other side. For example, by giving thirty-day notice to terminate a tenancy, a landlord imposes relocation costs on the tenant.[32] Conversely, a tenant who gives thirty-day notice imposes re-renting costs on the landlord. This mutual capacity to exit, by informally empowering both sides, fosters cooperation between landlords

31. See supra Chapter 12, note 27; Chapter 14, text accompanying notes 46–49.
32. When a tenant refuses to honor a thirty-day notice, a landlord is legally entitled to resort to a summary eviction action.

and tenants. Short of exit, each side also can readily administer small punishments to retaliate against misconduct by the other. For instance, a landlord can chisel on maintenance, while a tenant can chisel on rent payments and restraint from wear and tear.

Because both landlords and residential tenants can readily understand the advantages of informal governance of their relationship, their controller-selecting norms are predicted to forbid both sides from invoking formal legal rules or initiating a legal proceeding while the leasehold still has a future.[33] Indeed, ongoing residential landlord-tenant relationships are predicted to be generally cooperative.[34] A Rand Corporation study in Green Bay, Wisconsin, which reported landlord-tenant relationships there to be "relaxed and comfortable," supports this vision.[35]

Landlords and tenants who have reason to worry about their external reputations are likely to be even more civilized. In some housing markets, a landlord can purchase from a commercial data bank a report detailing a prospective tenant's prior involvement in housing litigation.[36] Some university student associations maintain files in which students report their experiences with specific landlords. Elementary game theory predicts that the existence of these sorts of information banks will tend to spur cooperation.

Conversely, ill-advised legal restructurings of landlord-tenant relationships can limit the participants' ability to exercise informal control. Rent control is particularly destructive of landlord-tenant relations because it takes from landlords the powers to set rent and to exit from the relationship. Tenants are unlikely to ignore rent control because it offers them a significant short-run gain without immediate fear of reprisal. In the long run, however, landlords typically respond to rent control by chiseling on services, which in turn angers tenants. Rent control thus foments adver-

33. The hypothesis also predicts that landlords and tenants would make a utilitarian mix of implicit norms and explicit lease provisions. See supra note 18, on how neighbors in a subdivision might similarly combine norms and express covenants.

34. Since the 1960s, legal-services attorneys have been heavily involved in representing poor tenants in landlord-tenant litigation. A tenant receiving free legal services is unusually prone to invoke legal rights because for him the costs of using the legal system are much reduced. Poor households are therefore more likely than nonpoor households to have legalistic and combative relations with landlords.

35. Rand Corporation, *Second Annual Report of the Housing Assistance Supply Experiment* 69 (R-1959-HUD May 1976) (discussing Brown County, Wisconsin). Rand's report did not offer a characterization of landlord-tenant relations in St. Joseph County, Indiana, its second experimental site.

36. See Pam Belluck, "Tenants Cry Foul as Screening Companies Help Landlords Spot 'Problem' Applicants," *Wall St. J.,* Dec. 27, 1985, at 13, col. 4.

sarial and legalized relations. This may be one reason why life in New York City, which has had rent control for almost fifty years, has an unusually nasty edge. If the media center of the United States happened to be Green Bay and not New York, the prediction that ongoing residential landlord-tenant relationships are generally informal and relaxed would be somewhat less in conflict with popular opinion.

The implied warranty of habitability. Focus on a specific issue in landlord-tenant relations will sharpen the discussion. Legal scholars have recently devoted much attention to the legal rules applicable to tenant complaints about latent defects in the quality of residential premises.[37] Before 1970 or so, the prevailing rule in the United States on this issue was caveat lessee. Absent an express lease provision, this rule held that a residential tenant was not entitled to abate rent when the landlord had failed to repair a latent defect.[38] For example, under caveat lessee, if the tenant's contract rent were $500 per month and a newly leaking roof were to cause the market value of the premises to fall to $300 per month, the tenant would still owe $500 per month.

During the late 1960s and early 1970s, a tidal wave of legal change obliterated caveat lessee.[39] Both state courts and state legislatures embraced the implication of a nonwaivable warranty of habitability in residential leases.[40] Many states adopted a damage formula that in some applications entitled a tenant harmed by breach of the implied warranty to abate rent to a level below the market value of the premises in their defective condition. The formula might entitle a tenant who had rented a patently substandard apartment for $300 a month and who had in fact received $300 a month in value, to reduce rental payments to, say, $100 per month for so long as the defect persisted.[41]

---

37. Unless otherwise noted, the ensuing discussion assumes that the tenant did not cause the defect and did not know of its existence when entering into the lease. It also assumes that the landlord could repair the defect more efficiently than the tenant could.

38. Even in a caveat-lessee jurisdiction, the threat of government housing-code enforcement might operate as a legal inducement for landlords to make repairs.

39. In retrospect, the impending demise of caveat lessee should have been evident at an even earlier date. Beginning with Pines v. Perssion, 14 Wis. 2d 590, 111 N.W.2d 409 (1961), no state supreme court that considered the issue applied caveat lessee. See Annot., 40 A.L.R. 3d 646 (1971).

40. See, e.g., Roger A. Cunningham, "The New Implied and Statutory Warranties of Habitability in Residential Leases: From Contract to Status," 16 *Urb. L. Ann.* 3 (1979); Edward H. Rabin, "The Revolution in Residential Landlord-Tenant Law: Causes and Consequences," 69 *Cornell L. Rev.* 517 (1984).

41. See, e.g., Green v. Superior Court, 10 Cal.3d 616, 638, 517 P.2d 1168, 1183, 111 Cal. Rptr. 704, 719 (1974); Hilder v. St. Peter, 144 Vt. 150, 161, 478 A.2d 202, 209 (1984). These decisions both contain dicta that would entitle a tenant to abate from the contract rent an amount equal to the difference between the market rent of up-to-standard premises and the

Despite all the hoopla about these legal events, the hypothesis predicts that neither caveat lessee nor the implied-warranty damage formula has ever in fact controlled the main run of ongoing month-to-month residential tenancies, especially those in which the tenant is not a consumer of free legal services. Instead, in the absence of an agreement to the contrary, landlords and tenants are predicted to follow an informal norm of objective equality—namely, that the market value of the housing services that the tenant receives should equal the rent that he pays. In common parlance, you are entitled to get what you pay for. This norm has two principal utilitarian advantages. First, by establishing the background principle that the aggregate exchange should involve objective equivalents, this norm frees the parties from having to specify in detail the rights and duties on both sides of the continuing contract. Second, unlike the two legal doctrines discussed, the norm of objective equality fosters cooperation by implicitly authorizing *both* sides to administer Tit-for-Tat sanctions to remedy partial nonperformance by the other. The application of the objective-equality norm would generate results other than those the legal system would reach in the two examples presented. Even if caveat lessee were the law, for instance, this norm would entitle the tenant who had contracted to pay $500 per month and who, because of a leaking roof, had received only $300 in value, to reduce rent paid to $300 per month so long as the roof continued to leak. And, even if the law were to recognize an implied warranty of habitability, this norm would forbid any rent abatement by a tenant who had rented patently defective premises at $300 per month, their market rent in that substandard condition.[42] To test these predictions, an investigator could interview landlords, management agents, and tenants about the formal and informal resolution of disputes arising from defects in residential buildings.[43]

---

market rent of the premises as-is. Under this formula, if the market rent of premises complying with implied-warranty standards were $500 per month, and the contract rent and market rent as-is were both $300 per month, the tenant would owe only $100 per month.

42. A tenant who enforces warranty rights receives shorter-term benefits than a tenant who enforces rent-control rights. The landlord can end a tenant's benefits from warranty doctrine by repairing the defect and then, after waiting long enough to ensure that the eviction is not illegally retaliatory, terminating the leasehold.

43. Field studies of landlord-tenant relations have mainly inquired into legally processed disputes. See, e.g., Samuel Jan Brakel and Donald M. McIntyre, "The URLTA in Operation: An Introduction," 1980 *Am. B. Found. Res. J.* 555; Allan David Heskin, "The Warranty of Habitability Debate: A California Case Study," 66 *Cal. L. Rev.* 37 (1978); Note, "The Great Green Hope: The Implied Warranty in Practice," 28 *Stan. L. Rev.* 729, 750–751 (1976).

16

* * *

Conclusions and Implications

In many contexts, law is not central to the maintenance of social order. This was the general finding in Part I, which described the domain and content of cattle-control norms in rural Shasta County, California. The evidence from that field study demonstrated the fancifulness of Ronald Coase's Parable of the Farmer and the Rancher, the most famous narrative in law and economics. Coase's parable correctly anticipates that the varying legal rules governing cattle trespass in Shasta County do not affect, for example, the quality of boundary fencing around pastures. The parable's explanation for the allocative toothlessness of the law, however, turns out to be exactly backward. According to the parable, the *absence* of transaction costs is what may make the law irrelevant; in Shasta County, however, the *presence* of transaction costs is what leads people to ignore law in many situations.

The Limits of Law

The strongest version of the Coase Theorem asserts that, as long as information and dealing are costless, people can be expected to bargain from any initial set of legal entitlements to achieve an identical, and optimal, allocation of resources. According to this vision, in a frictionless environment the market would roll like a river over the abject attempts of lawmakers to shape the world by changing rules of private law.[1]

Coase's parable has beguiled many analysts into believing that the law must matter when the unrealistic assumption of zero transaction costs is dropped. Bruce Ackerman, for example, regards the existence of transaction costs as serving up a rich opportunity for activist lawmaking to correct market failures.[2] More surprisingly, Coase, despite his steady pil-

---

1. The source of the river metaphor is Mark Kelman, "Consumption Theory, Production Theory, and Ideology in the Coase Theorem," 52 *S. Cal. L. Rev.* 669, 675 (1979).
2. See Bruce A. Ackerman, *Reconstructing American Law* 55–58 (1984). See also Stewart Schwab, Book Review, 87 *Mich. L. Rev.* 1171, 1198 (1989) (sympathizing with Ackerman's recasting of Coase).

lorying of A. C. Pigou for excessive faith in government,[3] also exaggerates the potential influence of law. Aware that transaction costs are in fact "large,"[4] Coase has asserted that lawmakers indeed affect the allocation of resources whenever the transaction costs of parties' exchanging initial legal entitlements exceed what the parties would gain from those exchanges.[5] In a representative passage from "The Problem of Social Cost," Coase writes: "In a world in which there are costs of rearranging the rights established by the legal system, the courts, in cases relating to nuisance, are, in effect, making a decision on the economic problem and determining how resources are to be employed."[6] In this sentence, as well as elsewhere, Coase overstates the influence of law. His error lies in his implicit assumption that people can effortlessly learn and enforce their initial legal entitlements, and that they confront transaction costs only when they attempt to bargain from their legal starting positions. In a world of costly information, however, one cannot assume that people will both know and honor law.[7] The Shasta County evidence indicates that people are aware that the legal system is a relatively costly system of dispute resolution and therefore often choose to turn a deaf ear to it. As a result, despite what Ackerman and Coase suggest, the introduction of transaction costs is not sufficient to make law matter.

The proposition that legal rules may lack bite is of particular importance to the legislators, lawyers, policy analysts, and others who aspire to be social engineers. These legal activists have been especially prone to exaggerate what the Leviathan can accomplish. For a wide variety of

---

3. Ronald H. Coase, *The Firm, the Market, and the Law* 20–30, 133–153, 179–185 (1988).

4. Id. at 26.

5. Id. at 115, 175–177.

6. Id. at 132–133.

7. Law may also fail when people are agreeable to using it. People disposed to honor law may nonetheless receive garbled legal messages, either because lawmakers have spoken unclearly or because human brains are fallible receivers. The passage of a closed-range ordinance in Shasta County, for example, influenced traditionalist cattlemen's practices only because the cattlemen misperceived its formal effects. See supra Chapters 5 and 6. The difficulty of communicating legal rules accurately suggests a possible revision in the famous Calabresi-Hirschoff test for identifying cheapest cost-avoiders. (See supra Chapter 11, note 8.) That test deals ingeniously with two transaction-cost realities: the costs of acquiring information about preventive technologies, and the costs of executing decisions. As formulated, however, the test pays no attention to the costs parties must bear to stay abreast of applicable rules of liability. Because actors' capacities to obtain legal information are often asymmetric, Calabresi and Hirschoff's test might be revised to recommend that liabilities be placed on the party in the best position (1) to make a cost-benefit analysis between accident costs and accident avoidance costs, (2) to act on that cost-benefit analysis once it is made, and (3) to learn about, and to be concerned about, where law has allocated accident risks. Of course, rulemakers must also be chary of rewarding deliberate or negligent obliviousness to the content of rules.

reasons, legal interventions can flop.[8] To avoid the frustration of trying to influence what is beyond their reach, legal instrumentalists would be wise to deepen their understanding of the nonlegal components of the system of social control.

Indeed, one reason people are frequently willing to ignore law is that they often possess more expeditious means for achieving order. For example, neighbors in rural Shasta County are sufficiently close-knit to generate and enforce informal norms to govern minor irritations such as cattle-trespass and boundary-fence disputes. This close-knittedness enables victims of social transgressions to discipline deviants by means of simple self-help measures such as negative gossip and mild physical reprisals. Under these circumstances, informal social controls are likely to supplant law.

Informal Social Control

Building on the Shasta County findings, Part II sought to develop a theory of informal norms. To place these informal controls in context, Chapter 7 disaggregated the entire social-control system into five principal subsystems: self-enforced personal ethics, two-party contracts, informally enforced norms, organization controls, and law. In practice, these subsystems are often not entirely distinct. Hybrid systems, under which one controller enforces another's rules, are common; a hybrid is in use, for example, when an individual internalizes his society's norms and then enforces those rules upon himself.

In addition, the rules of one controller often feed back to influence the rules of another. Innovations in norms may ultimately affect the content of law, and vice versa. These feedback loops are currently little understood. It is clear, however, that the loop from law to norms is not sufficient to make norms invariably converge toward law in all contexts. Particularly when lawmakers attempt to regulate workaday matters, they may fail to influence behavior not only directly, through law, but also indirectly, through influence on the content of relevant norms. In Shasta County, the legal designation of a territory as open (or closed) range had no apparent effect on how residents resolved trespass or estray disputes. The rancher Kevin O'Hara paid a neighbor for the loss of a corn crop

---

8. A generation ago, Lon Fuller, one of the truly wise legal scholars, identified "eight ways to fail to make a law." See *The Morality of Law* 33–39 (1964). Some of the pitfalls Fuller identified, such as failure to publicize a law and failure to make rules understandable, today would likely be articulated in the language of transaction costs. The phrase *transaction costs*, of course, did not enter legal scholarship until after the publication of Fuller's book.

because he "felt responsible," a feeling he said would not have been influenced by formal trespass law. Even Shasta County insurance adjusters paid virtually no attention to the legal distinction between open range and closed range when settling trespass-damage claims. The few landowners who actually knew there was a California statute dealing with the sharing of boundary-fence costs did not regard it as a source of entitlements. In sum, some spheres of life seem to lie entirely beyond the shadow of the law.

A centerpiece of the theory is the hypothesis that, to govern their workaday interactions, members of a close-knit group tend to develop informal norms whose content serves to maximize the objective welfare of group members. This hypothesis suggests that people often choose informal custom over law not only because custom tends to be administratively cheaper but also because the substantive content of customary rules is more likely to be welfare maximizing.

If verified, the hypothesis of welfare-maximizing norms will have several normative implications. The primary one is that, in situations where utilitarian considerations are paramount, lawmakers interested in the resolution of humdrum disputes that arise *within* a group are unlikely to improve upon the group's customary rules. Under these circumstances, a legal system would appropriately give deference to a group's informal practices. This conclusion supports, for example, the general impulse of common-law judges to give weight to custom, and Karl Llewellyn's efforts to incorporate merchant practices into the Uniform Commercial Code.

The Limits of Informal Control

From both positive and normative perspectives, norms have their limits, and law has its place. Legal rules in Shasta County commonly influence the resolution of disputes that arise after a motorist has collided with livestock on the highway. The examination of the settlement of these sorts of collision disputes helped to identify the variables that determine when the law matters. As prior investigators have found in other contexts, disputants are increasingly likely to turn to legal rules when the social distance between them increases, when the magnitude of what is at stake rises, and when the legal system provides an opportunity for the disputants to externalize costs to third parties.

From a normative standpoint, there may be good reasons for preferring the resolution of certain disputes through law rather than through norms. First, the hypothesis of welfare-maximizing norms provides no basis for expecting that norms will serve certain ends, such as corrective or distributive justice, that policymakers might regard as relevant, or even paramount. Second, because there is no reason for thinking that a group's norm-making process will give weight to the interests of those outside the group, a legal system properly can decline to pay any respect to how a group customarily treats outsiders. Third, the hypothesis is a positive proposition about the content only of workaday norms; it predicts nothing about the nature of a society's foundational entitlements.

Using Law to Invigorate Informal Control

Donald Black has offered the positive thesis that "[l]aw varies inversely with other social control."[9] In his view, the state has recently risen in importance as lawmakers have striven to fill the void created by the decline of the family, clan, and village.[10] Many current trends, such as increasing urbanization, the spread of liability insurance, and the advent of the welfare state, are continuing to weaken the informal-control system and expand the domain of law.[11]

It is worth stressing that legal policies themselves influence the vitality of informal systems of social control. To achieve order without law, people must have continuing relationships, reliable information about past behavior, and effective countervailing power.[12] Recast in the vocabulary of game theory, some basic variables in social structure are the numbers of players involved in an inning of a game, the number of innings in which current players later expect to encounter each other, the time span within which the players expect those innings to occur, the quality of the players' information, and the distribution of power among the players. Legal rules can influence all these attributes of social structure and thereby promote—or impede—informal cooperation.

Basic rules of land tenure, for example, can significantly influence both the number of parties involved in land disputes and the frequency of those parties' encounters. Harold Demsetz has observed that the subdi-

9. Donald Black, *The Behavior of Law* 107 (1976) (emphasis omitted).

10. Id. at 108–109. Black speculates, however, that law will decline in importance in the future, mainly because he anticipates that equality will increase. Id. at 132–137.

11. Recent cries of "hyperlexis" are nevertheless exaggerated. Despite the growth in the number of lawyers in the United States, private litigation between individuals, apart from divorce, remains surprisingly rare. See supra sources cited in Chapter 8, note 39. Indeed, during the nineteenth century, issues of cattle-trespass and boundary-fence law were more prominent in state courts and legislatures than they are today, in part because in the interim the amounts at stake in these sorts of disputes have fallen relative to household incomes.

12. See supra Chapter 10, text accompanying notes 35–49.

vision of a commons into private parcels abets cooperation by reducing the number of people concerned with localized externalities.[13] It can be added that land subdivision thrusts the remaining decision makers into repetitive relationships as immediate neighbors, and thereby is likely to enhance cooperation among them.

Foundational laws can also lengthen a person's perceptions of the time span, including periods after his own death, within which other people will have relationships with either him or his property. For instance, neighbors who own usufructuary interests (that is, rights to possess land so long as one uses it) are likely to have less permanent relationships than neighbors who have life estates (that is, rights to possess until death). Other legal rules can further extend a player's perception of the time period of play to beyond his own death. Laws that authorize inheritance by kin, disposition of property by will, and perpetual (fee simple) interests in land all encourage a living person to manage capital assets as if the game of life were infinite in length. By inducing players to adopt long planning horizons, these rules help to conserve resources for future generations.

Legal rules can also affect how easy it is for people to obtain the information they need to engage in informal social control. For example, recent advances in data processing make it easier to store and retrieve truthful public-record information about a person's previous failures to cooperate. Computerized data banks pose deeply troubling risks, of course, which are emphasized in law-review articles on the subject.[14] Nevertheless, just as the credible prospect of an omniscient and omnipotent god can deter sin, the improved circulation of accurate reputational information can deter fly-by-night opportunism. The arrival of the com-

13. Harold Demsetz, "Toward a Theory of Property Rights," 57 *Am. Econ. Rev.* 347, 356–357 (Pap. & Proc. 1967).

14. See generally Arthur R. Miller, "Personal Privacy in the Computer Age," 67 *Mich. L. Rev.* 1089 (1969); Spiros Simitis, "Reviewing Privacy in an Information Society," 135 *U. Pa. L. Rev.* 707 (1987). The legal scholars who have addressed the topic have been worried about the release of information that is either (1) false and defamatory, (2) intrusive on important privacy interests, (3) likely to result in retaliation against the good faith pursuit of legal rights, or (4) destructive of opportunities to make a fresh start. These are serious (and, for many types of information, decisive) considerations. The discussion here focuses on policies toward the release of truthful, public-record information about past misconduct toward others. The retention and release of this sort of information mainly implicates the last of the listed concerns. A central issue is the extent to which fresh-start objectives can be achieved by allowing the person to free himself of past transgressions, not by expunging them from the record after a period of time, but rather by supplementing the record with information about subsequent good behavior.

puter age thus creates the possibility that the informal-control system will be able to reclaim some territory from the legal system. Lawmakers should keep this in mind when they consider imposing new regulatory burdens on the collection and dissemination of truthful, publicly available information about past behavior.[15]

Finally, laws that serve to distribute power more broadly and equally are likely to bolster informal-control systems. For example, when lawmakers succeed in equalizing power within relationships such as landlord-tenant and husband-wife, they make it easier for those involved to work out problems informally. Conversely, lawmakers should avoid measures such as rent-control legislation and legal doctrines that treat wives as subordinate to husbands; these laws undermine symmetries of power and can be predicted to lead to more nastiness within relationships.[16]

This last point can be generalized: lawmakers who are unappreciative of the social conditions that foster informal cooperation are likely to create a world in which there is both more law and less order.

15. The Federal Fair Credit Reporting Act prohibits, with certain exceptions, a credit-information agency from reporting any bad debt, lawsuit, criminal conviction, or other adverse information that is over seven years old. See 15 U.S.C. §1681(c) (1982). Many states have similar statutes. See, e.g., Cal. Civ. Code §1785.13 (1989). Legislation aimed at improving the accuracy of information files is not necessarily worth the administrative costs involved. See, for example, the dubious statute proposed in Note, "Tenant Blacklisting: Tenant Screening Services and the Right to Privacy," 24 *Harv. J. Legis.* 239, 313 (1987) (a firm that provides landlords with information about prior evictions should be annually required to send each tenant a copy of his file).

16. See supra Chapter 10, notes 42–43 and accompanying text; Chapter 11, note 61; Chapter 15, text accompanying note 32.

Appendix

Index

* * *

Appendix:
Research Methods

Because the Round Mountain–Oak Run area of Shasta County had witnessed both an actual and a threatened closure of the range, it was an ideal site for a field study of the influence of law. The locale presented opportunities for both longitudinal and cross-sectional analysis. The longitudinal analysis would track the behavior of specific cattlemen and farmers over a span of years in the middle of which an applicable closed-range ordinance (such as Caton's Folly) had been adopted. The cross-sectional analysis would vary locations, not time periods; it would seek to determine whether on a particular date cattlemen and farmers behaved differently in open-range areas than in closed-range areas. The field study was designed to enable both types of inquiries.[1]

The fifty-six square miles of Caton's Folly almost equals the area of Washington, D.C. It was therefore prudent to concentrate the landowner interviews in a subarea within it, in order to be better able to judge the credibility of the information received. The most illuminating subarea, ideally, would be a band that straddled one of Caton's Folly's boundaries. Some of the interviewees within such a band would own lands in open range, some in closed range, and some (conceivably) in both.

For several reasons the southern border region of Caton's Folly became the obvious subarea within which to concentrate. First, the other three boundaries of Caton's Folly traverse lightly settled private forest. The southern border area, by contrast, was well settled and thus more likely to be conflict-ridden. Second, only the southern area included some territory that had been threatened with a closure. Third, an investigator conducting a cross-sectional study into the effect of law should pick a situation in which legal boundaries are essentially random with regard to the social and topographic features that might influence conduct. Were

---

1. An ideal research design makes use of time-series data for both experimental and control areas. See Richard Lempert, "Strategies of Research Design in the Legal Impact Study: The Control of Rival Hypotheses," 1 *Law & Soc'y Rev.* 111, 130–132 (1966).

the boundary not to be randomly drawn, any differences in landowner behavior the investigator discovered between the areas might be the result of preexisting conditions (which perhaps caused the line to be drawn where it was), and not the result of the difference in legal regimes. The southern boundary of Caton's Folly appeared to be a random line. None of the drafters of the Caton's Folly petition (the persons who selected this boundary) lived near it, nor did any appreciable number of the petition's signatories. Moreover, the terrain the southern boundary crosses is highly varied, rising from foothills at an elevation of 2100 feet at the western end, to mountain forest at an elevation of 4400 feet at the eastern end. An eight-mile east-west line drawn straight across diverse terrain seems unlikely to have been the product of a gerrymander.

The primary sources of data were government records and 73 interviews. Three types of government records—aerial photographs, traffic accident reports, and court files—were tapped for the study. Interviews were conducted both with landowners (mostly in the area near the south border of Caton's Folly) and with a somewhat greater number of specialists involved with stray-cattle disputes.

Federal agencies took aerial photographs of the western portion of the southern border area of Caton's Folly in both October 1973 and August 1980—that is, two months before and seven years after that closed-range ordinance was approved.[2] Although these photos were taken at too high an altitude to indicate the presence of fences or individual animals, they do reveal buildings and areas under cultivation. Copies of these photographs were obtained to provide objective evidence of changes in gross land-use patterns in and near the study area during the relevant time period. A geobotanist skilled in remote sensing was hired to analyze the two sets of aerial photographs. He detected no cross-sectional or longitudinal variations in land-use patterns that would cast doubt on the findings presented.

The California Highway Patrol made available its reports on vehicle-animal accidents occurring on the roads in unincorporated Shasta County between August 1978 and July 1982. The discussion of highway collisions in Chapter 5 makes use of these records.

The records of the state courts that serve the Northeastern Sector of Shasta County contain evidence of lawsuits arising out of stray-livestock incidents. Because none of the relevant state courts indexed their cases by

---

2. In October 1973 the Caton's Folly ordinance was pending and landowners might have anticipated its adoption. As a result, aerial photographs taken on an earlier date, had they been available, would have provided better evidence of the ex ante situation.

subject matter, I asked judges and court clerks if they could recall stray-cattle cases, looked for names of likely litigants in the plaintiff and defendant name indexes, and, in the Justice Courts, reviewed all complaints that had been filed during recent eleven-month periods.

Fifty interviews were conducted with specialists. Most of these interviews were completed before I embarked on the landowner interviews. The specialists were: the 4 state-court judges most likely to have been involved in livestock-related cases arising in the Northeastern Sector; 6 Redding attorneys who had rural landowners as clients; 5 members of the Board of Directors of the Shasta County Cattlemen's Association; 8 adjusters and salesmen employed by the insurance companies that underwrite most of the livestock risks in eastern Shasta County; 3 real estate appraisers and assessors; 11 county officials (including the brand inspector, the animal control officer, the livestock advisor, the former district attorney, and several supervisors, including John Caton); 4 fence contractors and fence-material suppliers; 6 agents of forest owners that lease their lands for grazing; and 3 grazing lessees. Eighty percent of these specialist interviews were conducted in person and the balance, by telephone. The face-to-face sessions averaged 40 minutes in length.

Twenty-eight persons owning rural land northeast of Redding were interviewed.[3] Eleven of these 28 owned land within Caton's Folly; 10 owned land outside it but within three miles of its southern border (mostly in areas that the Heinz closure petition would have affected); and 3 more—Hailey, McCall, and Shellworth—owned land both inside and outside it. Of the 28 landowners, 11 could be described as cattle ranchers, 4 as farmers (whose chief agricultural activity was producing feed for livestock), and 13 as ranchette owners (some of whom owned a few farm animals as a hobby).

Twenty of the 28 landowners were interviewed in person. Seventeen of these interviews were exhaustive sessions lasting about one and a half to two hours. A standardized survey instrument was not used, in part because a formal list of questions might have made respondents ill at ease.[4]

3. Because several interviewees qualified both as specialists and as landowners, the total number of interviews was 73, not 78.

4. The authors of several well-known law-and-society studies have used remarkably similar research methods. In his pioneering study of contracting, Macaulay interviewed 68 business executives and lawyers in Wisconsin, apparently without the aid of a standardized questionnaire. See Stewart Macaulay, "Non-Contractual Relations in Business: A Preliminary Study," 28 *Am. Soc. Rev.* 55, 55–56 (1963). Ross's interviews with his 67 insurance adjusters were also unstructured. H. Laurence Ross, *Settled Out of Court* 10 (rev. ed. 1980). Llewellyn and Hoebel's study of the Cheyenne was based on what sociologists call "memory cases"—

As in the specialist interviews, detailed handwritten notes were taken during the face-to-face sessions. The remaining eight landowner interviews were conducted by telephone; these telephone conversations averaged fifteen minutes in length.

The landowner interviews have several shortcomings as a data source. Twenty-eight is a rather small number. The people interviewed were not randomly selected, because conscious efforts were made to interview residents who had either owned cattle, been victims of trespass incidents, or been active in the political battles over closed-range petitions. Particular stress was placed on obtaining interviews with the owners of the largest farms and ranches in the study area. Compared with average foothill landowners, those interviewed were probably older, wealthier (though still of modest means), longer in residence in northeastern Shasta County, and more active in community affairs.[5] Although most respondents talked without hesitation—indeed, usually with enthusiasm—cooperative residents were undoubtedly somewhat overrepresented in the sample.

Interview data are not always reliable. Some memories were undoubtedly imperfect. One or two landowners also appear deliberately to have recast history to place themselves in a better light. Because the landowner interviews were concentrated in one locale and included some questions about events in the public record, however, it became possible to detect the most self-serving respondents.

---

tribal legends and tales related by interpreters. K. N. Llewellyn and E. Adamson Hoebel, *The Cheyenne Way* viii-ix (1941). Similar methods were also used in Thomas M. Palay, "Comparative Institutional Economics: The Governance of Rail Freight Contracting," 13 *J. Legal Stud.* 265, 271 (1984) (study based on 35 field interviews that were conducted without the use of a formal questionnaire in order to encourage the interviewees to be open in their responses).

5. To avoid developing a reputation for nosiness, I did not ask the landowners about either their religious convictions or their financial situations. Those factors may conceivably affect how they resolve their workaday disputes.

✳ ✳ ✳

Index

Harvard University Press is a member of Green Press Initiative (greenpressinitiative.org), a nonprofit organization working to help publishers and printers increase their use of recycled paper and decrease their use of fiber derived from endangered forests. This book was printed on recycled paper containing 30% post-consumer waste and processed chlorine free.